"Tommy Hays has spent a lifetime studying the place of prayer in inner healing. I have personally benefitted from his teaching, writing, and encouragement. This book gathers a wealth of helpful insights and experiences into one volume. I am honored to have it on my shelf and honored to call Tommy my friend."

—**Max Lucado**

"Tommy Hays combines a lawyer's keen logic with a spiritual intuition to bring inner healing to a practical, effective, and applied level. His proven techniques have been used in hundreds of ministry settings and can serve as simple yet profound tools in the hands of even the novice minister."

—**Andy Reese**
Author of *Freedom Tools*

"*Free to Be Like Jesus* will take you on a journey to learn more about the inner healing ministry. This book has many foundational spiritual truths and will help you if you want more healing in your own life, or if you want more tools to assist you in your inner healing ministry."

—**Randy Clark**
Global Awakening

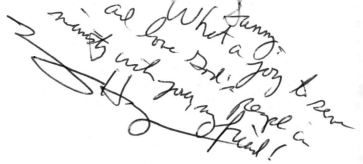

Free to Be Like Jesus

Transforming Power of Healing & Deliverance

Tommy Hays

Founder, Messiah Ministries
Pastoral Director, Rapha God Ministries

4 Dominion Drive, Building 1
San Antonio, Texas 78257

ISBN Number 978-1-60383-206-9

Published by
Holy Fire Publishing

www.christianpublish.com

Printed in the United States of America and United Kingdom

Table of Contents

Preface

I'm excited to share this revised edition of *Free to Be Like Jesus*. I published the original version in 2009 to share my understanding of the biblical principles and practices I'd learned through twelve years of prayer ministry, with particular emphasis on inner healing—what I call "healing from the inside out." Five years later, I'm still learning.

Prompted by the Holy Spirit, I'm gathering testimonies and insights to share from my daily experiences of prayer ministry with a book to come specifically on inner healing—called *Healing from the Inside Out*, one to come on my approach to deliverance prayer ministry from my background as a trial lawyer—called *The Final Verdict—Deliverance Ministry from a Lawyer's Perspective*, and one on the convergence of our lives on earth, in the earthly dimension, with our lives in heaven, in the heavenly dimension, that we already experience in both dimensions every day—called *The Eternal Dimension*. In the meantime, I want to share a few updates and insights to the core principles essential for understanding the biblical basis for healing prayer ministry.

I'm grateful for all who have encouraged me and prayed for me to share these principles that I've learned. For years, I primarily ministered through Messiah Ministries, which I founded after being ordained as a United Methodist Minister under special appointment to minister healing and equip the saints for the work of the ministry across denominational lines. In this new season, I'm ministering from my new home base in San Antonio, Texas as Pastoral Director of Rapha God Ministries, leading our ministry with my ministry partner, Tammy Watts. I'm blessed to have such anointed friends and partners in ministry every day. They have been the hands and heart of Jesus to me. Through them, I know my Redeemer lives.

I'm not finished yet. I need God's grace and the continual filling of the Holy Spirit to mature me into the person that God created me to be, firmly established in my identity as a child of God and committed to living out my destiny as a disciple of my Lord, Jesus Christ.

To God be all glory, honor, majesty, and praise!

—Tommy Hays
November 13, 2014

Introduction

Healing is wholeness in spirit, soul, and body. Deliverance is freedom from spiritual oppression. The Father heart of God is to heal us and free us from all that would hold us back from being all He created us to be. He is *Jehovah Rapha*, the God who heals us (Exodus 15:26).[1]

Ministering the Healing Love of God

In a broad sense, the ministry of healing and deliverance is helping someone come into agreement with what God has already done for them through the finished work of the cross. Jesus said, "It is finished" (John 19:30). Now with our hope and faith in Christ, we are "a new creation" and "everything has become new" (2 Corinthians 5:17). But sometimes in our weaknesses and doubts, in all our challenges and struggles of life in a broken, fallen world not yet fully experiencing the redemption of Christ, we need the Holy Spirit and someone who's willing to pray for us and help us embrace all the grace God has for us through Jesus Christ. Sometime we just need someone to minister the healing love of God to us. His grace is sufficient, but our part is to believe it and receive it, as best as we can, and all by the power of His grace (2 Corinthians 12:9).

Healing is at the heart of God, and healing is at the heart of the Gospel of Jesus Christ. It's not just a fringe benefit or ancillary experience. Isaiah 53 prophetically speaks of the coming of the Messiah who would take upon Himself all our sins and transgressions. Jesus the Messiah would be that "Lamb of God who takes away the sins of the world" (John 1:29). We commonly call this "the Atonement," meaning that Jesus was the atoning sacrifice for our sins so that we could be restored to right relationship with God.

But this same prophetic passage that speaks of the forgiveness of our sins through the sacrifice of the Messiah also speaks of the healing of our lives through that same sacrifice:

---

[1] Our inner healing prayer ministry in San Antonio that I help lead with Tammy Watts is named Rapha God Ministries, drawn from this Scripture and given by the Holy Spirit through a time of fasting and prayer.

9

Surely He has borne our infirmities and carried our diseases; yet we accounted Him stricken, struck down by God, and afflicted. But He was wounded for our transgressions, crushed for our iniquities; upon Him was the punishment that made us whole, and by His bruises we are healed. All we like sheep have gone astray; we have all turned to our own way, and the LORD *has laid on Him the iniquity of us all* (Isaiah 53:4–6).

Our transgressions and iniquities were laid upon Christ. And so were our infirmities and diseases. All done for us by our loving and forgiving God that we might be made whole—whole and free in every area of our lives. By His bruises, by His stripes, by His wounds, by His blood, we are healed and made whole (1 Peter 2:24).

Isaiah's Old Testament prophecy of the coming Messiah healing us and freeing us from our sins, our sicknesses, and our spiritual bondages was specifically fulfilled through the ministry of Jesus Christ, as precisely affirmed in the New Testament:

That evening they brought to Him many who were possessed with demons; and He cast out the spirits with a word, and cured all who were sick. This was to fulfill what had been spoken through the prophet Isaiah, "He took our infirmities and bore our diseases" (Matthew 8:16–17).

Through His transforming power of healing and deliverance, God wants to set us free to be like Jesus—to have His nature and continue His ministry in the power of His Holy Spirit. He wants us to be whole and holy, to be set free, and to see Him free others. This was at the heart of the ministry of the early church, and this is to be at the heart of the ministry of every church today:

Are any among you suffering? They should pray. Are any cheerful? They should sing songs of praise. Are any among you sick? They should call for the elders of the church and have them pray over them, anointing them with oil in the name of the Lord. The prayer of faith will save the sick, and the Lord will raise them up; and anyone who has committed sins will be forgiven. Therefore confess your sins to one another, and pray for one another, so that you may be healed. The prayer of the righteous is powerful and effective (James 5:13–16).

Our Father God wants to fill us with the Spirit of Christ, the hope of glory (Colossians 1:27). As His light shines through us, His glory will arise upon us (Isaiah 60:1). Then through us—the body of Christ, filled with the Spirit of Christ, growing in His nature and continuing in His ministry—the prophecy that the glory of the Lord will cover the earth as the waters cover the sea will be fulfilled (Habakkuk 2:14).

This is ultimately the purpose of the prayer ministry of healing and deliverance. The Father has sent His Holy Spirit to prepare a holy Bride, a holy people, for the coming of the Son. Whole and free, we will one day live with Him forever in His kingdom in heaven. At the same time He wants His kingdom to come now and His will to be done now, here on earth as it is heaven, as He presently and actively lives in us.

The kingdom of heaven is not only a place where we go when we die; it is also the place where the kingdom of heaven dwells within us now (Luke 17:21). It is righteousness, peace, and joy in the Holy Spirit (Romans 14:17). And the transforming power of healing and deliverance is a means of God's grace to welcome His kingdom to come and His will to be done in us and in all the earth, as it is in heaven. It is a means by which it will one day be true, that His Bride has made herself ready (Revelation 19:7) and that the Lord has brought many sons to glory (Hebrews 2:10 NKJV).

Inner Healing—"Healing from the Inside Out"

An essential dimension of healing and freedom in Christ is the healing of the heart. This is the healing and freedom from all that's buried down inside, from all the places where we're still stuck and bound up from the pain or shame of our past. This is inner healing, what I call "healing from the inside out."

Through our salvation in Christ and the power of the Holy Spirit abiding in our hearts, we are free to let go of the past so we can move forward to what lies ahead, pressing on for the prize of the heavenly calling of God for our lives in Christ Jesus (Philippians 3:13–14). Through our freedom in Christ we should be looking to Jesus, not to our past, laying aside the weights that try to crush our spirits and the sin that tries to entangle our souls to run the race that is set before us (Hebrews 12:1).

But the trouble is, most of us continue to drag our past along with us, stuff it down inside of us, or build big walls around us, all in our own strength, in our own wisdom, in our own control, in our own will. So we're exhausted and overwhelmed, even tempted to quit, instead of running the race we were destined to run. We need the inner healing that only God can give.

Unhealed Wounds, Unbroken Chains

Wounds of rejection, roots of bitterness, shadows of fear, walls of isolation, wells of abandonment, brokenness and sickness, shame of sin or abuse—the unhealed pain and shame of life steals the blessings of abundant life Jesus makes available through the power of the cross. Our unhealed wounds and brokenness block us from intimacy with God, divide us from loving one another, and imprison us from living out our destiny in Christ. We need healing from our wounds and deliverance from the chains of our bondage. We need to know our identity, purpose, gifting, calling, and destiny.

Through the ministry of healing and deliverance, we can experience wholeness in every dimension of our lives—in spirit, soul, and body—and also in our relationship with God, with one another, and within ourselves. This is the *shalom* of God—to be at peace with God, at peace with one another, and at peace within ourselves. This is part of the transforming process of sanctification, of being made holy and whole, delivered, free, sound, and blameless, by the power of God's healing love (1 Thessalonians 5:23).

Healing and deliverance comes as we submit every area of our lives to the Lordship of Jesus Christ. It's a process of breakthroughs that are part of the great awakening and arising of the pure, spotless, glorious Bride the Father longs to have for His Son. We are set free to be more like Jesus. As we become more like Jesus, the Lord can entrust to us more of the power of Jesus. Step by step, we are empowered to continue the ministry of Jesus as the body of Christ, filled with the Spirit of Christ, ministering the love of Christ to a broken and hurting world.

Jesus came to heal the brokenhearted and set the captives free, as He proclaimed the coming of the kingdom of God (Isaiah 61; Luke 4). Now as the Father sent the Son, so the Son sends us in the power of the Holy Spirit to the glory of God (John 20:21). This is the mission and ministry of the church: we are called to do our part to "prepare the way of the Lord" in our generation. We cannot prepare others unless we are prepared ourselves. Nor can we minister the healing and deliverance of Jesus to others unless we have received His ministry of healing and deliverance ourselves. We need to be free to be like Jesus.

Our Calling and Destiny—Free to Be Like Jesus

Our calling and destiny as children of God is to be like Jesus. The Father has sent His Holy Spirit to prepare a Bride for His Son. This Bride is called to be holy as He is holy (1 Peter 1:15–16; Leviticus 20:26), and to be perfected in the love and nature of Christ (Matthew 5:48).

> *Christ loved the church and gave Himself up for her, in order to make her holy by cleansing her with the washing of water by the word, so as to present the church to Himself in splendor, without a spot or wrinkle or anything of the kind—yes, so that she may be holy and without blemish* (Ephesians 5:25–27).

We are created and called to be conformed to Christlikeness. Our Father desires to heal us and deliver us so that we are free to be like Jesus. He desires to conform us into the image of Christ to "have the mind of Christ" (Philippians 2:5; 1 Corinthians 2:16), to have "the Spirit of Christ" (Romans 8:9), to be "the body of Christ" (1 Corinthians 12:27), and to be "participants of the divine nature" of Christ (2 Peter 1:4). He desires that we grow up "to maturity, to the measure of the full stature of Christ" (Ephesians 4:13), and that we "be filled with the fullness of God" (Ephesians 3:19).

That is "the high calling of God in Christ Jesus" (Philippians 3:14 KJV). That is the great desire of our Father: that the Bride of Christ "be conformed to the image of His Son" (Romans 8:29). For this reason, God is reawakening His church to receive and then to minister healing and deliverance to the body of Christ in these last days. To move forward into the fullness of our destiny, we must let go of the past—not just burying it or ignoring it, but intentionally, deliberately releasing it to God by leaving it at the foot of the cross and under the blood of Jesus.

"This one thing I do: forgetting what lies behind and straining forward to what lies ahead, I press on toward the goal for the prize of the heavenly call of God in Christ Jesus" (Philippians 3:13–14). The prayer ministry of healing and deliverance helps us let go of the past so we can press on for the prize of our calling and God's kingdom.

Preparing the Way of the Lord

The Holy Spirit is preparing the way of the Lord for the second coming of Christ in the earth, but first He is preparing the way of the Lord in our hearts through the prayer ministry of healing and deliverance. God wants to cleanse, redeem, heal, deliver, empower, and free us—free to be like Jesus.

When John the Baptist was on the earth, he was the voice of one crying in the wilderness, "Prepare the way of the Lord." And he had a very specific message: "Repent! For the kingdom of God is at hand." The word "repent" means to have a change of mind, a change of heart, to turn away from wrong actions, thoughts, and motives, and turn toward right ones. This includes turning away from sin, the past, false belief systems, wrong mind-sets, wrong attitudes, deception, self-deception, lies, confusion, self-centered pride, the ways of the world, and choosing to turn to the Lord. So the message of John the Baptist was preparing the way of the Lord for the first coming of Jesus.

Jesus said that John the Baptist carried the spirit of Elijah—the Spirit-anointing to prepare the way of the Lord by preparing the people of the Lord. And in these days, the Lord has poured out the spirit of Elijah in great measure upon the earth. It is the spirit of Elijah, through the Holy Spirit of the Living God, that is now preparing the way of the Lord for the second coming of Jesus. Malachi chapter 4 speaks about Elijah and that great and terrible day of the Lord, telling us that on that day when the Lord comes, "The Sun of Righteousness" will arise with healing in His wings.

The Sun of Righteousness speaks of the Son of God. He is the Righteous Holy One. And The Sun of Righteousness, the Light of Righteousness, is arising upon the people of God. He is righteousness, holiness, and purity. And His people will be a pure and a holy Bride. As

14

we arise with Christ in us The Hope of Glory, we arise with healing in our wings. The Sun of Righteousness arises with healing in His wings, and He's releasing healing and wholeness in every dimension of our lives. That includes healing within ourselves, healing with one another, healing in our relationships, and healing throughout the generations of people on the earth.

It says in Malachi 4:6 that God will come and return the hearts of the fathers to the children, and the hearts of the children to the fathers, lest He strikes the earth with a curse. God wants to bless us. He doesn't want us under the curse. He wants to cleanse us, free us, restore us, and return our hearts to Him and to one another so that He can release the blessings of God upon the earth. That's the spirit of Elijah that is preparing the way of the Lord. Through the ministry of healing and deliverance, the Father has sent the Holy Spirit to prepare the Bride of Christ. And through the transforming power of healing and deliverance, the Holy Spirit is preparing the way of the Lord. Revelation 19:7 tells us, "... for the marriage of the Lamb has come, and his Bride has made herself ready."

One day Jesus will return to the earth at His second coming to fully establish His kingdom on earth as it is in heaven. The kingdom of God is where God is King. Jesus is the King of Kings and the Lord of Lords. And when He returns, He will return in glory. He's returning for the Bride—He's returning for that marriage supper of the Lamb, with His holy Bride. But for the wedding supper, the Bride must make herself ready.

The Bride will be made up of His people who have come to Him for healing and deliverance. We can make a choice, by God's grace, to let the Holy Spirit come and minister to us and prepare us to be the Bride of Christ, holy and whole. We're making ourselves ready by agreeing with God. God has to do it. But God looks for us to embrace Him. God looks to us to be willing to humble ourselves and embrace His conviction and healing, letting him dig up the roots that bear bad fruit. He patiently waits for us to invite Him to lay the ax to the root and dig it up, so that He can cast into the fire all the chaff, leaving what is pure and holy remaining. This is how the Bride is called to make herself ready (Revelation 19:7).

15

As God heals and delivers us in His process of sanctifying and maturing us into the image of Christ, He is preparing us to be the church He created us to be. Jesus is coming back for a holy Bride who seeks Him with single-minded faith and whole-hearted devotion. Before He comes to receive His Bride, the world will know that His Bride has been in its midst—moving in the power of Christ because we are living in the nature of Christ.

As the body of Christ, filled with the Spirit of Christ, we are the temple of God on earth (1 Corinthians 3:16). The Lord has promised that the glory of the later temple will be greater than the glory of the former (Haggai 2:9). "Greater works than these" will He do in these last days than even in the days that Jesus walked the earth with His first disciples (John 14:12). God has saved His best wine for last (John 2:10).

These are the days of "the greater works" of God that He will do through His people as He has promised. And He seeks to have a people to whom He can entrust such great power—a people who will demonstrate both His power and His nature (2 Peter 1:4). Though the Lord can, and likely will, continue to use whomever He will, whenever He will, as instruments of His grace and power in the earth, He desires a holy people who will be a holy Bride to display His nature and His glory (Isaiah 60:1-3).[2]

These will be a people who have humbled themselves before Him to receive the cleansing and freedom they need through healing and deliverance to be holy and whole—people who are emptied of themselves and filled with His Spirit. They will be prepared, empowered, crucified in the flesh and sanctified in the Spirit.

One day Jesus will come in His glory in the skies, but at the same time, every day between this day and that day, Jesus wants to come in His

---

[2] Nothing in this teaching and understanding of these principles is intended to take away from the sovereignty of God to do as He will, including working His miraculous power through those He chooses—regardless of their desire for holiness or submission to the process of sanctification of the soul and crucifixion of the flesh. But at the same time, I do believe from God's Word that it is His desire to display His power through His ambassadors who have His heart and reveal His nature in ever-increasing measures, as will be explained in further detail throughout this book.

16

glory in our hearts. One means of that grace is through the transforming power of healing and deliverance, as we allow the Holy Spirit to set us *free to be like Jesus!*

Revealing the Diamond in the Rough

There are many approaches to the prayer ministry of healing and deliverance. I personally have learned much and received much from so many of the diverse ways that the Lord, in His mercy and love, ministers His healing and freedom to His people with the compassion of the Father heart of God. Different ministries often have different focuses, practices, and perspectives that fit who they are and how God intends to use them. One way does not invalidate another. God is infinitely diverse, and He has created us and ministers through us in a myriad of various ways, but all consistent with His Word and His nature.

Though the Lord uses me and our ministry in many diverse ways, He seems to have especially called me and gifted me to minister His healing love most often from the perspective of inner healing—healing from the inside out. Rather than starting instantaneous miracles of the body, He often leads me to begin with the process of healing the spirit and the soul, which then often manifests in the healing of the body. This is a process of transformation through prayer ministry, with breakthroughs of healing and deliverance along the way. And while I have seen, with great excitement and enthusiasm, God's miraculous healing power through our ministry many times, His healing power most often seems to come through the gentle but steady process of inner healing and deliverance, little by little, and step by step. So this will be the primary focus of this book, written from my perspective and experience of healing and deliverance prayer ministry.

One morning, the Lord began to speak to me during my prayer time about this approach of prayer ministry as "The Diamond in the Rough." I write out my morning prayers to share with others, posting them on my blog and sending them out to my free e-mail list. And I'll share with you the prayer the Holy Spirit led me to pray that morning. I began my prayer as I always do, "Good morning, Lord Jesus," to start off my day in contemplative prayer, centered on Jesus, embraced by the Father, and filled with the Holy Spirit:

From *Morning by Morning, A Prayer Journey with Tommy Hays*:

Good morning, Lord Jesus. You are My Lord and Savior, My Healer and Deliverer, My God, My King, and My Best Friend. You are the One who sees my heart and loves me anyway....

"He's a diamond in the rough." Those words have always stuck with me. I grew up on a cotton farm and then in little oil towns around west Texas and eastern New Mexico. I worked my summers in middle school, high school, and college mostly hauling hay and driving tractors. I even filled in a couple of weeks as a roughneck on an oil rig until one day the reality of losing a finger or a toe from hauling drill pipe up and out of a greasy derrick really sank in, and I went back to hauling hay.

But now I was being considered for a position as a trial lawyer in a Dallas law firm where I had worked part of my summer through law school as a law clerk. The lawyer who was pulling for me to be on the list of new hires from the graduating class passed along the summary of how I was seen by the hiring committee—"a diamond in the rough." It felt good and it hurt at the same time. They were willing to see my potential but not fooled by my present and my past.

That's how You are, Lord. With Your Father's heart, You see me as You created me to be. You see me in the fullness of the potential of my purpose and destiny, along with all the gifting, calling, and anointing You have given me and imparted to me by Your grace. But at the same time, You are not fooled by my present and my past. You see the diamond, but You also see the rough. You see my true self that needs to be nurtured and healed as You call forth my true identity and destiny, but You also see the false self that I have created and I have allowed others to create out of my own hurts and wounds, pride and insecurities, that needs to be broken off in order to reveal the diamond hidden beneath the rough.

When You called me to the ministry of inner healing—healing from the inside out— You began to remind me of those words and that image from long ago. You began to give me Your Father's heart to see Your sons and daughters as You see them, like a diamond in the rough. You taught me how to confront the "rough" and call the sin for the sin that it was in order to lead a person to confession and repentance in submitting every area of their life to the Lordship of Jesus Christ. You taught me how to help them acknowledge the pain and the shame that was still buried in the hurts and wounds of their past, from the things they had done and the things done to them. You taught me how to help them let Your Holy Spirit release it all to You—step by

18

step and layer by layer, like pealing the layers of an onion with patience and faith, persistence and truth.

You taught me how to speak life to the dry bones in the power of Your name and call forth their God-given purpose and passion to see and be who You created them to be. You began to teach me how to listen to You and speak Your heart to them, as You called forth the diamond and broke off the rough through inner healing. And You began to teach me how to minister deliverance—how to take the authority You had given me as Your disciple and Your ambassador over all the power of the enemy of our souls who seeks to keep us bound up in the idolatries and addictions of the bondage of self in our flesh. You were teaching me how to bind up the broken-hearted and set the captives free, as You proclaimed through my prayers the coming of the kingdom of God and the year of the Lord's favor in each person's life (Isaiah 61; Luke 4). Much of it You taught me as You used others to minister this kind of life and healing to me, as You gave me the courage and humility to set aside my pride and fear to receive the ministry of the healing love of God through those You had anointed to be Your healing hands and living words to me, as instruments of Your grace.

You reminded me how when You saw the woman at the well, You went much more deeply than the surface (John 4:1-42). You looked into her past and confronted her shame and her need for love and acceptance. You could have just ministered a miracle, but You ministered inner healing as You exposed her past, so she could release it to You. In her healing, her eyes were opened to see You as her Messiah; and in her joy, she hurried off to tell everyone she knew about the love of the One "who told me everything I have ever done!" (verse 4:29). "Many Samaritans in the city believed in Him because of the woman's testimony" (verse 4:39).

And You reminded me how the friends of the paralyzed man pressed through the crowds and every barrier to bring him to You for healing (Mark 2:1–12). You could have simply worked the miracle as said, "Rise and walk." But instead You looked beneath the surface of the problem to the root of the issue, ministering inner healing from the inside out. You spoke to the sins of his past as well as to the manifestation of that sin in his body; and he was healed. You expressed Your authority, divine insight, and revelation knowledge to not only work miracles, but also to expose the root and the source of all that keeps Your people from experiencing the healing and freedom of Your will. " But so that you many know that the Son of Man has authority on earth to forgive sins'—He said to the paralytic—'I say to you, stand up, take up your mat and go to your home' " (verse 2:10–11).

19

Thank You for the ministry of Your healing love. Thank You for the ministry of inner healing and deliverance. In the same way that You have ministered Your healing and deliverance to me, now You have given me the heart and the joy to minister Your healing love to others by the power and authority of Your Spirit living through me. In the same way we are healed and comforted by You, so You send us to be Your heart and hands of healing and comfort to others (2 Corinthians 1:3–4). There is still much to receive and there is still much to give. Freely have I received, now freely am I to give (Matthew 10:8). Lord, thank You for letting others see the diamond in the rough in me, so now I can minister that same Father's heart of Your healing love to others. In Jesus' name I pray, Amen.

Be encouraged today! In the Love of Jesus, Tommy Hays[3]

Perhaps through my prayer that morning, the Holy Spirit put into simple words the heart of all I'm trying to say and share in this book.

---

[3] One years' worth of these morning contemplative prayers is collected as a daily prayer devotional in my first book, *Morning by Morning, Prayer Journey with Tommy Hays*, available through our web site www.messiah-ministries.org. You can also see the prayers I continue to post each morning or sign up to receive these morning prayers each day by email through the Messiah Ministries website.

Part 1 — Prayer Ministry of Healing and Deliverance

Though there are many perspectives and approaches to healing and deliverance prayer ministry, I want to share with you in this book the ones I have learned so far along the way. As they say at home, "Take the meat and leave the bone." My prayer is that these principles and teachings will be a blessing for you in your own healing, as well as a means of God's equipping and empowering you for healing ministry to others, as He sets you free to be like Jesus.

I'd like to begin this section with a recent testimony that shows how God's Holy Spirit often moves through our approach to the prayer ministry of healing and deliverance.

Linda's Story—A Testimony of Healing Prayer Ministry

Linda: It's amazing to me that I could have lived half my life being Spirit-filled, baptized in the Holy Spirit, so hungry for more of God, and seeking the Lord with all my heart, serving God in ministry, and then realize that I may need inner healing and deliverance. Last summer the Lord led me to my first connection with Tommy Hays and Messiah Ministries through Aldersgate Renewal Ministries summer Conference on Spirit-filled Living. I ordered some resources, and as I watched his *Preparing the Way of the Lord* DVD series, God began bringing up memories and flashbacks of things that I hadn't remembered or thought about in many years. So began my journey of healing prayer ministry.

A bit of my personal history is that I was born the second of four children, only eleven months after my sister came into the world. My Mother always said she cried and was overwhelmed the entire pregnancy at the thought of two very small babies under a year old. Although I knew she loved me, I often heard that I looked like an Aunt that she didn't particularly like. I have dealt with some issues of rejection, and almost seemed to have a target on my back that drew rejection from those whom I needed to love me, affirm me, and support me. I have experienced deep rejection and abuse from every man in my life.

My Dad was very controlling and unable to express love, and he used silence and verbal abuse to control my Mother and the entire family. I became an extremely shy, introverted child who lacked confidence, and who always tried to be good at all costs to avoid my Father's anger. We attended church for several years when I was a little girl, and I accepted Jesus as my Savior at age seven. Very soon thereafter, my Dad became angry about something that happened at church and we stopped attending altogether.

Over time, I began to realize that some of the things that happened in my childhood opened the door that created the issues and strongholds that I've struggled with for most of my life. In many ways, my adult life seems to have been a roller coaster ride of grief, pain, and struggles. I was married to a man who was later diagnosed as bipolar and manic-depressive. Nevertheless, we had three beautiful children together; one daughter and two sons. When our first-born child, Heather, was diagnosed with a rare, aggressive form of cancer called rhabdomyosarcoma at the age of 10 years old, our lives came to a screeching halt. We spent over three years battling this deadly opponent called cancer, spending weeks in the hospital receiving chemo, radiation, and many surgeries.

My daughter's battle with childhood cancer brought me to my knees in prayer, as I was totally dependent on God to heal my child. Though we were initially told that her chances of survival were nearly nonexistent, God moved miraculously and Heather survived, grew up, and went on to fulfill her dream of becoming a childhood cancer nurse. The Lord had healed her and would use her as a healer for other children with cancer. He gave her such a heart of compassion to be able to know the pain and fear of these small children because of all that she had experienced herself.

After fifteen years of being cancer free, she was diagnosed with pulmonary lung fibrosis resulting from the late effects of the three years of chemo she had received years earlier. We began another battle against a life-threatening illness. She continued to work at the hospital for as long as she could, pulling her oxygen tank behind her. Eventually, she moved back home and my daughter was put on a list for a lung transplant. Day by day for more than a year, we awaited the call that could hopefully save her life. Heather's sweet, personal relationship with the Lord, and the wonderful times of prayer that we shared together will always be one of my most precious memories. Her childlike faith and trust in the Lord to heal her was a real witness and testimony of the healing power of the Lord. She just simply believed and trusted God for her every breath. Unfortunately, we didn't get the call in time and Heather went on to be with Jesus on Dec. 19 of 2000, at the age of 25. My daughter and I had always been extremely close and her illnesses had drawn us even closer. We were a Mother and daughter who were more like sisters and best friends. Her death eight years ago is the deepest pain and heartache of my life.

Through it all, my marriage had been very troubled from the start. With his rages, manic episodes, overspending, and extremes, followed by times of deep, dark depression, I walked on eggshells most of the time. I was constantly trying to keep the peace and avoid doing anything that would set him off. The relationship was always emotionally and verbally abusive but intensified to become physically and sometimes sexually abusive. Because I determined that my children were not going to grow up in a broken home, and I also didn't want to ruin my Christian witness by being divorced, this stressful marriage continued on. One day a friend asked me, "But what about your Christian witness if you stay *in* this marriage? What example are you showing other women who are in abusive relationships?" Her words helped set me free! One night when he threw me against the kitchen counter, my son pulled him off of me. Finally, at the insistence of both of my then adult sons, he moved out and decided to file for divorce. Our marriage of 29 years ended over seven years ago.

During the early years of our marriage, we were not in church. But in the later years when my children were older, I became very involved in my church and hungered for a closer relationship with God. God began drawing me into more areas of serving Him in ministry, and eventually led me to attend an Emmaus Walk. A few years later while serving on an Emmaus team, God called me into full time ministry. *God began to show me His plan: to use all those years of struggles and pain to help others, as He began equipping me for ministry.* I love being in ministry and enjoy my present appointment as the pastor of two churches where I have tremendous responsibility. Although I minister daily to others, preaching, praying, teaching and leading, God began revealing areas where I was not as effective as I wanted or needed to be in ministry.

As I watched the DVDs of *Preparing the Way of the Lord*, I realized that I was still "stuck" in some ways and had not been able to find freedom through my own prayers and efforts. Although I am a pastor, I had never personally experienced prayer ministry for inner healing and deliverance, nor did I know anyone who ministered in this particular way. I really did not know quite what to expect. I just thought that there must still be some healing that I needed as a result of the stress and trauma of my daughter's death several years ago, or from the abuse from my 29 year marriage and divorce. I didn't know that God would first begin the healing process by digging for even deeper roots that had been buried inside.

During my first prayer ministry session with Tommy and his team, I received healing from brokenness and the trauma of sexual abuse and a miscarriage that happened in my teen years. The Lord specifically began to bring up a memory of a traumatic incident that happened. I had been pursued by a much older guy and became pregnant at the young age of 16. We "had to" get married and just two weeks later, through an act of sexual abuse by this man, I began to hemorrhage profusely, and my tiny child within me was born into my hand. The shock and trauma of that incident was buried deep inside and had never been healed.

The Lord actually took me back to that time as I received prayer, and God did a very deep healing of that deeply buried pain, loss, grief, and trauma as He healed that broken part of me that had been broken off through that act of violence. Areas of buried shame, rejection, and unforgiveness were also healed by God's grace and love.

In that same prayer session, the Lord brought up other areas of word curses, and verbal abuse and hurt by men in my life. The years of negative words that have been spoken to me by men in my personal life and also in ministry, who had tried desperately to hold me back and press me down, have had a deep affect on my finding freedom and walking effectively in the authority to which God called me. I had come to believe the words and lies, "You're fat! You're ugly! Who do you think you are to be serving in ministry?" Through prayer, Tommy heard the words 'high value target' and he saw a picture of me in a cage that was submerged in water up to my neck. He saw me with my face turned upward to heaven in worship of God, but I was held as a captive, unable

24

to get out. That day the Lord began to open the door to release the captive!

I was led through prayers of forgiveness, and word curses were renounced and broken off. Then Tommy told me to begin to speak out those negative words and lies that seemed to continue to hold me hostage. As I began to speak them, he began to renounce them and cut and break them off. I then received deliverance from lying spirits that had seemed to be "brainwashing" me into believing the lies. I remember just feeling physically limp and falling forward through this process. Tommy prayed the Father's blessing over me, and spoke words of affirmation and truth and life. I was told that I am a general, a Deborah, a conqueror, an Ester! No longer held captive!

When he read from Isaiah 62:1–5, the words just washed over me, bringing cleansing and healing. He prayed for me to be filled with the love of God in all the places that were left empty. I felt such peace and strength come back into my body, and I could actually feel myself being physically raised up by the Lord as I was standing with arms stretched up to heaven in praise and worship! It was a very powerful experience of such beautiful peace and joy! What an incredible feeling to begin to find true freedom after all these years!

Afterwards, I noticed an immediate difference. I felt much more peaceful and slept better. My mind seemed clearer and I was drawn to read books on which I couldn't focus before. My preaching felt more powerful and the anointing much stronger! I even lost some weight when I stopped believing that lie! God is so good!

I felt much better, but I also knew that there were still areas that needed God's healing touch. I continued to struggle with walking in the authority of who I am in Christ, and stand up for myself many times. Fear is sometimes a problem, and I knew I still needed more freedom from other past trauma and abuse. For years I've struggled with back problems and have lived with almost constant pain in my back and neck.

I set up another prayer ministry session during a recent School of Spiritual Ministry.[4]

This time God took me way back and showed me a picture of myself when I was about 8 months old, sitting on the ground on a blanket all by myself. I was leaning forward trying to hold myself up. My Dad was in the background holding my older sister in his arms. I remembered that my Mom had always said she cried the entire time she was pregnant with me, with only 11 months between my older sister and myself. Although I knew my parents loved me, I realized that I had always felt some rejection and somewhat alone.

Tommy began to pray that I would be released from those thoughts and words of rejection, and be loosed and freed of any loneliness, jealousy, envy, or offense, and be filled with the truth of God's love for me.

The Lord then brought up another memory of a time when I was 14 years old and walking through our little town with my younger sister and brother. An older guy called to me and told my sister and brother to go on home. He then grabbed me and threw me down a levy bank and tried to rape me. I remembered fighting him so hard and finally he gave up. I walked home in shock, shaking and crying but I didn't tell anyone for a long time. He continued to harass me at school and threaten that he was going to finish what he had started. He was spreading lies and rumors at school about me, and I finally had to tell someone. When I finally told my Mom, she said I had to go tell Dad. Instead of my Dad supporting me and protecting me, he said it must have been my fault and called me a whore. I remember crying and saying I'd never tell him anything again!

The hurt, pain, and the poison of that trauma just began pouring out of me as the tears flowed without restraint. Tommy prayed that the Lord

---

[4]The Fountain School of Spiritual Ministry was a one-week intensive course, hosted by Messiah Ministries, and often attended by national and international students to be equipped and empowered as spiritual leaders for healing and deliverance prayer ministry. Today, we continue to teach and equip for ministry through Rapha God Ministries in San Antonio. I also continue to travel to other churches and conferences by invitation to teach and minister on healing prayer ministry through Messiah Ministries..

would go back into that moment and draw out the fear, terror, shock, and being vulnerable with no one standing up for me. He continued to pray and lead me through prayers of forgiveness for the boy, my Dad and my Mother—not making excuses—just speaking the truth of all that was done that was wrong and bringing it all to the Lord. We also prayed prayers of release from false words and false identity off of my spirit and mind, and broke any unholy soul ties. As prayers for healing of that brokenness and trauma continued, the Lord revealed to me even deeper roots of abuse of power that still seemed to have power over me, and was causing a block in my walking in the authority and power of God in me.

As Tommy began to pray for all damage of abusive powers to come off and out in the name of Jesus, I actually felt a pressure on my back physically pushing me forward! The more he prayed the harder it pushed. He continued commanding the abuse of powers to go! False powers, go! And he commanded it to come off in the name of Jesus. Then he prayed, "All of that which represents that big tall boot which is pressing down on her neck, you come off!" Suddenly, I felt a release and was able to begin to sit up. The oppression was being lifted and Jesus began lifting me up and I was sitting up straight and tall. The pressure and pain in my back and neck that had been there for so long was released and gone! No pain! Thank You Jesus! Praise God!

The love of Jesus being poured into me began to heal me and lift me into that place of honor and authority. Prayers and scriptures for power, authority, courage, new life, and an anointing of boldness were spoken over me. God filled me with His love and assurance of who I am in His eyes, as favor and grace, and blessing and the love of God just filled all the empty places. I began to hear the Lord gently speak to me telling me of His love for me, giving me a new name, "Beloved of the Lord"

The peace, freedom, and joy are indescribable! I still feel so light and free, and the pain and pressure on my back and neck are still gone! Others have also said that they can see a difference. Someone at church said that she could definitely tell that I was very different. She said, "I could hear it in your prayers. And your preaching is even more powerful than ever before, and the anointing was tangibly evident. Something has changed in you!" Praise God!

As a pastor I would encourage other pastors not to be afraid or to hold back from seeking the Lord's healing in their lives. God's desire is to heal, restore, and sanctify us for the purpose of making us more like Jesus, and so He can better use us to help and heal others. We all have things we may not even be aware of in our lives that may be blocking us from walking in the freedom, power, and authority that is ours in Christ. We can't be effective healers to others if we are bound up and wounded ourselves!

I would also encourage anyone who has wounds and hurts of the past that may be blocking or hindering your relationship with the Lord and with others to trust God to gently bring healing and restoration through healing and deliverance prayer ministry. God desires to bind up the brokenhearted and set the captives free! He's our amazing healing God!

I know that there is more that the Lord will need to do in the process of my sanctification, and I just say, "Yes, Lord! I am willing. More of Him, less of me!"[5]

---

[5] Linda recorded our prayer ministry session, saying it continues to bring layers of healing and freedom, along with a fresh filling of God's Holy Spirit, every time she rereads it. She graciously agreed for me to include the full transcript at the end of this book to give the readers a very specific, real-life understanding of this approach to healing prayer ministry. Every story and prayer ministry session is different, but this is Linda's story from her session. Praise God for His healing love and transforming power! Now Linda is better equipped and praying for others out of a deep place of healing and freedom in the fullness of her salvation in Christ.

Chapter 1

The Healing & Deliverance Ministry of Jesus

Healing and deliverance was at the heart of the ministry and message of Jesus. He not only taught the truth and the principles of the kingdom of God, He demonstrated them with power.

Jesus' Ministry Model

Wherever Jesus went, the crowds were soon to follow. He never missed an opportunity to proclaim the coming of the kingdom of God with both His words and His actions. He invited all who would come to learn about the kingdom and see it demonstrated in power. This was the ministry model of Jesus:

> *He welcomed them, and spoke to them about the kingdom of God, and healed those who needed to be cured* (Luke 9:11).

For Jesus, the ministry of teaching and the ministry of healing flowed together out of the ministry of compassion. He welcomed the people into the presence of God. "He had compassion for them, because they were like sheep without a shepherd; and He began to teach them many things" (Mark 6:34). As He taught them about the principles of the kingdom of God, they received understanding so that they could choose, of their own free will, to receive the grace of God in faith. This prepared the way for Jesus to minister the healing love of God to all who were in need.

As the Father sent the Son, so He sends us (John 20:21). This was Jesus' model of ministry, so this is to be our model of ministry. Though the particular details must vary with the uniqueness of the circumstances, there is a general pattern for our ministry. We are to welcome those who are seeking the grace of God, speak the words of the Lord to them, and teach them the principles of His kingdom. Then we are to minister the healing love of God to them as they have need—in the name of Jesus and in the power of His Holy Spirit. But we can only give away what we have received ourselves.

29

At times, our modern church can tend to separate teaching ministry from prayer ministry. Jesus didn't do that. He never intended His message to be separate from His ministry. We hear many sermons preached expounding upon the great teachings of Jesus to the crowds from His Sermon on the Mount. But it is often forgotten that the context of Scripture introducing Jesus' famous sermon makes clear that His teaching and preaching ministry was not separate from His healing and deliverance ministry:

> *Jesus went throughout Galilee, teaching in their synagogues and proclaiming the good news of the kingdom and curing every disease and every sickness among the people. So His fame spread throughout all Syria, and they brought to Him all the sick, those who were afflicted with various diseases and pains, demoniacs, epileptics, and paralytics, and He cured them. And great crowds followed Him from Galilee, the Decapolis, Jerusalem, Judea, and from beyond the Jordan* (Matthew 4:23–25).

> *When Jesus saw the crowds, He went up to the mountain; and after He sat down His disciples came to Him. Then He began to speak, and taught them, saying: "Blessed are the poor in spirit for theirs is the kingdom of heaven. Blessed are...."* (Matthew 5:1–4)

The end of Matthew chapter four speaks of the power of God being demonstrated through the ministry of Jesus. Then the beginning of Matthew chapter five speaks of the teaching and preaching ministry of Jesus. Jesus' teaching and preaching was backed up with God's power. That's why "the crowds were astounded at His teaching, for He taught them as one having authority" (Matthew 7:28–29).

Jesus wants His fame to continue to spread throughout the earth as He releases His power through His people who teach and minister in His name and for His glory. We are the body of Christ in the earth today. The ministry of teaching, preaching, and healing that He intends to do in the compassion and love of God, He intends to do through us. As Mother Theresa said, "He has no hands but our hands."

Jesus' Personal Mission Statement

We hear much these days about being focused and purpose driven. We have future committees, long range planning, vision summits, five-year plans, and dream teams. These are designed to, "broaden our horizons" and "lift our vision" to "see our future" so we can "be our future" because you "hit what you aim for." Right?

The movie *Jerry Maguire*, starring Tom Cruise, epitomizes this type of self-defining, future-driven quest. A cocky, young sports agent gets shaken by an awareness of the meaningless and shallow life he's living. Then he gets inspired to examine his life in the light of his destiny. He gets reminded about the core values and guiding principles that lead the decisions and direct the paths of people of integrity and conscience in a world of compromise and self-seeking, and he writes his Personal Mission Statement.

Before he has a chance to retract it, he finds himself living it. His sense of personal mission defines his destiny. And before he gains everything that really matters, he loses everything that he thought really did. In the end, of course, he gets the money and the girl and gets to feel good about who he has become—instead of feeling ashamed of who he was. It makes a cute movie, but it also makes the point of the power of knowing your purpose.

Jesus had a Personal Mission Statement as well. It's recorded in Luke 4:14–21. After thirty years of preparation, Jesus was ready to begin the ministry for which He came to this earth. He stepped out of the crowd and into the Jordan River, where He was baptized in the Holy Spirit and led away to be tempted by the enemy in the wilderness (Luke 3:21–38; Luke 4:1–13). With every test, Jesus proved Himself to be ready to fulfill His commission as He was emptied of Himself and filled with the Holy Spirit. Then He returned to Galilee, "filled with the power of the Spirit" and "began to teach" (Luke 4:14–15). He stepped from the wilderness into the synagogue—which was the center of the church, the marketplace, and the public square in His culture. He found in the scroll of Isaiah, chapter 61, where it was written of Him long ago and declared His personal mission statement for all to hear:

The Spirit of the Lord is upon me, because he has anointed me to bring good news to the poor. He has sent me to proclaim release to the captives and recovery of sight to the blind, to let the oppressed go free, to proclaim the year of the Lord's favor (Luke 4:18–19).

From that day until the day He ascended back into heaven, Jesus fulfilled His mission. He was teaching and preaching the gospel of the kingdom of God. He was binding up the broken-hearted and setting the captives free. He was opening the eyes of the blind, in spirit, soul, and body, and destroying the works of the kingdom of darkness and revealing the power of the kingdom of light. This was His purpose; this was His mission.

Jesus' Purpose and Destiny

Scripture declares that the Son of God was revealed for one purpose. What is that one purpose? To die on the cross for us? To forgive us of our sins? To reconcile us to God? To redeem all creation? Clearly, these are all *part* of the plan of God through the coming of Jesus to live and die and be resurrected in glory. But of all the things that Scripture could name as the "purpose" that "the Son of God was made manifest," what is that *one key purpose?* Scripture answers that question:

The Son of God was revealed for **this purpose***, to destroy the works of the devil* (1 John 3:8, emphasis added).

All that Jesus said and did on earth converges upon this great purpose and destiny. The miracles, the teaching, the sacrifice, all encompassed this calling: "to destroy the works of the devil."

What are "the works of the devil?" They are the temptation to sin; the separation of people from God though the choices made in response to his temptation; the defilement of all creation held bound and blind by his deception and evil. They are the attempt to distort and disrupt the plan of God to have a people living in a world of perfect relationship, intimacy, and love with their Creator. They are the schemes and devices of arrogance and pride to exalt himself in the heavens above the throne of God to make himself like the Most High, stealing the worship and glory that belong only to God.

32

All that God created was good and perfect. His children were whole and free, unafraid and undefiled. "The man and his wife were both naked, and were not ashamed" (Genesis 2:25). All that changed in the next verse: "Now the serpent was more crafty than any other wild animal that the LORD God had made" (Genesis 3:1). The works of the devil to distort and destroy God's creation had begun.

Jesus was revealed and made manifest on earth to destroy these works. This is the healing and deliverance ministry of Jesus—healing and deliverance of mankind through the redeeming blood of the Lamb so that there could be healing and deliverance of all creation—healing of the brokenness of a fallen world and deliverance from bondage of an oppressive enemy. Our Father allowed the willing sacrifice of His Son to redeem us to Him. He came to "deliver us from evil" through the sacrifice of His love on the cross of Christ. And He continues to deliver us from evil as we receive for ourselves and enforce for others the victory of the cross. Freed from the enemy, we are healed and made whole once again through the redeeming love of God.

There is healing and deliverance so "that at the name of Jesus every knee should bow, of things in heaven, and things in earth, and things under the earth; and that every tongue should confess that Jesus Christ is Lord, to the glory of God the Father" (Philippians 2:10–11 KJV). Jesus is destroying the works of the devil in all creation, through His cross and through His church, for God's redemption of all things in these last days (1 Corinthians 15:24–28).

All creation will be redeemed forever in a perfect relationship of love with God and with one another to the glory of His name. The redemption of all creation is accomplished through healing and deliverance—individually in our personal lives, corporately in the universal body of Christ, and throughout all generations and all creation. Healing and deliverance ministry is not on the fringes of the message and ministry of Jesus—it is at the very heart of all Jesus came to do and all Jesus is continuing to do by His Holy Spirit in the earth today and in the days to come.

Chapter 2

The Healing & Deliverance Ministry of Jesus' Church

Jesus is the head of His church. He is our head and we are His body. His mission and ministry are to be our mission and ministry. If healing and deliverance were at the heart of His ministry, they are to be at the heart of our ministry as well.

Jesus' Commission to All His Disciples

We speak about the Great Commission, that we are sent to go and "make disciples" as we are "baptizing them" in the ways and "teaching them" the words of Jesus (Matthew 28:18–20). But too often we focus on getting members and decisions rather than making disciples for Christ. We baptize them into a religion instead of a relationship and teach them our ways instead of His. We spread the gospel of our kingdom instead of the gospel of His kingdom. And then we wonder why no one is astounded at our teaching. It's because too often we don't teach as Jesus taught—as one having authority from living a life of personal and intimate communion with God.

—"As the Father Sent Me, so I Send You"

But Jesus also stated His commission to us this way: "As the Father sent me, so I send you" (John 20:21). In the same way the Father commissioned Jesus, Jesus has commissioned us. The things the Father sent Jesus to do are the things Jesus sends us to do. As the Father sent Jesus, so Jesus sends us.

So what is our mission? It's the same mission as Jesus'. His Personal Mission Statement is also ours. We are sent to proclaim the coming of the kingdom of God, demonstrate it with power, teach what Jesus taught with authority, bind up the broken-hearted, and set the captives free. We are sent as "ambassadors for Christ" to destroy the kingdom of darkness and reveal the kingdom of light as instruments of God by His grace (2 Corinthians 5:20).

This would seem prideful and blasphemous if this were not a direct command of God, "As the Father sent me, so I send you." That's why we can't understand, much less fulfill, this command and commission of God without understanding the role of the Holy Spirit. We must see and understand the purpose and power of the Holy Spirit in Jesus' ministry, and therefore, in our ministry. It's not about us; it's all about Him. We don't do the ministry; He does it through us. We are called and commissioned to minister in the authority of the name of Jesus, by the power of the Holy Spirit, to the glory of our Father in heaven.

The Holy Spirit—The Power and Presence of Christ within Us

The Holy Spirit is the power and presence of Jesus. He is the "Spirit of Christ," so that in Christ, "the Spirit of God dwells in you" (Romans 8:9). Through the indwelling power and presence of the Holy Spirit, you have "Christ in you, the hope of glory" (Colossians 1:27). We live the life of Christ and continue the ministry of Christ by the power of His Holy Spirit abiding in us.

This is the promise and inheritance of the disciples of Christ and children of God. We don't live or minister in our own power, but in the power of God made manifest through us. "If the Spirit of Him who raised Jesus from the dead dwells in you, He who raised Christ from the dead will give life to your mortal bodies also through His Spirit that dwells in you" (Romans 8:11).

This is why, at the same time that Jesus commissioned His disciples and sent them forth into ministry as the Father sent Him, He said, "Receive the Holy Spirit" (John 20:22). We can't minister in the name of Jesus without the power of Jesus. The Holy Spirit is the power and presence of Jesus—the Spirit of Christ within us, the hope of glory. If we're going to teach as Jesus taught, do what did, in the power that He had, it won't be in our own flesh, power and strength. We can only do that by the power and presence of the Holy Spirit, the Spirit of Jesus Christ living in us and through us to the glory of our Father. "'...Not by might, nor by power, but by My Spirit,' says the Lord of hosts" (Zechariah 4:6).

Jesus' Example for Us

Sometimes we fail to enter in to the ministry of Jesus as we have been commanded because we think, *Jesus was God and He could do anything. Who am I?* Of course, there is a measure of truth in this because Jesus said, "Apart from Me you can do nothing" (John 15:5). But as disciples of Jesus, we are not apart from Jesus. We have His Holy Spirit abiding within us. The same Spirit that flows through the Vine flows through the branches. So Jesus says, "I am the Vine, you are the branches. Those who abide in Me and I in them bear much fruit, because apart from Me you can do nothing" (John 15:5). We have justified our sin of disobedience by passively focusing more on doing nothing instead of abiding in Him. As a result, our lives and ministries do not "bear much fruit" at all. We have been satisfied with far less fruit than we were created, called, and commissioned to bear.

Forgive us, Lord. Help us see our sin and call it for the sin of disobedience that it is. Convict us so that we may repent and turn away from that way of thinking and ministering, so you can forgive us and redeem us, then use us to reveal Your glory to a broken and fallen world.

Both "Son of God" and "Son of Man"

Part of the problem is that we see Jesus in His glory as fully God without also seeing Him in His humility as fully man. Jesus is both "Son of God" *and* "Son of Man," both the nature of God *and* the nature of man—not one without the other. The key to understanding how Jesus sends His disciples as the Father sent Him is to understand that everything Jesus did on earth, He did by the power of the Holy Spirit as Son of Man. Jesus Himself said, "I can do nothing on My own. As I hear, I judge; and my judgment is just, because I seek to do not My own will but the will of Him who sent Me" (John 5:30). Yes, Jesus, Son of God, said, "I can do nothing on My own."

As Son of Man on earth, Jesus did everything He did—not as God—but as man. This was necessary so that He could truly offer His sinless life as a sacrifice for our sinful lives. This was necessary so that He could truly show us how human beings can live a life on earth in the power of God. Then He could truly set an example of how human beings can

37

minister to others on earth in the power of God. As Jesus said, "Very truly, I tell you, the Son can do nothing on His own, but only what He sees the Father doing; for whatever the Father does, the Son does likewise" (John 5:19).

God is One. And at the same time, He has revealed and manifested His nature to us in three dimensions of His One Being—God the Father, God the Son, and God the Holy Spirit. In the incarnation, God the Son set aside the glory of heaven and humbled Himself to take on human flesh and blood. To become "incarnate" is to become "flesh." John speaks of this mystery when he says, "And the Word became flesh and lived among us, and we have seen His glory, the glory as of a Father's only Son, full of grace and truth" (John 1:14).

Paul speaks of this mystery as well:

> *Let the same mind be in you that was in Christ Jesus, who, though He was in the form of God, did not regard equality with God as something to be exploited, but emptied Himself, taking the form of a slave, being born in human likeness. And being found in human form, He humbled Himself and became obedient to the point of death—even death on a cross. Therefore God also highly exalted Him and gave Him the name that is above every name, so that at the name of Jesus every knee should bend, in heaven and on earth and under the earth, and every tongue should confess that Jesus Christ is Lord, to the glory of God the Father* (Philippians 2:5–11).

As God the Son willingly chose to humble Himself in the sight of the Lord, God the Father lifted Him up and gave Him the name that is above every name. On earth, Jesus was "emptied" of His "equality with God" into the humility of "human form." As Dr. Robert Tuttle teaches, "Jesus' suffering didn't begin at the crucifixion, it began at the incarnation." God the Son humbled Himself to take on the "form of a slave, being born in human likeness." The Son of God then also became the Son of Man. On earth, this was the title Jesus chose for Himself far more than any other title. On earth, this was His name, His nature. It is important to see Him as He was and understand every dimension of His being.

When we see that Jesus spent so much time in prayer with the Father, it is not a fiction or some kind of holy shell game. We are not to read, "Jesus prayed" and then give a knowing wink that we really don't believe that because Jesus was God so he didn't really have to pray. Jesus really was praying. He really was seeking the Father's wisdom and direction. Jesus needed to pray as Son of Man to know the mind and heart and will of the Father. As He said, "I do nothing on my own, but I speak these things as the Father instructed Me" (John 8:28). Through prayer in the Spirit, Jesus received revelation knowledge and divine wisdom of His Father's will in heaven, so that Jesus might be a chosen instrument and yielded vessel to release His Father's will on earth as it is in heaven. As He said, "I declare what I have seen in the Father's presence" (John 8:38).

As Son of Man, Jesus sought the will of God the Father through prayer. In humility and submission, He willingly chose to trust and obey His Father in heaven. Then God the Father anointed Jesus as Son of Man with His power through the Holy Spirit to declare and demonstrate His will on earth. It is important to understand that God anointed Jesus with power as Son of Man, in His humanity as Jesus of Nazareth. Peter's words after Pentecost make this clear:

> How God anointed Jesus of Nazareth with the Holy Spirit and with power; how He went about doing good and healing all who were oppressed by the devil, for God was with Him (Acts 10:38).

God the Father anointed Jesus the Son with the Holy Spirit in order for Jesus to minister the will of God in the power of God on earth as Son of Man. It is important to see that Jesus, as Son of Man, needed to be "anointed" with the Holy Spirit and His power to accomplish His mission and ministry on earth. This was to teach us by the example of Jesus as a man, completely dependent on God in humility and completely obedient to God in faith, anointed with Spirit of God in power.

The Holy Spirit Anointed Jesus and Anoints Us

The same Holy Spirit who empowered Jesus as Son of Man to minister the will of God is the same Holy Spirit who empowers us as disciples of

Jesus to minister the will of God. Before Jesus ascended to heaven, He encouraged His first disciples, saying, "I am sending upon you what My Father promised; so stay here in the city until you have been clothed with power from on high" (Luke 24:49). This is what John the Baptist had foretold from the beginning, saying, "I have baptized you with water; but He will baptize you with the Holy Spirit" (Mark 1:8).

Jesus was speaking of the promise of the power to continue His ministry, commanding His disciples "to wait there for the promise of the Father" when they would be "baptized with the Holy Spirit" (Acts 1:4–5). He told them, "You will receive power when the Holy Spirit has come upon you; and you will be My witnesses in Jerusalem, in all Judea and Samaria, and to the ends of the earth" (Acts 1:8). Of all the promises, commands, or direction Jesus could have given before ascending to heaven to burn in their hearts and ring in their ears, these were His very last words.

As Jesus commanded His first disciples, so He commands all His disciples. We are to "wait" until we are "baptized with the Holy Spirit" on the day of our personal Pentecost. Then we are to be continually "filled with the Spirit" (Ephesians 5:18), that we may "abound in hope by the power of the Holy Spirit" (Romans 15:13), and live our lives in constant "communion with the Holy Spirit" (2 Corinthians 13:13). This is living in the kingdom of God and allowing the kingdom of God to be living in us. "For the kingdom of God is not food and drink but righteousness and peace and joy in the Holy Spirit" (Romans 14:17). This is allowing Christ the Healer to minister the healing love of God through us as the Body of Christ, filled with the Spirit of Christ, ministering in the power of Christ.

Our Role in God's Redemption of the Earth

God has chosen, in His sovereignty, to redeem the earth through the sacrifice of the life of His Son Jesus, who willingly chose to lay down His life for us as Son of Man. Through the obedience of His sacrifice, the Father has given "all authority in heaven and earth" to His Son (Matthew 28:18). Now the Son of Man has chosen to give "power and authority" to His disciples (Luke 9:1; 10:19).

Until we understand His role as Son of Man, we will not be able to understand ours. As we see Him more clearly in His calling and nature of Son of Man, we will begin to see our calling and nature as "sons of God" more clearly (John 1:12 KJV). It would almost be blasphemy if it weren't God's own word and will. Scripture clearly reveals that, "It is that very Spirit bearing witness with our spirit that we are children of God" (Romans 8:16).

As the Father sent the Son, so the Son sends us to continue His ministry of redeeming the earth in the power of the Holy Spirit. By God's will and grace, we have a role in redemption through our place in Christ, "For the creation waits with eager longing for the revealing of the children of God" (Romans 8:19). Jesus' prophetic declaration of the calling and purpose of His disciples will come to pass in the power of His Spirit living through us:

> *Very truly, I tell you, the one who believes in Me will also do the works that I do and, in fact, will do greater works than these, because I am going to the Father. I will do whatever you ask in My name, so that the Father may be glorified in the Son. If in My name you ask Me for anything, I will do it* (John 14:12–14).

How incredible that we will do even "greater works" than Jesus! As Son of Man, He was one man. As the body of Christ, we are one, but we are also many (Romans 12:5). We do the works that Christ did in the power that He had throughout all generations and all nations through His Holy Spirit within us. As Jesus promised:

> *I will ask the Father, and He will give you another Advocate, to be with you forever. This is the Spirit of truth, whom the world cannot receive, because it neither sees Him nor knows Him. You know Him, because He abides with you, and He will be in you* (John 14:16–17).

Personally and corporately, our bodies are now temples of the Holy Spirit of Christ dwelling within us (1 Corinthians 3:16 and 6:19; Ephesians 2:21). By the presence and gifts of His Holy Spirit, we bear the fruit of His Spirit—much fruit—as we abide in Him and He abides in us. We cannot do this on our own in human strength or power, but we can do all things through Christ who strengthens us with the power of His Spirit (Philippians 4:13). "For mortals it is impossible, but for God all things are possible" (Matthew 19:26). Even greater works than Jesus did are to be done through broken and fallen human beings, living in a broken and fallen world, to the glory of God.

This is our ministry, commission, and model. We are to be the body of Christ, filled with the Spirit of Christ, continuing the ministry of Christ. We are to teach what He taught, do what He did, in the power that He had. By His Spirit, He makes us one with Him, one with each other, and one in ministry to all the world, until we feast at His heavenly banquet. There we will celebrate forever with all who have been brought to the table of His presence through His compassionate ministry of love through His disciples. There we will hear, "Well done, My good and faithful servant; you have been found faithful over a few things, I will make you ruler over many things. Enter into the joy of your Lord!" Let us be found faithful when the Lord returns in glory to receive His glorious Bride—spotless and pure, healed and free, filled with the fullness of His power and His glory.

Part 2 — Understanding "Healing"

When we speak of "healing," most people seem to think of miracles—particularly physical healing miracles. Healing certainly includes the instantaneous and miraculous. And the Lord is increasing the move of His power through His miracles in the earth today. Praise God, that's really exciting! But at the same time, the biblical concept of healing is broader than that. Not all miracles involve healing, and not all healing involves miracles, in the sense that healing is not always instantaneous. In fact, in this season of the unfolding of God's redemptive plan of creation, most healing takes place in a process. And within the broader context of that healing process, we often see miraculous breakthroughs along the way by the power of God.

Ultimately, all true healing is from God. And in a very general sense, we might say that the Lord heals in at least five ways:

First, sometimes He heals instantaneously—in a moment through miraculous signs and wonders. Second, sometimes He heals in a process—little by little, step by step, layer by layer, through the process of restoration. Third, sometimes He heals through the gifts of human wisdom and natural remedies—using the truths of God we discover from science, medicine, and nature. Fourth, sometimes He heals through the grace to persevere—not wasting a moment of our suffering and redeeming it all, even when He does not will all we may endure. And fifth, sometimes He heals through the resurrection—when all sorrow and sighing shall flee away and we stand whole and forever free in His presence.

This past year, I've been excited to be invited by Max Lucado to share a time of preaching and ministry with him at a monthly worship and healing service at Oak Hills Church, his home church in San Antonio.[6] I like what he said to introduce these healing services to the church:

---

[6] This First Wednesday Service of worship and healing is open to the community, so please come join us. It's often live-streamed from the Oak Hills Church website at 7pm CST. Our Rapha God Ministries' prayer team joins the OHC elders and prayer team to pray for people individually after the worship and messages, with both English and Spanish prayer ministry teams.

43

"Sometimes God heals instantly; sometimes God heals gradually; but God always heals ultimately."

However and whenever true healing comes, it comes from the Lord. "Every good gift and every perfect gift is from above, and comes down from the Father of lights, with whom there is no variation or shadow of turning." (James 1:17). He is *Jehovah Rapha*, the God who says of Himself, "I am the Lord who heals you" (Exodus 15:26).

Our God is a healing God. And He has called us and empowered us to continue His healing ministry. So we really must begin to understand from God's Word just what "healing" is, and what the biblical, spiritual principles are in relation to "healing" and "deliverance."

There's much about healing that's a mystery, and at the same time, there's much we can learn from the Word of God. In our journey of understanding, it's so important to take the posture of humility before God, trusting that healing is ultimately in His way, in His time, by His power, and for His glory.

Chapter 3

What is Healing?

Healing is the process of being restored to wholeness by the grace of God, and includes being made whole in every dimension of our lives. As we will see, God has created the world in such a way that trust in His nature and obedience to His will brings about the restoration of all things. The key to this process of restoration is to "sanctify Christ as Lord" in our hearts and throughout the earth (1 Peter 3:15). As we obey His command to "submit yourselves therefore to God" we can "resist the devil and he will flee" (James 4:7).

Healing and deliverance for us and for all creation come through submission to the Lordship of Jesus Christ. This lifelong process of sanctification and holiness of heart and life releases the healing power of God to us, and then to all creation. When Christ is Lord of all, we will be healed and whole.

Healing is Wholeness

In the broad sense, healing is wholeness. To be healed is to be made whole. Every dimension of our being is being restored into created order, redeemed by the Blood of Jesus in the power of the Holy Spirit through trusting faith in God. We are healed in spirit, soul, and body. We are healed spiritually, emotionally, physically, and relationally. We are healed in our relationship with God, with one another, and within ourselves.

As Jesus comes to bind up the brokenhearted and set the captives free, He is ministering the healing love of God to make us whole and wholly His. Two ways this concept of healing as wholeness is conveyed in Scripture is through idea of "peace" in the Old Testament, and through the idea of "salvation" in the New Testament.

Salvation Includes Peace and Healing

In the Old Testament, one of the Hebrew words for peace is *shalom*. Even today, Jewish people use the word, "*shalom*" when they greet one another. *Shalom* is a blessing of peace that includes the idea of wholeness, being at peace with God, with one another, and within ourselves. So healing is not only wholeness, but it's also being at peace in every dimension of our lives.

In the New Testament, the same concept of wholeness is conveyed in the idea of salvation. And the Greek words, "*soteria*" (salvation) and "*sozo*," (be saved) are really the same concept. It's the idea of being made whole. In many of the scriptures where Jesus is talking about eternal life, this word "*sozo*" is used—be saved; have eternal life. But also, in some of the passages where He's ministering physical healing to someone, the word "*sozo*," be saved, is used even though it may also be translated "be healed," or "be cured" because the fullness of salvation includes healing—healing of our bodies, our souls, our spirits. And some of the accounts where Jesus sets someone free from spiritual oppression—a deliverance encounter—the same word "*sozo*" is used even though it's the context of deliverance or freedom from spiritual oppression. Jesus came to save that person from bondage. It's the same context. The fullness of salvation is eternal life, but it's also healing, deliverance, and wholeness in every level and depth of our being.

Two Different Gifts—Miracles and Healing

Sometimes healing comes instantaneously and that's exciting. When heaven comes to earth immediately, that's a miracle. But most of the time, especially in this season of time of church history, most healing is layer by layer, little by little, step by step. Miracles are increasing on the earth and in our lives. Praise God! And at the same time, God is still working to bring about the healing and wholeness of bringing our lives back into His created order, redeemed by the blood of Jesus. And most of that is healing through the process of restoration.

We couldn't really handle it if God did it all the healing and deliverance we need all at once. Even in the times where we've had a deep measure of deep healing in our lives, that was about all we could handle. It's like pealing the layers of an onion, layer by layer, step by step. As we give Him one layer, He brings up the next layer because He wants to heal us and make us whole.

The book of First Corinthians, chapter 12, talks about spiritual gifts. Some have the gifts of miracles. Others have the gifts of healings. These are two different gifts. Many times they move together, but they are different gifts. That's just one of the ways that God expresses the distinction of healing and miracles in His Word.

Healing is the Process of Restoration

Healing also includes the process of restoration—restoring our relationships with God, one another, and within ourselves. It includes eternal life, healing, and deliverance. We know the very familiar passage of Isaiah 53. Isaiah is speaking eight hundred years or so before the coming of Jesus, speaking of Christ the Messiah who would come to restore and redeem God's creation. Different versions translate this in different ways, but Isaiah 53 beginning in verse 4 says:

> *Surely He has borne our infirmities and carried our diseases, yet we accounted Him stricken, struck down by God and afflicted. But He was wounded for our transgressions, crushed for our iniquities, upon Him was the punishment that made us whole, and by His stripes we are healed.*

This is God's heart. This is the fullness of salvation. It's the fullness of what the Messiah has come to release to the people of God. He cleanses us of our iniquities, forgives us of our sins, bears our infirmities, our sicknesses, and our diseases. Everything that should have been upon us in this broken, fallen world has been laid upon Him that we might be made whole. So healing comes by the blood sacrifice of Christ because He laid down His life for us. The prophecy of Isaiah 53 was fulfilled in the healing and deliverance ministry of Jesus:

> *That evening they brought to him many who were possessed with demons; and he cast out the spirits with a word, and cured all who were sick. This was to fulfill what had been spoken through the prophet Isaiah, "He took our infirmities and bore our diseases." Now when Jesus saw great crowds around him, he gave orders to go over to the other side*
> (Matthew 8:16–18).

When the faith of John the Baptist grew weary and he wondered whether Jesus was the promised Messiah, the anointed One of God who would come to bring the fullness of salvation to the people of God, Jesus pointed to the fruit of His healing and deliverance ministry:

> *Jesus answered them, "Go and tell John what you hear and see: the blind receive their sight, the lame walk, the lepers are cleansed, the deaf hear, the dead are raised, and the poor have good news brought to them. And blessed is anyone who takes no offense at me"* (Matthew 11:4-6).

And so we're to receive the fullness of His salvation, eternal life, healing and deliverance in every level, every depth of our being. That's God's calling. That's God's will. And knowing the distinction between healing and miracles helps free us from disappointment when we don't always see a complete and immediate healing. Healing is transformation, and transformation takes time. Miracles are like God's microwave and healing is like God's crock-pot. Both are good and accomplish their purpose and get the job done, but they get it done in different ways and for different purposes.

Healing includes "Inner Healing"

When we talk about "inner healing," we're really talking about healing from the inside out. There are New Age practices that sometimes use this term regarding guided imagery, spirit guides, and the like; but that's not what we mean by the term. Through the Christian prayer ministry of inner healing and spiritual transformation, God is starting on the inside with our hearts. He starts in our spirit and moves outward from there to the soul and the body. Healing from the inside out is letting the Holy Spirit begin to search our hearts to expose all that is in us that is not yet like Jesus. It's like the cry of David's heart in Psalm 139: "O Lord, search my heart. O Lord, see if there is any wicked way in me. See if there is any brokenness, any pain, any bondage in me. See if there's anything in me that is not yet like you" (author's paraphrase).

Our part is to make a choice to welcome the Lord, let Him search us, and let Him heal us. It's letting Jesus look beneath the surface and into the depths of our being. Considering the woman at the well again, Jesus knew that she had sin and shame from her past. And Jesus still came to her. He looked beneath the surface, down into the Samaritan woman's soul and He basically said, "Yes, you've had five husbands, and the man

48

you're now living with is not your husband" (John 4:17). He was going beneath the surface to minister inner healing. He went into her past, exposed it, and brought it to the surface. Not because He wanted to judge her and condemn her and say, "You should be ashamed of yourself and your sin." It was because He loved her! Her had compassion for her. He was opening Himself to her, and wanted her to open herself to Him.

Remember the paralytic who was forgiven of sin in Matthew chapter 9? They lowered him down to Jesus, but Jesus didn't just walk up and release the healing miracle. He basically said, "Rise up and walk because your sins are forgiven you." Sin's not always the reason that our healing is blocked, but sometimes it is. Jesus was ministering inner healing to this man. And inner healing goes beneath the surface of the matter. It's dealing with the root of the matter, dealing with the barrier blocking God's will from being done on earth as it is in heaven. It's creating in us a clean heart as David prayed in Psalm 51, when he longed to have the joy of his salvation restored.

Our salvation includes eternal life, healing, deliverance, the fullness of life here on earth. Sometimes we need to have the joy of our salvation restored. As Paul said in Romans 14, "The kingdom of God is . . . righteousness and peace and joy in the Holy Spirit." We need the joy of our salvation; the peace of our salvation restored. Inner healing and deliverance restore that joy to us, and that kind of joy is contagious. When the world sees the peace and joy of God in us, then they will want to come to God.

"Bad Roots Produce Bad Fruit"

There can be roots of resistance to God's inner healing. We'll look at seven of those key roots in detail a little later because they come up so often in prayer ministry. For now, I just want to mention that the names of the roots we'll study are Pride and Rebellion, Bitterness and Unforgiveness, Rejection, Shame, Fear, Brokenness and Unresolved Trauma, and Infirmity. One of the healing prayer ministers that taught me about these roots was Jack Frost, who always taught, "Bad roots produce bad fruit."

One way of looking at getting free of these bad roots is comparable to the idea that we're agreeing with the Lord, or even partnering with Him, to dig up the roots that produce bad fruit. For example, in Hebrews 12:15 it says that through a "root of bitterness" many are defiled. A "root of bitterness" is a hardness of heart, often harboring deep-seated and simmering unforgiveness. And God makes it very clear in His Word that unless we forgive one another as our Father has forgiven us, our Father will not forgive us (Matthew 6:15). While it's true that we are saved by faith in Christ; Jesus himself said in teaching us the Lord's Prayer, "Unless you forgive one another, your Father in heaven will not forgive you."

So if we want to be free to be like Jesus, it's important that we choose to forgive. While salvation is certainly a free gift of God, He also says that, "If anyone loves Me, he will keep My word; and my Father will love him, and We will come to him and make Our home with him" (John 14:23 NKJV). This tells us that there's something more to salvation, something to this faith in God that includes obeying God and His spiritual principles—living as He's called us to live in accordance with His Word and His principles. So God wants us to experience the fullness of salvation, but to do that, sometimes He has to dig down to some roots that are producing bad fruit in our lives.

I also learned quite a bit from Jack about ministering the Father heart of God, as well as prophetically speaking the Father's blessing into someone's soul as the Holy Spirit leads. And that's what this kind of healing prayer ministry is. It's really letting God come to us and hold us, love us, and let His heart pour into us. It's letting the healing power of His love dig up the roots, dig up the shame, dig up the pain, and free us all of the things that keep us bound in the past so we can move on into our destiny (Philippians 3:13–14).

"Pain out, love in." That's kind of a simple formula of my perspective of healing prayer ministry. The approach I often teach is, "Here's Jesus; give it to Him." And then I listen for what the Father wants to do for His child, speaking it and praying it as He leads.

Many people in healing and prayer ministry say that unforgiveness is the number one barrier to God's healing grace in our lives. And I've seen

50

that many, many times. So God wants to dig up the roots. The Holy Spirit comes to put the ax to the root of that which is not bearing good fruit (Matthew 3:10). He wants to separate the wheat from the chaff with His winnowing fork (Matthew 3:11–12). He has His threshing floor. And when you come to His threshing floor, You come to the place where He's sifting out the wheat from the chaff. *His refining fire is purifying, sanctifying, and healing us, but sometimes for the healing, we have to embrace the flame.* Sometimes we have to let Him shake what needs to be shaken.

When God shakes everything that can be shaken, as His Word says He will, then whatever can't be shaken remains (Hebrews 12:27). Now that's not because He's mad at us, it's not because He's harshly judging us, and it's not because He wants to push us away. It's because He loves us. It's because He's a good and perfect Father who wants His best for His children (vv. 7-11). He wants us to experience the fullness of His salvation and restore us to the joy of our salvation. He wants us to "be healed" (v. 13). So we say, by His grace, "Yes, Lord! I come to the threshing floor. Yes, Lord, I come to the purifying fire. Dig up the roots. Prune every branch that does not bear good fruit. Heal me and restore me. Deliver me and free me. Make me whole and wholly Yours."

Now it's one thing to say, "Yes, Lord, I get that in my mind." It's another thing to say, "Yes, Lord, I'm letting you do that in my heart." So if we could, I'd like for us to take a moment and agree in prayer according to the principle of Matthew 18:19:

> *Yes, Lord. I do agree. I open my heart to you. I come to the threshing floor. Put your ax to the roots of everything in me that does not bear good fruit. Dig up the pain, the shame, the hurt, the fear, the anger, the bitterness, resentment, dig up the bondages, the addictions, the hardness of heart, the sorrow, the grief, depression, weariness, heaviness, dig it up, Lord. Draw it out and pour in your love. I'm asking for this. I'm asking you to do it now and in the days ahead. Restore unto me the joy of my salvation. I want to be part of Your glorious Bride who has made herself ready as You are bringing many sons to glory. In Jesus' name, Amen.*

As you read this book and consider these biblical, spiritual principles, I know the Lord will be answering that prayer. He will be guiding you and leading you to a deeper place of surrender, a higher place of faith, and a

51

fuller place of healing. There were miracles in Jesus' day; and by the same Holy Spirit who anointed Jesus for miracles in His day, there are miracles of Jesus in our day as well. And in this process and journey of healing and deliverance, I believe by faith that you will see miracles, healing, and breakthroughs in your life and through your life for others, all by the transforming power of God.

Chapter 4

God's Will to Heal

One of the ways the Lord revealed Himself in the Old Testament is through the name *Jehovah Rapha*, meaning, "I am the Lord who heals you" (Exodus 15:26).[7] And in the New Testament, Jesus comes as Son of God and Son of Man, perfectly revealing the Father heart of God in His ministry of teaching, preaching, and healing (Matthew 4:23). He was teaching, preaching and healing because it is God's will.

> *Now a leper came to Him, imploring Him, kneeling down to Him and saying to Him, "If You are willing, You can make me clean." Then Jesus, moved with compassion, stretched out His hand and touched him, and said to him, "I am willing; be cleansed." As soon as He had spoken, immediately the leprosy left him, and he was cleansed* (Mark 1:40–42 NKJV, emphasis added).

Still, sometimes people question the will of God for healing in a particular moment. People ask, "Well, should we pray for healing? It might not be God's will for healing." Sometimes that comes up whether we're talking about our body, or sickness, or disease, or even death. But God's Word reveals His will. God's Word shows us that it's His will for us to be healed and made whole. All of the things that should have been laid upon us have been laid upon Him so that we might be made whole (Isaiah 53:5; Matthew 8:17).

Jesus went about healing people—their spirit, soul, and body. He went about delivering them from evil because it was the will of God. It can't be the will of God for healing to happen and at the same time be the will of God for healing not to happen. A kingdom divided against itself can't stand. So God's Word is revealing His will.

---

[7] Healing is often conditioned upon obedience, though God often moves sovereignly out of His compassion when we least deserve it, but even then, His spiritual principles are at work in ways we don't often understand. Obedience brings the peace of healing and wholeness. We'll discuss the spiritual principle of obedience and alignment with God's will and ways in relation to healing in more depth in a later section.

Many times I find myself praying Psalm 103 over people in prayer ministry and encouraging people with this, because sometimes there's this doubt or this question about God's will for healing. And Psalm 103:1–5 is one of those places that makes His will for healing us very clear in His Word. We know the beginning of this very well:

Bless the Lord oh my soul, and all that is within me bless His holy name. Bless the Lord oh my soul, and forget not all His benefits who forgives all your iniquity, who heals all your diseases, who redeems your life from the pit, who crowns you with steadfast love and mercy, who satisfies you with good as long as you live so that your youth is renewed like the eagle's.

So for all who are willing to confess and to repent of their sins, the Lord is willing to forgive and cleanse if we'll bring it to Him. But are all the sins forgiven even though that's God's will? Only when we confess and repent. Only when we turn to Him are they forgiven. The precious, powerful blood of Jesus is what makes this available. But even though the blood of Christ is available for our complete forgiveness, we have to make a choice to apply the blood.

During the first Passover when God delivered His people out of Egypt and released all those judgments against Pharaoh, every time that Pharaoh chose to harden his heart against God, Pharaoh's heart became more and more callused. Then came the last judgment. The angel of death was released, and God told His people to slay the lamb that was spotless and without blemish, and apply the blood to the doorposts and the lintels of their homes so that the angel of death would pass over— the first Passover.

So the blood was available. But what would have happened to the Hebrew families had they not applied the blood of the lamb to the doorposts of the houses that the angel of death passed over? The same judgment of God would have come upon their home as well. So even though the blood is available by God because God makes it available, He's calling us to apply the blood—which is to agree with Him. That's our part—to agree to make the choice to open our hearts, lay down our sins and burdens, give Him our suffering, pain, sicknesses, diseases, iniquities and all that keeps us from being made whole.

He calls us to do our part, which is to agree with Him, to give it to Him, to apply the blood. We couldn't do it by our own power or our own strength, but by the sacrifice of Christ, the blood is available. So Psalm 103 verses 1–5 tell us that He forgives all iniquities, and He heals all our diseases. Just like it's God's will to forgive us of all of our sins, it's His will to heal all of our diseases. It's His will to redeem, restore, and cleanse our lives from destruction, brokenness, and sin.

Some of us might say, "Well, it doesn't always happen." Just like everybody doesn't always get saved, doesn't always get forgiven of their sins, everybody doesn't always get healed of all their diseases. But does that mean it's not God's will? This is really important to understand when we pray: we can agree with God's will, and that's as it is in heaven, where God is the King of the kingdom of heaven. Jesus teaches us to pray for God's will to be done on earth as it is in heaven, for His kingdom to come on earth as it is in heaven. God is wanting to bring forth heaven to earth, to bring earth into alignment and agreement with heaven. He does that through the prayers of individuals. He also does it through the body of Christ coming into agreement with God. So just because we don't see His will made manifest immediately and miraculously, are we supposed to give up? Are we supposed to conclude that it must not have been God's will, because if it was God's will it would have happened?

No! What God's calling us to do is to see His will and search out His Word. Since His Word reveals His will, we are to choose to come into agreement with His Word and His will. His Word tells us that He wants to forgive, to cleanse, and to heal us of all of our iniquities and all our diseases. His will is for us to be made whole because all that should have been laid upon us has already been laid upon Him. He wants us to believe that and receive that, as we come into agreement with that, because that is the truth.

Battling in the Heavenly Realm

The Bible speaks of Daniel as being a righteous man. He was taken captive out of Israel, taken over to Babylonia (which is modern day Iraq), and one day God dropped some understanding into Daniel's spirit about a prophetic truth uttered through Jeremiah that was recorded in that

55

scroll. In Daniel 9:1–2 it says, "In the first year of Darius son of Ahasuerus, by birth a Mede, who became king over the realm of the Chaldeans—in the first year of his reign, I, Daniel, perceived in the books the number of years that, according to the word of the Lord to the prophet Jeremiah, must be fulfilled for the devastation of Jerusalem, namely, seventy years."

Chapter 9 goes on to speak about how Daniel prayed and cried out to God on behalf of Israel. Another way to say that is that he was standing in the gap for them. (We'll teach more on that later when we talk about cleansing generational sin.)   Daniel identified with the sins of the forefathers that led Israel into exile and the judgment of God to come. Chapter 9 gives quite a bit of detail about how Daniel asked God to forgive them and cleanse them, not on the basis of their righteousness, but of God's. Then the Lord answered his prayer, and ultimately, Israel was set free out of Babylon and restored back to the promised land of Israel.

But what happens in the mean time? Daniel's fasting. Daniel's praying. Daniel's crying out to God, and we see the story in Daniel chapter 10 when the angel comes twenty-one days later—twenty-one days of fasting and praying and crying out to God. And then the angel comes and says in Daniel 10:12–14:

> *Do not fear, Daniel, for from the first day that you set your mind to gain understanding and to humble yourself before your God, your words have been heard, and I have come because of your words. But the prince of the kingdom of Persia opposed me for twenty-one days. So Michael, one of the chief princes, came to help me, and I left him there with the prince of the kingdom of Persia, and have come to help you understand…*

You see, there's a battle taking place in the heavens. It's not just us and God. We really do have an enemy. But God's will for us is to cleanse us, free us, heal us, deliver us, make us whole, restore all creation in His perfect order, redeemed by the blood of Jesus—that's God will, that's our God! And God has His people here whom He's putting on our hearts. He's moving us to pray, intercede, and stand in the gap. He's looking for anyone to intercede, to stand in the gap, to cry out for Him. And as we begin to pray, we seek God, we pray His Word, we know His

Word, and we seek Him for His will, we'll sometimes be faced with the enemy running resistance against us.

We really do have the thief who comes to kill, steal and destroy (John 10:10). And he has his army with its legions. Jesus said our enemy uses, he wields "the power of darkness" in this broken, fallen world where human beings and spiritual beings have a free will to act out of sin and rebellion (Luke 22:53). There is a battle taking place in the heavenlies that interferes with God's will being immediately done in our lives. We need to recognize that God has created a world where we are to pray, seek Him, and agree with Him. That's our part—to agree with God— to choose God. And God's releasing the Word, His will, and the blessings of salvation, healing, and deliverance. And in that battle in the heavenly realm, there's Michael the archangel and all of the heavenly warriors that are fighting for God and for us. They are ministering spirits, as the Word says, who do the bidding of the Lord to help us (Hebrews 1:14). During the intensity of that battle, sometimes the will of God is hindered, but He's calling us to agree with Him to pray through for the victory. Now sometimes we don't see the victory instantaneously. When we do, that's a miracle! heaven comes to earth. God's will as it is in heaven is done on earth—praise God! And that's exciting when we get to see those kinds of miracles. We're seeing more of them. But most of the time it's a battle. Most of the time, it's a fight.

Now God's going to use every battle. He's not going to waste a moment of our suffering or struggles. As we entrust it to Him, He's going to redeem it all. He just makes us hungrier for Him and that much more determined to press through for the victory. But we fight a very real enemy—the enemy who comes to steal, kill, and destroy. Our enemy is defeated by the cross, but our part is to enforce the victory of the cross against the so-called "god of this world" and his kingdom of darkness that is defeated by the light of the glory of God (2 Corinthians 4:4). That's another part of the ministry of healing and deliverance. It's applying the blood of Jesus and enforcing the victory of the cross. God's doing it with His power and authority, according to His will, but He's doing it *through* His people. And He wants us to agree with Him for our own healing and wholeness, but He also wants us to agree with Him as we minister healing and wholeness and deliverance to others. God's

Word reveals His will, and He wants us to agree with Him and His will for our healing and deliverance on earth as it is in heaven.

Chapter 5

Why God Heals Us

We've seen in Scripture that God's will is to heal us and free us. It's a joy to Him when we receive the fullness of salvation, not forgetting all that Christ has done for us through His sacrifice of love for us on the cross (Isaiah 53; Psalm 103; Matthew 8:16–18). "He himself bore our sins in his body on the cross, so that, free from sins, we might live for righteousness; by his wounds you have been healed" (1 Peter 2:24). But why does God heal us?

We are healed for a purpose. And I think that at least three of the purposes why our merciful God chooses to heal us are: God is compassionate to make us whole; God is conforming us into the image of Christ; and God is commissioning us to the ministry of Christ. His ministry of healing and deliverance is part of His plan of fulfilling these purposes in our lives.

God is Compassionate to Make Us Whole

Through healing, God reveals His Father heart of compassion for us. When Jesus saw the crowds of people hurting, hungry, broken, and bound, "He had compassion for them and cured their sick" (Matthew 14:14). Jesus perfectly reveals the Father heart of God, and our Father's heart is full of compassion. Psalm 107 is one of those powerful places in God's Word that reveals God's will to heal us and deliver us out of His compassion, mercy, and steadfast love.

God is Conforming Us into the Image of Christ

God is preparing a holy Bride. He's bringing many sons to glory and that's part of what the healing and deliverance ministry is. As He heals us of our wounds, our pain, and the ways in which we're bound up in our past, He also delivers us from evil—the world, the flesh, and the devil—so that we can be emptied of ourselves and conformed to Him. This is part of the healing process of transformation of spirit, soul, and body through the sanctifying work of the Holy Spirit to make us both "sound"(healed, whole, and free) and "blameless"(holy and conformed to the image of Christ) by His grace and in His power (1 Thessalonians 5:23–24).

When Christ returns in glory for a glorious Bride, it's His desire for her to be conformed into His image. And this ministry of inner healing, wholeness, and deliverance, is also the ministry of preparing the Bride, His people, to be a holy people ready to completely receive Him. We are to be "conformed to the image of Christ" (Romans 8:29). We are to have "the mind of Christ" (Philippians 2:5, 1 Corinthians 2:16). We are the "body of Christ" on earth (1 Corinthians. 12:27). We are to be "filled with the Spirit of Christ" (Romans 8:9). God the Father and God the Son have come to dwell within us through God the Holy Spirit. Every dimension of God is moving in us, flowing through us, conforming us into His image, into His nature, making us one with Him, one with each other, and one in ministry to all the world.

We are to be "sound and blameless" because God desires to "sanctify [us] entirely" in "spirit and soul and body" not just in heaven when we die, but now and "at the coming of our Lord Jesus Christ" (1 Thessalonians 5:23). We will discuss this in detail in the next section, as a foundational principle of this perspective and approach to healing and deliverance prayer ministry. But this is another purpose for healing.

God is Commissioning Us to the Ministry of Christ

As we are healed, He is also empowering and sending us to be His hands of healing and freedom for others. In the ways He comforts us, we will comfort others (2 Corinthians 1:3–7). As we are forgiven much, we then love much (Luke 7:47). As we have been healed and free, so He sends us to heal and free others with His authority in those very areas where we have overcome by the grace of God. As disciples of Christ, we are sent to continue the ministry of Christ (Luke 9:1–2; 10:17–19). To be truly effective in living and giving this ministry of healing and deliverance, we need to receive it first so that we can minister out of God's healing and freedom rather than out of our unhealed wounds and bondage.

60

Compassion Before Commission

God was teaching me these principles and purposes in my own journey of healing and freedom. In the beginning of my ministry, while deeply in the season of my own healing of some deep brokenness and bondage in my life, God began to put people around me that believed in praying right now and expecting God to move right now. I hadn't always been around people like that as I was growing up in the church. So I began to say, "Lord, I want that! I want to move in the gifts of your Spirit. I want to have the fullness of You living in my life, flowing through my life. I want to be used that way. I want my life to have purpose and meaning. I want to fulfill my calling and destiny."

And as I began to pray for this gift of healing, I began to understand more of what it was and understand that God did want to heal us and make us whole. This became something that I would really pray and strive about in my prayer time, because we're supposed to press in to pursue spiritual gifts. That's one of the confusing things in the church. You hear it said many times to "seek the Giver and not the gifts." And that sounds holy and good, but it's not really biblical. We're supposed to seek the Giver *and* seek the gifts, according to God's Word, rather than human, religious thinking.

Now you have to have that in the right order. If you're seeking the gifts first, that's out of order. That's idolatry. But we are to seek the Giver, seek God, and His Word makes it very clear that we are also to seek the gifts. We are commanded to "earnestly pursue spiritual gifts" (1 Corinthians 14:1). So God does want us to seek Him, and as we're seeking Him, we're going to want to agree with Him, flow with Him, be His vessel, His ambassador. We want both the nature of His Spirit to flow through us *and* the gifting of His Spirit to flow through us.

So I would cry out to God, asking Him for this gift of healing. And one day it was just really clear that He was speaking to me about this—it was just one of those life-changing, supernatural moments. Back then it wasn't always so clear to me when He was speaking to me. I've grown and matured in my prayer life since then. And as I was praying for the gift of healing, the Lord said very clearly to my heart, "First pray for the gift of compassion." And so I did. That led me into a prison ministry.

61

On Sunday nights I'd gather with those guys in a prayer circle—praying out loud, learning how to pray out loud as I prayed for them, learning how to preach out loud as I gave them a message. God began to put compassion in my heart.

At first, the significance of what the Lord was doing in me personally wasn't so apparent. But ironically, even though my Dad had been shot in a bar in Houston back when I was younger and still in law school, "coincidentally," the man who shot my father was sitting in a Texas prison while I was preaching, teaching, and learning to minister the healing love of God in a Kentucky prison. God was at work. God was working His compassion into my heart.

I shared that irony with the men for the first time on a cold Christmas Eve night, when none of them were expecting anyone to come out and minister to them that night. As I spoke of my father's murder and my family's pain and journey toward forgiveness and healing from the inside out, I could tell the Holy Spirit as speaking to their hearts. When I invited them to come receive Holy Communion as a step toward the love of God revealed in Jesus Christ, every man in that filled chapel came forward. Every one of them gave me a hug. And the light bulb came on that God was healing me as He was using me to heal others.

He was uprooting the unforgiveness and bitterness in my heart as I was releasing His love to them. God has a way of giving us compassion and mercy—sometimes for the very people, or the people in the same kind of circumstances who we feel have hurt us the most. That's just one of the ways that God works because He calls us to pray for those who have persecuted us, to bless those who have cursed us, and even to love those who have hated us (Luke 6:27–28). That's one of God's kingdom principles for turning the world upside down.

We are to grow in Christlikeness. That's our purpose on earth. Every struggle, every challenge, everything that we go through, they are opportunities to grow into the image Christ. And even Christ, as it says in the book of Hebrews, learned obedience through suffering. Now I wish that wasn't the case, but it is. We live in a broken, fallen world where people are going to hurt and wound us, and there are spiritual forces of wickedness warring against us. But as we keep our eyes fixed on Him, as we keep our heart open to Him, as we welcome Him into our pain, shame, brokenness, and bondage, then He heals us and frees us to be like Jesus. He is conforming us to His image. He's looking for a people who will be willing to let Him do that out of His compassion and purpose for us, because we will be His glorious Bride, his sons and daughters conformed to the glory of His image and learning to move in the authority of His power as we display His nature.

Unfortunately, many of us are still so focused on ourselves and bound by our past—our own pain, struggles, needs, and bondages. We're trapped there. We're ensnared to the depth that even though God's anointing may flow through us to a degree, He's prevented from flowing through us in the unhindered and powerful intensity that He desires. And we really do need healing and deliverance so that He may flow more freely through our lives. That's why in these days God is pouring out an amazing anointing upon ministries of healing and deliverance. He's using this to prepare the way of the Lord, to prepare the Bride of Christ, to cause the church to arise in power and in glory in these last days. That's one of the ways in which He will fulfill Habakkuk 2:14, that the glory of the Lord will cover the earth as the waters cover the sea—His glory covering His creation through His people.

Chapter 6

How God Heals Us

Our God is a healing God, and He heals us in many different ways. Much of healing is a mystery, but there are principles that I believe He wants us to learn from His Word, and characteristics of His nature that He wants us to learn from His ways. Sometimes God just moves sovereignly in His power and compassion, whether we ask for it, have faith for it, align ourselves with it—or not. Praise God! We can celebrate those times and celebrate a God who does that. But at the same time, God also desires to bring healing to us and to His creation through His people who are available to be His instruments of His healing love to others through prayer ministry.

God created each of us uniquely, and there are many unique and diverse ways that He chooses to heal through the prayers and ministry of His children. We are not all the same, and we each have a different gifting, calling, and anointing. Though together we are the body of Christ, having one Spirit of Christ within us, there are different ways that God moves through us for healing ministry at different times and in different people's lives. Here, I'd like to look at three different ways or dimensions that God heals through us: (1) prayers of faith, (2) enforcing our authority in Christ, and (3) helping remove barriers to healing.

Prayers of Faith

Sometimes God leads us to pray for others by asking Him to heal them. A key Scripture expressing this form of healing prayer ministry is from James 5:

> *Are any among you suffering? They should pray. Are any cheerful? They should sing songs of praise. Are any among you sick? They should call for the elders of the church and have them pray over them, anointing them with oil in the name of the Lord. The **prayer of faith** will save the sick, and the Lord will raise them up; and anyone who has committed sins will be forgiven. Therefore confess your sins to one another, and pray for one another, so that you may be healed. The prayer of the righteous is powerful and effective* (James 5:13–16, emphasis added).

Here's another example of God's Word revealing God's will for healing. Scripture asks, "Are *any* suffering. Are *any* sick?" If *any* are, "they should pray." God's will is to heal us. One way He heals us is for us to ask the "elders of the church to pray for us." I believe the context of "elders" is speaking of those in the church who are more spiritually mature in the faith and understanding of the ways of God's Word and Spirit.

In this form of prayer, the spiritual elders "pray over them." I think of this time of prayer as something like this: "Father, in the name of Jesus, we ask You heal Johnny from _____." Notice that anointing with oil is not merely a tradition of one part of the church or something that only "charismatic Christians" are supposed to do. It's named a means of God's healing grace to flow into anyone's life.

And this type of prayer is not merely prayer, but it is a "prayer of faith." The idea of "faith" and its necessity for healing is often very misunderstood among the body of Christ, I believe. It is a spiritual principle explicitly stated in Scripture that informs us of the importance of faith:

> *Without faith it is impossible to please God, for whoever would approach Him must believe that He exists and that He rewards those who seek Him* (Hebrews 11:6).

But it's very important to keep the right priorities and focus when understanding and applying our faith. First, God must be the primary object of our faith. He rewards those who seek *Him*. It's important to *first* seek Him and His righteousness, *then* all these things that we are seeking (healing, freedom, and all the blessings of God) will be added to us (Matthew 6:33). The order of our seeking makes a difference. We are supposed to bring our needs before God and seek His answers to our prayers in faith, but we must first seek Him and then the answer to our needs in faith. Otherwise, if we are putting our focus and priority on the things *we* are seeking first, then that's a form of idolatry—putting something else in the place of God. So we first seek Him, then we seek what we ask of Him.

And faith is primarily a matter of trust. We are trusting God and trusting His nature that He loves us and that He is for us. So even when the answer does not come when and how we want it, we should not let our circumstances determine our relationship with God. As we've discussed regarding the will of God for healing, not all healing will always happen on this side of heaven because the kingdom of God has come but it is not yet fully manifested. Still, we can choose to thank God for all He is doing, letting that be our focus, instead of criticizing Him for all that we think He's not doing and letting that steal our focus from what is really important—our relationship of trust in God who loves us and is fighting for us in ways we don't fully see or know.

While faith is important in our relationship with God, so is patience. "Through faith *and* patience [we] inherit the promises [of the kingdom of God]" (Hebrews 6:12). I've heard it said that we hear much these days about "the faith movement," but not "the patience movement!" But it's by both—faith and patience—that we inherit the promises. We are much more into microwaves and God is much more into crock-pots. We can praise God for the instantaneous answers to prayer when we see heaven come to earth in the miracle of a moment, but we can also praise Him for the patient process of healing and restoration that comes, layer by layer, step by step, and "little by little" (see Exodus 23:30).

As we pray in faith, believing and trusting God first, being patient in His answers and certain of His will, the Word declares that, "The prayer of faith *will* save the sick, and the Lord *will* raise them up" (James 5:15). These are declarations of God's Word revealing His will. Our part is to agree with God, to pray heaven to earth in faith. As we stand in the gap in Christ, allowing Christ to stand in us by His Spirit, we are praying for His kingdom to come and His will to be done "on earth as it is in heaven." In a broken, fallen world not yet fully redeemed and fully manifesting the consummation of the coming of the kingdom, we may not always see the answer come in the way and time in which we want it. But we are to keep on believing and praying in the faith and patience God gives us. And we will see much more healing happen than if we don't. The more healing we see happen, the more it increases our faith and increases our experiences of answered prayers of faith.

A key Scripture that has really helped me understand this tension of standing firm in faith and believing the promises of God, even when we don't yet see the healing manifested in agreement with God's will on earth as it is in heaven, is the spiritual principle of Ephesians 3:

Blessed be the God and Father of our Lord Jesus Christ, who has blessed us in Christ with every spiritual blessing in the heavenly places (Ephesians 1:3).

This Scripture brings together the idea of how the kingdom of God and our healing can be present already, but also not yet. It's not either/or; it's both/and. We already have this blessing in the heavenly realm, but at the same time, it is being called forth by faith in the natural realm.

This is a critical concept to understand, especially in healing prayer ministry. I used to get frustrated if I was praying for people and things didn't happen immediately, especially when God was giving me a witness in my spirit that He was doing it. And one day, this Scripture burst to life for me from Ephesians 1:3 to explain how we can declare something to be done by faith, according to God's Word, even while we don't yet see it manifested on earth, as it is in heaven.

This Scripture says that God "*has* blessed us." When did he bless us? Already! What did He bless us with? *Every* spiritual blessing! How many spiritual blessings? *Every* spiritual blessing! What are some spiritual blessings? Eternal life, healing of our body, healing of our emotions, peace and intimacy with God, security and provision, and so on. All of these are spiritual blessings. This Scripture is saying that God *already* has given us *all* these spiritual blessings. How? First of all, we must be "in Christ." It's only through Christ that we can receive any of God's spiritual blessings.

But *where* do we already have these spiritual blessings in Christ? It's "in the heavenly places"—in the heavenly realm, the heavenly dimension, the eternal, spiritual dimension of our lives. This coincides with the teaching of the Lord's Prayer when we pray, "Lord, let Your kingdom come, let Your will be done on earth as it is in heaven." It's already God's will, it's already established in heaven—in the heavenly dimension, in the eternal dimension. In that dimension, all things are already present to God eternally—past, present, and future. The heavenly dimension is an eternal dimension.

68

But we live in both the heavenly dimension *and* the earthly dimension when we are in Christ. We are here on earth, living our lives in the earthly dimension of chronological time, moment by moment, day by day, and year by year. But at the same time, we are also *in Christ*, not only living in this chronological dimension of earth, but also living eternally in the heavenly dimension. Christ is the intersection between the heavenly dimension and the earthly dimension. I personally think this is also part of what it means that Christ is both Son of God and Son of Man—He's always, eternally existed as Son of God, yet at the same time, He humbled himself in human flesh and blood to live a life of chronological years in history on earth as Son of Man. And when we are in Christ and Christ is in us, we also join in that intersection of the heavenly and earthly dimensions.

> *But God, who is rich in mercy, out of the great love with which he loved us even when we were dead through our trespasses, made us alive together with Christ—by grace you have been saved— and raised us up with him and seated us with him in the heavenly places in Christ Jesus*
> (Ephesians 2:4–6).

In Christ, we are already seated with God "at His right hand in the heavenly places, far above all rule and authority and power and dominion" (Ephesians 1:20–21). There, in the heavenly places of that eternal, spiritual dimension, we already "have redemption through His blood," and we have already "also obtained an inheritance" (Ephesians 1:7–12). In that eternal dimension, where we already live in Christ, everything that ever will be true is already true because it is eternally true. That's how something can be God's will and be done in heaven, even though we don't yet see it made manifest here on earth as it already is in heaven. That's how we can call things that are not as though they are, according to the Word of God and His promises that are always yes and amen, without being in some kind of denial. In this sense, everything that is true is eternally true, everything that ever will be true has always been true, and it is true now.

For example, that's how Jesus can declare from the cross, "It is finished" even before His resurrection. Eternally, it has always been finished in the heavenly places, and now it is being done on earth as it is in heaven. Now by the grace of God, we can come into agreement with that eternal

69

truth. We apply the blood of Jesus, eternally available, to every area of our lives, enforcing the victory of the cross and celebrating the glory and power of the resurrection. When we do, His kingdom comes and His will is done here on earth as it is in heaven—here in this earthly dimension as it is in the heavenly dimension. These are fairly deep concepts, and I'm still seeking the Lord's wisdom and understanding, but I sense that they are extremely important to grasp in the bigger picture and perspective. So I'm planning another book to be called *The Eternal Dimension.*

We can apply this kingdom principle to the ministry of healing. So let's take, for example, someone seeking prayer for healing from disease. We pray, believing that is God's will for this person to be freed of disease. His Word reveals His will, and His Word says that He is the God "who heals all your diseases" (Psalm 103:3). I had a series of battles with pneumonia a few years ago. Based on God's Word, I believed it was not His will for me to have pneumonia, that it was His will to heal me from pneumonia. There may have been some opening, some weakness, something going on in my body or my emotions or my family, my community, or the body of Christ in general that allowed an access point somehow for that attack to come. But God didn't send the pneumonia; the enemy did. And he may have used some physical weakness or opening in my immune system. There may have been a natural means or agent that was used, a virus or bacteria or whatever. But that doesn't rule out the spiritual component of a spiritual root or opening for the manifestation of the sickness in my body as well. It's rarely either/or; it's mostly both/and, I believe. This is a more holistic viewpoint that every area of our lives affects the other areas of spirit, soul, and body.

So as I began to pray for healing to resist that disease, to stand against the root and the source of it, I was coming into agreement and into alignment with the truth of God's Word and God's will for me. It was already done in the heavenly realm the moment I asked for it and agreed with God's Word about it because it was God's will.

> *And this is the boldness we have in him, that if we ask anything according to his will, he hears us. And if we know that he hears us in whatever we ask, we know that we have obtained the requests made of him* (1 John 5:14–15).

The moment that I began to pray for that and receive it and others joined me, I had that healing from pneumonia. It was already done in the heavenly places of the eternal realm in Christ Jesus where I am already and eternally seated. In that realm, I was already healed and whole, delivered and freed. In that realm, I was healed of that disease. But here in the earthly, in the chronological time of this dimension it had not yet worked itself out until after a season of time. It was done in heaven and was in the process of being done on earth as it was in heaven. But the day came where earth agreed with heaven, and I didn't have the disease of pneumonia anymore. Sometimes that kind of healing comes instantly and miraculously, sometimes it comes little by little in the process, and sometimes it comes in the healing of the resurrection. But in any event, God wants us to pray according to His Word, expecting in faith for His kingdom to come and His will to be done on earth as it is in heaven. When that's our perspective and our direction in prayer, we'll see heaven and earth move in ever-increasing measure to bring about God's Word and God's will or redemption and restoration.

So when we pray we can believe that God is at work. Every time we pray something happens. We are releasing the power of God, bringing the power of God to bear on what we are asking of Him, as we seek to be led by His Word and His Spirit in our prayers. And God calls us to persevere, to pray through. We should pray through until we see the victory or He releases us from the burden of prayer. Someone has said we should "PUSH" in our prayers—Pray Until Something Happens! Based on God's will revealed in God's Word, we can know that we are praying with confident faith rather than arrogant presumption because that's how He taught us to pray—"Your kingdom come, Your will be done, on earth as it is in heaven."

Enforcing Our Authority in Christ

A second way that God heals through prayer ministry is through enforcing our authority in Christ. A key Scripture to this form of healing prayer ministry is in Luke 9:

> *Then Jesus called the twelve together and* **gave them power and authority** *over all demons and to cure diseases, and he sent them out to*

71

proclaim the kingdom of God and to heal (Luke 9:1–2, emphasis added).

Jesus "gave *them* power and authority." There is a distinction between prayer and taking authority. There is a time for prayer and then a time for taking the authority that God has given us to exercise it on behalf of others in ministry. Once again, Jesus is our model for ministry. He said, "As the Father has sent Me, so I send you" (John 20:21). In other words, He says, "How I did it is how I want you to go do it." How did Jesus minister to people? He first spent time in prayer with the Father. Remember that he said, "I only do what I see my Father doing. I only speak the words that He gives me to speak." So Jesus spent a lot of time in prayer, intercession, and communion with the Father. He was praying for the people, praying to hear God's voice and know His Word. Then He went where the Father sent Him to minister in authority—the authority that can only come by spending time with God in prayer and in God's Word.

When you read the accounts of Jesus' ministry of healing and deliverance, binding up the brokenhearted and setting the captives free, there are some interesting things that you never see in the Bible: You never find Jesus going and laying hands on somebody and saying, "Father in heaven, would *You* heal Simon Peter's mother-in-law of this fever?" "Father in heaven, would you heal Bartimaeus of his blindness?" "Father in heaven, would you raise Tabitha back to life?" "Father in heaven, would you cleanse these ten men from their leprosy?" That's not in the Bible. That wasn't Jesus' primary model of prayer ministry, if at all.

What *is* in the Bible is Jesus coming from the place of prayer and going to the place of authority. Jesus spoke to the fever. He cast out demons with a word. He said, "Stand up and walk." He said, "Arise and take your mat and walk." Jesus touched someone and he was healed. Jesus took someone by the hand and lifted her up and the fever left her. What you see time and again is Jesus taking authority against sickness, disease, and spiritual oppression. Jesus had authority because the Spirit of God was upon Him. He was anointed by the Holy Spirit. He had spent time knowing what God was doing and then He did it. Not in His power, as

Son of Man doing everything on earth in the humility of the Son of Man, but in the power of God that was upon Him and moving through Him.

How God anointed Jesus of Nazareth with the Holy Spirit and with power; how He went about doing good and healing all who were oppressed by the devil, for God was with Him (Acts 10:38).

The ministry of Jesus is our model. As the Father sent Him, so He sends us. The same Holy Spirit that anointed Jesus of Nazareth is the same Holy Spirit who anoints us. So first we spend time in prayer. We spend time in intercession. We let God fill us. He increases as we decrease, in submission to His will and His way, to follow His leading. We draw near to him in intimacy so that we can be pure vessels, yielded to God's Word and God's will, functioning as His heart and His hands, ministering His healing love and power.

So along with prayers of faith, we are also called and commissioned, commanded really, to take our authority in Jesus' name. Jesus says, "I give you power and authority to heal the sick and cast out demons, as you proclaim the coming of the kingdom of God." He says, "Go. I give *you* authority. *You* heal the sick. *You* cast out demons. *You* proclaim the coming of the kingdom of God." It's all God's power and authority, and it's all in the power of His name, but He desires to release it to us and express it through us. It's part of our call to spiritual maturity, to "grow up in every way into Him who is our head" as the Body of Christ (Ephesians 4:15). Some say Jesus only commissioned the first twelve apostles with that kind of power and authority, but that's just not biblical. The very next chapter shows Jesus commissioning "seventy others" with the same power and authority to heal the sick, cast out demons, and proclaim the coming of the kingdom of God in His power and authority, expressed through His disciples (Luke 10:1–24).

One way of taking our authority is by speaking with His authority. Part of exercising faith is by speaking with authority.

Jesus answered them, "Have faith in God. Truly I tell you, if you say to this mountain, 'Be taken up and thrown into the sea,' and if you do not doubt in your heart, but believe that what you say will come to pass, it will be done for you. So I tell you, whatever you ask for in prayer, believe that you have received it, and it will be yours" (Mark 11:22–24).

Another expression of our authority in Christ is by "binding" and "loosing" with the power of our words, anointed by the Holy Spirit of God to accomplish the purposes of God:

And I tell you, you are Peter, and on this rock I will build My church, and the gates of Hades will not prevail against it. I will give you the keys of the kingdom of heaven, and whatever you bind on earth will be bound in heaven, and whatever you loose on earth will be loosed in heaven (Matthew 16:18–19).

God, in His sovereignty, has chosen to work out His purposes through His people who are surrendered and yielded to Him. He says, "I *give you* the keys of the kingdom of heaven." "The keys" speak of authority. They speak of the weapons of our warfare: Our faith in God; the name of Jesus; the power of the blood of Jesus; the Word of God; worshiping God in Spirit and truth; intimacy and protection through the communion of prayer.

We have been given these keys of the kingdom of heaven and God wants us to put the keys in the door. There are too many locked doors because we do not take the key, put it into the door, and turn the lock. We are waiting for God to take the key and put it in the door and open the door. But God is not going to do what He has commanded us to do. He says, "I gave *you* the keys to the kingdom of heaven. I am preparing a people who will rule and reign with Me forever. I am growing you up into spiritual maturity, as you learn to exercise the power and authority I have given you in My name. It's by My power, by My Spirit," says the Lord, "but you must do your part. I am calling you, Body of Christ, to arise and shine, individually and together as My Body to take the authority that I have given you. Go and obey My command. Go and heal and deliver and proclaim. Go and manifest my glory and my Word, as I lead you and empower you" (see Isaiah 60:1–2).

We are called to pray and we are called to take authority. Our prayers, actions, and body language can reflect the form of prayer ministry we are exercising. One way of expressing this is whether our eyes are opened or closed. When we exercise prayers of faith, we can close our eyes to focus on God, seeking Him, praying to Him, praying for ourselves, for others, and for the situations on our hearts. But when we go from the place of prayer to the place of authority, it's time to open our eyes. We are no longer praying and speaking to God. Now we are speaking to "the mountain." We are speaking to the spiritual forces of evil, to sickness, to disease, to situations that are less than God's perfect will on earth as it is in heaven.

With open eyes and a faith-filled heart, we speak in the power and authority we've been given by God: In the name of Jesus, we command this infirmity to go. Flu, leave my sister. Pneumonia, leave my Dad. Rejection and discouragement, come off of my Mom. Fear, get out of my son. God has not given him a spirit of fear, but a spirit of love and power and a sound mind. Cancer, be consumed in the fire of the Holy Spirit. And so on.[8] We are expressing the agreement of our words with the Word of God—by His stripes we are healed (Isaiah 53:5; 1 Peter 2:24).

When I was ordained an Elder in the United Methodist Church, the Bishop and the Elders laid hands upon me and said, in the historic words of our tradition for consecration of new ministers, "Take thou authority, Thomas Ray Hays." As part of the MorningStar Fellowship of Ministries, Rick Joyner also ordained me and commissioned me, declaring, "You will never retreat before the enemies of the cross." These were prayers of anointing and commissioning for ministry.

In Christ, we are all a kingdom of priests, anointed by God with authority as disciples of Jesus Christ. "To Him who loves us and freed us from our sins by His blood, and made us to be a kingdom, priests serving His God and Father, to Him be glory and dominion forever and ever!" (Revelation 1:5–6). In Christ, we are called to take our authority as the priesthood of all believers.

---

[8] Sample prayers and commands of authority are included after each chapter in the Potential Barriers to Healing section. Model Prayers for Inner Healing and Physical Healing are included at the end of this book.

But you are a chosen race, a royal priesthood, a holy nation, God's own people, in order that you may proclaim the mighty acts of Him who called you out of darkness into His marvelous light (1 Peter 2:9).

When Jesus gave Peter the keys of the kingdom of heaven He said, "Whatever you bind on earth shall be bound in heaven. Whatever you loose on earth shall be loosed in heaven." This speaks of our taking authority, as Christ's Body, filled with Christ's Spirit, to continue Christ's ministry. We do that with our words and actions through faith. When you bind something it is like taking a rope and tying it up. You bind it, restrict it, overpower it, overcome it. Jesus said, in the context of healing and deliverance ministry, that you bind up or tie up the strongman, which is the demonic spirit claiming access to a person's life.

But if it is by the Spirit of God that I cast out demons, then the kingdom of God has come to you. Or how can one enter a strong man's house and plunder his property, without first tying up the strong man? Then indeed the house can be plundered (Matthew 12:28–29).

First, you take authority over the demonic spirit in the name of Jesus when you "bind" him up. Then, you can cast him out and plunder his house "to destroy the works of the devil" (1 John 3.8). To cast him out is to "loose" the spirit, to break its' hold. As we will discuss in detail in the deliverance section, the spirit's hold and claimed legal right to remain in its "house" is broken when a person submits that area to the Lordship of Christ: "Submit yourselves therefore to God. Resist the devil, and he will flee from you" (James 4:7).

When we speak with authority in the name of Jesus, these spirits and their works are subject to the name of Jesus, subject to the power of the blood of Jesus, and subject to His authority being expressed and asserted through us as the Body of Christ (Philippians 2:9–11).

Removing Barriers to Healing

A third way that God also heals through our prayers is by using us to help remove the barriers to someone's healing. A key Scripture for this dimension of healing prayer ministry is from 1 John 3:

Little children, let us love, not in word or speech, but in truth and action. And by this we will know that we are from the truth and will reassure our hearts before him whenever our hearts condemn us; for God is greater than our hearts, and he knows everything. Beloved, if our hearts do not condemn us, we have boldness before God; and we receive from him whatever we ask, because we obey his commandments and do what pleases him
(1 John 3:18–22).

Though it's God's will to heal us, sometimes there can be barriers to our healing. God wants us to "receive from Him whatever we ask" but sometimes the trouble is "our hearts condemn us." When our hearts condemn us, we don't "have boldness before God" because something we sense inside is out of alignment with God's will and ways. He wants us to "obey His commandments and do what pleases Him." So God has created a world based upon His nature of love and holiness. God has created spiritual principles, revealed in His Word, to help guide us to bring our lives into alignment with the created order of His will. And when things are out of order and out of alignment, in His mercy, He allows us to sense it so that we can respond by grace to bring our lives back into His created order, redeemed by the blood of Jesus.

This dimension of healing prayer ministry involves teaching and understanding principles of the kingdom of God. This is a place where healing and deliverance prayer ministry coincides with discipleship and spiritual maturity. It doesn't take away from the miraculous healing of God with breakthroughs when we least expect it out of His sovereignty and desire to display His power. But it does respect God's plan for our lives to grow into Christ-likeness. "Since we have these promises, beloved, let us cleanse ourselves from every defilement of body and of spirit, making holiness perfect in the fear of God" (2 Corinthians 7:1).

Much the prayer ministry of inner healing—healing from the inside out—and deliverance is allowing the Holy Spirit to show us the barriers to our healing or roots of resistance to our healing and holiness. We'll discuss these potential barriers and key roots of resistance in some detail in later chapters, learning to apply God's biblical, spiritual principles to every dimension of our lives in the healing process of sanctification of spirit, soul, and body. This is one of God's ways of healing and freeing us, so that we may be both "sound"—to be healed, whole, and free—

and "blameless"—to be holy and pure, sanctified through and through by the Holy Spirit of God (1 Thessalonians 5:23).

When God is showing us the barriers to our healing, He's giving us an opportunity to bring our lives into agreement with His principles of the kingdom of God. Everywhere that Jesus went, He was proclaiming the coming of the kingdom of God and then demonstrating it in power. What is "the kingdom of God?" It's where God is King. It's where Jesus is Lord. Jesus is the King of the kingdom of God; He is "the King of kings and Lord of lords" (Revelation 19:16).

And Jesus wants to live now and be King of the kingdom in our hearts. "But in your hearts, sanctify Christ as Lord" (1 Peter 3:15). Paul said it this way in Romans 14:7, "The kingdom of God" is "righteousness and peace and joy in the Holy Spirit." "Righteousness" is right relationship with God, right relationship with one another, and right relationship within ourselves. When the kingdom of God is made manifest in our lives, we're going to have righteousness, peace, joy, and we're going to have the fullness of the Holy Spirit within us.

Jesus said, "The kingdom of God is within you" (Luke 17:21). It's not just when Jesus comes back one day. It's right now. It's already here with the first coming of Jesus and it's yet to come and be fully consummated with the second coming of Jesus. But right now, the will of God is for the kingdom of God is to be manifested within us. We can have peace even in the midst of turmoil; and we can have joy even in the midst of mourning and suffering deep down on the inside. We can have the Spirit of God within us giving us strength to come through everything that we face, and giving us grace to know the healing and freedom God longs for us to have now, not just when we get to heaven. That's why He teaches us to pray for His kingdom to come and His will to be done here on earth—here right now—just as it already is in heaven. Removing barriers to our healing helps His kingdom come in us, so that it can be manifested through us to the glory of God.

All three of these forms of healing prayer ministry are ways God may choose to heal us and free us: Prayers of faith, enforcing our authority in Christ, and removing barriers to healing. We don't have to pick and choose. And God may use us differently in our diversity of gifts to minister healing in the lives of others and receive healing ourselves. Our part is to humble ourselves before God, making ourselves available to Him to teach us His ways, lead us into His truth, and minister His healing love to us and through us, in His timing and His way.

Chapter 7

Ministry Model for Inner Healing:
The 3 Rs—Reveal. Remove. Replace.

When I joined Rapha God Ministries as the Pastoral Director, the ministry was using a model of inner healing prayer ministry based upon Andy Reese's book, *Freedom Tools*.[9] It's an excellent model and resource, which we continue to use today in our Level 2 School of Ministry. At Rapha, we now teach the foundational principles of *Free to Be Like Jesus* to firmly establish our ministry practices upon biblical principles in our Level 1 School of Ministry and then build upon that foundation with practical ministry training and experiences in our Level 2 School.

For some time, Andy Reese called his ministry tools *sozo* ministry tools for *sozo* ministry sessions, based on the Greek word *sozo*—meaning to save, heal, and deliver. He just recently revised and updated his *Freedom Tools* book and now refers to his tools as freedom tools for freedom prayer ministry sessions, avoiding confusion with the prayer ministry practices of Bethel Church, which they call *Sozo* Prayer Ministry. In large part, these ministries, along with many more, seek to teach and apply basically the same biblical principles reinforced by practical experience and expressing the unique personalities of each ministry. But all true healing is God's healing through Jesus Christ, by whatever name it's called. I personally prefer to use the terms healing, inner healing, and deliverance, though the terms *sozo* and *sozo session* are now deeply ingrained in our ministry vocabulary at Rapha from the initial days of the ministry.

When we began to teach our School of Ministry at Rapha using *Freedom Tools*, I had previously used similar principles and practices in prayer ministry, but I didn't generally call them by the same name or necessarily apply them in the same ways. One day in my morning prayer time, before we first taught our own School of Ministry at Rapha, I asked the Lord, "Lord, what is my ministry tool that I've been using all these years

---

[9] I'm very excited to now know Andy personally and to have had the opportunity to teach and minister with him. I'm incredibly honored to have his endorsement of this book, along with those of Max Lucado and Randy Clark.

in inner healing and deliverance prayer ministry?" And what came to me immediately as the Lord's reply was this: "The 3 Rs. Reveal. Remove. Replace." (Not to be confused with the 3 Rs of Readin', Ritin', and 'Rithmatic.)

As I've mentioned before, I journal my morning prayer times and send them out as a daily devotional to those who like to join with me on my *Morning by Morning* email list.[10] So I journaled my prayer and my conversation with the Lord that morning:

Morning by Morning, February 26, 2013 —
Reveal. Remove. Replace. The 3 Rs of Inner Healing

Good morning, Lord Jesus. I call on Your name and press in to Your Presence. ...

"These things God has revealed to us through the Spirit, for the Spirit searches everything, even the depths of God" (1 Corinthians 2:10).

Reveal. Remove. Replace. These are The Three Rs of inner healing—healing from the inside out. If we're willing to trust You enough to search our hearts, You'll show us the things in us that are not yet like You. In Your mercy and love, You'll show us the sins that need to be forgiven, the hurts that need to be healed, the bondages that need to be broken, the lies that need to be exposed, and the truth that needs to be embraced.

So first You reveal what You want to heal. Then You remove what needs to go. And finally, You replace what was never meant to be ours with everything You've always longed for us to have. You sanctify us in spirit, soul, and body (1 Thessalonians 5:23). You conform us into the image of the Son of God (Romans 8:29). You heal us and free us; You make us whole and holy, from the inside out (Psalm 139:24).

As we allow You to connect the events from the pain or shame of our past with the memories and the emotions buried down inside, You free us from where we're stuck, empower us to let go, and release us to advance into the fullness of who we are in

---

[10] If you would like to join me for my free daily devotional that I journal and send out most every morning, please sign up at the Messiah Ministries website at www.messiah-ministries.org. Also, I published one year's worth of my prayers in a 365 Day Devotional called *Morning by Morning, A Prayer Journey with Tommy Hays*, my first book.

Christ and all You've already done for us at the Cross. "Not that I have already obtained this or have already reached the goal; but I press on to make it my own, because Christ Jesus has made me His own; but this one thing I do: I press on toward the goal for the prize of the heavenly call of God in Christ Jesus" (Philippians 3:12–14).

As we allow Your Holy Spirit to reveal, remove, and replace, Your Kingdom comes and Your will is done, within us and then through us, on earth as it is in heaven. "For, in fact, the Kingdom of God is within (us)" (Luke 17:21). "For the Kingdom of God is ... righteousness and peace and joy in the Holy Spirit" (Romans 14:17).

Thank You, Lord. Remove every veil that covers our eyes, our hearts, and our minds from seeing You as You truly are and from seeing ourselves as You see us. As You reveal Your truth, remove everything less, and replace our broken and fallen lives with the fullness of Your life fully expressed through our lives fully surrendered to You, You are making us more like You each day. "And all of us, with unveiled faces, seeing the glory of the Lord as though reflected in a mirror, are being transformed into that same image from degree of glory to another; for this comes from the Lord, from the Spirit" (2 Corinthians 3:18).

As You heal the broken-hearted and set the captives free, You give us beauty for ashes, joy for sadness, and hope for despair, that our lives can then display Your glory (Isaiah 61:1-3). Then in the ways You've healed us and freed us, You send us to share and minister the healing love of God into the lives of others (Isaiah 61:4–6). Freed from our past, embracing our identity, You send us forth into our destiny, excited to give away all You've freely given to us (John 20:21; Matthew 10:8). And it all begins as we allow You to reveal, remove, and replace. In Jesus' name I pray. Amen.

The cry of my heart that morning expresses the cry of my heart today, as I continue to give myself to this ministry of inner healing and deliverance—healing from the inside out. I believe it's still one of the cries of the heart of God our Father, who has sent His Holy Spirit to prepare the Bride for the coming of His Son, Jesus Christ. As I've said before, one day Jesus will come in His glory in the skies, but at the same time, every day between this day and that day, Jesus wants to come in His glory in our hearts. One means of that grace is through the transforming power of healing and deliverance, as we allow the Holy Spirit to set us free to be like Jesus.

As we minister, we all develop our own styles of ministry, as the Holy Spirit expresses Himself uniquely through the unique personalities and experiences of each one of us. Laura Falconer, my great friend and colleague at Rapha God Ministries serving as our Director of Spanish Ministries, has developed a very helpful and powerful book with sample prayers she's collected in ministry from many different styles and patterns of prayer ministry. Her *Sozo Ministry Prayer Guide*, affectionately known as *The Little Book*, is available in English and Spanish at www.RaphaGodMinistries.com

At the end of this book, I've included a basic outline with some key principles and Scriptures for a Model for Inner Healing and also a Model for Physical Healing. I developed these as a way to teach the core principles with limited time for equipping settings of healing prayer ministry when I teach at home and abroad. Please feel free to copy them, use them, develop, and personalize them however the Holy Spirit leads you in His unique expression of His healing love and power through your ministry.

Also, I've included a prayer for impartation and anointing at the end of this book as well, based upon the biblical principles of impartation for ministry (Romans 1:11; 2 Kings 2:9; 1 Timothy 4:14; and 2 Timothy 1:6, among others).

Part 3 — Healing & Deliverance through Sanctification

Together, we are the Body of Christ (1 Corinthians 12:12). Every part of the Body is needed for us to be whole, for us to grow up "to the unity of the faith and of the knowledge of the Son of God, to maturity, to the measure of the full stature of Christ" (Ephesians 4:11–13).

Every part of the Body is unique, with varying expressions of who we are in Christ and who Christ is in us, and to minister and share the message of hope in Christ and the Kingdom of God in ways that fit our calling and destiny in our spheres of influence. No two preachers preach the same; no two teachers teach the same. No two churches worship the same or minister the same. Each is unique, so that we are united as one Body, not in uniformity but in a unity that's intended to embrace and celebrate our individual expressions of God through us, personally and corporately (1 Corinthians 12:4–11).

We have various perspectives and understandings of God's will and God's ways within the various streams and traditions of the Body of Christ, now and throughout all generations, as we all seek to know the one true God and His truth. This same is true for healing prayer ministry. There are many unique expressions of the ministry of healing and deliverance, but every true expression of the ministry of God through His Church to heal and free His people is powerful and essential, even though all are not the same.

My perspective and approach to healing prayer ministry is, of course, very similar to some and very different from others. Primarily, my perspective for healing and deliverance prayer ministry is founded upon the biblical principles of sanctification—that God is at work within each one of us to make us whole and free, emptied of ourselves and filled with His Spirit, making us more like Jesus in every dimension of our lives.

We are God's people. And God's glory will always arise as His light bursts forth to shine through us by the Presence of His Holy Spirit within us (Isaiah 60:1). The Father has sent His Holy Spirit to prepare a holy Bride for the coming of His Son. Our glorious Savior is coming for His glorious Bride!

But we will not be glorious without healing and deliverance, especially the ministry of inner healing—healing from the inside out—that sets us free from everything that would keep us from being all God created us to be. That's why the Holy Spirit is moving mightily in the earth to slay our pride and humble our hearts, to allow us to see our need for our own healing and deliverance. It's not just for the heathen and the spiritually immature; it's not just for the unbeliever and the unchurched. When Jesus said to pray, "Father, deliver us from evil," He was talking to the whole Church of God. Unfortunately, in many ways throughout many generations, we've been too proud to acknowledge that we need our own deep healing and cleansing deliverance.

God wants to free us, cleanse us, and make us whole in our bodies, our souls, our spirits, in all our relationships, and in every dimension of our lives. God is commissioning us to the ministry of Christ. As the Father sent the Son, so He sends us. He wants to send us—healed, whole, and free—so that we can truly be His ambassadors and disciples. He wants us to display His nature as His body, the people of His Church, in the midst of the increasing darkness of this broken, fallen world that needs the hope and light of the glory of God shining through us as never before.

> *Arise, shine; for your light has come, and the glory of the Lord has risen upon you. For darkness shall cover the earth, and thick darkness the peoples; but the Lord will arise upon you, and His glory will appear over you. Nations shall come to your light, and kings to the brightness of your dawn* (Isaiah 60:1–3).

Chapter 8

Healing as Sanctification of Spirit, Soul, and Body

Through the years of ministering the healing love of God through prayer ministry, the Lord has continued to teach me His principles of healing. He has continued to give me more understanding about the "keys of the kingdom of heaven" He has placed in our hands as His Church (Matthew 16:10). I have learned much in my own journey of healing and in ministering to others, and I am thankful for the teaching of the Lord through prayer, mentors, training, and through experience along the way. Like all of us, I have much more to learn. As much as anything, we learn as much through our mistakes; and we can praise God that He loves us enough to redeem our mistakes, as we entrust even those to Him.

Understanding the bigger picture of healing in the context of sanctification is one of the most significant key insights that the Lord has ever given me. Being sanctified is being made holy and whole by the grace of God, being set free to be all He created us to be. He sets us free to be like Jesus.

From my perspective, understanding healing and deliverance through the process of sanctification of every part of our being—spirit, soul, and body—ties it all together and begins to make sense out of an area seemingly steeped in mystery. Healing *is* a mystery; yet at the same time, there are principles from the God's Word and ways that He wants to teach us.

In a broad sense, the process of healing and freedom in Christ is the process of sanctification—God the Father, sanctifying us by His Holy Spirit, to conform us into the image of Christ, that we may be the Body of Christ, filled with the Spirit of Christ, to continue the ministry of Christ until the kingdom of God is established on earth as it is in heaven. In the bigger picture of an eternal perspective, God is healing and sanctifying His people and all His creation through the redeeming grace of the blood of Jesus, and the sanctifying power of the Holy Spirit, to the glory of God our Father.

With this understanding, we begin to see why healing and deliverance were at the heart of Jesus' ministry and should be at the heart of ours. As we are healed of the wounds of the past and set free from the bondage that holds us back, we are set free to be like Jesus. We are healed and made whole as we are being conformed into the image of Christ and released into the fullness of our destiny to glorify God with our lives. Ultimately, He is redeeming and restoring our eternal relationship with God, with one another, and with all creation. What God is doing in us, He is doing in every dimension of His creation. (Romans 8:18–23).

Over the years of prayer ministry, I have learned that it helps people come into agreement with the prayers for healing when they understand the concepts. Remember the ministry model of Jesus: He welcomed them, He taught them about the kingdom of God, and then He healed them as they had need (see Luke 9:11). Teaching brings understanding and agreement. When we are able to agree in prayer, God answers and healing comes (Matthew 18:18–20).

As I have learned from others, developed my own style of ministry and teaching, and grown in my understanding of the spiritual principles of healing, the Lord has put tools in my hands to help teach and bring understanding to those coming for ministry. One of these tools is a diagram explaining the process of healing and deliverance through the process of sanctification. I have refined and modified it over the years. After almost twenty years of ministry, I can now say I've literally taught it all over the world.

A lot of people who have received our ministry and teaching through the years call it "the three circles." Though other ministries and teachers sometimes use the concept of circles or other images to try to express these spiritual concepts, this particular way of expressing it is a little unique to the other expressions that I have seen. People seem to find this conceptualization very helpful in grasping the bigger picture of healing and deliverance in the context of sanctification, discipleship, and the journey of spiritual maturity.

Three Dimensions of Our Being: Spirit, Soul, and Body

According to 1 Thessalonians 5:23, there are three aspects or dimensions of our being: Spirit, Soul, and Body. My diagram shows each part of our being as a separate circle, but they are interwoven because these three parts of our being are intimately and intricately connected. As we will see, what affects one affects the others:

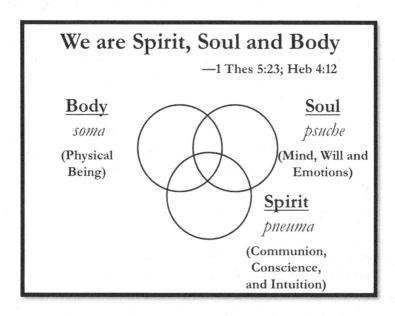

God's Trinity and Our Trinity in Three Dimensions

My diagram of three circles comes from a traditional symbol of the Trinitarian nature of God: God is One; and at the same time, God has revealed Himself to us in three different dimensions, three Persons of His Being—God the Father, God the Son, and God the Holy Spirit. There is only one God, yet He manifests and reveals Himself in these three dimensions or aspects of His Being.

The three interlocking circles represent the Triune nature of God as One God in Three Persons. There are three aspects of His Being, intimately interrelated in perfect agreement and unity, yet also having distinct identity. We call this "the Trinity." Though the term in not specifically in the Bible, the revelation of this concept of God is very biblical, as shown in many contexts of Scripture revealing these three dimensions of the One Being of God. A few Scripture references would include: Matthew 28:19; Luke 3:21, 22; Acts 2:32-26; Galatians 4:6; Titus 3:4–7; and 1 Peter 1:2.

Likewise, we also have three aspects or dimensions of our human being. In a sense, this is one of ways in which we are created in the image of God (Genesis 1:26–27). He is Father and Son and Holy Spirit—three Persons, yet One God. We are spirit and soul and body—three aspects of our being, yet one person. We are each one person having three intimately, interrelated parts of our being which form the whole of our personhood. Scripture explicitly teaches this concept of our being in 1 Thessalonians 5:23–24:

> *May the God of peace Himself sanctify you entirely; and may your **spirit and soul and body** be kept sound and blameless at the coming of our Lord Jesus Christ. The One who calls you is faithful, and He will do this* (emphasis added).

"The God of Peace"

We'll look at these key verses, clause by clause to see how they relate to healing and deliverance. The first clause of verse 23 says, "May the God of peace Himself sanctify you entirely." This is Paul's expectant prayer and word of blessing for God's people. Moved by the Holy Spirit with the Father heart of God, He wants God's very best for the people the Lord has entrusted to His care. He wants them to know their God and to know His peace.

"The God of peace" is the God of *shalom*, the God of healing and wholeness. He comes to bring His perfect peace, His *shalom*, to every area of our lives so that we are at peace with God, at peace with one another, and at peace within ourselves. Ultimately, He is redeeming all creation into an eternal rest of an eternal *shalom*. He comes that we may know and experience the fullness of salvation, without measure. He comes that we may have life and have it abundantly (John 10:10).

The God of peace is the God who sanctifies. He is a holy God, who desires a holy people. He says, "I am the Lord; I sanctify you" (Leviticus

90

20:8). He says, "I am faithful and I will do it" (see 1 Thessalonians 5:24 above). The God of peace wants to bring the fullness of His peace into our lives and all creation. His sanctification brings His peace. Our "Wonderful Counselor, Mighty God, Everlasting Father" is also our "Prince of Peace," as our Creator made manifest to His creation in the nature of our Messiah, Jesus the Christ (Isaiah 9:6; Matthew 16:16). As they say, "Know Jesus, know Peace; no Jesus, no peace."

Verse 23 says God desires to keep His people "sound and blameless". To be "sound" is to be whole—healed and free. The alternate translation for "sound" in the NRSV is "complete." This wholeness includes our healing and deliverance—to have the fullness of salvation. To be "blameless" is to be holy. The God of peace, who sanctifies us, desires His people to be both "sound and blameless"—to be whole and holy. We are "sanctified by the Spirit" of God (1 Peter 1:2).

"Sanctify You Entirely"—Wholeness is Holiness

The Holy Spirit of God comes to sanctify us "entirely" (verse 23). Some versions say "wholly," or "completely," or "in every way." The idea is that God wants to make us whole and wholly His. He wants to make us whole and holy. To God, wholeness is holiness. Every part of our being is brought into alignment and harmony with Him. Nothing is left out and nothing is held back. This is peace; this is *shalom*. This is His will according to His Word. "For this is the will of God, your sanctification" (1 Thessalonians 4:3).

The truth is, God is not willing to settle for anything less. That's what 1 Thessalonians 5:24 makes very clear: He is faithful and He will do it. We won't do it. We can't do it. But He will do it—*if* we let Him. His part is to work it out in us and our part is to willingly choose to embrace Him and His process—the process of sanctification and healing that brings wholeness and holiness.

We will come back to this call to be "sanctified entirely" in a moment. There are different perspectives in the body of Christ about what this

91

means, and when we may attain this level of holiness and sanctification.[11] But for the moment, let us see from Scripture that this is Paul's prayer and God's will to sanctify us entirely—to sanctify **all** of us, **every** part of us.

"Your Spirit and Soul and Body"

The second clause of 1 Thessalonians 5:23 is the continuation of Paul's prayer and blessing, "and may your **spirit and soul and body** be kept sound and blameless at the coming of our Lord Jesus Christ." This is the explanation of what is meant by "entirely." These are the three aspects of our being which make up the whole person. In the original language of this verse in Greek, these are three different words with three different meanings, referring to three different dimensions of our being.

The Greek words from the original langue of this passage are *pneuma*, *psuche*, and *soma*, meaning spirit, soul, and body. The meaning of each separate word and concept is found and expressed in the context of each word in the various passages where they are found. In a moment, we'll look in some depth at each of these distinctions and see why our understanding makes a significant difference in both the process of spiritual maturity as well as the process of healing.

Some people teach that human beings are really "bi-partite" (two-part) beings instead of "tri-partite" (three part) beings. Their understanding is that the spirit and soul are really the same thing—interchangeable words and concepts—in contrast to our body. This is actually a fairly common belief, and there are certain passages of Scripture that do use these two terms interchangeably this way. But significantly, that's not the case in this passage of 1 Thessalonians 5:23.

---

[11] If you've been pushed away or wounded from a misunderstanding or mistaken application of the principles of holiness and sanctification in the past, please don't let that deter you. As you will see, the correct understanding of our call to seek this and our gift to receive this is something to which God intends to bring healing and not fear—acceptance and not rejection. This is much more about relationship than religion, and an attitude of the heart rather than a legalistic performance of duties. There is a beauty of holiness He wants us to seek and receive in His power and strength—not ours. True holiness brings healing.

Scripture makes an important distinction in this verse and elsewhere between the spirit and the soul, between the *pneuma* and the *psuche*. The original words translated "spirit" and "soul" in the Greek of the New Testament are not the same; and the original meanings are not the same. The contexts of the Scripture passages where these words are found define their meanings.

Hebrews 4:12, for example, makes this distinction very clear:

> *"Indeed, the word of God is living and active, sharper than any two-edged sword, piercing until it **divides soul from spirit**, joints from marrow; it is able to judge the thoughts and intentions of the heart"* (emphasis added).

To "divide" in this context is to expose in order to examine and to set in order. The state of our spirit and soul and body needs to be examined and set in order in accordance with the Living and the Written Word of God.

This kind of "dividing" is not like taking a meat clever and dividing one piece of meat from another. It's more like the concept of dividing the Word of God—exposing it, examining it, seeking to understand it, and applying it.

Understanding this difference is extremely important in healing prayer ministry and in spiritual direction. I've come to believe it is profoundly significant both for receiving our healing and for growing in spiritual maturity. There is a "created order" and a "priority of authority" in the relationship of our spirit, soul, and body. Just as in the order of this Scripture, there is also an order in our lives: first the spirit, then the soul, and then the body. We will come back to this important point after we define and understand each of these three components of our being.

The Human Spirit

The human spirit, the *pneuma*, is the innermost part of our being. It is the place of communion with God where His Spirit fellowships with our spirit. As the Psalm says, it is the place where "Deep calls to deep" (Psalm 42:7). It is the place of intimacy within our being that rises up in our prayer and worship of God. "God is spirit, and those who worship Him must worship in spirit and truth" (John 4:24). We are primarily spiritual beings living in physical bodies, created for a spiritual relationship with our spiritual God. Together with one another, we are the body of Christ, filled with the Spirit of Christ, living in relationship to God through Christ (1 Corinthians 3:16 and 6:15–20; Romans 12:1–8).

The book of Hebrews teaches how the pattern of the earthly tabernacle under the Old Covenant was but a shadow of this spiritual reality (Hebrews 10:1). This pattern of the tabernacle speaks of the pathway of drawing near to God—from the outer court to the inner court to the holy of holies. In a sense, it also speaks of the created order of our human nature. The body is the outer court; the soul is the inner court; the spirit is the holy of holies. In the holy of holies of our human spirit, we behold the Presence of God. Our bodies are God's temples, our heart is His home (1 Corinthians 3:16 and 6:19). Our spirit is the holy of holies of the temple where the Ark of the Covenant of God's manifest Presence dwells within us—within the court of the body and beyond the veil of the soul. This is where Christ sits enthroned upon the mercy seat of our heart. "Christ *in you*, the hope of glory" (Colossians 1:27).

The Chinese spiritual leader Watchman Nee in his book, *The Spiritual Man* describes three aspects or functions of the human spirit. The human spirit is the innermost place of our being where we are to primarily experience the communion, the conscience, and the intuition of relationship with God's Spirit. These categories of understanding are based upon a thorough review of these terms and phrases from their contexts in Scripture, tested out in ministry and confirmed by experience in the journey of spiritual maturity. Using these categories, we will look at each dimension of the human spirit: communion, conscience, and intuition.

—Godly Communion

In our human spirit, we experience "the communion of the Holy Spirit" (2 Corinthians 13:13). "Communion" with God is the intimate fellowship of our trusting relationship with Him. "God is faithful; by Him you were called into the fellowship of His Son, Jesus Christ our

94

Lord" (1 Corinthians 1:9). In our spirit, we become one with Christ in the unity of His Holy Spirit with our human spirit. "But anyone united to the Lord becomes one spirit with Him" (1 Corinthians 6:17). It is *primarily*[12] in our human spirit that we join with the Lord in the intimacy of worship and prayer. We worship the Lord "in spirit and truth" for "God is Spirit" (John 4:24).

Through the abiding presence of God's Holy Spirit within our human spirit, we come to know Him. "This is the Spirit of Truth, whom the world cannot receive, because it neither sees Him nor knows Him. You know Him, because He abides with you, and He will be *in* you" (John 14:17). This knowing of God is something that takes place deep within our spirit, before it is confirmed in our thoughts. It is a knowing in our heart before it is a knowing in our mind. The Holy Spirit is a Person of God and He comes to abide in us personally.

—Godly Conscience

"The human spirit is the lamp of the Lord, searching every inmost part" (Proverbs 20:27). The Holy Spirit speaks to our human spirit to quicken the discernment of our conscience (see Romans 9:1). By the blood of Jesus the Holy Spirit comes to "purify our conscience" to "worship the living God" (Hebrews 9:14).

In the song "Give a Little Whistle," Disney's Jiminy Cricket sings about being guided by your conscience. This is the world recognizing a spiritual truth. We really do have a conscience—a sense of what is holy and unholy, what is true and false, what is right and wrong. This is to take place *primarily* in our spirit. The sense we have "down in the gut" is really "down in the spirit." This is the place of godly discernment. "Those who are *spiritual* discern all things" (1 Corinthians 2:15). Our conscience discerns down in the depths of our human spirit by God's "Holy Spirit bearing witness with our spirit" (see Romans 8:16).

---

[12] I say "primarily" to continually emphasize that our spirit and soul and body are interrelated and interwoven, though distinct in identity and function. We must always strive to hold the tension between understanding the parts and understanding the whole, as in trying to grasp the spiritual reality of both the parts and the whole the Trinity, with the limitations of human minds and human language.

—*Godly Intuition*

In the human spirit, we sense the leading of the Holy Spirit. "For all who are *led* by the Spirit of God are children of God" (Romans 8:14). This is how the Lord leads us beside the still waters in His paths of righteousness (Psalm 23:2–3). We intuit the sense of prompting by the Holy Spirit in our human spirit. This is the nudging of the "still, small voice" (1 Kings 19:13 KJV). Our Lord Jesus says, "My sheep hear My voice. I know them, and they follow Me" (John 10:27).

We speak of "women's intuition." Once again, this is the world picking up on the reality of a spiritual truth. We are created to sense the truth, and the Truth is a Person (John 14:6)—a Person who wants to lead us into all truth by the leading of His Holy Spirit within us. We intuit the truth by the leading of the Holy Spirit speaking to our human spirit through the communion of prayer and the daily journey of faith. The more time we spend with Him, the more sensitive we are to recognize the sound and the leading of His voice from Spirit to spirit and Deep to deep. The godly intuition aspect of our spirit is primarily a hearing and a knowing in our human spirit, as we sense the leading and direction of the Lord. "Therefore, as the Holy Spirit says, 'Today, if you hear His voice, do not harden your hearts…' " (Hebrews 3:7–8). We are to hear in our human spirit and then respond in our human soul as God's Holy Spirit leads.

As we hear and obey the voice of the Lord in our spirits, our hearts are opened to the leading of the Lord; but if we choose to resist, our hearts become hardened. The more we resist Him, the more difficult it is to sense His leading. The hardening of the heart is the effectual process of our choices of disobedience in resisting the leading of the Lord. God opens our heart to Him by degrees as we grow in trusting Him and obeying Him. Our hearts are hardened by degrees as we resist Him and disobey Him (see Exodus 8:15 and Romans 11:25–32).

God desires to sharpen our spiritual hearing through our obedience to listen and obey the leading of His Spirit through the intimacy of relationship with Him. The freedom to obey or disobey is intertwined with the freedom to love or not love in order to have the potential of a relationship of true love with a God who is love and who created us for that purpose in His image. We are presented with the choices of obedience and love as we intuit the leading of His Spirit in our spirit.

The Bible says we have a choice to "hear" God's voice and not "harden" our hearts (Hebrews 3:7–8). But some look to the biblical account of Pharaoh in Egypt where it says God hardened Pharaoh's heart or to the account of Israel where it says their hearts have been hardened. The whole counsel of God makes it clear that Pharaoh and the people of Israel each "hardened" their own hearts with each choice of disobedience in rebellion to the will of God. "He hardened his heart and would not listen to them, just as the Lord has said" (Exodus 8:15). Israel's heart was hardened "because of their disobedience" (Romans 11:30). These Scriptures must be viewed in the light of the overarching spiritual principles and application of those principles in the Word of God as a whole.

It can be said that God "hardened" their hearts in the broad sense that God created this world based upon His spiritual principles, one of which is that disobedience and rebellion harden our hearts to Him in resistance to His grace. "God opposes the proud but gives grace to the humble" (James 4:6). Here, it is important to hold the tension between God's sovereignty and God's gift of free will. In His sovereignty He has created us for a relationship of love; and for a true relationship of love, we must *always* have the freedom to receive it or reject it, to obey or disobey— otherwise it would not be a true relationship of love. Instead we would be enslaved robots rather than free humans.

As discussed in the context of understanding God's will, this becomes a critically important perspective for healing prayer ministry in discerning the source and cause of evil and tragedy—things we often blame as God's will, that were never God's will at all. Instead, these are the tragic and painful consequences of free choices made by free humans and spiritual beings, affecting themselves and one another throughout the generations that are necessarily permitted in order to have the potential for a relationship of love with a God who is love and who created us in His image. We'll discuss this further in relation to the human soul, where our free will resides.

The Human Soul

The soul, the *psuche*, is our mind, our will, and our emotions. This is *primarily*[13] the essence of the expression of our human personality. The word "soul" in our translations of Scripture comes from different words. The underlying words in the Hebrew language of the Old Testament sometimes are in the context of the mind, sometimes in the context of the will, and sometimes in the context of the emotions. The same is true for the underlying words in the Greek language of the New Testament. So, the realm of our soul is our mind—how we think; our will—how we make choices; and our emotions—how we sense and feel our surroundings.

As I will describe in some detail in moment, the soul is the great battlefield for our sanctification, healing, and deliverance—the battlefield of the mind, will, and emotions. There is a war going on in our souls between the flesh and the Spirit. This is where our mind, will, and emotions are either being conformed by the Spirit of Christ into the image of Christ or where our flesh rises up in rebellion against the will and ways of the Lord, influenced by the unholy spirits at work in this world trying to conform us to the image of the world, the flesh, and the devil. We will now look at briefly at these three aspects of the human soul: the mind, the will, and the emotions.

—Our Mind

Our mind is the realm of our thoughts. This is our means of thinking about God, about ourselves, about the world around us. God wants to renew the thinking of our minds and conform our minds into the image of Christ. "Let the same mind be in you that was in Christ Jesus" (Philippians 2:5). By the Holy Spirit, the Apostle Paul says:

> *Do not be conformed to this world, but be transformed by the renewing of your minds, so that you may discern what is the will of God—what is good and acceptable and perfect* (Romans 12:1–2).

---

[13] Once again, I am expressing the tension of the whole and the parts—that the soul is primarily, but not exclusively, the point of expression of the personality and the other functions of the soul.

The mind is where we are called to fight the battle "to take every thought captive to obey Christ" (2 Corinthians 10:5). As we begin to choose to agree with God, bringing our thoughts into submission to the mind and nature of Christ, we begin to quit agreeing with the world, the flesh, and the devil. Then we begin to know the peace and the power of God, as He changes the way we think about Him and everything else.

> *And the peace of God, which surpasses all understanding, will guard your hearts and your minds in Christ Jesus* (Philippians 4:7).

Though the battle can be intense, we can choose, by God's grace, to "think on these things" that are holy, good, and true, rather what is unholy, evil, and false (verse 4:8). And clearly, there is a close relationship between the mind and the will, as well as the emotions.

—Our Will

Our human will is the means of our power to choose. God is love and He created us for a relationship of love. To have true love, the real thing, He must give us the freedom to willingly choose to love Him and obey Him or not. To create us in His image, it was necessary to create us with free will; otherwise we would just be robots choosing the choices we were conditioned to choose. Life would be a façade and our relationship with God would be a farce. So, at the pain of knowing all the wrong and painful choices we would make—affecting ourselves and one another throughout all the generations of humanity—God still chose to create us with the freedom of choice and the power of free will. Love could have it no other way and still be love; and "God *is* Love;" and God will never change His nature (1 John 4:8 and 4:16).

God sets before us the choice of obedience and disobedience, life and death, the power to choose good or choose evil, to choose His ways or our ways (Deuteronomy 30:15–20; Joshua 24:15; John 8:44; and Luke 11:28). We have His grace to help us, and we have His Spirit to lead us; but ultimately the choice is ours. There are consequences for our actions and spiritual principles that come to bear, but ultimately we must choose our own path. He will not override the free will of His creation; because the moment He did, He would be removing the potential of a relationship of love. He will not ever do that because He cannot ever do that and still be Love, being true to His nature which never changes, and creating a people for a relationship of love.

As we know, there are significant differences of opinion among Bible-believing and Spiritually-committed Christians throughout the traditions of the Church on this point of the tension between the sovereignty of God and human free will. Both are true. In my perspective of Scripture and experience in ministry, I believe this is a critical issue to understand that God, in His sovereignty, has chosen to create humans and spiritual beings with free will. It is critically important for healing prayer ministry with wounded people who are either consciously or subconsciously very angry with God for something He neither did nor willed. When they hear and embrace the truth of the nature of free will, the truth sets them free. They can then choose to release God from their judgments of Him and focus their anger on our spiritual enemy—where it belongs. Then they can choose to release and forgive the human beings who were influenced by evil spiritual beings to make bad choices in rebellion to the will of God, causing so much pain, destruction, and bondage.

So instead of forcing our will, God redeems the effects of the choices of will we make and others make in our lives. This is one of the most important purposes of healing prayer ministry—the redemption of the effects of disobedient choices made by us and by others, in our lives and the lives of the generations before us, as we bring them to the foot of the cross and under the blood of Jesus. The exercise of free will in response to God's grace is a key to wholeness and holiness in our journey of salvation and sanctification.

—*Our Emotions*

Our emotions are the means by which we sense and feel and engage the world around us. God wants us to learn to be led by His Spirit, rather than driven by our emotions—to follow Him rather than the passions and desires of our flesh that have not yet been sanctified by the transforming power of God. The "passions of our flesh, following the desires of flesh and sense" lead us to be "disobedient" rather than faithful to the leading of God's Spirit (Ephesians 2:1–7).

As we allow the Lord to bring our soul into submission to His Spirit, the emotions of fear, anger, shame, lust, greed, jealousy, strife—and all other emotions of the flesh—begin to be crucified with Christ. "Live by the Spirit, I say, and do not gratify the desires of the flesh" (Galatians 5:16). Then our lives begin to bear less fruit of the flesh and more fruit of the Spirit (vv. 19–23). "And those who belong to Christ Jesus have crucified the flesh with its passions and desires. If we live by the Spirit, let us also be guided by the Spirit" (vv. 24–25).

As we discuss in more detail below, what Scripture often refers to as "the flesh" is not the literal flesh of our human bodies. Rather, it is the unsanctified areas of our soul—the areas of our mind, will, and emotions that are not yet like Jesus. This is the "flesh" that must be "crucified with Christ," so that the life we live is no longer our own, but the life that is lived by the faith of the Son of God (Galatians 2:20).

The Human Body

Our human body, the *soma*, is our physical being. This is the outward, visible part of us, as well as the inward sum of every organ, tissue, fiber, and cell. Our bodies provide the physical house of our spirit and soul, forming the mortal and perishable dimension of our being (1 Corinthians 15:53). We were created by God from the dust of the earth; and as He has said, "You are dust, and to dust you shall return" (Genesis 3:19).

Our bodies are our mortal flesh. They will (likely)[14] pass away like the grass of the earth and the flowers of the field, yet they are our means of experiencing the earthly dimension of our lives. They are our "earth suits," as some have called them. Even Jesus took upon the likeness of human flesh and blood, as He set aside the glory of heaven, to humble Himself and live among us, that He might bridge the gap between heaven and earth for us (Philippians 2:5–8). God cares about our bodies and calls us to faithfully steward them as His instruments and vessels,

---

[14] Likely, but not necessarily. See 1 Corinthians 15:51–55 and 1 Thessalonians 4:13–18 for the promise that a day will come when death, our enemy, will be defeated and even the mortal bodies of those blessed to greet the Lord face to face will never perish even in the natural realm. "The last *enemy* to be destroyed is death" (1 Corinthians 15:26).

even though they are but dust, holding the treasure of His presence and His power in these humble jars of clay
(Romans 6:12–13).

Yet, even so, we must allow God to continually bring us into His created order, redeemed by the blood of Jesus—first the spirit, then the soul, then the body. Our earthly bodies are the vessels into which God pours His Spirit to accomplish His purposes. But to over-emphasize the body at the expense of the spirit and soul is to be out of God's created order, which we will discuss shortly. God cares about our mortal bodies; and at the same time, He cares about us having our bodies in proper alignment, redeemed in His created order. They have a purpose as long as we have a purpose on this earth. So He desires to sanctify our bodies, along with our spirits and souls.

Using this concept of "the three circles" of spirit, soul, and body, I would often draw this out for someone coming to receive healing and deliverance prayer ministry. It would help them understand the concepts and how we would be praying for the God of Peace to come and make them whole.

In order to help explain the concepts of how one area of our lives can affect other area of our lives, how spiritual roots can produce bad fruit in our health and well-being, how our flesh can battle against the Holy Spirit even in the Christian soul, how strongholds of the enemy can get established, and why Christians need inner healing and deliverance, I developed a whole series of "the three circles" to help explain the process. Through the years, this has now become the core of my teaching and approach to healing and deliverance prayer.

I'll discuss in some depth each of these sets of circles and the concepts they convey in the following chapters, but it should be helpful to set out the whole series I normally present now as an overview. These are basically the same series of diagrams we use to teach these principles in our Level 1 School of Ministry, and I often use them when speaking at various retreats and conferences.

These figures of the three circles are intended to convey the idea of how the Holy Spirit comes into our lives to save us and to begin the process to sanctify us—to make us more like Jesus, to make us whole and set us free from everything that would hold us back from being all God created us to be. The same principles that apply to our healing and deliverance when we are bound by the past are also the same principles that help us grow into maturity now in the present. All the while, we are basically choosing, by the grace of God and power of the Holy Spirit, to come into agreement with all God has already done for us through the sacrifice of Jesus Christ and the finished work of His cross.

Overview of The Three Circles Teaching:
Healing and Freedom, Wholeness and Holiness
in Spirit, Soul and Body

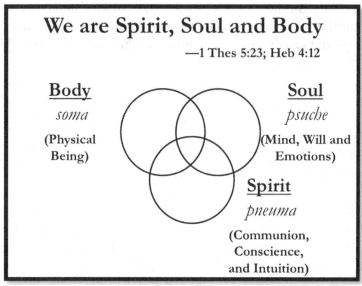

We are Spirit, Soul and Body
—1 Thes 5:23; Heb 4:12

Body
soma
(Physical Being)

Soul
psuche
(Mind, Will and Emotions)

Spirit
pneuma
(Communion, Conscience, and Intuition)

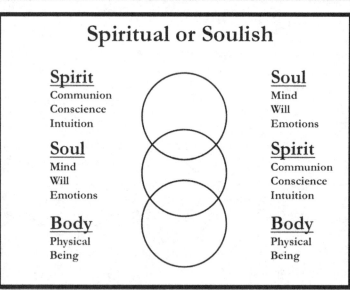

Spiritual or Soulish

Spirit
Communion
Conscience
Intuition

Soul
Mind
Will
Emotions

Soul
Mind
Will
Emotions

Spirit
Communion
Conscience
Intuition

Body
Physical Being

Body
Physical Being

Holy Spirit Saves and Sanctifies
—1 Thes 5:23; Titus 3:3-8; 2 Cor 7:1

Body

soma

(Physical
Being)

Soul

psuche

(Mind, Will and
Emotions)

Spirit

pneuma

Holy
Spirit

Salvation
& _Beginning_ of Sanctification

(Communion,
Conscience,
and Intuition)

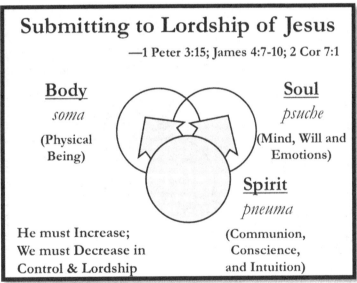

Submitting to Lordship of Jesus
—1 Peter 3:15; James 4:7-10; 2 Cor 7:1

Body

soma

(Physical
Being)

Soul

psuche

(Mind, Will and
Emotions)

Spirit

pneuma

He must Increase;
We must Decrease in
Control & Lordship

(Communion,
Conscience,
and Intuition)

Pockets of Resistance

War in the Soul of the Spirit and the Flesh

—James 4:1; Rom 7:14-25; 1 Peter 2:11

Body

soma

(Physical
Being)

Bad Roots &
Barriers to Healing

Holy
Spirit

Soul

psuche

(Mind, Will and
Emotions)

Spirit

pneuma

(Communion,
Conscience,
and Intuition)

Footholds of the Enemy

In the Unsanctified Flesh of the Soul

—Mt 6:13; Eph 4:27; 2 Cor 11:3-4 and10:3-5

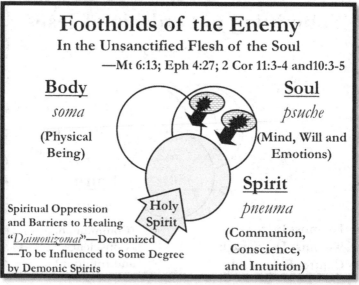

Body

soma

(Physical
Being)

Spiritual Oppression
and Barriers to Healing
"*Daimonizomai*"—Demonized
—To be Influenced to Some Degree
by Demonic Spirits

Holy
Spirit

Soul

psuche

(Mind, Will and
Emotions)

Spirit

pneuma

(Communion,
Conscience,
and Intuition)

Goal: Wholeness and Freedom

—1 Thess 5:23-24; Duet 30:6; Mark 12:28-31

Body

soma

(Physical
Being)

Filled with the Holy Spirit
Whole and Free
Sanctified Entirely
Loving God, One Another, and
Ourselves Completely

Soul

psuche

(Mind, Will and
Emotions)

Spirit

pneuma

(Communion,
Conscience,
and Intuition)

Chapter 9

Created Order of Spirit, Soul, and & Body

We are "spirit and soul and body" (1 Thessalonians 5:23). These are the three dimensions of our being, and the order of these three dimensions is very significant. It affects our spiritual maturity, the process of sanctification, and the process of healing. Now we will explore in more depth the correlation between wholeness and holiness.

God is the Creator, and creativity is at the heart of His very essence. He created us to express His creativity in ways that we have not even begun to imagine, much less live out in the fullness of our calling and destiny in the earth. Yet at the same time, God is a God of order. Even in the freedom and creativity of the expression of our spiritual gifts, He reminds us, "all things should be done decently and *in order*"—in *His* order (1 Corinthians 14:40).

God's order releases freedom and encourages the free flow of His Spirit within the bounds of His laws and His leading. His freedom and creativity is intended to move in His order, just as the banks of a river allow the river to flow beautifully and freely, without overflowing its banks and destroying the very lands and lives it's meant to bless. As someone has said, "We need both God's law and God's grace. The banks of God's law allow the river of God's grace to flow."

God's freedom is a blessing, yet we can only receive the fullness of the blessing when we bring our lives into His order, by His grace. As Paul said in explaining the blessings of both freedom and order, "I say this for your own benefit, not to put any restraint upon you, but to promote good order and unhindered devotion to the Lord" (1 Corinthians 7:35). God does not desire to unnecessarily restrain us by His principles of order, but uses them to allow us to experience the blessings of unhindered devotion to Him.

In the days of Moses, the Lord specified in great detail the order for the earthly tabernacle that would welcome His presence in the midst of His people (Exodus 40:1–33). Moses set everything in order, and "did everything just as the Lord had commanded him" (Exodus 40:16). When everything was brought into God's created order, in line with God's commandments, "the glory of the Lord filled the tabernacle" (Exodus 40:34–35).

We are the tent of meeting; we are the tabernacle of the presence of God's glory in the earth. As the body of Christ, filled with the Spirit of Christ, we are the temple of the Holy Spirit of the Living God (1 Corinthians 3:16–17 and 6:19; Romans 8:9; Philippians 1:19). God desires to set His temple in order, to bring His people into His created order, redeemed by the blood of Jesus and filled with the Holy Spirit (Ephesians 5:15–20). Christ in us, the hope of glory (Colossians 1:27).

Redeemed to God's Created Order:
First the Spirit, then the Soul, then the Body

Our spirit, soul, and body must be restored and redeemed to God's created order for us to live in the peace of healing. "Created order" is when we allow His Holy Spirit to direct our human spirit. Then our human spirit directs our soul, and our soul directs our body. Another way to express this is that we are living in God's created order when our body is in submission to our soul, our soul is in submission to our spirit, and our spirit is in submission to God's Holy Spirit. We are out of order when our soul rises up to force the spirit into submission against the leading of the Holy Spirit. And we are out of order when our body rises up to the place of priority, above the leading of the spirit and soul.[15]

We are created to be "spiritual Christians" and not "soulish Christians." Paul speaks of the joy of life lived in the Spirit in the eighth chapter of Romans. But first, he describes the struggles of life lived in the dominion of the soul rather than the Spirit in the seventh chapter of Romans. Paul talks about a "war" that is taking place within the life of the believer (Romans 7:23), using his own struggle as an example. The unsanctified areas of the soul—"the flesh"—war against the areas of the soul yielded

---

[15] I'm grateful to the following mentors who helped shape my perspective in these areas from the resources of their teachings and ministry: Watchman Nee; David Seamands; Steve Seamands; John Sanford; John G. Lake; Rick Joyner; Francis Frangipane; Francis MacNutt, Randy Clark; Fuchsia Pickett; Paul Keith Davis; Margaret Therkelsen; Peter Horrobin; Charles Kraft; Steve Chua; Mike and Becky Chaile; Jack Frost; and others.

to the Spirit of God—"the spirit." Peter speaks of this "war" of the soul as well, challenging us to "abstain from the desires of the flesh that wage war against the soul" (1 Peter 2:11).

Both Paul and Peter are speaking to Christian believers, those who already have welcomed Jesus into their hearts and have the Holy Spirit living in their lives. These believers have been washed by the blood of the Lamb; their names are written in the Book of Life; and they are going to heaven when they die. They are already experiencing a measure of the presence, power, gifts and fruit of the Holy Spirit in their lives, yet there is a "war" going on in their souls.

The "war" is between the nature of the "spirit" and the nature of the "flesh". Paul says, "For we know that the law is spiritual; but I am of the flesh, sold into slavery under sin" (Romans 7:14). When Paul refers to "the flesh" he is not talking about the "body" our physical being. Rather, he is talking about the human soul that rises up in self-will against the will and leading of the Lord, who desires to lead our human spirit by His Holy Spirit. I have come to define "the flesh" as "the unsanctified area of the soul."

Spiritual or Soulish Christians

A "fleshly" or "carnal" Christian is a "soulish" Christian. This is our state when our soul takes the place of authority and forces the spirit to submit. In God's created order, there is a priority of authority where our soul should willingly submit to our spirit, as our spirit willingly submits to the leading of God's Holy Spirit. We are created and called to be "spiritual" Christians. We are *spiritual* rather than soulish when our soul willingly submits to the authority of our spirit, being led by the Holy Spirit. Then our spirit is permitted by our soul to take the place of priority of authority. This is restoration to "created order," which brings peace and order in our lives, rather than war and strife.

111

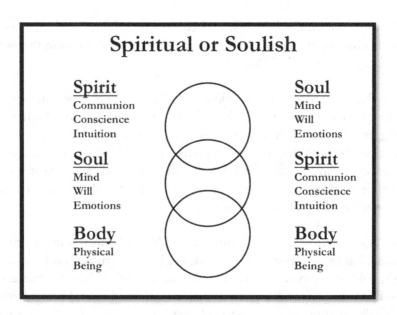

Spiritual or Soulish

Spirit
Communion
Conscience
Intuition

Soul
Mind
Will
Emotions

Body
Physical
Being

Soul
Mind
Will
Emotions

Spirit
Communion
Conscience
Intuition

Body
Physical
Being

This diagram shows another way of looking at the three circles that represent the three dimensions of our being—spirit, soul, and body. When they are aligned in the order shown on the left, this represents a *Spiritual* Christian. The human spirit is sitting in the place of authority, in submission to the Holy Spirit. Then the soul is in submission to the spirit, and the body is in submission to the soul: first the spirit, then the soul, then the body. This person is restored to created order—living in peace with God, peace with others, and peace within himself.

When the circles are aligned in the order shown on the right, this represents a *Soulish* Christian. This person's life is out of order. The soul has risen up, has taken the place of priority of authority, and has pressed the spirit down into submission rather than being led by the Spirit of God. The soul is in rebellion when it is doing the directing and leading. But when the human spirit leads the soul and the body, then a person will be in line with God's will and purpose. So the soulish Christian is someone who is being led by his own mind, will, and emotions; rather than by his human spirit in communion with God's Holy Spirit. Soulishness produces varying degrees of strife rather than order; war instead of peace. In a sense, this Soulish Christian is at war with God, at war with others, and at war within himself. He is not led by the Holy

Spirit leading his human spirit; instead, he is led by his soul in rebellion against the leading of the Holy Spirit.

Our soul is our mind, will, and emotions. So our will is in the soul. We have free will. In our soul, we have the power to rise up and take the place of authority if we so choose. We all know times when we are "self-willed" and driven by our own will instead of God's. In our own minds, we think we know what is best. In our own will, we decide that we are going to do what we want to do, no matter what the Lord or anyone else wants us to do. In our emotions, we feel like doing what we want to do; and we don't feel like doing what we don't want to do.

All of this is "soulish." It's a manifestation of pride that says, "I'm going to do what I want to do." The soul is asserting authority and projecting its own will upon the spirit and body. This is submission to the law of sin because we are rising up in disobedience and rebellion to the leading of the Lord. The "flesh" is in rebellion against the "spirit" in this inner "war" of the soul (Romans 7:21–25). We'll also discuss this in more detail looking at pride and rebellion as "roots of resistance" to God's will and healing grace in our lives in a later chapter.

Willing submission to the Lordship of Jesus Christ delivers us from this struggle and brings our spirit, soul, and body back into God's created order. God rescues us from the way of death when we submit to Jesus Christ as Lord in the area of our soul in conflict with our spirit. We are "spiritual" when our human soul willingly chooses to submit to the leading of our human spirit, which is being led by the Holy Spirit—the Spirit of Christ within us, the hope of glory (Colossians 1:27).

> *But you are not in the flesh; you are in the Spirit, since the Spirit of God dwells in you.... (And) if Christ is in you, though the body is dead because of sin, the Spirit is life because of righteousness. If the Spirit of him who raised Jesus from the dead dwells in you, He who raised Christ from the dead will give life to your mortal bodies also through His Spirit that dwells in you. So then, brothers and sisters, we are debtors, not to the flesh, to live according to the flesh—for if you live according to the flesh, you will die; but if by the Spirit you put to death the deeds of the body, you will live. For all who are led by the Spirit of God are children of God*
> (Romans 8:9–14).

113

The *soulish* Christian spends his life in the inner war of Romans 7, but the *spiritual* Christian spends his life in the inner peace of Romans 8. We can choose "life in the flesh" or "life in the spirit." The spirit does not force the soul to submit; the soul has the power to choose because the "will" resides in the soul.

When our soul willingly submits, we begin to receive more of the mind of Christ, obey the will of God, and sense the world around us with emotions led by the Spirit. The Holy Spirit can lead our human spirit, which can lead our soul, which can lead our body. The communion and peace of intimacy and communion in right relationship with God in our spirit is then manifested in our soul and our body. We are restored into created order, redeemed by the blood of Jesus, and sanctified by the Holy Spirit. The key to restoration in created order is submission to the Lordship of Christ, rather than asserting the lordship of self. One way is living by the law of the Spirit; the other is living by the law of the flesh. One way brings life, the other brings death. One way brings peace, the other brings war.

If we are willing to be really honest, we would have to admit that much of our Christian life is spent as *soulish* Christians. Rather than waiting on the Lord for the leading of His Spirit to guide and direct our human spirit in His ways, our soul rises up to take charge. At times we give our mind the place of authority rather than our spirit. At other times we give our will the place of authority rather than our spirit. Sometimes we give our emotions the place of authority rather than our spirit. We are out of order, in rebellion to the order of God, when we have the wrong priority of authority.

Much of our teaching, preaching, and ministry in the church is actually very soulish, rather than spiritual—driven by the exaltation of the mind rather than the spirit. We often receive the knowledge in our heads, but not in our hearts. We receive it in our souls, but not our spirits. In created order, our minds are to confirm and understand what our *spirits* have received from the Lord. Not the other way around. Too much of our lives are *soul*-driven, rather than *spirit*-driven. Too much of the body of Christ is soulish, rather than spiritual. We suffer and the world suffers because of it. We are living our lives and following our own plans and agendas, rather than the Lord's. We are fulfilling *our* great ambition,

114

rather than the Lord's great commission. We are building our own kingdoms rather than the kingdom of God.

Our minds are important, as are our wills and our emotions. But we must have all things in order to grow into spiritual maturity and wholeness. The more we willingly choose to submit to the leading of the Spirit, the more our minds are transformed into the mind of Christ, the more our wills are conformed to the will of our Father, and the more our emotions are yielded to the sensitivities of the Holy Spirit.

> *I appeal to you therefore, brothers and sisters, by the mercies of God, to present your bodies as a living sacrifice, holy and acceptable to God, which is your spiritual worship. Do not be conformed to this world, but be transformed by the renewing of your minds, so that you may discern what is the will of God—what is good and acceptable and perfect*
> (Romans 12:1–2).

So the spiritual life is not rejecting the soul. The mind and will and emotions are not rejected or displaced, but everything is brought into its proper place and order: first the spirit, then the soul, and then the body. In every area of our lives, we are called to "promote good order and unhindered devotion to the Lord" (1 Corinthians 7:35). When the soul submits to the spirit, the hindrances to the flow of the Spirit of God through our lives are removed. The life of God is then free to be manifested in our spirit, soul, and body. Then we are redeemed and restored into created order—at peace with God, with one another, and within ourselves.

Some Practical Effects of Restored Order

This concept of God reordering our spirit, soul, and body begins to bring an understanding of the purposes of many of the spiritual disciplines and practices. A few years ago, the Lord began to show me this is much of what is happening in contemplative prayer and fasting, experiencing the presence of the Lord in the Holy Communion of the Lord's Supper, true worship in spirit and truth, and even praying in the tongues of the Spirit. These are ways the Lord draws us nearer to Him, as we willingly choose to submit the mind, will, and emotions of our soul and the physical being of our body to the leading of our human spirit in communion with His Holy Spirit.

—*Contemplative Prayer*

One of the main purposes of prayer is this reordering of our spirit, soul, and body. There are many different facets and forms of prayer. One of these is what many call contemplative prayer—the kind of prayer where we get still and quiet, to watch and wait for the leading of the Lord. At times we are called to "be still, and know that I am God" (Psalm 46:10); to "be still before the Lord and wait patiently for Him" (Psalm 37:7); and to come to the place where "I have calmed and quieted my soul" (Psalm 131:2).

This is a form of prayer in the silence of surrender. We surrender the desires of our soul to simply watch and wait in the stillness and silence of submission to God. In this form of prayer, we let the Holy Spirit center our thoughts on the Lord rather than on ourselves, our needs, or even our burdens for others. There is room for all of that, and the Lord often calls us to these other forms of prayer in petition, supplication, intercession, and even spiritual warfare, but contemplation is a different form of prayer with a different purpose.

Its purpose, I believe, is to bring us back into created order and intimacy in our relationship with God, and back into the communion of the Holy Spirit. Then this becomes the source of our passion to rise and go forth in the fullness of the power of God in all these other forms of prayer and ministry.

When we get quiet and still before the Lord in contemplative prayer, we enter into His "rest." The Scripture of Hebrews 4:12 which speaks of "dividing soul from spirit" is actually in the context of entering into the divine place of *rest* the Lord has prepared for us (see Hebrews 4:1–12). When we enter in to this rest, through the quiet surrender of our soul, ceasing from our fleshly striving, the Lord brings us back into created order. Our body submits to our soul; our soul submits to our spirit; and our spirit submits to God's Holy Spirit. Worry, stress, anxiety, and fear begin to fade away. Confusion begins to give way to clarity; and heaviness begins to give way to praise and peace. Then when we arise

116

from the place of prayer, we arise to be led by the Spirit of God, rather than being driven by our own soul, or by the world, the flesh, and the devil. This way, He restores our soul and leads us beside the still waters in His paths of righteousness, no matter what circumstances we face in the world around us (see Psalm 23). We are steady and secure in the peace that surpasses all understanding, and we begin to know again the joy of the Lord as our strength.

—Fasting

The spiritual discipline of fasting is another means of grace the Lord uses to bring our lives back into created order. Fasting humbles our soul (see Psalm 69:10). Through fasting, our soul and body are willingly choosing to submit to our spirit. This is why prayer and fasting go together; otherwise, fasting would just be a bad diet! During a fast, our body is hungering for food; yet we willingly choose to submit our physical hunger to our spiritual hunger.

Our soul wants to rise up in rebellion to the leading of the spirit in the call to sacrifice in obedience to the Lord. Our mind continually wants to think about eating and all we are sacrificing for no outward or obvious gain, trying to rationalize away our commitment to obedience. Our will wants to choose to eat and satisfy our desires, to assert its freedom to choose to forgo the challenge and test of our faith. Our emotions try to drive us to eat, in frustration and irritation, feeling all the sensations of hunger and sacrifice.

Yet, by the grace of God and the leading of His Spirit, we willingly choose to submit our desires to the desires of the Lord. This is a sacrifice of obedience, which brings joy to the Lord and peace to our lives. Our spirits rise up as our soul submits, and we are drawn more deeply into the intimacy of relationship with God. As we humble ourselves in the sight of the Lord, He lifts us up (James 4:10).

—Holy Communion of the Lord's Supper

Receiving the sacrament of Holy Communion in the Lord's Supper is another means of grace for the Lord to bring our spirit, soul, and body back into created order. When we confess our sins and repent from our

117

own ways of thinking and living apart from God's ways, we are forgiven and cleansed of all unrighteousness by the blood of Christ (1 John 1:9). When we humble ourselves through repentance, the Lord then lifts us up into His presence, as we partake of the living Presence of the living Christ (1 Corinthians 11:23–26). "The cup of blessing that we bless, is it not a sharing in the blood of Christ? The bread that we break, is it not a sharing in the body of Christ?" (1 Corinthians 10:16)

Whether we understand the Scriptures to speak of a literal reality, a spiritual reality, a time of memorial, or a combination, we can all agree that Jesus intended to use this sacrament as a means of drawing us nearer to Him in humility and faith. Redeemed into created order, we become "one with Christ, one with each other, and one in ministry to all the world." We experience the "communion of the Holy Spirit" through "the grace of our Lord Jesus Christ" and "the love of God" (2 Corinthians 13:13). The humility of our confession and the obedience of our faith, as we receive the life of His body into our bodies and the life of His blood into our blood, bring our souls and bodies into submission to our spirits. Proper alignment brings deeper intimacy.

—True Worship in Spirit and Truth

Another means of the Lord's grace for restoring our spirit, soul, and body into God's created order is worship. In true worship, we bring every part of our being into focused adoration and praise of the Lord. Willingly, we allow our bodies to be living sacrifices and we worship the Lord with all our might "in spirit and truth" (John 4:23–24).

As "true worshipers," our mind and thoughts are actively directed to the Lord. Our will is engaged to choose to honor Him and love Him with all our heart, soul, mind, and strength. Our emotions are flooded with a sense of His Presence. And our spirits rise to soar into the heavenly realm of His Spirit. *Spiritual* worship, rather than *soulish* worship driven by our own mind, will, and emotions becomes another way of bringing our body and soul into submission to our spirit, so that our spirits rise into the intimacy of worship of our God.

The gift of praying or speaking in tongues is one of the biblical gifts of the Holy Spirit for the body of Christ. All of the gifts are given for the common good and for the building up of the body of Christ, to minister in the love of Christ, by the power of the Spirit of Christ with us (1 Corinthians 12:4–11).

According to the Word of God, there are "various kinds of tongues" (1 Corinthians 12:10, 28). One kind is when someone speaks in a language unknown to the person speaking in tongues, but is understood by others in their own language (Acts 2:1-13). Another kind is when the Holy Spirit moves upon someone to speak out a message to the gathering of believers in a language of the Holy Spirit. When this gift is exercised, there needs to be an interpretation of the tongues so that the church body knows what the Lord is speaking and "so that the church may be built up" (1 Corinthians 14:5). "Therefore, one who speaks in a tongue should pray for the power to interpret," (1 Corinthians 14:13), or another person who has the gift of "interpretation of tongues" should declare what is said so that the prophetic word of the Lord is heard and can be obeyed.

> *When you come together, each one has a hymn, a lesson, a revelation, a tongue, or an interpretation. Let all things be done for building up. If anyone speaks in a tongue, let there be only two or at most three, and each in turn; and let one interpret* (1 Corinthians 14:26–27).

But another kind of tongues is the personal prayer language of one who is praying in the Spirit. The purpose of this kind of tongues is not to share a prophetic word of the Lord with the body of believers, but to grow in spiritual maturity and intimacy with God.

> *But you, beloved, build yourselves up on your most holy faith; pray in the Holy Spirit; keep yourselves in the love of God; look forward to the mercy of our Lord Jesus Christ that leads to eternal life* (Jude 20–21).

It is the nature of tongues, that we are not praying with the mind, but in the spirit—God's Holy Spirit is praying through our human spirit what is the will of God.

119

For if I pray in a tongue, my spirit prays but my mind is unproductive
(1 Corinthians (14:14).

Likewise the Spirit helps us in our weakness; for we do not know how to pray as we ought, but that very Spirit intercedes with sighs too deep for words. And God, who searches the heart, knows what is the mind of the Spirit, because the Spirit intercedes for the saints according to the will of God (Romans 8:26–27).

In the gathering of believers where the Lord wants His message to be interpreted and understood, we need to pray in the spirit but with the mind also, so that the prophetic message is clear and understood. But in personal prayer, the Lord is building us up personally in spiritual maturity.

For those who speak in a tongue do not speak to other people, but to God; for nobody understands them, since they are speaking mysteries of the Spirit....Those who speak in a tongue build up themselves
(1 Corinthians 12:2–4).

So, the gift of tongues has its place in the assembly of believers when there is interpretation and it has its place in the personal prayer life of the believer as a means of being personally built up in spiritual maturity. Paul spoke and prayed in tongues and wished that all of those under his care would speak and pray in tongues (1 Corinthians 12:5). Through Paul, Scripture specifically commands us, "Do not forbid speaking in tongues" (1 Corinthians 14:29).

The spiritual gift of tongues is a biblical means of God's Spirit leading His people. We are available to pray God's perfect prayers as we make our spirit and tongue available to God. We are submitting our control to His control, bringing the mind of our soul into submission to our spirit, being led by the Holy Spirit. So as we pray in the Spirit, this becomes another means of God's grace to restore us into created order: our body in submission to our soul, our soul in submission to our spirit, and our spirit in submission to God's Holy Spirit.

Created Order is Distorted Through Sin

Original Perfection

"In the beginning God created the heavens and the earth" (Genesis 1:1 NKJV). God is the Creator of all things; and all that He creates is "good" (vv. 10, 12, 18, 21, 25). Then in the midst of His perfect creation, He created mankind in the very image of His own perfection and "God blessed them" (vv. 26–28). After creating humanity, "God saw everything that He had made, and indeed, it was very good" (v. 29). All things were created and established in God's created order—holy, pure, and perfect. "Indeed, it was *very* good."

Original Sin

Then sin entered in. The first man and woman disobeyed God (Genesis 3:1–7). God's holy creation was distorted and tainted by sin. The sin of disobedience brought all creation under a curse (vv. 14–19). And the curse of sin is death—death to God's perfection and defilement of His created order (Genesis 2:17; Romans 6:23). The original sin of our first ancestors, along with the curse of those consequences, was passed down through the generations, continuing to distort God's creation and disrupt God's created order.

> *Therefore, just as sin came into the world through one man, and death came through sin, and so death spread to all because all have sinned* (Romans 5:12–14).

Both the Goodness of Creation and the Tainting of Sin

God created each one of us. And everything God creates is holy and pure; it is "very good"—actually "perfect" in every way (Genesis 1:29; James 1:17–18). Yet, at the same time, we are marred by the tainting of original sin, which is inherited through the generations so that we are "born guilty," sinners from conception in our mothers' womb (Psalm 51:5). How can God's creation be both perfect and fallen at the same time? Understanding the concept of our personhood as spirit, soul, and body can help us understand how all that God creates is good when He creates us, while tainted by sin from our generations before us at the same time.

God created the first man, Adam, as a sinless and holy creation. "And the Lord God formed man from the dust of the ground, and breathed into his nostrils the breath of life; and the man became a living soul" (Genesis 2:7 KJV). The dust of the earth became Adam's body. The breath of life was his human spirit, which God breathed into existence. When God formed Adam's body and breathed into him his human spirit, Adam became "a living soul."

So it is with us. God takes the dust of the earth from the bodies of our mother and father—the egg and the sperm. He chooses the moment of conception to breathe into existence our human spirit—the innermost part of our being with identity and destiny, gifts and graces. And we become a living soul, knit together by the hand of God, with our unique personality and purpose (Psalm 139:13). When God creates our human spirit, it is holy and pure, breathed forth from the very mouth of God with the seal of His image and nature.

Yet, while the human spirit God creates is holy and pure, the embryo of our body is formed from the bodies of our parents—tainted and defiled by original sin and the sins of the generations passed down at every conception in the ancestral line, all the way back to Adam and Eve. From Adam's firstborn son on down the generational line, we are created in the image of God, but also tainted in the image of fallen man at the same time (Genesis 5:30).[16]

Diamonds in the Rough

As I began to pray with people in ministry, the Lord began to show me the heart of each person like a "diamond in the rough," as I mentioned earlier. Through the prayer ministry of inner healing and deliverance, He was calling forth the diamond, while breaking off the rough. The diamond of our spirit is unique and pure, designed to shine with the

---

[16] At the same time, God is also passing down the generational blesses that come down through the heritage of faith. For the sake of simplicity, we will discuss the principles of generational blessings and curses in depth in a later chapter.

radiant glory of the image of God through our lives. This is how He creates us. But the diamond is also encrusted by stone and impurities that hide its beauty and block the light from shining with fire from every facet and cut.

The "rough places" begin with the generational line. This is an image of how we are, at the same time, created holy and pure by God, but also tainted and defiled by sin. And then those rough places also emerge as we go through life and experience our own sins and the sins of others that affect us. But God comes to make "the rough places smooth" (Isaiah 40:4 NKJV). He begins to break and chisel away all that hinders us from displaying His glory if we will embrace Him and His process of healing and sanctification, of wholeness and holiness.

At Conception and Birth, None are Righteous

What God has created is holy and pure, with purpose, gifting, calling and destiny. It is unique and beautiful; but at the same time, it is defiled and tainted, hidden and enclosed by the consequences of sin. Because of the tainting of sin through the generations, we each start off our lives at conception both gloriously created in the image of God and yet, defiled and tainted by the sins of our ancestors at the same time. We are created by God, but we are also conceived and born out of God's created order. We all have need of a Redeemer, a Savior who will redeem us through the blood of the sacrifice of His own life for us.

> *As it is written, "There is no one who is righteous, not even one." ... For there is no distinction, since all have sinned and fall short of the glory of God* (Romans 3:10; 3:22–23).

Only in Christ do we "become the righteousness of God" (2 Corinthians 5:21). We each need the salvation that comes when we are redeemed by the blood of Jesus and brought back into created order, by the Spirit of God at work within us.

At the moment of conception, we are created with a spirit and soul and body, yet we are each detached and separated from God the moment our human spirit is breathed into a human body, defiled and tainted through the generational curse of original sin. As David declared,

"Indeed I was born guilty, a sinner when my mother conceived me" (Psalm 51:5).

Even before we make our first choice in the freedom God gives us, we are separated and detached from God, in a sense, through the sins of the generations before us. We are created for relationship with God, yet we each begin life without the fullness of His presence within us, because of the defilement of the sins before us. A way of viewing our state at conception is that the three circles of our human spirit, soul, and body are empty of the Spirit of God, as shown in the following diagram:

We are Spirit, Soul and Body
—1 Thes 5:23; Heb 4:12

Body
soma
(Physical Being)

Soul
psuche
(Mind, Will and Emotions)

Spirit
pneuma
(Communion, Conscience, and Intuition)

God Desires All to Come to the Knowledge of the Truth in Christ

Like each one before us, we must come to the place of choosing to humble ourselves and seek the mercy and grace of God made available to all through the blood of Jesus Christ. God the Holy Spirit is already at work in every life, trying to draw each person near to God the Father through God the Son, Jesus Christ. His will is that we all receive His gift of grace and love, that we may be restored into the loving relationship with Him that our first ancestors knew before sin entered the world and tainted the lives God created.

*This is right and is acceptable in the sight of God our Savior, who desires everyone to be saved and to come to the knowledge of the truth. For there is one God; there is also one mediator between God and humankind, Christ Jesus, Himself human, who gave Himself a ransom for **all**—this was attested at the right time* (1 Timothy 2:3–6, emphasis added).

*The Lord is not slow about his promise, as some think of slowness, but is patient with you, not wanting any to perish, but **all** to come to repentance* (2 Peter 3:9, emphasis added).

We have the freedom to choose God; and it is God's will that we choose Him. But the choice is up to each of us (John 3:16–18).

The Holy Spirit Comes to Save Us and Sanctify Us

When each of us comes to the place of humility and trusting faith, that we receive the love and grace of God revealed in Jesus Christ at salvation, the Holy Spirit of God enters inside of us. This is the Spirit of Christ in us, the hope of glory (Colossians 1:27).

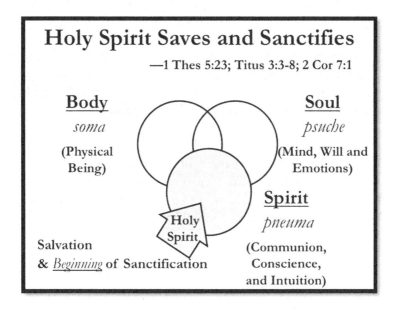

At salvation, we are changed. In my diagram, the golden light (when this diagram is in color) represents the indwelling presence of the Holy Spirit. We were lost, but now we are found; we were dead in our spirits but now we are alive to God's Spirit—the Spirit of Christ—who we have now welcomed to live in us. Our heart becomes His home.

> *But you are not in the flesh; you are in the Spirit, since the Spirit of God dwells in you. Anyone who does not have the Spirit of Christ does not belong to Him. But if Christ is in you, though the body is dead because of sin, the Spirit is life because of righteousness. If the Spirit of Him who raised Jesus from the dead dwells in you, He who raised Christ from the dead will give life to your mortal bodies also through His Spirit that dwells in you* (Romans 8:9–11).

We are now in Christ and Christ is in us, by the presence and power of His Holy Spirit. Now the Holy Spirit *begins the process* of renewing us and transforming us into His nature—the nature of Christ.

> *For we ourselves were once foolish, disobedient, led astray, slaves to various passions and pleasures, passing our days in malice and envy, despicable, hating one another. But when the goodness and loving kindness of God our Savior appeared, He saved us, not because of any works of righteousness that we had done, but according to His mercy, through the water of rebirth and renewal by the Holy Spirit. This Spirit He poured out on us richly through Jesus Christ our Savior, so that, having been justified by His grace, we might become heirs according to the hope of eternal life* (Titus 3:3–8).

By exercising the freedom of our will and choosing to submit to the Lordship of Jesus Christ, we are choosing to embrace the will and nature of God. As we give God permission to convict us and to change us, His Holy Spirit begins the process of sanctification and healing—to make us more like Jesus.

> *Since we have these promises, beloved, let us cleanse ourselves from every defilement of body and of spirit, making holiness perfect in the fear of God* (2 Corinthians 7:1).

126

Temples of the Holy Spirit

We cannot cleanse ourselves in our power or self-determination, but "God is faithful and He will do this" (1 Thessalonians 5:24). That is God's part. Our part is to make the choice to embrace Him and His process. Once we receive Christ and His Holy Spirit, this is not the end of the process, but *the beginning*.

In my diagram from the previous section, I am showing the Holy Spirit coming in to possess and completely fill the human spirit. Our spirit was dead, but now it is alive; we were disconnected from God, but now He dwells within us. Our bodies are now the temple of the Holy Spirit. We are bought with a price, by the blood of Jesus, and our lives now belong to God—if we have truly submitted to the Lordship of Christ (1 Corinthians 6:19–20).

The Beginning of the Process of Sanctification and Wholeness

Though our bodies are now temples of the Holy Spirit; at the same time, the Holy Spirit has not yet sanctified us "entirely" (1 Thessalonians 5:23). Instead, He has only begun the process of sanctification and wholeness when we come to Christ and receive Him as Lord. This is what I am showing by the diagram, where the light of the glory of the Holy Spirit only fills the human spirit but does not yet completely fill the body and soul. At salvation, *our soul* is partially filled with the Holy Spirit but not entirely; we are partially sanctified and healed, but not entirely.

In the diagram of my three circles, the golden light of the Holy Spirit covers part of the soul, but not all. What I am intending to convey by this is that not all of soul—our mind, will, and emotions—is completely sanctified. We are not yet completely like Christ at the moment of our salvation. If we were really honest, we would have to admit that when we were saved, we did not immediately have the mind of Christ—completely. Not all of our thoughts were the thoughts of Jesus. We did not immediately have the will of God—completely. Not all of our choices were the choices Jesus would make. In fact, we might not even bother to ask, "What would Jesus do?" much less actually do it. We did not immediately have the emotions of Christ—completely, as we encountered every obstacle and offense in our Christian walk.

At salvation, we want to be like Jesus, but the truth is (for most us), we were not—and are not even yet—completely like Jesus. We are beginning to be sanctified, but we are not yet entirely sanctified at the moment of salvation.

The "renewing" of our mind and will and emotions is a process (Romans 12:2). In fact, if we are really honest, we have to admit that even today, we likely do not fully have the mind of Christ in every area of our lives. Nor do we fully have the will and emotions of Christ in every area of our lives. Sanctification is a process. It begins when we are saved, but it does not end there. Though there may be significant spiritual encounters, experiences, and breakthroughs along the way, sanctification is a life-long process in the journey of spiritual maturity to Christlikeness. It's also the journey to healing and freedom.

The Kingdom of God is Where God is King and Jesus is Lord

In a sense, "the kingdom of God" is where God is King, not us. It is where Jesus is Lord, not us. This is the sense in which, "the kingdom of God is within you" (Luke 17:21). The kingdom of God is where we submit to and honor Jesus as our King—where we agree with the Word of God that He is the "King of kings and Lord of lords" (Revelation 17:14 and 19:16; 1 Timothy 6:15). When we are saved, we choose to recognize Jesus as King and Lord. But most times, this is in a general sense. He wants to be King and Lord of all—in every particular sense.

We would be foolish and naïve to believe the victory of the flesh over our spirit does not affect our healing and wholeness and the level of our joy and peace. There is no true peace without submission to the peace of God, no true joy without embracing the joy of God. When our human spirits are yielded to the leading of God's Holy Spirit, we experience the blessings of the kingdom of God. But when our human soul rises up in rebellion to the leading of the Spirit and in submission to leading of our flesh, we "will not inherit the kingdom of God" in that area of our life (Galatians 5:21).[17]

---

[17] Some argue that we will not inherit the Kingdom of God at all if there are areas of sin in our lives. This is the mistaken view that we must be entirely sanctified to go to heaven. Yet this misses the point of the progressive process of the sanctification of our souls, as revealed in the whole counsel of God.

When we set aside our own desires in submission to the desires of the Spirit of God, the King of kings is enthroned as the Lord of lords of our soul. He comes to rule and reign in righteousness, and then we are free to experience the peace and joy of His reign within us. "For the kingdom of God is not food and drink but righteousness and peace and joy in the Holy Spirit" (Romans 14:17). Healing and wholeness comes with the peace and joy of the Lord, as we allow Him to restore our lives into His created order. (Matthew 6:33).

Sanctified Entirely—Healed, Whole, and Filled with the Spirit

We begin life empty of God and full of ourselves, each one in desperate need of God's mercy and grace. He draws us near to Him and helps us to trust Him, enough to commit our lives to Him in humility and faith. When we do, His Holy Spirit comes into our human spirits to begin changing and conforming our nature into His nature.

Pressing on to Perfection in God's Grace

The Lord meets us where we are, but He will not leave us where we are. Faith is a journey—we are either moving forward or moving backward, moving down His path or off the path. God loves us too much to settle for anything less than the fullness of our trust, the fullness of our love, and the fullness of our surrender. He knows we were created to never be satisfied with anything less, because He created us that way. He accepts us and loves us as we are, but His love for us and His desire for us to become all we were created to be will not allow Him to leave us passive or complacent about moving forward in Him. He moves in our hearts to continually "press on toward the goal of the prize of the heavenly call of God in Christ Jesus" (Philippians 3:14).

It is God's will to sanctify us entirely—that our spirit and soul and body may be sound and blameless at the coming of the Lord Jesus Christ (1 Thessalonians 5:23). This is not a man-made doctrine, not one of the traditions of men, not some legalistic platitude invented by the authorities of the church to make us always feel guilty because we can never live up to their standards. In fact, God could not have declared His will in His Word in this matter any more clearly:

For this is the will of God, your sanctification.... For God did not call us to impurity but in holiness. Therefore whoever rejects this rejects not human authority but God, who also gives his Holy Spirit to you
(1 Thessalonians 4:3–8).

In Christ, God has chosen us "as the first fruits for salvation through sanctification by the Spirit and through belief in the truth..." so that we, "may obtain the glory of our Lord Jesus Christ" (2 Thessalonians 2:13-14). As those who have chosen to receive the love of God revealed in Jesus Christ, we "have been chosen and destined by God the Father and sanctified by the Spirit to be obedient to Jesus Christ and to be sprinkled with His blood" (1 Peter 1:2).

Filled with the Glory of God

We "obtain the glory of the Lord Jesus Christ" to the degree that we are filled with fullness of the Spirit of Christ. God desires to sanctify us entirely and fill us completely with the fullness of the glory of His presence living in us.

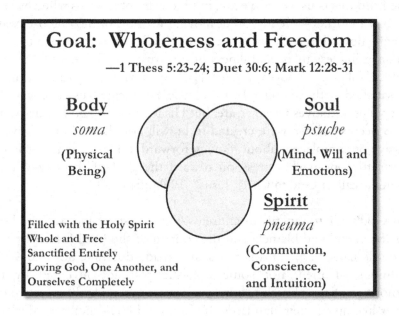

Goal: **Wholeness and Freedom**
—1 Thess 5:23-24; Duet 30:6; Mark 12:28-31

Body
soma
(Physical Being)

Soul
psuche
(Mind, Will and Emotions)

Spirit
pneuma
(Communion, Conscience, and Intuition)

Filled with the Holy Spirit
Whole and Free
Sanctified Entirely
Loving God, One Another, and
Ourselves Completely

Whole and Holy, Healed and Free

In this diagram, I am showing the golden light of the Holy Spirit completely filling every dimension of our being—spirit and soul and body. This is the goal: wholeness and holiness—to come to the place of absolute trust and absolute surrender. This is where we love God and love one another completely. (Mark 12:28–31).

We are commanded by God's Word to "be filled with the Holy Spirit" (Ephesians 5:18). This is to be filled with the nature of Christ because the Holy Spirit is "the Spirit of Christ" (Romans 8:9; 1 Peter 1:11; Philippians 1:19). To be filled with the Holy Spirit is to be sanctified into the nature of the Holy Spirit—to be saturated, immersed, and baptized in the Holy Spirit. "Sanctified entirely" means to be sanctified completely in spirit, soul, and body (1 Thessalonians 5:23).

Baptized in the Holy Spirit

As we are baptized into the fullness of the nature of Christ, we are emptied completely of ourselves—our self-will, that we may be filled completely with Him—His will. The word "baptism" comes from the Greek word *baptizo*, which means to saturate, to submerge, to dip repeatedly, and to cleanse thoroughly. It is not a one-time dipping, but a life-long dunking. It is not so much like wading in the water, as it is like getting washed away in the river.

John the Baptist prophesied of this coming ministry of Jesus, saying:

> *I baptize you with water for repentance, but One who is more powerful than I is coming after me; I am not worthy to carry His sandals. He will baptize you with the Holy Spirit and fire* (Matthew 3:11).

In Jesus' last words on earth, He told his first disciples to wait to be *"baptized with the Holy Spirit."* This is not merely the language of some tradition or denomination of the Church; it's the language of Jesus:

> *While staying with them, He ordered them not to leave Jerusalem, but to wait there for the promise of the Father. "This," He said, "is what you have*

heard from Me; for John baptized with water, but you will be baptized with the Holy Spirit not many days from now" (Acts 1:4–5).

Called to be Holy

To be filled with the Spirit is to be baptized with the Spirit. The nature of the Holy Spirit is, of course, holiness—"Holy" is the His first name. He comes to live in our hearts and fill us with His nature to make us more like Jesus. This is God's means of sanctifying us—making us holy as He is holy, making us perfect as He is perfect. Some scoff at the idea, but these are actually *commandments* of God. He declares it in the Old Testament and affirms it in the New Testament:

> *For I am the Lord your God; sanctify yourselves therefore, and **be holy**, for I am holy* (Leviticus 11:44, emphasis added).

> *Consecrate yourselves therefore, and **be holy**; for I am the Lord your God. Keep my statutes, and observe them; I am the Lord; I sanctify you* (Leviticus 20:7–8, emphasis added).

> *Instead, as He who called you is holy, **be holy** yourselves in all your conduct; for it is written, "You shall **be holy**, for I am holy"* (1 Peter 1:15–16, emphasis added).

The climax of Jesus' Sermon on the Mount is this call to "Christian perfection," declared as a *command*: "*Be perfect*, therefore, as your heavenly Father is perfect" (Matthew 5:48, emphasis added). Holiness is sanctification; and sanctification is the work of the Holy Spirit, who comes to make us holy and whole—restored into God's created order in every dimension of our lives—free to be like Jesus.

The objection of many is that human beings cannot possibly be holy and perfect this side of heaven. In response to the Scriptures and commands of God in His Word that seem to say otherwise, they take a passive stance that we already are holy and perfect in Christ in some kind of positional way—even if our current reality reveals we are far from it. The idea is that we are already *positionally* holy in Christ, so there is really nothing more we are called to embrace. Yet, that kind of theological understanding sets us up for a kind of spiritual schizophrenia, where

God clearly commands something of us, but does not ever really expect it of us. Or somehow this command is something that gets taken care of in heaven, while we are expected to obey all His other commands here on earth.

Our Part and God's Part in the Process

A key is to understanding what the Scripture means by these concepts of holiness, perfection, and entire sanctification is to understand how they relate to the *process* of being filled and baptized with the Holy Spirit. As in everything else in our journey to spiritual maturity and Christlikeness, the key involves the decisions of our will in response to God's grace.

> *Since we have these promises, beloved, let us cleanse ourselves from every defilement of body and of spirit,* **making holiness perfect** *in the fear of God* (2 Corinthians 7:1, emphasis added).

We are called to make *a choice* by a free act of our will—all by the help of God's grace and in response to God's grace, made available to us by the sacrifice of Christ at the cross. God gives us the freedom to choose to obey Him or not, and there are consequences for our choices.

The Key: "As Much as I Can, All by His Grace"

This is the choice God wants each of us to make: to give Him as much of myself as I can, and to receive as much of Him as I can, all by the leading and power of His grace.

To give Him anything more than this would be impossible; and to give Him less than this would be sin. "As much as I can" is the key to understanding the principle and the command. If I make the choice, by the grace of God, to give Him as much of me as I can at every moment of my life, what more could I give? If I make the choice, by the grace of God, to receive as much of Him as I can at every moment of my life, what more can I receive? Nothing—therefore, nothing more is required. To me, this is the place of complete trust and complete surrender—as complete as I can make it for where I am at every stage of the journey.

133

To me, this is the call to personal holiness, to entire sanctification, to Christian perfection—to be filled and baptized with the Holy Spirit.[18]

The Life-Long Journey

The process of sanctification is a life-long journey with breakthroughs along the way. If I give God all I can give Him today, I will be able to give Him more of myself tomorrow. If I receive as much of God as I can today, I will be able to receive more of Him tomorrow. At times along the journey of deep brokenness, desperation, or passionate conviction, there may be great breakthroughs where His grace and mercy come rushing in like a flood or a mighty rushing wind. These are the great spiritual experiences of divine encounters in our lives. Most of the time, though, it is more like the gentle journey of two friends growing in their loyalty and trust over time.

We receive sanctification just like we receive salvation—by our response to God's grace. We receive the baptism of the Holy Spirit just like we receive every other gift of God—by asking and receiving, in faith believing. This is God's gift and He has revealed His will to give us this gift in His Word. Yet He will not force us; He will not override our free will. But He will use all the circumstances of our lives to call us, nudge

---

[18] I deeply appreciate the writings of John Fletcher, who wrestled with these issues until the Lord showed him this perspective. He was John Wesley's theologian and vindicator of the Methodist movement, and Wesley's designated successor to carry on the Methodist revival after his death, but Fletcher predeceased Wesley. Fletcher came to equate the baptism of the Holy Spirit with entire sanctification. Many of the writings and sermons of Wesley on these points did not fully make sense to me, because of his own progressive, developing understanding of these terms over the years of his life, until I began to read Fletcher's writings as part of my devotions for a year. In Wesley's last years, he fully embraced Fletcher's understanding that to be "baptized in the Holy Spirit" is to be sanctified entirely in spirit, soul, and body, being perfected in Christian love by God's grace. Please see Dr. Larry Wood's book, *The Roots of Pentecostalism in Methodism*, incorporating many of Fletcher's personal writings and correspondence with John and Charles Wesley, along with a historical development of these terms. A good case can be made, as Dr. Wood presents in his book, that the move to embrace the "baptism of the Holy Spirit" in modern times can be traced back to an awakening of this scriptural call through the writings of John Fletcher. These concepts have become key to my perspective of God's transforming power of healing and deliverance prayer ministry.

us, and draw us to this place of trust and surrender, so that we "may be filled with the fullness of God" (Ephesians 3:19).

The Journey Continues

Many times, people believe they have already received the blessing of the baptism of the Holy Spirit. And indeed, many have—because they have come to a place of trust and surrender, where they trust God at a deeper level than before and entrust a deeper measure of themselves to Him than before. His Spirit comes in like a mighty rushing wind. The fullness of His presence and His gifts are flowing like never before. But some stop there and don't keep pressing on. They think it's done because they have given Him all they could give Him, without realizing they will be able to give Him more and more as His grace abounds more and more in the journey of spiritual maturity.

These are not one-time events, but a lifetime series of events from choosing to commit our lives to God—moment by moment and day by day. This is a lifestyle of holiness; this is living life in the fullness of the Spirit—holiness of heart and life. This is the journey Christians are called to join as we walk in the steps of Christ. Though these choices are simple, they are powerful. As we will see, these simple choices of surrender make a tremendous difference in our journey of healing, deliverance, and wholeness. They affect our spirits, souls, and bodies. They affect our relationships with God and with one another.

The Key to Wholeness and Holiness:
Submission the Lordship of Jesus Christ

The next diagram shows the light of the Holy Spirit rising up from the spirit into greater levels of the soul and body of the believer. Remember, when we are saved and receive the Spirit of Christ in us, the hope of glory, our soul is beginning to be sanctified, but is not yet entirely sanctified. The light that completely fills the spirit is only partially filling the soul and the body. God is in the process of bringing us back into His created order. The key to this process is submission to the Lordship of Jesus Christ.

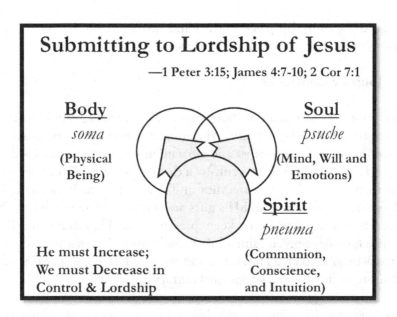

Submitting to Lordship of Jesus
—1 Peter 3:15; James 4:7-10; 2 Cor 7:1

Body
soma
(Physical Being)

Soul
psuche
(Mind, Will and Emotions)

Spirit
pneuma

He must Increase;
We must Decrease in
Control & Lordship

(Communion,
Conscience,
and Intuition)

God Increases as We Decrease

John the Baptist said of Jesus, "He must increase, but I must decrease" (John 3:30). God increases as we decreases—in terms of submission of our will to His will. He fills us with Himself *to the degree* that we are emptied of ourselves—emptied of our self-will apart from His will. Every believer has made Jesus Lord of his life—*in general*, but Jesus also wants to be Lord of every area of our lives—*in the specifics*, in every level and depth of our being. To advance in the kingdom, the King must advance in us. If He is to increase, then we must decrease. To grow in spiritual maturity, and grow into the fullness of our salvation, healing, and deliverance, the nature of the Spirit must grow in us.

> *Rid yourselves, therefore, of all malice, and all guile, insincerity, envy, and all slander. Like newborn infants, long for the pure, spiritual milk, so that by it you may grow into salvation—if indeed you have tasted that the Lord is good* (1 Peter 2:1–3).

"Lordship" is a relational term. To say someone is my Lord is to say I submit to his authority. To say Jesus is my Lord is to say I am not—He is in charge, and I'm not; He is in control, and I'm not. This is a decision of humility and faith. It is humility because I am humbling myself to

136

renounce my own control as I put Him in complete control. It is faith because I am entrusting my life to Him, believing He loves me and knows what is best for me. With the humility of trusting surrender, we answer the call of the Holy Spirit. This is a key principle:

In your hearts, sanctify Christ as Lord (1 Peter 3:15).

By His grace, we turn our faces and open our hearts to the Lord. Then the light of His glory presses out the darkness of our self-centeredness and self-focus. As He is increasing, we are decreasing. As He is filling us with Himself, He is emptying us of ourselves. But He is not casting us away or replacing us; He is transforming us and conforming us into His image and His nature (Romans 8:29 and 12:1–2)

> *But we all, with unveiled face, beholding as in a mirror the glory of the Lord, are being transformed into the same image from glory to glory, just as by the Spirit of the Lord* (2 Corinthians 3:18).

"From glory to glory" emphasizes the *process* of transformation. That transformation takes place as we behold the Lord. We become like what we worship. The point of our focus becomes the point of our destination. We are consumed by what we allow to consume us, and we are embraced by what we allow to embrace us. God our Father wants that to be His Holy Spirit through our increasing yielding to the Lordship of Jesus Christ.

Receiving God's True Spirit, not a False Spirit

The order and the focus of His increasing and our decreasing is important as well. If we get this process backwards—so that we are decreasing before He is increasing—there can be danger of receiving another spirit besides the Holy Spirit (2 Corinthians 11:3–4). This can be a false religious spirit, masquerading as the Holy Spirit. We must actively look to the Lord—not passively waiting on anything that may come along, but actively looking to Him alone. This is one of the dangers of New Age practices and eastern religions, which encourage a form of meditation or prayer where the mind and spirit is passive rather than active. We discuss this in detail later.

Spiritual Maturity

We are to grow up, personally and as the body of Christ, into spiritual maturity as we are being made healthy and whole. By God's grace and through the ministry of His people, He is "building up the body of Christ, until all of us come to the unity of the faith and of the knowledge of the Son of God, to maturity, to the measure of the full stature of Christ" (Ephesians 4:12–13).

> *We must no longer be children, tossed to and fro and blown about by every wind of doctrine, by people's trickery, by their craftiness in deceitful scheming. But speaking the truth in love, we must grow up in every way into Him who is the Head, into Christ* (Ephesians 4:14–15).

In God's kingdom dynamics, the way to grow up is to bow down; the last shall be first; and those who lose their lives will find them. All of this speaks of the process of humbling ourselves in the sight of the Lord that He may lift us up. We are not humbling ourselves before just anything that seems to be more spiritual, fascinating, or powerful than us. We are *specifically* humbling ourselves before the Lord. And as we humble ourselves in trusting surrender and obedient faith, He lifts us up into the intimacy of His presence and the calling of our destiny. "Humble yourselves before the Lord, and He will exalt you"
(James 4:10).

Filled with All the Fullness of God

The Holy Spirit wants to fill us with the fullness of the nature of Christ. He must increase and we must decrease. We must be emptied of ourselves so we can be filled with Him. In praying for others to embrace this process of healing and wholeness through humility and faith, I have often sensed the Holy Spirit leading me to pray a Scriptural prayer that Paul prayed for those under his care. This is often the final prayer and word of blessing I will speak over someone's life to seal the healing work of God during our prayer time together:

> *For this reason I bow my knees before the Father, from whom every family in heaven and on earth takes its name. I pray that, according to the riches of His glory, He may grant that you may be strengthened in your inner being*

with power through His Spirit, and that Christ may dwell in your hearts through faith, as you are being rooted and grounded in love. I pray that you may have the power to comprehend, with all the saints, what is the breadth and length and height and depth, and to know the love of Christ that surpasses knowledge, so that you may be filled with all the fullness of God. Now to Him who by the power at work within us is able to accomplish abundantly far more than all we can ask or imagine, to Him be glory in the church and in Christ Jesus to all generations, forever and ever. Amen (Ephesians 3:14–21).

As we submit to the Lordship of Jesus Christ in our hearts and in every area of our lives, we are being strengthened with the power of the Holy Spirit in our inner being, we are being rooted and grounded in God's love, and we are in the process of being filled with all the fullness of God. As we do, our Father God is glorified in us and in His Son, forever and ever.

Chapter 10

The War of the Soul—Our Flesh Resisting God's Spirit

For God to increase in our lives, we must decrease. The trouble is our "flesh" does not want to decrease. Our flesh—the unsanctified areas of our soul—wants to rule and reign, rather than willingly submit the Lordship of Jesus Christ. This is the battlefield in the war of the soul, because the flesh is at war with the Spirit.

The Flesh—The Unsanctified Areas of Our Soul

In my next diagram of the three circles, part of the soul is filled with the light of the Spirit and part of the soul is not, part of the soul is sanctified and part is not. From this perspective, every unsanctified area of our soul is "the flesh." Our flesh is like a brick wall of resistance guarding our strongholds of pride—areas where we have declared that we are lord, where we have refused to bow our hearts to the Spirit of Christ. Pride rallies its troops in the resistance movement of our flesh against God's Spirit.

And within our flesh, we also have specific areas where we have hardened our hearts against the Lordship of Christ in our soul. They form what I call "Pockets of Resistance." They are like an insurgency of our flesh against the advance of the Holy Spirit and the kingdom of God in our lives.

Pockets of Resistance

War in the Soul of the Spirit and the Flesh

—James 4:1; Rom 7:14-25; 1 Peter 2:11

Body

soma

(Physical Being)

Soul

psuche

(Mind, Will and Emotions)

Spirit

pneuma

Holy Spirit

(Communion, Conscience, and Intuition)

Bad Roots & Barriers to Healing

Our Flesh at War with the Spirit

Our flesh is every area of our lives where we are still in rebellion against the will and ways of God, even though we have received Christ as Lord and now have the Holy Spirit at work within us. This is the area of our life where we are still "lord" and where we are in control, asserting our lordship instead of submitting to His. In these areas, we have not yet fully trusted Christ to fully submit to the "Lordship of Christ," fully yielding to His control and the leading of His Spirit in our lives. We are still saved; we still have the Holy Spirit; we are still going to heaven when we die; but we are not yet entirely sanctified. And "pockets of resistance"—as I call them—emerge as the battlefield where the "war" of the soul is fought.

> *For I delight in the law of God in my inmost self, but I see in my members another law at war with the law of my mind, making me captive to the law of sin that dwells in my members* (Romans 7:22).

"The desires of the flesh" are opposed to the desires of the human spirit that are to be submitted to the desires to the Holy Spirit.

142

Beloved, I urge you as aliens and exiles to abstain from the desires of the flesh that wage war against the soul (1 Peter 2:11).

Our flesh wants to rise up in rebellion against our spirit in the war for the Christian soul. To the degree that the flesh wins this battle, our soul will rise up in the place of authority over our spirit. (See the earlier diagram and discussion). We will be more soulish than spiritual to that very degree.

We Have a Choice

Once we receive the Spirit of Christ in our hearts through faith, this war for the Christian soul is fought one battle at a time. We win or lose these battles between the Spirit and the flesh in the war of the soul by the choices we make. In essence the war is waged in the will of our soul. Remember, the will is in the soul—the mind, will, and emotions. The soul must choose to submit to the Spirit or not. By God's grace, we have a choice: to live by the leading of the Holy Spirit or to live by the leading of our flesh in each specific area of our life.

To willingly submit to the leading of the Spirit is to submit to the Lordship of Jesus Christ in that area of our soul. To submit to the leading of the flesh is to rebel against the Lordship of Jesus Christ to that very degree that we rule as lord of that area of our lives instead of submitting to His rule.

> *Live by the Spirit, I say, and do not gratify the desires of the flesh. For what the flesh desires is opposed to the Spirit, and what the Spirit desires is opposed to the flesh; for these are opposed to each other, to prevent you from doing what you want. But if you are led by the Spirit, you are not subject to the law. Now the works of the flesh are obvious: fornication, impurity, licentiousness, idolatry, sorcery, enmities, strife, jealousy, anger, quarrels, dissensions, factions, envy, drunkenness, carousing, and things like these. I am warning you, as I warned you before: those who do such things will not inherit the kingdom of God* (Galatians 5:16–21).

In this war, we're actually being called to a place of complete surrender—trusting surrender to the will of God. And what God asks of every one of us is that we give Him all of us that we can, as we reach

each level in the process of sanctification in our life. And He wants us to receive all of Him that we can receive at that moment. That's what He means by be holy, be perfect, be sanctified entirely – be perfected in Christian love. That's where I choose to give God as much of me as I can. And I receive as much of Him as I can at that moment. The key phrase in that is "as much as I can."

There is a level for every single one of us right now which is a level of surrender that each of us can give God right now. No matter how many roots still need to be dug up, no matter how many bonds need to be broken, no matter how much more sanctified I need to be, there is a level that I can choose right now. By a free act of my will I can choose to say, "God, I give as much of me as I can give you right now." And to the very degree that we have emptied ourselves before Him, to that very degree He can fill us with the fullness of Himself.

The idea here is to give Him as much as I can right now, and then as much as I can tomorrow. I'll be able to give Him more of me tomorrow than I can right now. And more next week than I can this week, more next year than this year because it's the *process* of being sanctified—level by level, degree by degree. Then that process takes place as I sanctify Christ as Lord in my heart. I can say, "Lord, I give you as much of me right now as I can." Anything more is impossible. And anything less than as much as I can right now is sin.

Right now, for every one of us—no matter what we've been through, no matter what our generational line looks like, no matter what struggles and battles and obstacles we've endured, no matter how badly the enemy has tried to destroy us—there is a level for every single one of us that we can choose to surrender to God right now. And to that degree, we'll receive as much of Him as we can at this moment. Now that is the level that determines how much we are sanctified entirely and how much we are perfected in Christian life. And God wants to bring us to the place of complete surrender. So at that moment where we have given God all that we can give Him, we're entirely sanctified. We are perfect in Christian love. That doesn't mean that there's not another layer to give Him tomorrow, because it's a lifelong journey. But He's asking us, He's calling us, He's commanding us to give Him as much of us as we can at that moment.

Pockets of Resistance

In our flesh, we have a "resistance movement" going against the high command of God. Some of us have been guarding some of those areas and some of those layers. We've still been asserting our authority, our lordship, our control in those areas. Sometimes directly, sometimes subconsciously, sometimes guarding it like you'd guard a wound that's still tender—almost subconsciously, automatically, but we're still guarding it. And the Lord wants to expose that so that we can release our control, slay our pride, and humble ourselves in His sight. As He sanctifies us entirely, He also wants to fill and cleanse us so that our spirit, soul, and body may be found blameless and holy at the coming of the Lord Jesus Christ; and that we love the Lord our God with all our heart, soul, mind, strength and love our neighbor as ourselves. That's the goal.

Some Specific Examples of Pockets of Resistance

The most obvious examples of "pockets of resistance" are the areas of persistent sin. In the passage above, Paul gives a list of "the works of the flesh" in his exhortation to *the believers* in the church at Galatia. These are words to believers, not unbelievers; and this list is obviously not exclusive. We can't deny that we see these works of flesh at times in our Christian neighbors' lives; and if we are really honest, we have to admit we continue to see some of these works of flesh in our own lives at times. The more we persist in sin by engaging in these works of the flesh, the more our hearts become hardened with pockets of resistance and strongholds of pride against the Lordship of Jesus and the filling of His Holy Spirit.

This perspective of understanding the flesh and the Spirit explains how a Christian who has received Jesus as Lord can have the Holy Spirit and still have an area of sin in their life. Some would say that the person who persists in sin is just not saved, but the truth is more likely that the person is saved but not fully sanctified. Thankfully, we don't have to be perfectly holy and sanctified entirely in order to be saved. But these pockets of resistance become the focus of the Holy Spirit. God, in His mercy, will make us miserable in these areas from suffering the consequences of our sin which brings us to our knees in the humility of confession and repentance. Then He can release the fullness of His grace to us in that area of our life.

—Example of Unforgiveness

Unforgiveness is probably the most common "pocket of resistance" I encounter in prayer ministry.[19] Paul names "enmities, strife, jealousy, anger, quarrels dissensions, factions, envy" as some of the "works of the flesh" (Galatians 5:19-21). These are all potential roots and fruit of unforgiveness. Unforgiveness is sin. It is a manifestation of the pride of our flesh and self-will resisting the will of God. Jesus said:

> *Forgive, and you will be forgiven* (Luke 6:37)

> *For if you forgive others of their trespasses, your heavenly Father will also forgive you; but if you do not forgive others, neither will your Father forgive your trespasses* (Matthew 6:14–15).

Jesus taught his disciples to pray in the Lord's prayer, "Forgive us our trespasses *as* we forgive those who trespass against" (see Matthew 6:12). It is a spiritual principle that we are forgiven in the same way that we forgive others. "For the measure you give will be the measure you get back" (Luke 6:38). God requires our forgiveness because He has forgiven us, as Jesus pointedly explains in the parable of the unforgiving servant, who is handed over to the tormentors for his sin of unforgiveness, warning each of us: "So My heavenly Father will also do to every one of you, if you do not forgive your brother or sister from your heart" (Matthew 18:35).

Unforgiveness is our self-centered pride saying, "I know what You and Your Word say about forgiving this person, but I will not forgive them for what they have done. So I'm going to do what I want to do, no matter what You and Your Word say." This is an attitude of rebellion and sin, where we have hardened our heart and blocked the grace of God. By our choice. We are preventing the filling of God's Holy Spirit in this area of our life.

---

[19] We will cover the topic of Unforgiveness and Bitterness in some detail later when we discuss Seven Key Roots of Resistance and also in the section on Potential Barriers to Healing in my "Seven Categories for Prayer Ministry."

—Example of Pornography

With the explosion of popularity of the internet and the cover of anonymity it brings, struggles and addictions to pornography are an increasingly common pocket of resistance, especially among men. The word comes from the same root word translated as "fornication" as a work of the flesh in Galatians 5:19, meaning all forms of illicit sexuality. Even many mature believers, spiritual leaders, and pastors I have prayed for fight major battles in this area. And their lives are marked by the guilt and shame of their secret sin that is defiling their marriages, destroying their consciences, tainting their gifts, and damaging their relationships with God.

These men, and sometimes women, are drawn into this devastating trap for a number of reasons—sometimes it's simply arrogance and rebellion or lust, but many times there are deeper issues. Often, it is a form of false intimacy where they *perceive* true intimacy is lacking, frequently compounded by loneliness, isolation, weariness, or stress. And, of course, the relentless pornography industry attempted to draw men into the web of impurity through temptation and lust to profit from their weakness and sin. Then the cycles of sin and remorse, sin and remorse, draw their victim into a downward spiral of condemnation and guilt until there seems to be no hope of freedom.

With every encounter with the images, their consciences become more seared and their hearts become more hardened. And all their relationships suffer from both the defiling sin itself and the outward manifestations of the inward remorse. These are believers, saved and being sanctified, having the Holy Spirit and a measure of the gifts of the Spirit operating in their lives, while at the same time, there is an area of their soul that they are not submitting to the Lordship of Christ and the cleansing power of the Holy Spirit.

—Unhealed Emotional Wounds

Persistent sin is not the only way pockets of resistance are formed. Unhealed emotional wounds from past hurts are another primary source. Here, the person often begins as the victim of sin, rather than the sinner, when they are hurt and wounded by another. For example, a

147

wound of rejection by a trusted friend or former spouse can cause us to pull back from all relationships and become less trusting of everyone. We can begin to form attitude in our heart that says, "I'll never trust anyone," or "I'll never let someone get that close to me again." These are examples of "inner vows," which we will discuss in more detail later.

These attitudes seem like natural or even wise ways to protect us from being hurt again. But the trouble is that this is another form of pride— "I'm going to do what I think I need to do to take care of myself." We are trusting in ourselves, not God, to take care of us. We take control rather than depending upon God to be in control. We assert our lordship in that area, rather than submitting to the Lordship of Jesus and the leading of the Holy Spirit in that area. Then the sin of someone else who hurt us leads us to commit our own sin in response—the sin of pride. Like a scab that forms over a sore, a pocket of resistance forms around an unhealed hurt, locking the pain or anger or other damaged emotion inside.

Pockets of Resistance and Strongholds of the Mind

Life's experiences affect every dimension of our soul. At times, we may be more of the instigator, and other times we may be more of the recipient. In any event, they affect our mind and how we think, our will and how we make choices, and our emotions and how we feel. God intends these experiences to be challenges and opportunities for our spiritual growth and maturity into the fulfillment of our calling and destiny. Our spiritual enemy—the enemy of our souls—intends these experiences to be opportunities to distract and destroy us, hindering and blocking the purposes of God in our lives.

Generally, we begin to process these experiences—both good and bad—through our emotions as we sense and feel the pain, shame, passions, desires, excitement, joy, and all the myriad of feelings that we have in response to the events and opportunities of life. Then we begin to process them through our mind, thinking about what has happened, what it means, how we're affected and how we might respond. Finally, we process them through our will as we choose our course of action in response to the processing of the events through our emotions and our mind. Some of this takes place almost instantaneously with the event, while some we process over the moments and hours, if not days and years to follow. Some events may have a seemingly fleeting impact and some may seem to last a lifetime. But in one degree or another, every experience of life will affect every dimension of our soul.

A key factor in how well we will act or react regarding any experience or opportunity is how we filter it from our emotions, through our mind, to the actions or reactions of our will. The mind is the filter. With our mind, we will analyze and rationalize, remember and recount, rightly or wrongly, until a decision is made. Even indecision is a decision of sorts. Then we may continue in that chosen course or not.

After our decision is made, then we will filter through our thoughts about our own decision. And of course, how we have processed all the past experiences and decisions, as well as how we remember them—accurately or not—affects how we'll process the current experiences.[20]

Scripture speaks of "strongholds" in the context of a battle of our thoughts. Our thoughts lead us to make a decision. They can lead us to obedience or rebellion, to submission or sin.

> *Indeed, we live as human beings, but we do not wage war according to human standards; for the weapons of our warfare are not merely human, but they have divine power to destroy strongholds. We destroy arguments and every proud obstacle raised up against the knowledge of God, and we take every thought captive to obey Christ* (2 Corinthians 10:3–5).

In the biblical sense, "strongholds" are the "arguments and every proud obstacle raised up against the knowledge of God." Once again, pride is at the source of sin. Pride says, "I will do what I think I should do because of what I am feeling and what I am thinking, no matter what God says." The more we entertain those arguments and appease those thoughts contrary to our knowledge of God's will and ways, the stronger those thoughts become. Soon, our rebellious thoughts become actions, our actions become habits, and our habits become lifestyles of sin and rebellion against the will and ways of God. Both our actions and our

---

[20] This is also part of how our belief systems are formed, which we will discuss in more detail later.

reactions can become strongholds of sin if they are contrary to the will of God and leading of His Holy Spirit. The more we give in to these strongholds and allow them to remain, the stronger their hold becomes. These strongholds of the mind become pockets of resistance in the war being waged between our flesh and the Spirit.

We are called to "destroy strongholds" as we "destroy arguments" and "we take every thought captive to obey Christ" (vv. 4–5). God gives us grace to resist these thoughts before they take root and begin to build the strongholds of rebellion and sin. As we are in the communion of relationship of God's Holy Spirit with our human spirit, we are able to discern with godly conscious and godly intuition the source and nature of the thoughts that come to our mind. If we discern they are not from God, we are to resist them and reject them. When we do, we are in obedient submission to God, and when we don't, we are in the prideful rebellion of sin.

In prayer ministry, the Lord gave me an image one time that I have used many times to explain the principle. I think of the enemy drawing back his bow and shooting an arrow of a negative thought or lie contrary to the will and Word of God. The Holy Spirit gives us discernment to look up and recognize the thought for what it is. We reach up and grab the arrow, taking the thought captive. Then we break it and throw it down, bringing it into submission to the obedience of Christ.

The more we do this, the more easily this becomes our habit and lifestyle of obedience and holiness. God redeems these challenges into opportunities to strengthen and renew our minds in conformity with the mind of Christ. But if we don't, the opposite is true. These challenges become opportunities for the enemy of our soul to gain ground and establish his strongholds, making it even harder to resist the confusion and deception of his rebellious thoughts. The thoughts that lead us to sin, as well as the thoughts that lead us to respond sinfully to the sins and actions of others, stir up the rebellion of our flesh in the war against the Spirit. The rebellion of our flesh then opens the door the enemy, who quickly comes in like a flood to take advantage of any pockets of resistance to occupy and fortify the strongholds of pride and rebellion against our knowledge of God and His will for our lives. In the next

150

section we identify some key root issues that feed into these pockets of resistance and strongholds of the flesh.

Chapter 11

Seven Key Roots of Resistance to Healing & Holiness

Bad roots produce bad fruit. Jesus expressed this spiritual principle of healing prayer ministry and spiritual maturity in these terms:

> *In the same way, every good tree bears good fruit, but the bad tree bears bad fruit. A good tree cannot bear bad fruit, nor can a bad tree bear good fruit. Every tree that does not bear good fruit is cut down and thrown into the fire. Thus you will know them by their fruits* (Matthew 7:17–20).

In our prayer ministry, especially in the realm of inner healing from the inside out, we've found that there are very similar root issues in most people's lives that seem to manifest in different ways depending upon the particular circumstances and experiences of life. And these roots bear fruit. If they are bad roots, they bear bad fruit. It is biblical, spiritual principle that we reap what we sow.

> *Do not be deceived; God is not mocked, for you reap whatever you sow. If you sow to your own flesh, you will reap corruption from the flesh; but if you sow to the Spirit, you will reap eternal life from the Spirit*
> (Galatians 6:7–8).

If we just pray for healing of the fruit without dealing with the root, we may remove the fruit instantly in a miraculous prayer and even for a season, but the fruit will be back if the root is not dug up and removed. Part of the ministry of "preparing the way of the Lord" is to allow the Holy Spirit to put the axe to the root of every tree that does not bear good fruit (see Matthew 3:10). Then, rather than the fruit of the flesh, the tree can bear the fruit of the Spirit.

Seven Key Roots of Resistance

Though I'm sure there are many more, I tend to center my prayers for people around seven key roots of resistance to healing and holiness. These are the roots that feed into the pockets of resistance and tend to grow into strongholds in the flesh of the unsanctified areas of the soul:

(1) Pride and Rebellion
(2) Bitterness and Unforgiveness
(3) Rejection
(4) Shame
(5) Fear
(6) Brokenness and Unresolved Trauma
(7) Infirmity

These are seven bad roots that bear bad fruit and seven barriers that block the healing presence of God. We'll look at the seven barriers in a later section. The good news is that Isaiah 11:2 speaks of the seven Spirits of God. The seven Spirits of God will help us to overcome these seven roots and seven barriers.

Pride and Rebellion

I'm beginning with the root of pride because pride is most often the deepest root of all. And the spiritual roots of pride and rebellion are actually intertwined together. They're like two sides of the same coin—to turn inward to ourselves is pride, and to turn away from God is rebellion. "Pride" isn't necessarily referring to things like: I'm proud to be an American or that I was born in Texas; I'm proud of the San Antonio Spurs or the Kentucky Wildcats; or I'm proud of my grandkids.

Here, we're talking primarily about the kind of pride that accentuates "self"—self-centeredness. It's an attitude that's something like: *I'm* going to do what *I* want to do because *I* think *I* know what's best for *my* self. See all the references to "I" in that? That's the sin of pride. Even in its name, "I" is at the center of "pride." And that kind of pride of self-centeredness and self-idolatry is rebellion against God. This is the pride that is the opposite of humility. It's a form of idolatry because we exalt ourselves into the place of authority and focus reserved for God alone.

We may not always consciously say, "God, I'm rebelling against You. I'm rejecting You." But the truth is, any area of our lives where "I" have taken control, then Jesus *isn't* in control. Any area where we decide, "I am Lord," then Jesus isn't Lord in those areas of our lives. That's pride, and there's a spiritual principle in James 4:6 that says, "God resists the proud, but He gives grace to the humble."

154

So a large part of this ministry is letting God expose our pride, expose the places where we take control, put up a walls, set up barriers, and where we're making decisions based on what we think we need to do to take care of ourselves. We need to choose to humble ourselves before God and pray, "Lord, *show* me what to do! Show me where to draw the boundary line in this relationship. Show me who to push away, who to draw near, who to trust and who not to trust, and when to change that level of trust." If we're not humbling ourselves before God and letting Him lead us, then we're moving in pride. And that's one of the deepest roots that bears bad fruit that there is.

In a sense, pride is the taproot. It goes the deepest and feeds into all these other things. In one way or another, it seems the other roots often grow out of this root. Wasn't that the very thing that got Satan, who was Lucifer, thrown out of heaven? Pride was found in him. Now he's trying to work that pride into us and cause us to focus on ourselves rather than God, deceiving us into thinking that we're taking care of ourselves.

There may be reasons, even good reasons, why we feel we have to assert ourselves and take care of ourselves. Maybe we feel nobody else will and maybe nobody else has. Ultimately, deep down inside, maybe even subconsciously, we have decided that we cannot even trust God to be in charge, so we have to be in charge. We think we're being wise and responsible. But the problem is this—wherever I am in charge, God is not. Wherever I am lord, Jesus is not. So, in the very places where we need God's grace the most, we are blocking God's grace by our own pride (see James 4:6; 1 Peter 5:5).

The Graven Image of the False Self

Our pride is our false self, not the true self. This is the graven image that we have created with our own hands or that has been created at hands of others that we bow down to and worship. And this is what the pride of our false self wants others to bow down to and worship—"worship" in the sense that we want it acknowledged and affirmed, blessed and respected. This is the false self that God wants to be broken so that the true self arises and grows into maturity and intimacy with Him.[21]

Godly brokenness is when we come to the place of the end of ourselves, and the end of our self-centered pride, to entrust ourselves to Him. This is the place where our false self is broken and our true self is healed and restored and redeemed. Rather than worshiping ourselves—our power, our wisdom, and our desires—we worship Him and Him alone (see Deuteronomy 5:6–10).

For believers, the "false self" is often the "religious self." It's that part of us that tries so hard to find our sense of identity, significance, and self-worth in what we do, especially when it's "for God." Spiritual pride is just as sinful as any other form of pride, and just as devastating in its power to hinder the true power of God in our lives. We often mask our true selves with the façade of the false self. We often act like we are living the victorious Christian life, when the truth is that we are hurting, broken, and defeated inside—underneath the mask of the religious self.

We might even sit calmly in our pew, attempting to convey to everyone around us the peace of God that surpasses all understanding when the altar is opened for those who need prayer. But inside, our guts are churning with anxiety, worry, stress, and fear. We might jump, shout, and wave our banners in praise and worship as if the joy of the Lord was our strength. But underneath our fake smile and forced laughter, we're weary, tired, depressed and discouraged.

Our Pride Blocks God's Grace

If we won't acknowledge that we need God's grace, we can't receive it. Pride blocks grace. Pride says, "No thanks, Jesus. I don't need Your help. I'm doing just fine." So we continue to struggle, suffer, and try to

---

[21] I remember Steve Chua powerfully teaching this concept as the Holy Spirit brought deep conviction to expose these areas in my own life. I began to see "pride" in a new light, seeing how devastating its power can be to block the grace and power of God in our lives. Steve was teaching at Singing Waters Ministries in Orangeville, Ontario at their retreat center, formerly Ellel Ministries of Canada, when I was there for the nine-week school of ministry. I am very grateful for all the teaching, ministry, and impartation that I received from my teachers and mentors with this powerful ministry.

get by in our own power and strength because we are too proud to ask God for His. God loves us and often ministers His healing love to us through one another. So when we are too proud to humble ourselves before one another to ask for prayer or ask for help, we are not only pushing others away, we are pushing God away.

Because God is love and created us for a relationship of love, He will not override our free will manifesting itself in pride. In His mercy, He will let us suffer the consequences of our pride, which is blocking His grace, until we come to Him in humility and brokenness to receive His healing and transforming power.

Until I started ministering to others in prayer and allowing God to expose these areas in my own heart, I never really understood the passage on pride and humility in James 4:6–10. It begins with a call to humility and then a call to intimacy, and verse 8 specifically says, "Draw near to God and He will draw near to you." And it seems like the next verse would say something like, "So rejoice and be glad, for the joy of the Lord is your strength. Enter into His rest and know the peace of God that surpassing all understanding, for He is your comfort." Wouldn't that be a good way to finish off this passage? That's how I would have written it, but that's not how God wrote it! Instead, the Word of God says:

> Draw near to God, and He will draw near to you. Cleanse your hands, you sinners, and purify your hearts, you double-minded. Lament and mourn and weep. Let your laughter be turned into mourning and your joy into dejection. Humble yourselves before the Lord, and He will exalt you (James 4:8–10).

Like Isaiah, as we draw near to God, God begins to expose everything in us that is not yet holy (see Isaiah 6:1–8). Out of His mercy and love, in a desire for intimacy with nothing between us, He wants to cleanse our hands from all sin and purify our hearts from all double-mindedness. If we are double-minded, we cannot seek Him in whole-hearted devotion; and we cannot love Him with all our heart, mind, soul, and strength.

We cannot deceive God, and He loves us enough to not allow us to deceive ourselves. As we see how holy He is, He allows us to see how unclean we are (Isaiah 6:5)—not because He is angry with us, not because He wants to shame us, but because He loves us. God doesn't condemn us, but He does want to change us. He wants to free us to be like Jesus.

If we are willing to honestly "lament and mourn and weep" before the Lord, He'll free us from the curse and burden of false joy, false peace, and false self. As we humble ourselves before Him in truth, He'll lift us up and call forth our true self to experience His true joy and peace. So when we pray, "Lord, search my heart, open up my past, my pain, and every age and moment of my life. Open every level and depth of my being to you. I'm welcoming you in. In your timing and in your way, draw out the pain, the shame, expose the bondages, bring me to a place of wholeness," that's humility, surrender, and a place of trusting faith in God. Pride is slain and uprooted. Then the grace and power of God arise in its place.

2. Bitterness and Unforgiveness

One of the most poisonous roots that bears bad fruit in our lives is bitterness. It's closely related to unforgiveness, resentment, and hardness of heart toward another, toward God, or toward ourselves. Scripture explicitly identifies the destructive power of this root with a command to be vigilant in refusing to let it have any place in our lives:

> *See to it that no one fails to obtain the grace of God; that no root of bitterness springs up and causes trouble, and through it many become defiled* (Hebrews 12:15).

Nurturing the sin of a root of bitterness not only defiles us, affecting our relationship of intimacy with God, it also defiles "many." It affects everyone around us, not just the person toward whom we are bitter and unforgiving. Ironically, it defiles and destroys ourselves more than anyone else.

It's said that bitterness and unforgiveness is like drinking poison and waiting for the other person's guts to burn out! Or as I heard recently,

158

it's like eating rat poison and watching for the rat to die! When we hold on to grudges or harden our hearts over what someone has done to us, we think we're judging them, punishing them, holding them accountable, or even hurting them. But the truth is that it's killing us. It's eating us alive on the inside.

Bitterness and unforgiveness affect every dimension of our lives—our spirit, soul, and body; our relationships with God and with one another. So God, in His mercy and wisdom, commands us to "forgive each other, just as the Lord has forgiven (us)" (Colossians 3:13; Ephesians 4:32). God commands us to choose to forgive because He loves us and knows what bitterness and unforgiveness will do to us.

God's Command to Forgive from the Heart

In the Lord's prayer, Jesus leads us to pray for forgiveness of our trespasses, just as we forgive those who have trespassed against us, asking God to forgive us of our debts, just as we forgive our debtors (Matthew 6:12). And the Lord goes on to speak of the seriousness of this decision to forgive one another and cancel one another's debts:

> *"For if you forgive others their trespasses, your heavenly Father will also forgive you; but if you do not forgive others, neither will your Father forgive your trespasses"* (Matthew 6:14–15).

It's true that we are saved by grace, through faith. And at the same time, these "red-letter words" of Jesus are also true: "If you do not forgive other, neither will your Father forgive your trespasses." There is something about having an authentic, saving relationship with Jesus Christ that would seem to require a heart of forgiveness at the heart of our faith, having grace for one another as God has grace for us.

To dramatically drive home the point of just how significant this command of God to forgive one another really is, Jesus told the parable of the unforgiving servant (Matthew 18:23–35). When the unforgiving servant insists on his rights, refusing to forgive and cancel the debts of another in the way his own debts were canceled and forgiven by the master, he suffers the consequences of his unforgiveness. "His lord handed him over to be tortured until he would repay his entire debts"

(v. 34). His master "delivered him to the tormentors" (v. 34 KJV). And in these astounding, harrowing words, Jesus says: "So My heavenly Father will also do to every one of you, if you do not forgive your brother or sister from your heart" (v. 35). God is very serious about His command to forgive from the heart.

Most people that I know who are experienced with healing prayer ministry believe, as I do, that this root of bitterness and unforgiveness is probably the most common barrier to our healing, blocking the free flow of God's grace in our lives. So I also include this topic of Unforgiveness in the chapters on Seven Potential Barriers to Healing. I also include it in my discussion of deliverance, because when we are handed over to "the tormentors" by consequence of our choices of holding on to bitterness and unforgiveness, we make room for the demonic tormentors who come "to steal and kill and destroy" (John 10:10). We could write a book on this one topic alone!

Forgiveness is a Choice

The heart of forgiveness is simply a choice. It's not necessarily simple or easy, but it is a choice. And it's essential for our health and healing. God requires it because we need it. God is so serious about it because it has such serious consequences when we refuse to obey God make the choice to forgive.

Forgiveness is choosing to do for others what God has done for us. When I'm leading someone in the steps of forgiveness I'll discuss in a moment, I often lead them to say: "Lord, I choose to give them a gift they don't deserve, just like You've given me a gift I don't deserve—forgiveness, mercy, release from my judgments. I choose to cancel their debts, just like You've cancelled my debts. I choose to cancel every debt I feel they owe me. So even if they never admit they were wrong, never admit how much they hurt me, never ask me to forgiven them, never make things right, I still choose to forgive them from my heart in the name of Jesus. No matter what they do, this is what I choose to do, as best as I can and all by Your grace."

160

So forgiveness is *not* saying it's ok, or saying it doesn't matter, or saying they're free to do it again. Forgiveness is *not* saying all is well or all is reconciled. Forgiveness is *not* an emotion or a feeling or a hope that one day it will be all better or just go away. Forgiveness is *not* forgetting— *not* forgetting the facts of what really happened, *not* forgetting the hurtful or cruel or wicked or criminal action of the person who hurt us, *not* forgetting the pain or shame or fear or damage of all they've done.

And forgiveness is *not* saying it's all done. Sometimes it's much more like a process than an instantaneous event. Sometimes it's more like pealing the layers of an onion, layer by layer, step by step, as we are able, in the time we need. And God has grace to meet us where we are, but not leave us where are, as we choose to ask Him to help us. Sometimes a good place to start is "Lord, help me be willing to be willing to forgive."

Forgiveness is simply a choice—a choice we are required to make as best as we can in the power of the grace of God He will give us if we will ask Him. Forgiveness is saying that even though what they did was wrong, even though they hurt me so deeply, I still choose to forgive them, just like God has forgiven me.

Forgiveness is Different from Boundaries

Just because we choose to forgive does not mean we have to choose to continue to let the person hurt us or to let them potentially hurt others. We must forgive from the heart, but then we must let the Lord determine what are to be the boundaries in that relationship and when He wants to change the boundaries based upon how safe He determines them to be and how trustworthy He determines they are.

God resists the proud but give grace to the humble (James 4:6). Humility is the attitude of the heart that says, "Lord, I willingly choose to be desperately dependent on You alone. So You put Your thoughts in my mind and Your desires in my heart. You show me where the boundary lines are to be in this relationship." Pride says, "I will do what I think I should do to take care of myself, so here's what I'm going to set the boundaries and here's where I am going to put up the walls so that they will never hurt me again."

To the degree that we let God set the boundaries, He can give us His grace to keep on forgiving and to keep healthy boundaries in the relationship. But to the degree that we let our pride rise up and we take control, we block God's grace from guiding us and helping us. And that leads us back to our own bondage again.

It's helps me to remember the principle of Micah 6:8: "What does the Lord require of you but to do justly, to love mercy, and to walk humbly with your God?" God cares about justice. Righteousness and justice are the foundations of the throne of God (Psalm 89:14). But God also cares about mercy just as much. "The steadfast love of the Lord never ceases, His mercies never come to an end" (Lamentations 3:22).

So the only way we can walk in both justice and mercy is to walk humbly with our God. That's letting Him set the boundaries. That's trusting Him to set His boundaries for us and those who have hurt us "in pleasant places"—in the pleasant place we let Him set for us because we choose to trust Him to know what's best for us (Psalm 16:6).

Forgiving Others, Forgiving Ourselves, "Forgiving" God

Sometimes we need to forgive others. But sometimes the person we need to forgive the most is ourselves. Sometimes we are so ashamed of what we've one we can't quite forgive ourselves. Or sometimes we even begin to think there is something holy or righteous about continuing to judge ourselves or condemn ourselves. Often we even hate that part of ourselves. But God wants us to love Him with all our heart, all our mind, all our soul, all our strength (Mark 12:30).

So He gives us grace to forgive ourselves. He reveals the truth that refusing to forgive ourselves is one of the greatest sins of all. It's like rejecting the sacrifice of Jesus Christ, rejecting God's love for us and all He has done for us.

And sometimes we need to "forgive God." It's not really *forgiveness* because God has never does anything wrong. But sometimes we blame

162

Him and judge Him, saying, "Why did You do this? Why did You allow this? Why didn't You stop this?" And we harden our hearts against Him, sometimes so far down deep inside we don't even know it's there, or we're too ashamed or afraid to admit it's there.

We need the truth to come and set us free. We need to know, deep down in that place that is so hurt or angry with God, that human beings have free will and spiritual beings have free will. A relationship of love requires the freedom to choose, so God in His nature of love, having created us for a relationship of love, does not reach in the control someone's free will, even if the consequences are so devastating. But if we will welcome Him into that place and give it over to Him from the heart, He will not let that sinful choice that someone made have the last word.

Sometimes we need to see with the eyes of our hearts the truth that God was there even when we felt we were alone, fighting for in ways we couldn't see and helping us in ways we didn't know, ready to take on to Himself all we will release to Him.

So God doesn't need our forgiveness. But sometimes we need to release Him from our judgments. We need to confess and repent of the ways we've hardened our heart against Him, judging Him that He didn't care or He's not good. And as we receive His forgiveness for our sin of judgment against Him, we can be restored to a relationship of trust and love with Him again, especially deep down in that place in our heart that's been so hurt with Him.

Seven Steps of Forgiveness

In ministry we've developed a few steps we often walk someone through to help them let go of bitterness and unforgiveness, to help remove this potential barrier to their healing. It's not really a step-by-step formula, but rather a way to cover seven key elements of a process of forgiveness so that it's forgiveness from the heart instead of merely from the head. It's a way to help the person have a kind of cathartic release of the pain or shame or anger that's buried down inside and even manifesting in their body as well as in their other relationships.

163

I started out with five steps, but through the years of ministry, we've developed seven steps we now call the Seven Steps of Forgiveness.[22] These basic steps make it easy for me to remember when I'm helping somebody in prayer or going through it in my own life:

(1) Admit the wrong
(2) Admit the hurt
(3) Release the person to God[23]
(4) Release the hurt to God
(5) Repent of our sinful responses
(6) Bless the person who hurt us
(7) Receive God's blessing for us

These steps are simply choices we can make, as best as we can and all by God's grace. At the end of the day, forgiveness is a choice, not a feeling, emotion, or acquiescence that what was done to us was right or ok; it's simply a choice. God gives us the grace to see our need to forgive and the grace of His power to choose to do it if we're willing to let Him help us.

But to really forgive someone from the heart, we have to first admit that we felt like what they did was wrong, and we also have to admit that we feel that wrong hurt us. You can't really forgive someone of something that you won't admit was wrong, and you can't really release hurt and pain to God that you won't admit is there. It's part of the process of

---

[22] My ministry partner at Rapha God Ministries, Tammy Watts, and I recently had an incredible opportunity to teach and minister these Seven Steps of Forgiveness in ministry with Christian music artist Matthew West in San Antonio after he sang his powerful songs *Forgiveness* and *Child of the One True King*. We were all stunned how much the unexpected, standing room-only crowd, hungry for God's truth and hope, was an expression of the desperate need for this message of healing and freedom through forgiveness.

[23] In our ministry, we generally lead people to release the person and the hurt to Jesus, but sometimes people are more comfortable praying and speaking to the Father or the Holy Spirit. Of course, God is One and God has revealed Himself in the three persons and dimensions of His Being as God the Father, God the Son, and God the Holy Spirit. In prayer ministry, the main thing is to help the person connect with God however best they can.

trusting God enough to let go of our control—letting go in humility instead of holding on in pride.

Sometimes we try to control our pain by making excuses for people. In our pain, we say, "Oh, they didn't mean to;" or "Oh, it's just what they do in our family;" or "Oh, everybody does that, it shouldn't be such a big deal." These are all defense mechanisms, self-protection, where we are trying to control our pain, all in our power, all in our strength, instead of giving it to God. It may be very unconscious. But it's a form of pride, in the sense of asserting our own will and our own way of handling our pain, that is manifesting in control.

That control is a form of pride that blocks God's grace in the place we need it the most (James 4:6). So the first step to truly forgive from the heart is to admit the wrong and stop denying it or making excuses. You can't release what you won't admit is there. And many times we don't even know it's there until we take the time to ask the Lord to reveal it us. Then He can reveal, remove and replace.

Another way we try to self-protect from the pain is by denying the pain or minimizing the pain. We say, "Oh, that didn't really hurt me;" or "Oh, I didn't really need their love or their attention or their time or their physical expression of love or their verbal expression of love." These are ways this form of pride, manifesting in control, blocks the grace of God from the places we need it the most. So the next step to truly forgive from the heart is to admit the hurt, just like we admit the wrong. You can't release what you won't admit is there.

Then once we've admitted the wrong and admitted the hurt, from deep down in the place of our heart in the ages and moments of our lives where the event occurred, we can choose to release it to God. We release the person to God. Then we can release the hurt to God. This is the heart of the matter, the heart of forgiveness is making the choice to release it to God. And sometimes, it's so deep and so hard, it's more like letting God come and take it from you.

As we're choosing to let the person and the pain go to God and out of our heart, then we need to ask God to forgive us. We may have been completely innocent in the original event, completely the victim and not

165

the perpetrator, but our sin can be our sinful response to what they did. Our sin is holding on to the unforgiveness, the bitterness, to resentment, the hardness of heart in judgment, the desire for vengeance. So in humility we must repent of our sinful responses. We might say, "Lord, now forgive me for holding on to any of that, even if I didn't really I was. I ask for Your forgiveness for my unforgiveness and I receive it now in the name of Jesus."

Now we can ask God to give us His heart to pray for that person, to bless the person who hurt us. That's a means of God's grace to help us let it go and heal our heart by changing our heart. It's part of what Jesus meant when He teaches us to pray for those who persecute us, bless those who curse us, love those who hate us (Matthew 5:44). Sometimes it's hard to pray those prayers and speak those blessings for those who have hurt us or those we love, sometimes even with great cruelty, wickedness, or evil. So we don't have to start our prayer by saying, "O God, give them a great life." We need to "keep it real" if we are to forgive from the heart.

So sometimes we need to start out by praying, "Lord, reveal the truth to them, show them what they've done and how much hurt they've caused. Convict them of their sin." But we can't stop there; we must press on by the grace of God with God's heart. God's heart is that all would repent and come to a knowledge of His truth and receive His grace. So we go on to pray, "And Lord, let Your conviction lead them to repentance and their repentance lead them to Your mercy. In Your mercy I pray for them, as far as Your grace will go, that they will know the fullness of Your salvation through Jesus Christ, that You would heal them and deliver them from what evil influenced their choices, so that they may be all You created them to be. Give me Your heart for them in the name of Jesus."

Even if the person who hurt us is no longer in our life or has died, we want to have the right heart toward them and put it all into God's hands. He's the "judge of the living and the death," not us (Acts 10:42). And He's "not willing that any should perish but that all should come to repentance" (2 Peter 3:9). And in some sense, He's perhaps not even limited by the physical death of those under His judgment, suffering the consequences of their sins (1 Peter 4:6). That's God's business,

166

according to God's grace. Our part is to ask for God's heart toward that person so that we release them from our judgment and entrust them to God's judgment, as far as God's grace will go. We want God to find mercy, not judgment, in our hearts because by the measure we judge, we also will be judged (Matthew 6:2).

Once we let it all go, we can choose to begin to receive the blessings God has for us. What we've let Him reveal and remove, now He can replace with His grace, His peace, His Spirit, and all that He has for us instead of all we've been holding on to down inside of us. "Blessed are the merciful, for they will receive mercy" (Matthew 5:7).

Example of the Destructive Power of a Root of Bitterness and Unforgiveness

One of the first examples that I saw of how a root of bitterness and unforgiveness so extensively affects someone's life came very early in my ministry when I was just out of seminary. As my mentor, Dr. Steve Seamands was helping me get Messiah Ministries established, we used to lead a weekly healing and renewal meeting along with Martin Mallory, our friend and a Christian counselor. Steve and I would take turns giving messages on areas of healing and then pray for people at the end. One night, an elderly lady came up for prayer ministry in response to a message about unforgiveness.

When I asked her how I could pray for her, she said, "Well, I'm realizing tonight that I've still been so angry at my mother. Just all the things she said. I could never do anything to please her and I never did anything right for her. I've said I've forgiven her, and I thought I had forgiven her. But the Lord is showing me tonight that there's another level of bitterness that I've buried down deep inside and another layer of unforgiveness to peel off."

So I guided her through a prayer of releasing her bitterness and unforgiveness. Basically, I walked her through the steps of forgiveness, leading her to pray phrase by phrase after me but from her heart. Then to finish up, I prayed a prayer of blessing with the words the Holy Spirit gave me to pray.

Romans 8:26 even says that we don't know how to pray as we ought, but the Spirit who knows what is the mind of the Father prays through us according to His will. God's doing it, but we're the vessel. He's looking for compassionate vessels to be His ambassadors of His healing love to others. So I prayed with her, prayed a blessing over her, gave her a hug, and she headed out the door.

About a month later, I was sitting in the back of Steve's class on the campus of Asbury Seminary, waiting to go have lunch with him after his class. Then I saw the lady from the prayer meeting. I had no idea that she was a second-career seminary student attending Asbury. When she saw me, she came over and said, "Hey, remember me? You prayed for me the other night. I was releasing all that bitterness toward my Mother."

And I said, "Yes, yes, I do."

"Well, I didn't tell you," she began, "but there at the end, you prayed for my hands. I hadn't specifically asked you to pray for my hands. I've had lots of people pray for my hands because I've had crippling arthritis in my hands for years. I've been anointed with oil; I've been prayed over; I've asked God to take this away from me for years. But that night, when I released that bitterness and unforgiveness toward my Mother, God began to heal me! He began to take away that pain, and today I have no pain in my hands!"

Praise God! Now God could have sovereignly come in and worked a miracle. He could have instantaneously taken that away. It seems there had been lots of opportunities. But there was something way down, deep inside of her that He apparently needed to take care of first. That issue of arthritis in her body was a manifestation of something that was going on much more deeply down in her soul and her spirit. God's will was to heal her, but there was something blocking that healing—a bad root feeding into the bad fruit in her hands.

In her spirit, she was not right with God in that area of her life, because God says to forgive one another. In her soul, the thought of her mind, the will of her choices, the emotions of her feelings, those were not in right order because they were still controlling her; binding her in unforgiveness. All of that was being manifested in her body in the form of the disease of arthritis. Her heart and her hands were hardened and in pain, longing for release. And God loved her enough to put His finger on that area, bringing it up to the surface. As she released it to God, she received healing in her spirit, soul, and body.

Now I'm not saying that everybody who has arthritis or any other disease has bitterness in their heart, but I am saying that we need to pray and ask the Lord if it's there. Many diseases are rooted in things like bitterness, fear, anxiety, stress. There can be spiritual roots of disease that feed and fuel it.

God's truth revealed in science has shown that many immune system diseases go back to stress; and stress is typically caused by worry, doubt, and unbelief—which is really the opposite of faith. So we need to ask the Lord to reveal the roots of these things because our spirit, soul, and body all relate one to another. Bad roots produce bad fruit. So the key is confession, repentance, and releasing to Him all that He shows us. Reveal, remove, and replace.

3. Rejection

The root of rejection, along with a related root of the fear of rejection, comes up over and over again when we are rejected, wounded, hurt, or abandoned by others. Perhaps it even begins in our mother's womb. Sometimes we feel unwanted, unvalued, unnoticed, or unwelcome. When we grow up through life, we're pushed away or pushed aside. But deep down inside, we're created for acceptance and a sense of significance. We're created to love, and for people to love us. It's God loving us through people. And when we don't receive that, something is lacking in us. There's an empty hole waiting to be filled. And if it's not filled with love and the holy things of God, that hole will be filled with something else that will be far less holy or healthy for our soul.

It may seem like we are being wise when we sometimes say, "Well I won't trust anybody or need anybody. People always disappoint me. Sooner or later they will reject me or not want me anymore." Or we say in our hearts, *I get my security, my acceptance, my love, from God and God alone.* Now doesn't that *sound* wise? It *is* from God that we receive our love, acceptance, and security; but at the same time, God has created a world where we are to love one another, and where we need one another. That's not because we are too weak or needy or co-dependent. He created us that way. God loves us and accepts us through one another. He encourages us, affirms us, and calls us forth into our gifting, anointing, and destiny through one another.

It's not just God and us. There's a community relationship to faith and life. So we really do need God to be our sense of affirmation, security, and peace, as well as needing Him to love us through others. Now, like anything, that can be distorted or become unhealthy to varying degrees. If we put the primary emphasis on "one another" instead of first on God, that can lead to codependency, which leads to idolatry. That's putting people in the place of God; and it's sin. We must look *primarily to God* and allow God to love us and affirm us through others. It's not either/or; it's both/and. But the order is very important.

So to any degree that we begin to harden our hearts and push people away out of our rejection, woundedness, or our past, and say, "I don't need your love, time, or acceptance," that's just another form of the sin of pride. It's very important to recognize that. Most of us in the body of Christ don't realize that the ways in which we are protecting ourselves— our defense mechanisms, our barriers, our wall—are all forms of pride and control: "I'm in charge, I'm in control, I'm taking care of my needs because, God, You didn't." Or, "My father didn't, my mother didn't, my husband didn't, so I'm going to do it myself."

We Need a Father's Blessing

It's God's will for earthly fathers to reveal the Father heart of God to us. A father's primary role is to call forth the gifting, call forth what's good, and call forth what God has put into His children. A father's role also includes correcting, disciplining in love and encouragement, and teaching those who are younger the ways of the Lord. We're created for that. We need that! And when we don't have that because the father has sinned; we need to call it for the sin that it is. That sin against God creates a wound of rejection in us. Then we begin to try to fill that void and seek comfort from that pain in other ways such as other relationships that are unholy, alcohol, drugs, food, spending, unholy

170

sexual relationships, or any combination of these things and others. We may even seek for that in our work or in ministry. A wound of rejection is a deep wound that can drive us to seek out and chase after acceptance in whatever way we have not been affirmed and loved. And I would say that everyone who reads this has been wounded with wounds of rejection. I know that I have.

The Lord wants to go deep down into these roots, deep down into these levels of pain, shame, and hurt so that He can draw that out and pour in His love. Many people need that, and it's one of the key things the Lord wants to do through healing prayer ministry. As we confess and release to Him the people that disappointed us, hurt us, failed to respect and love us or recognize God's gifts and calling in our lives, God's grace, mercy, and love begin to wash over us. When we choose to release them to God, then we are choosing to slay our pride. We're also choosing to release our judgments and our control toward those who have hurt us, wounded us, and failed to love us.

God can do in a moment what we've not received in a lifetime. In one moment of prayer, surrender, and release; His Holy Spirit can pour into us what we've been yearning for from the very depth of our being; since the moment of our conception. He pours it in and it's supernatural— "Pain out, love in; shame out, love in." Sometimes it happens miraculously and it's just overwhelming. Most of the time, it's little by little and layer by layer in a process of healing and restoration. God begins to fill us and renew us with His love, as He reshapes our thoughts about Him and ourselves. And then we can begin to walk out that freedom and healing.

As we do, we'll begin to sense a security and peace with God and within ourselves. Now we're no longer going to need to seek after all that affirmation and blessing primarily from others because we're receiving it from God (Proverbs 29:25). And as we're receiving it from Him, an amazing thing starts to happen. We begin to receive it from others. It's God doing it through others. Then we don't seem so needy, insecure, manipulative, and controlling, constantly trying to call forth acceptance, significance, and get our sense of value out of how others see us. That's because God Himself has given that to us inside. Now it's from God, but God releases these things through others as well as directly from

171

Himself. It's when we don't have it through others, that it's a wound. There's a deep root that needs to be dug up, pulled out, and replaced with God's truth and love.

We Need a Mother's Nurture

God created mothers and designed them to love, nurture, hold, and comfort us; as well as wipe away the tears from our eyes and correct and discipline us in love. But we don't always receive all of that. It's supposed to be God loving us through our mothers, but sometimes our mothers fail. They sin, because anything less that the perfect will of God is sin and all fall short of the glory of God. Maybe they have good, rational reasons why it happened, but we have to acknowledge the fact that they sometimes fail. When they do, we can feel rejected or abandoned.

We Need Godly Companionship

So many times, a sense of rejection comes out of broken relationships like marriage and friendships. Feeling rejected, abandoned, unloved, or even betrayed can make us feel unworthy of love. We can fear being rejected again or develop an expectancy of being rejected again, which can become like a self-fulfilling prophecy. And all this can feed into bitterness and manifest as heaviness, discouragement, and depression. So we need to hear what God says about us and remember that He is the God who never leaves us or forsakes us, even if others do. And when others do, we don't have to let that control us and how we see ourselves. We can release them to God and freely receive whatever blessings He chooses to pour into us His.

4. Shame

Sometimes there's a root of shame because of the sins that we have done in our lives. We're ashamed of ourselves. And sometimes we're ashamed because of things that have been done to us from others. Perhaps we've been completely innocent, completely the victim, but yet, there's a cloak of shame that seems to cover us. We feel dirty, defiled, used, impure, or unholy. That's a deep root that's in most of our hearts, and the Lord wants us to be willing to let Him go to the root of the shame.

Sometimes we feel ashamed, experiencing the bad fruit from the bad root of shame in an area where we have sinned. We've done something wrong. It's possible that we didn't even know that it was sin at the time. Maybe we were little or we were confused. Perhaps we weren't yet a Christian or didn't know God's Word, but we did something and it was not God's perfect will. That's sin.

"Sin" is anything less than the perfect will of God. We can have the broadest possible definition of sin because God has the broadest possible definition of grace. There is no sin He will not forgive if we admit it and give it to Him. The only sin God can't forgive is the sin we won't admit and give to Him. But He can only cleanse and forgive the sin that we're willing to call sin (1 John 1:9).

Sometimes we are mistaken in the world and in the body of Christ that our compassion for one another means that we just coddle one another—even when we have sinned and we're doing things wrong. We think it's loving to not be judging; but the truth is, God can't cleanse and forgive anything that we won't call sin. So it's actually not loving or compassionate at all to leave someone in their sins when we're in relationships with them and say, "Well, that's okay. That's what everybody does. It's what the world does and that's how our culture is."

When we dismiss sin in this way, attempting to prevent people from feeling bad about themselves or what they've done, then we're leaving that person under the burden of shame. Deep down inside, they know it's wrong and they feel defiled, ashamed, and distant from God. And they might think in their minds, "I'm okay because everybody else is doing this." But deep down inside we know when we've sinned and we're dying inside, ashamed, guilty, and condemned—and that continues to condemn our hearts:

> *Beloved, if our hearts do not condemn us, then we have boldness before God and we receive from Him whatever we ask* 1 John 3:21–22).

In shame, we don't get to experience the joy of boldness and intimacy with God when we're ashamed and our hearts condemn us deep down inside. God loves us enough to reveal that, bring it out of the darkness, into the light, to remove it, digging up the bad roots to set us free of the bad fruit.

So when we have sinned, we need to agree with God. That's what confession is—to agree with God and speak it out to God, saying, "God, I have sinned. I have done wrong."

Once we confess our sin, we can repent of our sin. Repentance is changing our mind, changing our heart. Repentance is turning from our sin and turning to God, turning away from our past and turning toward all God has for us. When we do, we can embrace His promise and His grace for us:

> *If we confess our sins, He who is faithful and just will forgive us our sins and cleanse us from all unrighteousness* (1 John 1:9).

That's grace! That's the power of God's love and grace to forgive us and cleanse us from **all** unrighteousness! By the forgiveness that comes through our confession and repentance, we have a clean slate and a fresh start, the dawning of a new day! By the power of the grace of God, we are "justified" —"just-as-if" we had never sinned. Praise God!

But God cannot cleanse us if we will not repent. And we cannot repent unless we are willing to call the sin for the sin that it is:

> *If we say that we have no sin, we deceive ourselves, and the truth is not in us.... If we say that we have not sinned, we make him a liar, and his word is not in us* (1 John 1:8–10).

We can't let "unsanctified mercy" or "false compassion" keep us from the seeing and admitting the truth of our sin, whether for ourselves or in praying for others. We must see and speak the truth in love (Ephesians 4:15). And then the truth can set us free (John 8:32).

James 5:16 says, "Confess your sins one to another ... that you may be healed." We'll talk about this a little later in the section of removing the potential barrier to healing of personal sin. But this verse *doesn't* say, "that you may be *forgiven*", it says, "that you may be *healed*." God forgives us the very moment that we confess our sins and repent, whether anybody else is around or not. We're forgiven; we're cleansed. It's cast into the sea of forgetfulness as far as the east is from the west, praise God (Psalm 103:12).

But sometimes, even though God has fully forgiven us, we've not fully forgiven ourselves. We've not released ourselves. Sometimes even though God wants to heal us, we've not fully received that healing. We might need to confess our sins to one another, even confessing our pain, shame, and past to one another so that we may be healed.

Through confession and repentance of sin, God heals us, cleanses us, frees us from shame, and begins to restore the joy of our salvation (Psalm 51). Then we begin to become a safe person to whom others can come and open up. There's something spirit-to-spirit, deep-unto- deep, where that hurting person senses that you are a safe person, that You're transparent and humble, not judging and condemning, though willing to speak the truth in love. And as you have trusted yourself to God with you own sins, others will trust themselves and their sins to God with you in prayer ministry.

Shame from the Things Done to Us

As mentioned before, sometimes the shame comes because of something that somebody has done to us. And this comes up many times. So many who come for inner healing prayer ministry have had something done to them that has left them in deep shame.

Sexual abuse, for example, is so much more common than we realize. It seems to me that it's just a few that have not experienced that at some level. So if we have experienced it, the enemy likes to lie to us and make us think that we're the only one—that we're different or that nobody else has experienced that. There are many levels of abuse, and any level we've experienced can leave us feeling defiled, ashamed, and dirty— even if we were completely the victim and even totally innocent in the matter.

So the enemy comes, lies, cloaks us with shame and with a sense of unworthiness, dirtiness, and defilement. And sometimes, getting free

175

takes speaking it out loud to someone else, one-on-one, with someone we love or someone we trust. It's kind of like speaking it to "God with flesh on" or "God incarnate" in another human being.

Speaking it out loud brings up the root. It brings the root out of the darkness and into the light so that we can let it go. That's part of how healing prayer ministry helps us get free. It's a safe place where we can let these dark, painful, shameful things finally come up and out and release them to God.

Much of the ministry of inner healing—healing from the inside out—is helping someone be set free from the things that defile them and shame them and prevent them from knowing how much God loves them and longs for them to know their identity as His child and live into their destiny of the good plans He has for them.

Release from the pain and shame of the past is often the key, letting God remove what He reveals, so He can replace it with His truth and His love. It's an attitude, a perspective, even a choice of the heart. That's really our part in all that we're talking about—it's to release it to God by saying something like, "I let this go; I give this to You, Lord. Come and take it from me. Help me not take it back up."

5. Fear

Medical science and common sense reveal that many physical conditions are often rooted in fear, stress, worry, and anxiety. The same is true with many emotional conditions, mental conditions, relational conditions, or even spiritual conditions. Fear is a root that can produce bad fruit in our lives. We need to understand it so we can allow God to reveal it, remove it, and replace it.

The Emotion of Fear

Fear is an emotion. And in a broken, fallen world where we are surrounded by people and things that make us afraid, insecure, worried, stressed, or even terrorized, it's easy to encounter fear on almost a daily basis. Also, in a sense, we should have "a healthy fear" of things like playing in the street or getting into cars with strangers when we're kids.

But even then, it's not really "fear" we want to have, but a "a healthy respect" for what can harm us.

We are supposed to have a godly fear—that's "the fear of the Lord." "The fear of the Lord is the beginning of wisdom" (Psalm 111:10). But that's not the unhealthy emotion of fear. Rather, that's simply a sense of awe that we have toward God, to respect Him, revere Him, and obey Him. In the fear of the Lord, we realize there are consequences for our actions and choices, so we fear Him and respect Him by choosing to obey Him, because we choose to trust Him and believe He knows and wants what's best for us.

Counterfeit Fear of the Lord

In a sense, the unhealthy fear that can be a root of bad fruit in our lives is the enemy's perversion and counterfeit of the healthy fear of the Lord God has given us. The enemy of our souls wants to give us a an unhealthy, unholy fear instead of the holy fear of the Lord. There's only a counterfeit because there's the real thing that the enemy wants to pervert and distort. He tries to do this in the area of fear as well as all other aspects of our lives.

There's a spiritual principle of the real and the counterfeit. For example, there's a Christ and an antichrist; One's real and one's the counterfeit (1 John 2:18). God is the *only* Creator. *He* created us. We can't create anything ourselves. Likewise, our enemy, Satan, cannot create anything on his own. He himself was a created being. The name Lucifer means light-bearer. Lucifer was the light bearer of God, but he still had freedom. Lucifer had a choice and he chose in that freedom to rebel against God. And in his rebellion, he is now the accuser of the brethren. The name "Satan" means "the accuser." The enemy comes to accuse us before God. Since Satan cannot create anything on his own, what he has to do is to take God's principles that God created and skew them and pervert them to use against us.

God created the spiritual principle of fear—the fear of the Lord, godly fear, godly reverence, godly awe. But the enemy comes and twists that, perverting it into an unholy, tormenting fear that paralyzes us, hinders us, and holds us captive. And in every activity in our lives, the enemy

177

wants to bring fear as a means to attack us, control us, and subdue us. Jesus comes that we would have life, but the thief, our enemy, comes to steal and kill and destroy (John 10:10).

The Sin of Fear

While fear is an emotion, fear can also be a sin. The Bible says, "Fear not" (Isaiah 41:10 NKJV). And what do we can something that we do when the Bible says not to do it? Sin. To be attacked or tormented with fear is not a sin, but to give into it, to fail to resist it, is a sin. Where the emotion of fear becomes the sin of fear is when we allow it to control us.

> *Do you not know that if you present yourselves to anyone as obedient slaves, you are slaves of the one whom you obey, either of sin, which leads to death, or of obedience, which leads to righteousness?* (Romans 6:16)

Things that often along with fear are stress, anxiety, worry, insecurity, doubt and unbelief. In a sense, all of these aspects or levels of fear are sin to the extent we give in to it or allow it to control us because it is less than the perfect will of God for us. So God, who knows what's best for us lovingly commands us: "Fear not" (Isaiah 41:10 NKJV). "Do not worry" (Matthew 6:25). "Be anxious for nothing" (Philippians 4:6 NKJV).

In these ways, fear is not fully trusting God. And God wants us to trust Him in all things so that "in everything by prayer and supplication with thanksgiving (we can) let (our) requests be made known to God. And the peace of God, which surpasses all understanding, will guard (our) hearts and (our) minds in Christ Jesus" (Philippians 4:6–7). Rather than giving into fear and insecurity, He wants us to "trust in the Lord with all (our) heart, and lean not on (our) own understanding" (Proverbs 3:5 NKJV). Then He can be our rock and refuge, our strong tower and mighty fortress, our shield and savior (Psalm 18:2).

So we may need to confess and repent of our sins of fear, worry, doubt, unbelief, and every way we've not been fully trusting God, just as any other sin. Then He can forgive us and deliver us.

The Spirit of Fear

Fear can also be a spirit—an unholy, demonic spirit that attacks us, torments us and tries to enslave us, stealing our peace and joy through fully trusting God. The spirit of fear is not from God:

> *For God has not given us a spirit of fear, but of power and of love and of a sound mind* (2 Timothy 1:7).

So if we have opened the door, so to speak, for a spirit of fear to have access in our lives, we need to renounce it and reject it. We need to command it to get out of our lives in the authority we have in Christ, by submitting ourselves to God, resisting the devil, and commanding him to flee (James 4:7). Then we can allow God to replace that spirit of fear with faith and God's love, as we choose to fully trust Him in faith and embrace the grace of His love that keeps us secure in Him, no matter what we endure in this world.

> *There is no fear in love, but perfect love casts out fear; for fear has to do with punishment, and whoever fears has not reached perfection in love* (1 John 4:18).

A Personal Experience of Victory Over Fear

I'll give you an example from my life of how the enemy tried to bring fear to keep me from fulfilling my destiny in Christ. God created me to be someone who ministers on the front lines in deliverance and inner healing prayer ministry. I didn't know this all of my life, but I've come to realize that this area is one to which the Lord has called me, as well as to train and equip others to battle in spiritual warfare, to set the captives free and to see the Body and Bride of Christ arise as a mighty army for the kingdom of God to display God's glory through our lives throughout the earth. He's also been teaching me to battle in levels with others in the heavenly realms as He leads and teaches us in those ways.

Now it's important to realize that whatever our calling of God is, whatever our gifting of God is, the enemy is going to try to do just the opposite. He's going to be arranging circumstances in our lives, (beginning in our generational line) to try to crush that gift out of us, to bury it and make sure that we never walk in that gift. Or if by chance we somehow start to walk in that gift, he'll do everything he can to twist, pervert, and misuse it for his own purposes.

I was terrified of the dark for most of my life. Especially anything that was in any way related to the supernatural. This included movies that had anything to do with Damian, demons, the antichrist, ghosts, or any of that. I was scared to death of it. I think I was away at college before I finally stopped sleeping with the lights on! I thought I was just this wimpy little boy most of my life, but I eventually realized that the enemy was recognizing this gifting, this calling of God upon my life, and was trying to crush that out of me, trying to do just the opposite.

But there are times when the enemy will overplay his hand in his arrogance and pride, and he thinks that he's got us and he takes a gamble. If he strikes that blow at us he's gambling that he can take us out and we'll never get back to God. You see, he knows that if we do, if we will humble ourselves before God, bringing Him the battles, the pain, sin, and all the things that the enemy's done in our life, God will redeem it. And when God redeems it, He doesn't just replace it one for one. He releases "a hundredfold" anointing when he gives back what the enemy has stolen (see Matthew 19:29)! That's one of the ways that the enemy is his own worst enemy.

So he takes these calculated risks when he comes against us in an attempt to take us out. The enemy knows that he has to take us out because if he doesn't, and by God's grace we bring it to the foot of the cross and under the blood of Jesus, we'll arise in resurrection power. We'll arise with the anointing and authority from God to overcome the enemy's kingdom in that very area, with deep compassion for others who struggle in that same area. We'll have understanding and wisdom from the school of hard knocks, and now we're knocking his head. God loves that! God loves to take what the enemy has intended for evil and then use it for good. But it's not just a one-for-one trade off, it's a hundredfold return.

My personal battle with fear come to life in my first deliverance ministry encounter. But I praise God that the enemy overplayed his hand. Now I'm sure that I had experienced deliverance many times in my life because most of the time, deliverance, freedom from spiritual bondage, happens without us ever knowing it. That's a misunderstanding in much of the body of Christ. We think that deliverance has to be somebody foaming at the mouth, or cutting themselves, throwing up in a trash can, or on your floor or wherever. Now sometimes deliverance happens that way. But most deliverance happens without us even knowing.

When we worship, deliverance is happening; when we confess our sins and receive the Lord's Supper, deliverance is happening. James 4:7 is really a key deliverance principle: "Submit yourselves therefore to God, resist the devil, and he will flee from you." Whenever we're submitting ourselves to God, whenever we're humbling ourselves in the site of the Lord and He's lifting us up, the devil is fleeing because his right, his legal claim is being broken by our surrender, our submission to God.

So my first encounter with deliverance ministry where I knew it was happening because it was very much on the surface and manifesting before my eyes was at Asbury Seminary. A good friend of mine, one of my prayer partners actually, had been reading all these books on deliverance. (My friend told me I could share his story if I didn't mention his name.) And I'd been reading all these books on healing. I was feeling that I was being called to healing, and he was being called to deliverance. We'd begun to see over time that these were two sides of the same coin: Healing and deliverance are two sides of sanctification. It's God bringing us into freedom, wholeness, and holiness.

One day my friend informed me, "You know, I've been seeing Dr. Steve Seamands and he's been praying for me for deliverance."

"Oh, that's interesting," I said.

My friend added, "I've been seeing Dr. Seamands for about six months or so and the Lord told me that I'm supposed to include you now."

The reason my friend was seeing him was that before my friend knew the Lord, he used drugs. Now that opens many doors to the enemy all by itself, but these particular drugs had been cursed through witchcraft in South America for the specific purpose of trying to draw Americans into drug addiction. This fact came out in the process of deliverance. So even though my friend had the Spirit of Christ within him, he was an evangelist, loved to share the gospel with people, he himself was bound up in some areas of his life. He needed deliverance. He needed to pray the prayer that Jesus taught His disciples to pray, "Father, deliver us from evil."

And so Dr. Seamands was meeting with him and digging up the roots and going through the process. This experience was the beginning of a journey where Dr. Seamands ended up being one of my mentors. I leaned from him, and he learned from Dr. Charles Kraft, who was a missionary and then a professor at Fuller Seminary. He's written several good books which I would encourage those who are interested in this type of ministry to study.

Charles Kraft teaches deliverance like this: It's like having a garage, and over in the corner of the garage is a pile of garbage. Then rats come in and they feed off the garbage. The rats are like the demonic spirits—unholy spirits that are tormenting us in our lives. And God wants to have "a rat killing." He wants to come in and get rid of the rats and drive them out of our lives. The problem is that if we only deal with the rats and we don't deal with the garbage in the corner, the rats just come back.

Just like Jesus taught, even though you get rid of a demonic spirit, if you don't deal with the house, then they'll be back with seven even worse than that one (Matt.12:45). So we follow the process of submitting ourselves to God, then resisting the devil, and then he must flee, (see James 4:7). Submitting ourselves to God is part of letting God deal with the garbage, or the roots of resistance, and the things in our lives on which the enemy feeds.

Getting back to my friend's testimony, Dr. Seamands was taking him through this process of confessing sin, and releasing hurt and pain in his life so that we could take authority over the enemy and drive him out, and welcome in his place the Holy Spirit. So we all met in Dr. Seamands' office at Asbury Seminary in Wilmore, Kentucky. My friend was sitting in a chair and I was sitting in a chair next to Steve Seamands. Dr. Seamands likes to begin with Holy Communion, consecrating the elements of bread and juice, and welcoming the living presence of the living Christ. As my friend began to take the elements, this spirit rose up in my good friend! Now it's one thing to read about this in the Bible, or to hear somebody tell a story about it, but it's another thing to be sitting right there! You're looking at your friend, someone whom you know as your prayer partner, and all of a sudden this spirit rises up in him and speaks through his voice saying, "Get away from me!"

You see, my friend would not say that. That was not him speaking, it was an unholy spirit that had access to him and was rising up in the unsanctified area of his soul. I'll get back to that in a moment. For now, I want to point out that it's in our flesh that the enemy has access to us. The flesh is the part of our lives that is not yet submitted to the Lordship of Christ—the part of us that's resisting or rebelling against God in the flesh. As we will cover extensively from the Scriptures and biblical principles in the deliverance section, a Christian cannot be possessed by a demon but can certainly be tormented by a demon.

So this spirit rises up in his flesh, speaks through his mouth, and causes him to resist receiving the living presence of the living Christ through the sacrament of Holy Communion. That will open your eyes to a new dimension of Communion, too! It's more than a memorial service. Jesus said, "This is My body, this is My blood" (Matthew 26:26). We may have our own understandings and traditions about all that, but Jesus said, "This is My body, this is My blood." And apparently, that's what the demons think.

So finally, that's when I began to see that deliverance doesn't have to be all yelling and screaming, and all these big manifestations. Very calmly, Dr. Seamands said, "I command you to be bound, whatever spirit is causing this disruption; you stand back. You will not stop this child of God from receiving the presence of Christ." Then I watched my friend and prayer partner take the elements, the bread and the wine, the body and the blood, and we moved on with the procedure.

Someone has testified in one of my conferences about how this ministry is like God doing a surgical procedure. He does it precisely, gently, and just in His way. He knows just where we are, what we need, and just how to handle it. We can trust Him in this process of healing and deliverance.

We pressed on a little further. Dr. Seamands sometimes interrogates the spirits. Not everybody does deliverance ministry this way, but there' is an example in Luke 8:30 of a time when a demonically afflicted man met with Jesus, and Jesus said, "What is your name?" That was Jesus interrogating a demonic spirit. So there is a biblical basis for this, but you don't always have to do it that way. There are reasons to do it and not to do it, different schools of thought about that. At the time, we were led by the Holy Spirit to interrogate this spirit, to find out its name, because its name reveals its nature. Its nature reveals what you're dealing with. Sometimes it's good to find out how they got in because that's the open door, that's the root, that's the garbage on which they're feeding. Knowing what we're dealing with gives us insight on how to pray. But when you interrogate them, you still need to take everything with a grain of salt.

From my law practice, when I was cross-examining a witness on the witness stand, I was asking questions of my opponent's witness. I would take everything the witness said with a grain of salt, but what they said in response to my questions would help me prove my case. I was using my questions to get to the truth of the matter. And you know how God redeems anything? I have found that He's redeemed my skills as a lawyer to basically cross-examination and interrogate demonic spirits in deliverance ministry! And when the spirit that rose up in my friend, trying to block him from receiving God's grace and presence, Dr. Seamands asked it a series of questions, "What is your name? How did you get in? What is your function?"

He was pressing in. And we took it with a grain of salt, but ultimately, we took that information and turn it into a prayer. My friend submitted himself to God, confessed his sin, and renounced what needed to be broken off and uprooted from his life. When we submit ourselves to God, resist the devil, he will flee (James 4:7).

Well, somewhere in the process, another demonic spirit rose up and said, "I hate him!" He was pointing his finger up in the air in this seminary professor's office—a Ph.D. from Princeton. So we're not talking about over in Africa or India. We're talking about a couple of seminary students in their white button downs and a seminary professor with a Ph.D. sitting there interrogating a demon.

Now my friend didn't hate me. I knew he wouldn't say that.

Dr. Seamands said, "Who are you talking about?"

"Him! I hate him! He's always tormenting me."

Now Satan was trying to scare me to death. He was trying to bring up every memory from my childhood, every movie, every time I was scared of the dark and anything supernatural. The enemy was just trying to nip this little deliverance thing in the bud right there! And that might have been the biggest, most brazen, most ferocious thing in my friend and it was rising up!

"I hate him! He's always with him! He's always tormenting me!"

Dr. Seamands said, "Who are you talking about?"

"Him! His angel!" He was pointing way up high over my head.

That was one day when Satan overplayed his hand because I've never had another moment of fear in ministry, as far as I know. Why would I be afraid when I have these angels with me! Big angels! Mighty angels! Warriors of God! And they are with you, too. From the time we were little children, our "angels" were assigned to us as seeing the face of our Father (see Matthew 18:10). We seem to have these teams of angels that work with us in our calling and purpose. They are holy, ministering spirits who do the bidding of the Lord. "Are not all angels spirits in the divine service, sent to serve for the sake of those who are to inherit salvation?" (Hebrews 1:14)

These mighty angels are there to assist us. They're there to lift us up into the hand of God, under the shadow of the Almighty, so that we don't dash our foot against a stone (Psalm 91:1–12). And they're here with us, surrounding us right now. They're here ministering to us, worshiping God, releasing an atmosphere of worship and praise; and they're warring against the enemy of our souls as God sends them. They're worshippers of God's Presence, warriors on our side, and witnesses of God's glory. They are ministering spirits, "spirits in the divine service, sent to serve for the sake of those who are to inherit salvation" (Hebrews 1:14). The

185

Lord is teaching us how to minister with the angels alongside us on our team, as we serve Him without fear.

Different forms of Fear

One perspective I've learned is that the enemy works to do the opposite of God's gifting or calling concerning our lives. God will redeem and use anything, and He looks for those opportunities when the enemy will overplay his hand. Then He frees us and even redeems that attack against us. For me, it was fear of the dark, the enemy, and the supernatural in different ways. For you it might be fear of rejection, fear of pain, fear of death, fear of spiders, fear of crowds, or anything else.

The Fear of Man

Another form of fear I've personally wrestled with is "the fear of man"—which is being overly concerned with what other people think of me. This type of fear is an insecurity that leaves us feeling like we have to be "somebody" or do something impressive to be accepted by people. That's a terrible trap because we'll wind up playing up to the people, playing up to what we think we need to do to be accepted and affirmed, instead of looking up to God and finding our security, identity, and significance in Him. "The fear of others lays a snare, but one who trusts in the Lord is secure" (Proverbs 29:25).

The Lord wants to uproot our fear of man, and uproot those things in our lives we're fearing and honoring more than fearing and honoring Him. "Do not fear those who kill the body but cannot kill the soul; rather fear Him who can destroy both body and soul in hell," Jesus said in Matthew 10:28.

Whatever our fears are, God wants to uproot them and deliver us from them. Fear, as well as each one of these roots of resistance involve choices, emotions, and feelings. They can be sins, but there can also be demonic spirits in these same areas. And if the spirits are there, they are there because they are feeding on something in our lives—the things that need to be uprooted, the garbage that needs to be cleaned out, the wounds and emotions that need to be healed. We need to have a rat killing, but first we need to submit every area to God through the inner healing of our souls in our mind, will, and emotions (James 4:7). And as the Lord reveals it in our lives, He wants to come and replace what He removes with His truth, His life, and His love. "Perfect love casts out fear" (1 John 4:18).

6. Brokenness and Unresolved Trauma

The traumatic experiences of our lives are those times that leave us physically or emotionally broken and wounded. They are very often fearful, painful, or shameful experiences—the kind we'd like to forget. And that's the problem. Sometimes we bury those experiences and everything associated with them down in our minds, where they may be locked in our emotions or sealed in our bodies. We may not think about them or even remember them, but they are there. And they continue to influence and affect us in many ways we don't even know.

Brokenhearted and Double-minded

Brokenness from unresolved traumas in this sense is a form of being "double-minded." And it's a spiritual principle that a "double-minded person" is "unstable in every way," keeping us from receiving all the fullness of the peace and healing of the Lord (see James 1:8). We may not have chosen it, but we may be experiencing it.

This is another way in which we can be "broken-hearted" (Isaiah 61:1). It's like part of our heart is broken, shattered, not whole because of traumatic experiences in our lives. We will also discuss these concepts of Brokenness in more depth in the chapter on Seven Potential Barriers to Healing.

What can happen is our soul can become broken and shattered, in a sense, to varying degrees. Our mind, will and emotions bound up within that event can become detached. It's almost like a means of God's mercy and grace in that moment, like a form of survival to get through the traumatic event as best as we can. Our way of surviving and getting through that can be a mindset that's something like, "I'm going somewhere else. This isn't happening to me." And it's like that part of our soul at that age and moment kind of breaks off and goes down into

187

our unconscious realm so that we kind don't feel it, we don't experience it, and perhaps we don't even clearly remember it.

These are unresolved traumas when we've not resolved them by fully releasing them to Jesus. The roots can be deep, reaching back to long ago, or just last week, but they can continue to bear fruit that can control or heavily influence our current lives. Perhaps these traumatic events happened long ago, and that person has moved on with life to a degree. But at the same time, to another degree, "part of that person," so to speak, may still be stuck there in the experience of that trauma.

These traumatic experiences are often the most fearful, painful, or shameful experiences of our life. They often occur at very vulnerable times, such as when we are very young, or exposed to dangerous circumstances beyond our control, or where we are unprotected, rather than safe and secure. Some frequent examples in prayer ministry of traumatic experiences are sexual abuse, severe emotional turmoil from infinite sources and circumstances, or physical accidents.

In a sense, these traumas are still unresolved because we have not been able to fully trust God to release it to Him. Sometimes this is very deliberate and conscious, but many times it's a subconscious decision or even an unconscious act. We don't want to think about it or remember it, and certainly don't want to feel it, experience, or relive it. So it stays buried and unresolved.

In a way, though not usually consciously deliberate, this is a form of self-centered pride, manifesting as control. And any area where we are in control, God is not in control. Any area where we are being lord, Jesus is not Lord. So, whether we intend it or not, it becomes another way we can be resisting and blocking the grace of God in the areas we need it the most (James 4:6). And these roots can produce bad fruit in our lives.

We'll also address this topic of unresolved traumas in the context of Brokenness as in the chapters on Potential Barriers to Healing, when these traumas are at an even deeper level that's sometimes called dissociation or detachment in the realm of the unconscious mind. This is often when memories are blocked or very deeply buried. I think of this as a kind of sliding scale of degrees of detachment. In any event, the healing prayer process is similar—to welcome Jesus into the moments and memories to help the person entrust it all to Him.

The good news is that Jesus is still healing the brokenhearted and setting the captives free. His Holy Spirit is still at work in our lives to bring us back to a single-minded, pure devotion to Christ as our savior, healer, and deliverer. This can be a fairly deep topic that's often misunderstood, and I'm writing a very specific book to discuss this area in much more detail. Our ministry continues to encounter this deep level of brokenness on an almost daily basis in our ministry of inner healing and deliverance. But God is with us, and God is healing His children in powerful, loving ways that only He can do.

7. Infirmity

In broad terms, an infirmity is anything that keeps us from being completely whole. This can be any form of physical brokenness, sickness, or disease. God wants to go to the root and source of that because He wants us to be made whole. As we have seen, His will according to His Word is to forgive us of all of our iniquities and heal us of all of our diseases (Psalm 103:3).

When Jesus healed the sick and cast out demons causing spiritual oppression, the Gospels declare that He was fulfilling the prophecy of Isaiah 53 of the coming Messiah: "He took our infirmities and bore our diseases" (Matthew 8:17). It doesn't always happen instantly—that's the miraculous when it does. But He does want us to agree with His will for healing. And as we come into agreement with His will, then we'll continue to be brought into alignment with His will. Now sometimes we must wait until the resurrection to see that healing fully manifested. That's the ultimate healing. But God does want healing of infirmity, sickness, and disease. He wants that to happen here on earth as it is in heaven.

Jesus taught us to pray for the Father's kingdom to come and His will to be done on earth as it is in heaven (Matthew 6:10). So whenever we wonder whether something is God's will or not, we should ask ourselves, "How is it in heaven?" because that's God's will for earth, according to His Word. Is there infirmity in heaven? Is there sickness in

189

heaven? Are there diseases in heaven? Are there demons or spiritual strongholds in heaven? If not, then it's not God's will for that to be on earth because it's not as it is in heaven. Healing and deliverance is part of the redemptive process of bringing God's kingdom of heaven to earth, in us and in all creation.

Death is Our Enemy

In a sense, the sickness and disease of infirmity are just death on the installment plan. That's death little-by-little and step-by-step. It's the reverse of healing, and it's the reverse of life. Jesus came that we might have life and have it abundantly. It's the thief who comes to steal, kill and destroy (John 10:10). Death is not from God; it only entered this world through the open door of sin (Romans 5:12).

But there is great confusion about death in the Body of Christ. And many continue in sickness and disease, on their way to death, because they passively accept it instead of resist it as an enemy. Many believe that if someone dies, it must be God's will, without knowing the whole counsel of God in His Word. If a Christian dies, death does not win. Death is like an enemy who snatches that person from life, but Christ reaches out to snatch that one who died in Christ from the grip of death, declaring, "No! This one's mine!" and delivers us into the arms of the Father. According to the Word of God, Satan—the thief who comes only to steal and kill and destroy—"has the power of death"—and he tries to hold us captive "in slavery by the fear of death":

> *Since, therefore, the children share flesh and blood, He himself likewise shared the same things, so that through death He might destroy the one who has the power of death, this is, the devil, and free those who all their lives were held in slavery by the fear of death* (Hebrews 2:14–15).

So death is not our friend and not something to be desired. Death is our "enemy" according to Scripture: "The last enemy to be destroyed is death" (1 Corinthians 15:26). Death is the work of the devil, "the one who has the power death" according to the Word of God. But the good news is that Jesus came and still comes by the power of His Holy Spirit to destroy his works through the power of the blood of Christ. "The Son of God was revealed for this purpose, to destroy the works of the

190

devil" (1 John 3:8). And because of Christ, we now have this promise of life over death: "Death will be no more; mourning and crying and pain will be no more" (Revelation 21:4). "Death and Hades will be thrown into the lake of fire" (Revelation 20:14). And I can't wait for that day!

Our Lord Jesus Christ willingly endured death so that we might live with Him forever (John 11:25–26). In Christ, "Death has been swallowed up in victory" (1 Corinthians 15:54). So until that day of final victory and ultimate redemption of this broken, fallen world tormented by the one who has the power of death, death is an enemy to resist and defeat. On this side of heaven, we "go through the valley of the shadow of death" and into the victory of life in Christ—we don't stay there, camp out there, or celebrate the principalities and rulers of darkness and death there (Psalm 23:4).

Instead of agreeing with death and passively giving in to its power, we are called as disciples of Christ to stand against death in prayer and by the power of the name of Jesus. Death is one of the gates of hell that cannot prevail against the Church of Jesus Christ (Matthew 16:18). And wherever we see it manifested—through infirmity, sickness, disease, and anything less than the fullness of life, we have been given the keys of the kingdom to bind it up and cast it out in the name of Jesus (Matthew 16:19). We're called to embrace that calling and grow up into that level of maturity, authority, and faith. We're called to have faith enough to literally "raise the dead" in Jesus' name and power of the Holy Spirit, as a display of Christ's victory over death and the devil. This is part of the fulfillment of the promise of the coming of the kingdom of heaven on earth, as it is in heaven:

> *And as you go, preach, saying, "The kingdom of heaven is at hand." Heal the sick, cleanse the lepers, raise the dead, cast out demons. Freely you have received, freely give* (Matthew 10:7–8 NKJV).

There will one day be a generation on the face of the earth who will never even "taste of death" (Matthew 16:27–28). And one day soon Jesus Christ will literally return in the glory of the clouds of heaven, and we will see a world-wide display of the victory of Life over death (1 Thessalonians 4:16-17). Until that day, we want to be found faithful, fighting death and embracing Life—embracing the One who is Life and

191

has defeated death and every form of infirmity (John 14:6).

We can't effectively pray for healing and see the kinds of miracles of life from the dead that Jesus said we would see unless we agree with life and reject death—in our own lives and in the lives of those for whom we are praying in faith. Many have made a pact of agreement with death, either by embracing it directly as their lot or allowing it access by their passivity. And that gives death, along with every form of infirmity, the legal right to remain by the permission we grant. We need to renounce that and allow God to uproot death and all infirmity from our lives.

Death is not from God. Death only has access into this world because death entered this world through sin. All those who have been held by the fear of death are those who are held in bondage to that slavery. (Romans 5:12–15). So that doesn't necessarily mean death entered the world through *our* sin, it means death entered the world through *the* sin of Adam and Eve. But God is doing just the opposite. He's bringing and calling forth life. Even as all of creation groans and awaits the revealing of the sons of man, He's redeeming and cleansing so that creation itself can be set free from the process of death
(Romans 8:19–23).

The problem is that too many of us have come into agreement with death. We see death as our friend and not our enemy. Paul makes it very clear in 1 Corinthians 15:26 that the last enemy to be destroyed is death. In Revelation 20:14, we see death and Hades cast into the lake of fire in the end. Death is our enemy. Sickness, disease, infirmity, and all that is less than the wholeness of life are our enemy. It's not to be embraced, and we're not to be passive. We are to actively war against it.

Death, even for a Christian, is a doorway that we must pass through. Death is not to be embraced. It's something to be endured as we press through. Now God loves to redeem all things. He redeems even our death and our passing through death. But I like to think of it like this: death comes and snatches a life, but when we are dead in Christ, Christ comes and snatches us out of the hand of death and delivers us into the hand of the Father.

So we can celebrate life, but not death. We're to celebrate the life of God and we're to war against death. Infirmity, sickness, and disease, are just the process of death. We're to treat it as our enemy and overcome our enemy through life.

Good Roots Bearing Good Fruit

A good tree bears good fruit (Matthew 7:17). And like it or not, our roots determine what kind of "tree" we are growing up to become. In His love, Jesus calls us to abide in Him and in His truth and love so that our lives will bear much good fruit (John 15:1–5). All of this is so that our "joy may be complete" (John 15:11).

But too much of the time, we are continuing to just get by as a wounded and defiled Body and Bride of Christ Too often we've really just tried to deny these wounds, deny the pain, press on and act like something's happened that *hasn't* really happened. It's available to us through the blood of Jesus Christ and the victory of the cross, but we must apply the blood. And if we begin to recognize some of these roots producing bad fruit in our lives, we can pray, "Lord, come and dig down and dig them out. Come uproot everything in me that's producing bad fruit in my life." And He will begin to release us, cleanse us, and heal us from these things and then fill us with His peace, security, and love.

God wants to minister to us. He's lifting things up and He's drawing them. But we must make a choice. We can shut it down, set it aside, leave it for another day; or we can begin to open our hearts to the Lord and let Him go in and draw up the pain, draw up the shame, draw out the pride, bitterness, rejection, shame, fear, trauma, and infirmity. He can draw all these things out and pour in His love, if we'll be willing to ask Him and trust Him enough to let go of our control, giving ourselves to Him in trusting surrender and faith. Let's agree in prayer:

Heavenly Father, I am Your child and You love me. You have called me by name. You've formed me and shaped me in my Mother's womb. You desire good for me. You have plans for me, to prosper me for good and not for harm. And I welcome Your plan for my life. You want to heal me and deliver me. You want me to give permission to You to come into every age and moment of my life; to put Your finger on the place of my pain, shame, hurts, wounds, and walls; to uproot what is unhealed and unholy in my life; to fill me with Your love. My hope and trust is in You. You are my Rock and my Refuge. You are my Strong Tower. And You are mighty to save, mighty to heal, and mighty to deliver. If my God be for me, who can be against me? For I am loved; I am forgiven; and I am called by name to fulfill my destiny in Christ for the glory of God, healthy, free, healed, and whole.

So I welcome you now, Lord. Come, Holy Spirit. I submit myself to You and Your Lordship, Lord Jesus Christ, in every area of my life and I resist the devil from any place where he has claimed ground. In the name of Jesus, I command him to be bound. I overcome him by the blood of the Lamb and the word of my testimony. I command him to come out of me, to come off of me, to come out of every area of my life now. I send him to the feet of Jesus to be judged now, never to return. And in it's place, I receive Your life, Your healing, Your truth, Your freedom, and You Holy Spirit and all the fullness of God. In Jesus' name I pray, Amen.

Chapter 12

Footholds of the Enemy of Our Souls

Our "flesh" is where we give access to the enemy of our souls. Not our spirit that's been possessed and filled with God's Holy Spirit, not the surrendered and sanctified areas of our soul that are yielded and entrusted to the Lordship of Christ, but through "the flesh." These are the unsanctified, unhealed areas of our lives. As we have seen, sometimes it's because we are still resisting the Lordship of Christ in an area through the assertion of our own will and ways. But sometimes, it's because those are unhealed wounds or self-guarded areas that we have not yet been able to fully release to the Lord—whether intentional or not.

Spiritually Vulnerable

Our spiritual enemy who "comes only to steal and kill and destroy" does not fight fair, and he strives to take advantage of us in our most vulnerable places. He comes to steal from us the "abundant life" that Jesus longs for us to have, and for which He has already paid (John 10:10). Because the "flesh"—the unsanctified areas of our souls—is not yet fully submitted the protecting, cleansing, healing Lordship of Jesus Christ, that's our most vulnerable place, where we're most vulnerable to spiritual attack and oppression.

Jesus had no "Flesh" in His Soul

Jesus fearlessly faced death on the cross, knowing nothing in the kingdom of darkness had any power over Him. His heart was sinless and pure as the holy Lamb of God, "without defect or blemish" (1 Peter 1:19). He was perfectly one with the Father, perfectly anointed and filled with fullness of the Holy Spirit (John 14:11; Luke 4:18). "Jesus, full of the Holy Spirit ... was tempted by the devil," but never gave in to temptation or sin (Luke 4:1). Therefore, Jesus was able to confront and overcome all the wickedness and power of hell itself, declaring in truth, "The ruler of this world is coming. He has no power over Me" (John 14:30). Translated another way, "He has nothing in Me" (NKJV).

Jesus is the "one who in every respect has been tempted as we are, yet without sin" (Hebrews 4:15). Therefore, Satan—the enemy of our souls—had nothing in Jesus, had no power over Him, because Jesus had no "flesh." Every area of His life was perfectly yielded and submitted to the Father, in complete obedience to God. Jesus was "entirely sanctified" in spirit and soul and body. He had no "pockets of resistance" or "strongholds of pride."

But that was Jesus. We are on a journey of becoming more like Him through the process of sanctification, being conformed into the image of the Son of God. Between now and then, there is "flesh" in our souls to be crucified, and there are self-centered strongholds of pride to be pulled down and put to death.

The Flesh Makes Room for the Devil

Our flesh is where we unwittingly give place to the enemy of our souls, giving him a measure of power over us. This is where even Christians can "make room for the devil," as Paul warned Christian believers in the church at Ephesus (Ephesians 4:27). Some translations call this a "foothold" (NIV) or giving "the devil a way to defeat you" (NCV). These are the places of the flesh in the Christian soul where we can open the door to the devil and the demonic spirits of his kingdom of darkness. Jesus says, "I stand at the door and knock; open it up and let Me in" (from Revelation 3:20).[24] So does Satan.

The demonic spirits gain access to our lives through the doors of the flesh. What is clean draws the One who is clean, but what is unclean draws the ones who are unclean. These are the areas of our life where we have not fully opened the door for Jesus to come in and be Lord—the areas where we still claim to be lord—sometimes consciously and deliberately or not. Jesus may be our Lord in general, but He wants to be Lord of every specific area of our lives. And He loves us enough to

---

[24] Though we often use this Scripture in terms of evangelism to unbelievers, the biblical context is that Jesus is speaking to His believers in His church at Laodicea, calling them to open the door of repentance for their lukewarm hearts and let Him in. He is speaking of deeper levels of surrender and submission to His Lordship in their lives that the Holy Spirit may restore their passion for Christ (Revelation 3:14–22).

allow us suffer the consequences of living in the flesh until we will repent and seek the freedom and healing of life in the Spirit.

Pockets of Resistance Provide Footholds for the Enemy

In my next illustration of the three circles, I am showing the pockets of resistance darkened with black spots. These are the demonic spirits that feed on our flesh. They try to influence our souls to further resist the Lordship of Jesus and the filling of His Holy Spirit.

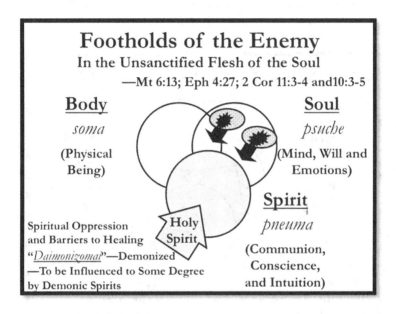

Satan's Plan for Us

Satan's plan and purpose for our lives is, of course, the exact opposite of God's plan and purpose for our lives. God wants to fill us with His Holy Spirit; the enemy wants to fill us with his unholy spirits. This is the battle of good and evil, between the flesh and the Spirit, between our agreement with God and our agreement with the enemy. But with the Holy Spirit of Christ living in us, greater is He who's in us than he who's in the world (1 John 4:4). And we overcome our spiritual enemy by the blood of the Lamb and the word of our testimony, not holding on to our lives, but laying our lives down in willing submission and trusting surrender to the will of God (Revelation 12:11). We must continue to

197

overcome, enforcing the victory of the cross and applying the blood of the Lamb in every area of our soul.

This battle doesn't vanish the moment that we pray the sinner's prayer, receive Christ in our hearts, and are saved. It continues throughout the life-long process of God crucifying our flesh, sanctifying our souls, and delivering us from evil—as Jesus taught His believers and disciples to pray. God wants His presence and influence to increase in our lives, and our enemy wants his to increase. This war for the Christian soul is the purpose of the ministry of deliverance—a needed ministry of Jesus intended as much for believers as it is for unbelievers.

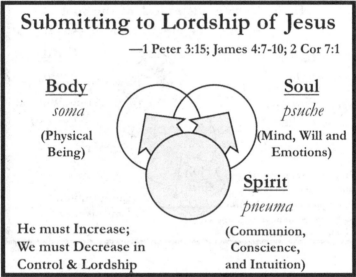

fruit

roots

Submitting to Lordship of Jesus

—1 Peter 3:15; James 4:7-10; 2 Cor 7:1

Body

soma

(Physical Being)

Soul

psuche

(Mind, Will and Emotions)

Spirit

pneuma

He must Increase; We must Decrease in Control & Lordship

(Communion, Conscience, and Intuition)

God's Plan for Us

God wants to lift us up into the arms of His Presence; Satan wants to push us down into the depths of despair. God wants to fill us with the fullness of His Spirit and the blessings of His kingdom; Satan wants to hinder and steal them. One kingdom comes through obedient humility and trusting faith; the other, through self-centered pride and rebellious sin. We are spiritual beings created for a spiritual relationship, living in a physical body. As God's principles of physics teach, "Nature abhors a vacuum." These bodies of mortal flesh will be filled in the spiritual

198

dimension of our beings with something—either something holy or something unholy. In our journey to press on to perfection, there is usually a mixture of both, as we will see.

Christians Can Be Influenced and Oppressed, Not Possessed

Demons are unholy spirits. A Christian cannot be possessed by a demon, because Christians are possessed by the Holy Spirit. We were bought with a price by the blood of the Lamb.

> *Or do you not know that your body is a temple of the Holy Spirit within you, which you have from God, and that you are not your own? For you were bought with a price; therefore glorify God in your body*
> (1 Corinthians 6:19–20).

While unholy spirits can't own us or possess us, that doesn't mean that they can't have any power of influence over us. And it does not mean that they can't dwell in the unclean areas of our flesh. Christians can be influenced, in varying degrees, by the unholy spirits. Wherever we are effectively in agreement with the will and ways of the enemy (and therefore in rebellion to God's will and ways) we have given the enemy access because we are functioning in our flesh in those areas—whether we know it or not.

As we will discuss in more detail in the next chapter on deliverance, Jesus taught the Church to pray, "Deliver us from evil" in the Lord's Prayer. So this isn't a theory or doctrine, that Christians need deliverance from evil. These are the words of Jesus and the cry of the Father's heart, that we would be healed and free. That's why Jesus is still binding up the brokenhearted and setting the captives free.

Can a Christian "Have" a Demon?

Some ask, "How can a Christian have a demon?" or "How can an unholy spirit live in the same body with the Holy Spirit?" This is how: The flesh is where they feed and the flesh is where they live. So the better question to ask is: "How can God's Holy Spirit live in the same body with my stinking flesh?" It's only by God's grace! And by God's grace, we can be cleansed and set free from the spiritual oppression of unholy spirits to

199

be more fully filled with God's Holy Spirit. As someone has said, "Can a Christian have a demon? Yes, but why on earth would you want one!"

Actually, the Bible never says that Christians *can't* have demons. That's our pride that says that. Instead, the Bible says Christians can "make room for the devil" (Ephesians 4:27) and "be led astray from a sincere and pure devotion to Christ" if we "receive a different spirit than the one [we] received" (2 Corinthians 11:3–4). We will look at these important passages in more depth in a moment, but it is important to note from the beginning that it's a philosophy of man or just wishful thinking rather than the Word of God, that says believers don't need deliverance because Christians can't have demons. If you know many Christians, you probably know what I mean!

Foundational Principles to Understand Demonic Oppression

The Bible makes it clear that the journey of sanctification into the fullness of God's salvation is a process. We take it step by step, as we choose to take up our cross and follow Him, one decision at a time. Like peeling an onion, God peels back one layer of our flesh at a time—only about as much as we can handle, in His mercy. And like clearing a field by picking up one stone at time, what we find living under it in the dark isn't always very pretty. So, God gives us the grace to allow Him to expose the hidden places in His timing and in His way, bringing all things out of the darkness, into His light, and under the blood of Jesus. And if we say, as Christians, that we have no flesh, we are likely mistaken. Just ask your spouse or best friend! Just read your Bible:

> *This is the message we have heard from Him and proclaim to you, that God is light and in Him there is no darkness at all. If we say that we have fellowship with Him while we are walking in darkness, we lie and do not do what is true; but if we walk in the light as He himself is in the light, we have fellowship with one another, and the blood of Jesus His Son cleanses us from all sin. If we say that we have no sin, we deceive ourselves, and the truth is not in us. If we confess our sins, He who is faithful and just will forgive us our sins and cleanse us from all unrighteousness. If we say that we have not sinned, we make him a liar, and His word is not in us* (1 John 1:5–10).

In this passage, God is speaking through John to Christian believers. We know from our own experiences that we do not always walk in the light, sometimes walking instead in the darkness. The blood of Jesus "cleanses us from all sin" to the degree that "we confess our sins." We walk in the light to the degree that we refuse, by God's grace, to walk in the darkness. We "have fellowship" with the one we are walking with. Our flesh seeks the fellowship of the darkness and if we say we never walk in the fellowship of the darkness, we are saying "we have no sin" and "we deceive ourselves."

Thank God, that He doesn't demand that we be perfectly holy or perfectly whole before He will come into our bodies of mortal flesh and begin the process of crucifying our flesh and sanctifying our soul! He meets us where we are, but never leaves us as we are.

Healing and Freedom Comes "Little by Little"

The stories and struggles of God's people under the old covenant teach us His spiritual principles under the new covenant. At one level, the story of God driving out the nations before His people as they came into their Promise Land speaks of God driving out our spiritual enemies as He brings us into our Promise Land of the fullness of His kingdom—"righteousness and peace and joy in the Holy Spirit" (Romans 14:17). In His mercy, He drives them out "little by little" as we can handle it, increasing His Holy Spirit and He delivers us from every unholy spirit.

> *I will not drive them out from before you in one year, or the land would become desolate and the wild animals would multiply against you. Little by little I will drive them out from before you, until you have increased and possess the land* (Exodus 23:29–30).

Divided Loyalties of a Divided Kingdom

One of Satan's strategies is to drive a wedge in our soul, and to divide our loyalties between our flesh and God's Spirit. Where we refuse to fully trust the Lord and submit to His authority, we are deceived into thinking that we are keeping control to ourselves. But in effect, where we refuse to submit to the Lordship of Christ, we are submitting the lordship of the enemy. These divided loyalties between the flesh and the

201

Spirit keep us from standing firm in the Lord and experiencing the abundant life Jesus sacrificed for us to receive. They give our enemy access to come in like a thief "to steal and kill and destroy" (John 10:10). Jesus spoke of these spiritual principles, warning us:

> *Every kingdom divided against itself is laid waste, and no city or house divided against itself will stand* (Matthew 12:25, with Jesus speaking specifically in the context of deliverance ministry).

> *No one can serve two masters; for a slave will either hate the one and love the other, or be devoted to one and despise the other* (Matthew 6:24).

> *Whoever is not with Me is against Me, and whoever does not gather with Me scatters* (Luke 11:23, with Jesus again speaking specifically in the context of demonic oppression and deliverance from evil).

Spiritual Warfare Within

Likewise, the Apostle Paul speaks of the spiritual warfare we face every day as believers under assault from our spiritual enemy. He says we "wage war" with the "weapons of our warfare" which have "divine power to destroy strongholds" (2 Corinthians 10:3–4). We wage this war especially in the battles for our "thoughts," where we are to "take every thought captive to obey Christ" (2 Corinthians 10:5). Since our thoughts are formed in our mind, this is a battle for our soul—the mind, will, and emotions.

In the very next chapter, Paul speaks of the enemy's ability to deceive us and lead us astray, even as Christians, if we falter in the battle for our thoughts, and receive a different spirit than the Holy Spirit:

> *But I am afraid that as the serpent deceived Eve by its cunning, your thoughts will be led astray from a sincere and pure devotion to Christ. For if someone comes and proclaims another Jesus than the one we proclaimed, or if you receive a different spirit from the one you received, or a different gospel from the one you accepted, you submit to it readily enough* (2 Corinthians 11:3–4).

In this passage, Paul is speaking to Christian believers in the church at Corinth when he says "your thoughts." These are believers who have had "a sincere and pure devotion to Christ" but they can be "led astray." It is "the serpent" who deceived Eve who continues to try to deceive the sons and daughters of Eve. And Paul is speaking of Christian believers, not unbelievers, who can "receive a different spirit from the one you received." Of course, the Spirit we received in Christ is the Holy Spirit. But we see here, according to the Word of God, even Christians can "receive" a demonic spirit—we can receive "a different spirit" if we "submit to it," rather than submitting to the Lordship of Christ in that area of our lives.

The context of these passages is the spiritual warfare for the battle of our souls. A clear strategy of our enemy is to keep us from "a sincere and pure devotion to Christ." We are not "pure" in our devotion to Christ to the very degree we allow a mixture of the flesh and the Spirit in the unsanctified areas of our souls.

Our crafty, deceptive enemy knows that if he can divide our loyalties, he can rattle us and shake us until we cannot stand in the strength of the Lord to fulfill our calling and destiny in Christ. Our enemy seeks to divide and conquer. He seeks to divide our loyalties as a kingdom divided against itself, so that we cannot stand, much less overcome the gates of hell with the keys of the kingdom of God in fulfillment of our destiny (Matthew 16:18–19). He seeks to divide every area of our soul from whole-hearted devotion to Christ—our mind, our will, and our emotions.

—Divided in Our Mind

We are to have "the mind of Christ" (1 Corinthians 2:16). The Holy Spirit wants to lead us into the fullness of the promises of God's kingdom, but the unholy spirits of the enemy's kingdom work in our flesh to cause us to doubt in our minds the wisdom and goodness of God. But the crafty and wicked serpent is still speaking to our flesh, "Did God really say that?" (from Genesis 3:1). If he can get us to question and doubt the wisdom of obedience to God and submission to His will, then he can get us to resist the very blessings of God's promises that God longs to give us.

203

If any of you is lacking in wisdom, ask God, who gives to all generously and ungrudgingly, and it will be given you. But ask in faith, never doubting, for the one who doubts is like a wave of the sea, driven and tossed by the wind; for the doubter, being double-minded and unstable in every way, must not expect to receive anything from the Lord
(James 1:5–7).

In the original language of this passage, the Greek word translated "double-minded" is *dipsuchos* from the root word *psuche*, which means soul. So the expression literally means "two-souled."[25] From the perspective of my three circles, the circle of the soul is divided between the two areas of the soul—the Spirit and the flesh. One part is the area submitted to the Lordship of Jesus and sanctified by Holy Spirit, while the other part is the flesh—the unsanctified area of the soul. The soul is the mind, will, and emotions. A "two-souled" person is a double-minded person. To that very degree, we are unstable in our devotion and submission to God, giving the enemy power and influence in our lives to keep us from fully receiving from the Lord.

—Divided in Our Will

Paul was obviously a Spirit-filled believer. Yet, even Paul—the great apostle who would write so much of what would become the New Testament—personally wrestled in his own will with the battle of the flesh, as he pressed on in his calling and destiny in Christ. He confessed his frustration with the unsanctified areas of his own soul:

For we know that the law is spiritual; but I am of the flesh, sold into slavery under sin. I do not understand my own actions. For I do not do what I want, but I do the very thing I hate. Now if I do what I do not want, I agree that the law is good. But in fact it is no longer I that do it, but sin that dwells within me. For I know that nothing good dwells within me, that is, in my flesh. I can will what is right, but I cannot do it. For I do not do the good I want, but the evil I do not want is what I do. Now if I do what I do not want, it is no longer I that do it, but sin that dwells within me. So I find it to be a law that when I want to do what is good, evil lies close at

---

[25] *Vine's Complete Expository Dictionary of Old and New Testament Words* (Strong's Lexicon, 1374).

204

hand. For I delight in the law of God in my inmost self, but I see in my members another law at war with the law of my mind, making me captive to the law of sin that dwells in my members. Wretched man that I am! Who will rescue me from this body of death? Thanks be to God through Jesus Christ our Lord! So then, with my mind I am a slave to the law of God, but with my flesh I am a slave to the law of sin (Romans 7:14–25).

As we have seen, our will is that dimension of our soul where we choose what we will do—to follow God's will and ways or not. That part of Paul and that part of us that does not do what we want to do in obedience to God is "the flesh." Part of us wants to do what is good and part of us wants to do what is not. And "evil lies close at hand" to take us "captive to the law of sin that dwells in our members." It is in our flesh that we are "a slave to the law of sin." Where does sin dwell in the members of a Christian? It dwells in our flesh. Satan seeks to divide our will, so that he can hold us captive in our flesh, bound to the law of sin rather than free to delight in the law of God.

—Divided in Our Emotions

Emotions are a gift of God to sense and feel and experience the fullness of life. Our enemy seeks to pervert and distort our emotions and desires to draw us away from experiencing life as God intended. We are continually tempted to desire the ways of the world instead of the ways of God, to express ourselves in unholy ways rather than holy ways. But the Lord warns us against the division of the desires and expressions of our emotions.

Do not love the world or the things in the world. The love of the Father is not in those who love the world; for all that is in the world—the desire of the flesh, the desire of the eyes, the pride in riches—comes not from the Father but from the world. And the world and its desire are passing away, but those who do the will of God live forever (1 John 2:15–17).

God wants to free us from our damaged emotions, wounds from our past, and deliver us from the desires and lusts of our old way of life. A term for being controlled and driven by our own emotions and desires rather than the Lord's is "lust." The biblical term of "lust" is much broader than impure sexual thoughts; it is really any covetous or unholy desire—the desires of the flesh.

The Lord wants to transform us and renew us so that His thoughts become our thoughts and His desires become our desires. He wants us to learn to express our hearts as an expression of His heart.

> *That is not the way you learned Christ! For surely you have heard about Him and were taught in Him, as truth is in Jesus. You were taught to put away your former way of life, your old self, corrupt and deluded by its lusts, and to be renewed in the spirit of your minds, and to clothe yourselves with the new self, created according to the likeness of God in true righteousness and holiness* (Ephesians 4:20–24).

Example of a Stronghold formed from the Emotion of Anger

Paul gives us another biblical example of how our flesh can open the door for the enemy to build his strongholds in our lives, using the example of the emotion of anger.

> *Be angry but do not sin; do not let the sun go down on your anger, and do not make room for the devil* (Ephesians 4:26–27).

First of all, we need to note that here in this passage the Word of God actually *commands* us as Christians to "be angry"—"Be angry but do not sin." It doesn't say, as many assume, and as many even teach, "Do not be angry, because that is sin." To the contrary, it says, "Be angry but do not sin." In other words, we are to be fully alive to the true emotions and pain of the encounters and circumstances of life. But we are not to be controlled by those emotions and pain. We are to be controlled by Christ, through the deliberate surrender of our emotions and pain to the leading of the Holy Spirit. Anger, in and of itself, is not wrong or sin. It's what we do with our anger that determines whether we are acting holy or unholy, making room for the devil or making room for the Holy Spirit.

206

Godly Expression of Anger

Jesus, as always, is our example for a godly expression of our emotions, including the emotion of anger. The moneychangers in the temple made Jesus angry. When they turned the temple of God into a den of thieves instead of a house of prayer, it made Him mad. In fact, He was so angry that John 2:15 tells us that Jesus made a "whip of cords" and "drove them out of the temple" as He "overturned their tables." He was fully alive to His emotions and pain, consumed with zeal, but not consumed by anger (John 2:17). As Son of Man, Jesus submitted to the Father and yielded to the leading of the Holy Spirit. Jesus was angry, but He did not sin in his anger. He was not out of control; He was walking in godly self-control by entrusting His emotions completely to the Spirit. He allowed Himself to "be angry," while at the same time, He didn't "make room for the devil" (see Ephesians 4:26–27).

By the way, Scripture doesn't say exactly how Jesus used this whip, as "He drove all of them out of the temple." But somehow, He did this without sin! The point is that there are times when we are supposed to be angry. There is a zeal of the Lord that is supposed to consume our emotions—even the emotion of anger at times. Many of the things in our culture and in our lives should make us angry. Maybe we ought to even get a whip sometimes. But remember, we are called to be *like* Jesus, but we can't *be* Jesus. In other words, "Don't try this at home!"

The example of Jesus gives us permission, and the Word of God gives us a command to "be angry" in a godly, Spirit-led way. The problem is that we Christians don't get angry about the things that ought to make us angry. There are ways of being angry that are sinning, but then there are also ways of being angry without sinning.

When we suffer injustice or get hurt and wounded or if someone we love suffers injustice or gets hurt and wounded, we're supposed to feel angry. When we see things that aren't right, things that are wrong in our lives, our culture, our nation, we're supposed to feel angry. God gave us the emotion of anger. To "be angry" is not necessarily bad. In a sense, we can't really control the actual feelings and emotions we have, anger or otherwise. What we can control is what decisions we make and what actions we take in light of those feelings.

Release Our Anger to God

But when we get angry, we're supposed to release the anger to God. If something makes us angry, hurts us, or wounds us, or stirs us in anger over what's happened to another, we are to release that anger to God. And then we are to respond and react as He leads us. Sometimes it's to speak the truth in love to the person who's made us angry (Ephesians 4:15). Sometimes it's to be led by the Spirit to take action, as Jesus did. But first, we need to release our anger to God. Sometimes it's good to step away and tell God, "Lord, that makes me so angry! I'm so angry when she does that! Why does he do that? That makes me so angry!" God wants us to release those emotions of anger to Him. That's okay. In fact, that's obedient—"Be angry."

This releasing is a choice. It's a perspective or an attitude of, "I'm choosing to release this to God." In prayer ministry, sometimes it helps people to speak it out loud and express what's really inside without fear that it's "wrong" to have anger. Sometimes it helps to hit a pillow or even take a baseball bat to old log or pound the ground until all the anger comes out. There are different ways to release it. But it's better to hit a log than kick the dog!

Ungodly Anger

Unfortunately, we often respond to the temptation and influence of the enemy of our souls to release our anger is wrong ways. While God does command us to "be angry," when appropriate, we have to be careful that we don't sin in our anger, "lest we make room for the devil" in our flesh and "give the devil a foothold" (Ephesians 4:27).

Rather than releasing our anger to God and then following the leading of His Holy Spirit in what to do about it, we often sin in our anger or "let the sun go down on (our) anger" by releasing it in wrong ways, either outwardly or by burying it in wrong ways inwardly (Ephesians 4:26). Either way, it can be very destructive and open the door for a demonic stronghold.

—Wrongly Releasing Anger Outwardly

Sometimes we release it with the violence of our bodies or our words. We may lash out with our clenched fists or a slamming door. Or we may lash out just as fiercely with our sharp tongues, harsh tones, biting criticism, accusation, judgment, condemnation, or shame. We might even withdraw in stone cold silence or cruel indifference.

We are not to retaliate in vengeance or violence out of our own response apart from God's leading, not matter another has done. We are not to repay evil with evil or battle tit for tat out of our angry flesh.

> *Do not repay anyone evil for evil, but take thought for what is noble in the sight of all. If it is possible, so far as it depends on you, live peaceably with all. Beloved, never avenge yourselves, but leave room for the wrath of God; for it is written, "Vengeance is Mine, I will repay, says the Lord." No, "if your enemies are hungry, feed them; if they are thirsty, give them something to drink; for by doing this you will heap burning coals on their heads." Do not be overcome by evil, but overcome evil with good* (Romans 12:17–21).

Instead, we admit our anger is there, release it to Him, and let His Spirit lead our actions. We let Him put His thoughts in our minds and His desires in our hearts. We let Him draw the boundary lines and show us when to change the boundary lines of relationship and trust as He wills, not as we will. This is the way of humility, rather than pride, being led by the Spirit, rather than consumed by our flesh.

—Wrongly Releasing Anger Inwardly

Another way that we're angry and we sin is just the opposite reaction: We bury it down inside. We deny that it's there and let it slowly simmer inside like a pressure cooker waiting to pop off the steam or explode. That's sin as well. It's another form of pride that's manifested as control. We can't' really release it if we won't' admit it. So whether we deny or suppress it, we're controlling it out of our own power in self-centered pride, instead of releasing it to God. We often control it by saying things in our heart like: *I won't let them see my anger. I won't let them know they get to me. I won't show them the weakness of my emotions, that they've hurt me, wounded me, offended me, so I will be silent. I will bury it. I will do the Christian thing and act like I'm forgiving them.* All of that's in the power of "I"—the sin of pride.

But the truth is, we're just burring it down inside, and that's just as sinful as hitting somebody in the mouth because we're angry. And it has consequences, too. Just like the ungodly expression of outward anger through violence, anger turned inward, buried inside, is often a key root that bears the bad fruit of depression. It's eating away at our bones deep down inside, ready to fester into bitterness. It saps away all our peace and joy, leaving us weary and heavy of heart and life.

So the sin of control that comes out of pride is a very subtle sin. We may think we're doing the right thing, "the Christian thing," by denying or suppressing our anger, but we need to be releasing it to God in the ways in which He leads us. In any area of my life where I'm in control, God's not. Any area where I am lord, Jesus isn't. That's my human flesh rising up instead of submitting to His Holy Spirit. We must deliberately choose to come back into alignment and communion with the Holy Spirit, allowing God's wisdom to fill our minds, and God's Spirit to lead our actions as He will, instead of how we will.

Fruit of the Spirit instead of Fruit of the Flesh

"Like a city breached, without walls, is one who lacks self-control" (Proverbs 25:28). But godly self-control is not the attitude of "I'm going to control this myself." Godly self-control is submitting our control to His control. We can't control the people and circumstances around us, but we can control our responses by the grace of God and the leading of the Holy Spirit. Then these become opportunities for us to grow in spiritual and emotional maturity. Then our nature becomes more like the nature of Christ, consumed by the zeal of His Holy Spirit rather than consumed by the zeal of our human flesh. Godly "self-control" is a "fruit of the Spirit." An uncontrolled temper, sinning in anger, weather outwardly or inwardly, is a fruit of the flesh (Galatians 5:22–23).

The Lord wants our lives to be filled with His Spirit, so that we bear the fruit of His Spirit. Then, even when God doesn't change our circumstances, we can trust Him to change us through those circumstances that become opportunities for our growth in spiritual maturity. He increases; we decrease as we willingly surrender in trusting submission to His will and ways.

Flesh and Spirit at the Same Time

When we make room for the devil, we're making a choice in our soul to agree with Satan and his plan for us, and we're willingly giving him access and allowing him that place. The places where we make room for him are the places we haven't laid down at the foot of the cross and put under the blood of Jesus. The Holy Spirit cannot fill any area of our lives that the blood of Jesus has not cleansed.

None of this diminishes the truth and reality of the godly spiritual experiences we've had: salvation, baptism of the Holy Spirit, surrender to God, breakthroughs, healing, deliverance, intimacy with God—all of that is very real. But what's happened at those key moments in our lives where we've had spiritual mountaintops, breakthroughs, and encounters, is that we've made a choice in the will of our soul to submit ourselves to God at a deeper level. And there's always more!

When we're seeking more of God and humbling ourselves before Him, we're submitting to Him at another level—another layer of our soul is given over to the lordship of Christ. And God shows up, breaks through, comes in like a flood, and the light and the glory of God rises up within us. So we don't have to be afraid of admitting that we have areas of the flesh that still need to be crucified, and areas of our mind, will, and emotions where we are not fully experiencing the abundance of life in Christ. In addition, we don't have to be prideful or insecure about admitting we still may have unsanctified areas of our soul that still need to be brought to the foot of the cross, cleansed by the blood of Jesus, and filled with the Holy Spirit, as He delivers us from evil and sets us free from the oppression of the thief and enemy of our souls, who comes "only to steal and kill and destroy" (John 10:10).

Then there's a deeper measure of our life that's available for God's gifts to flow, His power to flow, His fruit to flow through our lives. But that doesn't mean that we don't have some more layers that need to be exposed. Nor does it mean that there aren't some more roots that need to be dug up. And it doesn't mean that there aren't still some pockets of

211

resistance to be exposed and removed, where we are still lord and still in charge.

The Bigger Picture of God's Plan

What I'm saying here is that we must remember the big picture of God's plan in our lives to conform us into the image of Christ. Our need for healing and deliverance as Christians doesn't take away at all from being saved, baptized with the Spirit, having a deep and true walk of intimacy and friendship with God or any of those things because all of those things are simply a choice of deeper surrender and submission to God. That's a lifelong process of healing and freedom, wholeness and holiness, with mighty breakthroughs all along the way.

God loves us just as we are, and loves us enough to never leave us as we are. So by the power of His Spirit and the compassion of His healing love and transforming power of healing and deliverance, He loves to set us free to be like Jesus.

Chapter 13

Deliverance from Spiritual Oppression

Submit yourselves therefore to God. Resist the devil, and he will flee from you (James 4:7).

The biblical calling and command to actively submit ourselves to God and to actively resist the devil is a key verse and spiritual principle to experience God's transforming power of healing and deliverance. Here, the Holy Spirit is speaking through James to the Church, to each of us as believers in Christ, in this vital passage giving us a great key to the kingdom of God and a mighty weapon of our warfare.

When we humbly, desperately cry out to God in trusting faith, "Search me, O God, and know my heart; test me and know my thoughts. See if there is any wicked way in me, and lead me in the way everlasting," we are praying for deliverance (Psalm 139:2). When we give the Holy Spirit permission to reveal the "pockets of resistance" of our "flesh" in the unsanctified areas of our soul that have allowed the thief to come steal, kill, and destroy, we are praying for deliverance. We are simply praying the prayer Jesus taught us to pray: "Deliver us from evil" (Matthew 6:13). For the Christian, the evil attacks us, oppresses us, and tries to get a foothold in us in our "flesh"—the unsanctified areas of soul.

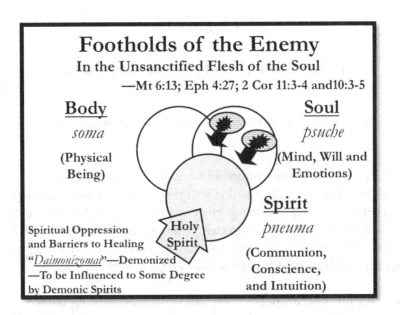

Footholds of the Enemy

In the Unsanctified Flesh of the Soul

—Mt 6:13; Eph 4:27; 2 Cor 11:3-4 and10:3-5

Body

soma

(Physical
Being)

Spiritual Oppression
and Barriers to Healing
"*Daimonizomai*"—Demonized
—To be Influenced to Some Degree
by Demonic Spirits

Holy
Spirit

Soul

psuche

(Mind, Will and
Emotions)

Spirit

pneuma

(Communion,
Conscience,
and Intuition)

"Deliver Us from Evil"

The term "deliverance" comes from the Lord's Prayer—"deliver us from evil" (Matthew 6:13 KJV). So it's important to take note at the outset that Jesus was teaching His disciples and all of the disciples of His church to come and pray for deliverance. He wasn't teaching the heathen, the unbelievers, the ones who did not yet have the Holy Spirit living in their hearts to pray this. He didn't teach us to pray, "Father, deliver *them* from evil." On the contrary, He taught us to pray, "Father, deliver *us* from evil."

As we saw in the previous chapter describing how Christians can be oppressed by demonic spirits, the idea that Christians don't need deliverance is simply not biblical—no matter how nice a thought that might be. As we've seen in God's Word, Christians can "make room for the devil" (Ephesians 4:27). Christians can be "deceived" and "led astray" form "sincere and pure devotion to Christ" and "receive a different spirit from the One (we) received" when we came to Christ and received the Holy Spirit (2 Corinthians 11:3–4). That's why Jesus teaches *us* to humble *ourselves* and admit that *we* need deliverance from evil.

The literal translation of the phrase is actually "deliver us from the evil one," as reflected in many of the modern translations. The Lord is leading us to pray for deliverance from a very personal form of evil. The "evil one" is, of course, Satan—the enemy of our souls, the enemy of the children of God.

> *We know that we are God's children, and that the whole world lies under the power of the evil one* (1 John 5:19).

> *I have given them Your word, and the world has hated them because they do not belong to the world, just as I do not belong to the world. I am not asking You to take them out of the world, but I ask You to protect them from the evil one. They do not belong to the world, just as I do not belong to the world* (John 17:14–16).

Also, the term "deliverance" comes from the King James Version of Jesus' Personal Mission Statement in Luke chapter 4. As Jesus began His earthly ministry in the anointing of the Holy Spirit, He took the scroll of the prophet Isaiah and found the place in chapter 61 where it foretold His coming ministry, declaring:

> *The Spirit of the Lord is upon Me, because He hath anointed Me to preach the gospel to the poor; He hath sent Me to heal the brokenhearted, to preach deliverance to the captives, and recovering of sight to the blind, to set at liberty them that are bruised, To preach the acceptable year of the Lord* (Luke 4:18–19 KJV).

Spiritual Oppression

To "preach deliverance" comes from the Greek word *aphesis*, meaning liberation from captivity; a release from bondage.[26] This is the idea of freedom from spiritual oppression. As Peter said of Jesus and His message of the fullness of God's salvation:

> *You know the message he sent to the people of Israel, preaching peace by Jesus Christ—he is Lord of all. That message spread throughout Judea, beginning in Galilee after the baptism that John announced: how God*

---

[26] Vine's, Strong's 859.

anointed Jesus of Nazareth with the Holy Spirit and with power; how he
went about doing good and healing all who were oppressed by the devil, for
God was with him (Acts 10:36–38).

"Oppressed" means "to exercise harsh control over one; to use one's power against one."[27] Christians and non-Christians alike can be "oppressed by the devil." But Jesus is "Lord of all" and the ministry of the power of His Holy Spirit is for all who will come to Jesus. In fact, deliverance is "the children's bread," a gift of God's love for His people (Matthew 15:22–28 NKJV). In this story of the Canaanite woman seeking healing and deliverance from demons for her daughter, Jesus at first says that that deliverance was only intended for believers in covenant relationship with God during that season, until He saw her desperation, expressed in deep humility and faith. Then He said, "Woman, you have great faith! I will do what you asked" (Matthew 15:28).

"Demonized"—To be Influenced or Afflicted, Not Possessed

Jesus is still binding up the brokenhearted and setting the captives free, by the power of His Holy Spirit for all who will turn to Him for help. But there is much confusion about the availability of Jesus' deliverance ministry for believers. Much of that confusion comes from the translation of the Greek word *daimonizomai* to mean "possessed by demons," when the word really means to be influenced or afflicted by demons in varying degrees of spiritual oppression.[28] The word can be translated, "one who has a demon" (John 10:21), which conveys a more accurate description of demonic "oppression" than the idea of "possession." More accurately, we should say a person is "demonized," not "possessed" by the evil one or his demonic spirits.

We see the connection between sickness and demonic oppression in the ministry of Jesus:

When Jesus entered Peter's house, He saw his mother-in-law lying in bed
with a fever; He touched her hand, and the fever left her, and she got up and

---

[27]Vine's Complete Expository, quoting Strong's 2616.
[28] Vine's Complete Expository, Strong's G1139.

began to serve Him. That evening they brought to Him many who were possessed with demons; and He cast out the spirits with a word, and cured all who were sick. This was to fulfill what had been spoken through the prophet Isaiah, "He took our infirmities and bore our diseases" (Matthew 8:14–17).

Because of healing passages like this, Christians around the world and throughout the generations have sought Jesus for healing of fevers and other sicknesses and diseases. But the context of this passage also speaks of Jesus casting out spirits in this ministry of healing. Sickness is one of the afflictions caused by demons. Someone who is sick is rarely "possessed" by a demon, but is often "oppressed," in terms of being influenced or afflicted in that way by demonic spirits.

For some reason, a distinction is made by some that Christians can have a fever or a sickness but Christians cannot have a demon. When the passage in Matthew says "*this* was to fulfill what was spoken through the prophet Isaiah," "*this*" includes both healing and deliverance. And the passage Matthew says is fulfilled in Jesus Christ, that "He took our infirmities and bore our diseases," is from the famous passage of Isaiah 53 that foretells Jesus dying on the cross for our sins as the suffering servant of God.

> *Surely He has borne our infirmities and carried our diseases; yet we accounted Him stricken, struck down by God, and afflicted. But He was wounded for our transgressions, crushed for our iniquities; upon Him was the punishment that made us whole, and by His bruises we are healed. All we like sheep have gone astray; we have all turned to our own way, and the Lord has laid on Him the iniquity of us all* (Isaiah 53:4–6).

As we discussed earlier, the fullness of "salvation" includes healing, deliverance, and eternal life. Upon Jesus was laid "the punishment that made us *whole.*" The word translated "whole" in this passage is the Hebrew word *shalom.* To be whole is to be healed in spirit, soul, and body; it is to be at *peace* with God, with one another, and within ourselves. For this reason, Jesus is our "Messiah"—the "anointed One of God," who came to bind up the broken-hearted and to set the captives free (Isaiah 61:1; Luke 4:18). Deliverance is a ministry needed as much by believers, as unbelievers.

Jesus "Cast Out" Demonic Spirits

One of the difficulties of understanding spiritual oppression and spiritual freedom is that we have to try to use categories of words from the natural realm to explain spiritual realities in the supernatural realm. In explaining deliverance, sometimes people use the concepts of whether the person is "possessed" or "oppressed." Sometimes the concepts are whether the demonic spirit is on the "inside" or the "outside." Likewise, some speak of whether we "cast out" or "drive away" demonic spirits.

When we talk about spiritual realities, we are talking about "dimensions" which overlap. We live in both the physical dimension and the spiritual dimension; we live in both the natural realm and the spiritual realm. We live out our lives here on earth where time is chronological, but we are also already seated with Christ in the heavenly places where time is eternal (Ephesians 2:4–7). From that standpoint, these categories of whether a spirit is on the "inside" or the "outside" may not really matter. The important point is the degree to which the Holy Spirit and demonic spirits have access and influence in our lives. As we have been discussing, this is primarily determined by the degree to which we are submitted to the Lordship of Jesus Christ.

We encounter our spiritual enemies at each of these levels—in the physical realm and the spiritual realm; in the natural dimension and the supernatural dimension; on the outside and on the inside. There is a hierarchy of spiritual beings with varying levels of authority and territory. There are "rulers and authorities in the heavenly places," "the cosmic powers of this present darkness," "thrones or dominions or rulers or powers," "principalities and powers," and others (Ephesians 3:10; 6:12; Colossians 1:16; 2:15 NKJV).

Demonic spirits are basically the ground troops and foot soldiers in the battle. From the many examples we have of encounters with demonic spirits throughout the New Testament, we see they are assigned to individuals. They desire to inhabit flesh (Matthew 8:31; 12:43). And throughout the encounters between Jesus and demonic spirits, Jesus "cast out" the spirits. He said, "But if it is by the Spirit of God that I cast out demons, then the kingdom of God has come to you" (Matthew

218

12:28). To "cast out" comes from the Greek word *ekballo*, which is a very forceful word meaning to expel, eject, or thrust out.[29]

In the context of deliverance ministry, Jesus described the process of casting out demons with the analogy of raiding a house:

> *But if it is by the Spirit of God that I cast out demons, then the kingdom of God has come to you. Or how can one enter a **strong man's house** and plunder his property, without first tying up the strong man? Then indeed the house can be plundered* (Matthew 12:28–29, emphasis added).

The "strong man" is the ruling demonic spirit assigned to a person. *Satan and his kingdom is a counterfeit of God's kingdom.* From the time we are little children, the Lord has assigned guardian angels to us who continually see the face of our Father in heaven (Matthew 18:10). The strong man is Satan's counterpart. God's angels are there to protect us, and Satan's spirits are there to destroy us (Psalm 91:11–14). In prayer ministry sessions of inner healing and deliverance, these spiritual realities become very clear. The strategy of deliverance for tying up the strong man and plundering his property involves the understanding of the kingdom of God and our keys of the kingdom. It is very significant that Jesus links the process of deliverance with the coming of the kingdom of God.

When the kingdom of God comes in the power of the Spirit of God, the demons are cast out. As the body of Christ on earth in the power of His Holy Spirit, we have "the keys of the kingdom of heaven" to bind up the enemy and cast him out. His gates and defenses will not prevail to keep the disciples of Jesus Christ from plundering the home and property he claims as the kingdom of heaven is opened up.

> *And I tell you, you are Peter, and on this rock I will build My church, and the gates of Hades will not prevail against it. I will give you the keys of the kingdom of heaven, and whatever you bind on earth will be bound in heaven, and whatever you loose on earth will be loosed in heaven* (Matthew 16:18–19).

---

[29] New Strong's Dictionary of Hebrew and Greek Words, G1544.

The kingdom of heaven is where Jesus is King. There will come a day when the kingdom of God is fully manifested throughout the earth, but at the same time, the kingdom of God is being manifested in the heart and soul of the disciples of Jesus Christ. He is the King of Kings and the Lord of Lords. We make him the King of the kingdom of our hearts when we submit to His Lordship as the Lord of Lords within us.

> Once Jesus was asked by the Pharisees when the kingdom of God was coming, and He answered, "The kingdom of God is not coming with things that can be observed; nor will they say, 'Look, here it is!' or 'There it is!' For, in fact, the kingdom of God is within you" (Luke 17:20–21).

> For the kingdom of God is not food and drink but righteousness and peace and joy in the Holy Spirit (Romans 14:17).

The kingdom of darkness is overcome by the kingdom of light. The strong man and his workers are bound up and cast out to the degree that Christ is welcomed in. The unholy spirits must go out as the Holy Spirit comes in. But we must choose if want the Holy Spirit of the kingdom of light to influence us or the unholy spirits of the kingdom of darkness. Both God and Satan will "honor" our choices.

Our lord or master is the Spirit or spirits we agree can have access in our lives. As we have seen, we can "make room for the devil" or make room for the Lord. Both stand at the door and knock. Which one we let in is up to us. That's our legal right and freedom to choose, with the gift of free will the Lord has given to us from His heart for a true relationship of love with us.

The Holy Spirit invites us to open us the door and lift up the gates of our hearts and minds so that the King of Glory may come in! (see Psalm 24:7–10) The enemy of our souls wants us to open up the doors and gates of our hearts and minds to him and his kingdom of darkness. Both the Lord and the enemy seek our permission. The choice is ours.

Legal Rights of the Enemy

Satan is a legalist. I am sure some who have had bad experiences from those in my prior profession as an attorney would say it this way, "Satan is a lawyer." What I mean is that he knows God's law and uses it against us and to his advantage. Any ground that we give to him through our sin against God's ways or our agreement with his ways can and will be used against us.

Our spiritual enemy does not fight fair. "He is a liar and the father of lies" (John 8:44). Satan will not be reading us our rights before he entraps us by his lies and schemes, in order to condemn us by the guilt of our sin.[30] The thing that he fears the most is that we will learn our rights from the Word of God and begin to assert them against him. He prefers that we remain "ignorant of his designs" so that we are "outwitted by Satan" (2 Corinthians 2:11). The last thing he wants is for us to call our "Advocate" to come and deliver us (John 14:26). For our God will come and contend with those who contend with us when we call upon His name.

> *But thus says the Lord: "Even the captives of the mighty shall be taken, and the prey of the tyrant be rescued; for I will contend with those who contend with you"* (Isaiah 49:25).

The Accuser of the Brethren

Satan is "the accuser of the brethren" (Revelation 12:10). He accuses us before God of our sin, as he presses charges against us with his legal grounds, based upon God's law and our violations. The name "Satan" means "adversary."[31]

> *Like a roaring lion your adversary the devil prowls around, looking for someone to devour* (1 Peter 5:8).

Like a lion, Satan and the spirits of his kingdom of darkness take advantage of our weaknesses and devour our "flesh." We are the most vulnerable in our "flesh" because these are the unsanctified areas of our soul, the areas of our lives not yet fully submitted to the Lordship of Jesus Christ. By resisting God and refusing in our self-centered pride or

---

[30] Sin is perhaps the most obvious way we can open the door to the enemy and give him legal rights to oppress us, but we will discuss in more detail later several other ways.

[31] Vine's Complete Expository, Strong's 4567

control to submit to the Lordship of Christ in these pockets of resistance in our flesh, we are giving our adversary legal rights to accuse us before God, using the law of God's own Word against us. Satan knows God's Word well; he even tried to use it against Jesus (Luke 4:9–11). And he used it effectively by questioning it to Eve (Genesis 3:1–7). By his cunning and deception, Satan tries to tempt us and trick us into submitting to him in our flesh, so that we receive one of his unholy spirits in his schemes to ensnare us and entrap us, to lead us away from Christ (2 Corinthians 11:3–4).

Overcomers by the Blood of the Lamb

Satan knows his legal rights and the thing he fears the most is for us to know our legal rights.

> *Then I heard a loud voice saying in heaven, "Now salvation, and strength, and the kingdom of our God, and the power of His Christ have come, for the accuser of our brethren, who accused them before our God day and night, has been cast down. And they overcame him by the blood of the Lamb and by the word of their testimony, and they did not love their lives to the death"* (Revelation 12:10–11 NKJV).

This is the key to victory against our accuser—"the blood of the Lamb." No matter what our sin, no matter what legal rights we may have given our accuser to use to contend against us before the judgment seat of God, "we overcome him by the blood of the Lamb." To "overcome" means to "conquer."[32] We are "more than conquerors through Him who loves us" (Romans 12:37).

> *And when you were dead in trespasses and the uncircumcision of your flesh, God made you alive together with him, when he forgave us all our trespasses, erasing the record that stood against us with its legal demands. He set this aside, nailing it to the cross. He disarmed the rulers and authorities and made a public example of them, triumphing over them in it* (Colossians 2:13–15).

---

[32] *Vine's Complete Expository*, Strong's 3528.

When we have opened the door to the enemy and given him "legal demands" against us in our "flesh," God calls us to bring that "record" to Him through confession and repentance. As we turn away from our sin and shut the door to the enemy, God erases "the record that stood against us" by "nailing it to the cross." He disarms our adversary through the triumph of the blood of the Lamb and the victory of the cross of Christ

Enforcing the Victory of the Cross

Jesus defeated our accuser through the victory of His cross. Jesus' victory becomes our victory as we humble ourselves at the foot of the cross and bring our lives under the blood of Jesus. Our victory begins at the moment of salvation, but we continue to enforce the victory of the cross throughout the process of sanctification. Through confession and repentance of our sins, we continually apply the Lamb's blood and overcome our enemy. By taking up our cross daily, we continually turn away from the world, crucify the flesh, and defeat the devil in every area of our life that we bring under the Lordship of Jesus Christ.

Although the blood of the Lamb has been available to us for over two thousand years, we must apply the blood to our own lives for Christ's victory to become our victory. This is one of the spiritual principles of the New Covenant that the Lord teaches us through the stories of the Old Covenant. In Exodus 12:1–14, God's people were given specific instructions about applying the blood of the Lamb to the doorposts of their homes. If a family did not apply the blood of the Lamb, then they would suffer judgment rather than mercy.

So it is with us. We first apply the blood of the Lamb to the doorposts of our lives in general when we come to Christ in repentance and faith. Then we continue to apply the blood of the Lamb when we bring our specific sins to the foot of the cross and under the blood of Jesus in the specific area of our lives. The pockets of resistance in our flesh are the areas that we have not yet brought to the foot of the cross in repentance. So in a sense, we have not brought those areas under the blood of Jesus. We are still under God's judgment rather than His mercy in those specific areas of our lives. Those are the areas that give legal ground to

223

our adversary to accuse us and condemn us, enforcing God's spiritual principles against us.

> *Do not be deceived; God is not mocked, for you reap whatever you sow. If you sow to your own flesh, you will reap corruption from the flesh; but if you sow to the Spirit, you will reap eternal life from the Spirit* (Galatians 6:7–8).

> *For the time has come for judgment to begin with the household of God* (1 Peter 4:17).

God, in His mercy, will judge us and allow us to suffer the consequences of our resistance to His will and His ways in order to bring us to the place of humility at the foot of the cross. As we turn to the Lord in repentance and faith in those specific areas, His "mercy triumphs over judgment" (James 2:13).

> *He himself bore our sins in his body on the cross, so that, free from sins, we might live for righteousness; by His wounds you have been healed. For you were going astray like sheep, but now you have returned to the Shepherd and Guardian of your souls* (1 Peter 2:24–25).

Deliverance: Resist the Devil and He will Flee

Submission to the Lordship of Jesus Christ is what breaks the power of the enemy and cancels his legal rights to remain. Where we had submitted to an unholy spirit and its unholy nature in our flesh, we now submit to the Holy Spirit of Christ with in us, the hope of glory. Our adversary no longer has any accusation against us. Now we can resist him, command him to go, and he must flee.

> *Submit yourselves therefore to God. Resist the devil, and he will flee from you* (James 4:7).

This is a *promise* of God. The devil "will flee" when we resist him. But it is important to see the full context of this Scripture. We cannot effectively resist the devil unless we first submit to God. We are not resisting the enemy if we are in agreement with his nature. We cannot effectively command the unholy spirit to go until we submitted ourselves

224

to God in that area. The enemy will not flee if he still has legal rights to be there.

Will the devil flee if we do not resist him? The Word of God specifically commands us to "resist the devil." To "resist" is to actively take a stand against our enemy. From the context of the Scripture, this is not a request from God if we feel like it or think it's necessary, it is a command—"Resist him!" *When* we resist him, *then* "he will flee."

There are two important things to note about the command to "resist the devil." First, to "resist" is a very active posture, not passive at all. Some teach that we should not pay any attention to the devil and keep our focus on Jesus. That sounds spiritual and wise, even biblical; but it's not. We are to keep our *primary* focus on Jesus, but this Scriptural command—among others—also calls us to actively resist the devil. We can't resist him if we can't direct our attention to him.

Second, there is a very specific and personal object of our resistance— "resist *him*," the devil. Some would say we just focus on resisting the enemy's lies or thoughts or temptations. But, once again, that's not what the Bible says. We are to "resist *him*." The Scriptural context is not some amorphous evil or evil practice; it is evil personified. It refers to Satan and the demonic spirits of his kingdom of darkness assigned to torment us and distract us from our calling and destiny in Christ.

How do we make the devil flee? By resisting him. How do we resist him? We begin by submitting ourselves to God and His holy nature, by no longer submitting ourselves to the enemy and his unholy nature. Then we can effectively command him to flee, in the name and authority of Jesus. According to the deliverance ministry pattern of James 4:7, submission to God is the first step, resisting the devil is the second step.

Old School Deliverance

Sometimes people attempting deliverance ministry skip the first step. They try to command a demonic spirit to be bound up and cast out in the name of Jesus. We will discuss in a moment some principles about the logistics of the actual process of casting out a demon. But we must realize that when we're helping someone to submit themselves to God

225

in the area where they are being tormented, the demon is not likely to go any time soon. Why should it? It still has a legal right to be there. In a sense, it has been invited there, continuing to be welcomed there because the person is submitting that area to the flesh, and effectively, that spirit, rather than submitting that area to Jesus' Lordship.

I have come to call this "old school deliverance." When the Lord began to reawaken ministries of healing and deliverance in the body of Christ, people were just beginning to learn the spiritual principles of effective ministry. We are still learning. But as a prayer minister of the people in a home group might began to address a demonic spirit in a direct way that was perceived to be at the source of someone's struggle in an area of their life, the demonic spirit would begin to manifest itself in a direct way.

We say a spirit is "manifesting" when it no longer remains hidden, still, or silent behind the scenes in the spiritual dimension, but begins to expose and express itself in the physical dimension as well. Manifestations can take endless forms. Some mild examples would be trembling, headache or pressure, change in body temperature, rolling the eyes toward the back of the head, unholy or deceptive thoughts coming to the persons mind. Some more dramatic examples would be physical movement, shouting, screaming, throwing up, supernatural strength or other phenomena, or the spirit speaking directly in the first person through someone's voice in either the person's voice or a different voice. I have seen a little bit of all of this. It can be pretty exciting, not necessarily in a fun way.

"Old School" practice would generally greet these manifestations with attempts to aggressively take authority in the name of Jesus and command the spirit to be cast out. This battle might go on for several hours or most of the night until either the demon or the deliverance ministers are exhausted and somebody gives up the fight. Even with the different approach we will discuss, sometimes these kinds of battles are hard to avoid, because we can't always pick the time of the battle. But these kinds of extended encounters can be much less common in the ministry of freedom, when we first address the legal rights of the spirit to be there before commanding it to go.

226

The trouble with "Old School" is that the person and the prayer team are resisting the devil with the authority we have, but not first helping the person submit that area of oppression to God. A more effective model of deliverance ministry is the ministry model of James 4:7. First, submit yourself to God; then, resist the devil and he will flee.

Example of "Old School" Deliverance Ministry in India

I will use an example from an experience in ministry to explain some of the spiritual principles I have learned of deliverance ministry. I am choosing a case that's a little more extreme because it involves so many different principles. But first, let me just say that I know that there are probably ways that I have learned and am learning that may not be exactly how the Lord intends. We are all learning and growing in spiritual maturity and spiritual gifting. And one of the primary ways that the Lord teaches us is through learning from our mistakes and the mistakes of others. Thankfully, His grace covers a multitude of sins and redeems many more of our mistakes than we may ever know.

Also, the Lord uses us all differently and gifts us all differently to suit those to whom we are ministering. I know that I personally have much more to learn and maybe even unlearn. Ministers and teachers who become rigid in their own practices can often hinder the creativity of the Spirit and become bound up in a form of religious pride that stifles their spiritual growth and the growth of others. The important thing is that we are willing to learn as we try to obey the leading of the Lord as best as we can. That helps us and those to whom the Lord sends us as ministers of His healing love and freedom.

I have had the joy of being sent by the Lord to minister in India four different times so far—three times as preacher and teacher with ministries, and one time as an attorney, with International Justice Mission. In many parts of India and eastern cultures, the spiritual realm is much more obvious, being more "on-the-surface" and "in-your-face" than in most western cultures. The religious beliefs in the southern province of Tamil Nadu, India, where I have spent most of my time, is a folk religion form of Hinduism. There are many forms of Hinduism, but this form is basically a religion of sacrifice and appeasement—they worship the millions of different "gods" and "idols" which are personal manifestations of the things they fear, for the most part. They worship the snake god, the elephant god, and the various mystical gods that they believe have power over their lives.

"Worship" is going to their temples, which are often small, decorated buildings everywhere, though there are also huge, major temples in some cities. The people give money and food they can scarcely afford to give to the temple god or the temple priest. Sometimes more sadistic sacrifices are required. These are not really "gods" at all; these are "the elemental spirits" confronted by the truth of the gospel of Jesus Christ (Galatians 4:8–10; Colossians 2:8). These are the "idols" and "so-called gods" who take advantage of our God-given desire for spiritual relationship and then deceive the people by misrepresenting and counterfeiting the true identity and nature of the one true God; for "there is no God but one" (1 Corinthians 8:4–6).

On my first trip, I went with Larry Coker as part of his team of teachers and ministers, along with Joe Connelly and Bob McCauley. Larry and I had both received part of our training for ministry, as well as some of our own personal ministry, at the Canadian retreat center for Ellel Ministries of England. That center is now called Singing Waters. It is a powerful ministry of biblically based principles and practices, very similar to the ministry of inner healing and deliverance where I had learned from my first mentor, Dr. Steve Seamands, at Asbury Theological Seminary. This was a time of learning and also confirmation of the things I felt the Lord had been teaching me through my own ministry experiences before going to Canada.

With Larry's team, we held two-week seminars at a number of locations, teaching and ministering to pastors, evangelists, ministry leaders, and their spouses. Our basic approach was to teach them the spiritual principles of inner healing and deliverance, then guide them in prayers to receive ministry as a group and in small groups ministering to one another. It was very effective and powerful. It seemed that in this part of India among these people there was such a great desperation meeting such a high level of faith that healing and deliverance often came instantaneously, though also in the process of little by little and step by step.

We saw many physical healing miracles as well, which was very exciting. Though we went in to much more depth, our basic approach then and still is the deliverance ministry pattern of James 4:7—helping each person submit themselves to God in every area of their lives, as best as they could, and then resisting the devil and commanding him to flee. This was *not* "old school" deliverance.

On my next trip, I taught and ministered with Larry's team again. Then, I had been invited to join another very powerful and effective ministry further south in India after Larry's team went home. This was Gospel Friends, led by Ghuna Kumar, a Spirit-filled man of God who oversees hundreds of churches throughout five states of southern India. Their ministry sends evangelists into poor villages, where the gospel has never been preached. Then they build small churches to make disciples of Jesus Christ. They endure incredible persecution, including beatings and even threats of death to stand firm in the faith, but carry an amazing joy of the Lord. Part of their ministry includes a Bible School and orphanage at one of their bases where I was teaching the leaders on these principles of inner healing and deliverance, though brother Kumar was away in America at the time. It was some of the young students of the Bible school who demonstrated what I call "old school deliverance."

I was teaching during the day, but in the evenings, we were going out to some of the villages to share and preach the gospel. I traveled in a van with the ministry leaders, followed by a bus of the Bible school students who wanted to learn how to evangelize and preach. After preaching one night, our vehicles stopped on the way back to the base. Several of the students came from the bus to get us. A young Bible school student who had just come to join the school was wailing and screaming, swinging her arms wildly in the back of the bus. The students said a demon was taking over her body. I was asked to minister deliverance.

In the courage of Christ alone, I went to the back of the bus to find everything they had said was true, only much more extreme than I had imagined. The young students were trying to take authority over this demon as best they knew how, but their method was fairly crude. They were all screaming at the demon, "Come out of her in the name of Jesus!" At the same time, they were using a form of "the truth encounter" approach to deliverance. They were taking God's truth in the form of their black Bibles and were banging the girl over the head with their Bibles as they commanded the spirit, "Come out!" When it didn't, more aggressive "truth encounters" ensued.

I slipped in next to the girl in the back seat and asked everyone to holster their weapons and be in silent agreement in prayer for the Lord to lead us in ministry to set her free. I explained to them that we war against the spirit, but we love and respect the person. This is a primary rule of deliverance ministry—always think of the person first, and then the enemy. In the "old school," sometimes love and respect for the person takes a back seat to the battle to drive out the demon. We ministered to her all the way back to the mission campus and then in the church until late in the night and early morning.

Knowing Our Authority in Christ

Demons can hear just fine without any yelling or screaming. They don't usually respond to that; they respond to the Lord Jesus Christ and His servants who faithfully assert their authority in Christ—which is really the authority of Christ in us, being asserted through us.

> *Therefore God also highly exalted Him and gave Him the name that is above every name, so that at the name of Jesus every knee should bow, in heaven and on earth and under the earth, and every tongue should confess that Jesus Christ is Lord, to the glory of God the Father* (Philippians 2:9–11).

> *Then Jesus called the twelve together and gave them power and authority over all demons and to cure diseases, and he sent them out to proclaim the kingdom of God and to heal* (Luke 9:1–2).

> *After this the Lord appointed seventy others and sent them on ahead of Him in pairs to every town and place where He Himself intended to go.... The seventy returned with joy, saying, "Lord, in Your name even the demons submit to us!" He said to them, "I watched Satan fall from heaven like a flash of lightning. See, I have given you authority to tread on snakes and scorpions, and over all the power of the enemy; and nothing will hurt you"* (Luke 10:1–19).

And these signs will accompany those who believe: by using My name they will cast out demons ... (Mark 16:17).

Without raising my voice, but with as much confidence and faith as God's grace would allow, I commanded the spirit to be bound in the name of Jesus. I commanded there would be no manifestations, except as Jesus required, declaring there would be no shouting, no screaming, no unclean speech, no throwing up, and nothing that would cause any harm to the girl or to us. I commanded the spirit to be overcome and weakened by the blood of Jesus. I released the holy angels on my ministry team to execute judgment as Jesus led against any act of disobedience.

I wanted the girl to agree with me in her will that she was seeking the help of Jesus and resisting the demonic spirit as best as she could. She didn't speak English, so through an interpreter I spoke in a gentle and firm voice that I was there to help her I needed her to help me by being in agreement with the words and commands I would speak. As I tried to speak, though, the demon began to speak through her voice in a very angry, almost masculine voice in the girl's native Tamil language. The interpreter said the spirit was very angry at my preaching in the village about God's generational blessings. The spirit was claiming power in this girl's life because of generational curses, that no one in her ancestral line had ever received Christ before.

In the ensuing battle, I took the information the demon revealed in its pride and arrogance and used that very information against it. Demons are liars because they serve the father of lies; and anything they ever say must be taken with a grain of salt; but at the same time, they often give themselves away by bragging about their legal rights to remain in a person and continue to torment them. I commanded the demon to stand back from her mind and tried to lead the girl in prayers of confession on behalf of her generations for rejecting God and submitting to false gods, giving the enemy a foothold in her life and in the lives of her family.[33] In a deliverance setting like this, there is a sort of dual consciousness where the person is aware of what is going on even when the demonic

---

[33] We will speak about the biblical basis for generational prayers when we discuss barriers to healing and open doors to the enemy.

spirit is asserting itself through the person's thoughts or voice. Her will was not yet strong enough to speak the prayers out loud, so I had her agree with me in her spirit and soul as best as she could, as I guided her to help me through an interpreter.

I repeatedly commanded the demon to stand back from her mind so I could speak to the girl. Some people who have not done very much deliverance ministry assume that demons must automatically and immediately obey our commands. Sometimes they do, but most of the time, we must persist in asserting our rights. The demons have free will too—Satan and his fallen angels had the freedom to choose to obey God and serve Him and His creation as the "ministering spirits" in the "divine service" they were created to be (Hebrews 1:14 NKJV). Even Jesus was not always able to force the demons to come out with his first command (see Mark 5:8, where Jesus "had said" to the spirit, "Come out of the man," but the demon continued to resist).

There are consequences for their choices, but the demons have a measure of free will even though they are subject the authority of Jesus and His disciples. That's why everything does not always happen as instantaneously as we would like. But with every choice a person makes to submit to God and resist the devil, the sprit's legal rights are being broken and its power is being weakened, as the power of the blood of Jesus is applied and the victory of the cross is enforced.

One time when I was speaking to the girl to tell her what to confess and renounce to break the enemy's hold, the spirit rose up in her, turned her head to look me straight in the eyes and screamed *in English*, "Get away from me!" We all knew this young girl did not yet speak English. While intended to bring fear, those kinds of moments always serve to bring faith to me, as they confirm to me how real the supernatural realm really is. It also revealed how effective our prayers were at weakening the hold of the demon.

Different Schools of Thought and Approaches to Ministry

Let me pause a moment in this story to say there are different schools of thought in deliverance ministry about whether we should speak to a demon, since they are liars. The Bible gives us principles to follow, but not specific guidelines in how to conduct the ministries of healing and deliverance. Jesus healed in many different ways, but using similar principles. Sometimes He spoke a command, sometimes He touched someone, sometimes He spit in the dirt and rubbed mud their eyes. The point is that there is no cookbook; we must be led by the Spirit within the boundaries of the principles of Scripture.

In deliverance, Jesus not only spoke the truth of the Word of God, He also spoke to the demons as He commanded them to come out on many occasions. On at least one occasion He interrogated a demonic spirit, demanding that it reveal information (Mark 5:9). I don't think it is a coincidence that this is on an occasion when the demon did not immediately obey Jesus' command to come out (verse 5:8). Sometimes if one approach doesn't work well, we shift approaches as God leads.

In deliverance, I always try to bring the person into agreement with the truth of who they are in Christ—and much more importantly, who Christ is in them. "You will know the truth and the truth will make you free" (John 8:32). But, like the model of Jesus, I also speak to the demons, at times, and "cast out the spirits with *a word*" (Matthew 8:16 emphasis added). So I don't think that we should be dogmatic about ministry styles or insist that everyone minister in our mold or model alone.

We must each try to follow the biblical principles and the leading of the Holy Spirit, who will never lead us to contradict Scripture, but will lead us many times in creative ways that are consistent with Scripture, if not detailed in Scripture. The cognitive therapy approach of a "truth encounter" is great and effective because God is renewing our minds, and that's why this was a part of Jesus' ministry model. But he also had many "power encounters" when He directly confronted demonic spirits and commanded them to obey Him.

Paul followed Jesus' principles and model of power encounters with demonic spirits when a girl "who had a spirit of divination" was following them, interfering in their ministry:

> *While she followed Paul and us, she would cry out, "These men are slaves of the Most High God, who proclaim to you a way of salvation." She kept*

233

doing this for many days. But Paul, very much annoyed, turned and said to the spirit, "I order you in the name of Jesus Christ to come out of her." And it came out that very hour (Acts 16:17–18).

Once again, it is interesting to note that the spirit did not necessarily come out that very minute, but "that very hour." Also, the spirit was speaking through the voice of the girl, but Paul addressed the spirit in her directly. Here the spirit was speaking the truth about them, so it is also incorrect to say demons never speak the truth or demons are not capable of speaking the truth. Many times, it is the truth they do speak that provides a key to break their legal grounds. Sometimes, the Holy Spirit will reveal this kind of information by "word of knowledge," especially if someone on team operates in this spiritual gift, but He does not always (1 Corinthians 12:8).

The Holy Spirit "allots to each one individually just as the Spirit chooses," not as we choose (1 Corinthians 12:11). Many times the Lord calls us to use different gifts and depend upon Him in different ways, so that we grow up into maturity in many different ways, together with others of other gifts (Ephesians 4:11–13).

In my career as a trial lawyer, I often encountered witnesses who would lie about certain key facts. In cross-examination I would press them for the details. For a lie to be believable, it almost always has to have a measure of truth. But I would use the kernels of truth to unravel the lie. Getting a spirit's name reveals its nature; and knowing its nature can help reveal how it got in or its legal rights to remain. Though not everyone would necessarily be comfortable or be led to use this style, I have found interrogation of demonic spirits to be a very effective tool to have available at times in my tool-belt for deliverance ministry. So did Jesus (see Mark 5:9).

On earth, Jesus spoke the words the Father gave Him to speak and minister in the ways the Holy Spirit led Him. We don't have a written record of all Jesus did and said, nor do we know all the details of how He ministered healing and deliverance in every situation (John 21:25). But we can learn from the examples we have and the principles they teach, as we listen for the leading of the Lord to minister to others.

234

Back to the Story of Deliverance in India

The Lord meets us where we are. This young girl's will to choose God and resist the devil was severely restricted by the power this spirit had over her. But the Lord did not expect of her more than she could give Him at each step of the battle. But the more she exercised her will to agree with God and resist the devil, the more her will was freed to join in agreement with us in the battle. With every choice to submit to God and resist the devil, the demonic spirit was being weakened and its power to resist diminished.

I felt led to interrogate the demonic spirit. I commanded it to reveal any legal grounds it claimed to have. I declared that if the spirit could not claim any legal right to remain, then its silence was consent, which meant it had no legal right and it must go. In the classic arrogance and pride of spirits who are not used to Christians taking their authority in Christ to outwit them, the spirit finally revealed a number of keys that would soon led to its own demise.

Finally the demon bragged that its power to remain in her was that she was dedicated as a young child to the temple of Kali. The spirit also claimed that when she came to the Bible college, her relatives that dedicated her were furious and were sending witchcraft curses against her in retaliation for her conversion to Christ. The spirit kept claiming, "She's mine! She's mine! And I won't let her go." And at the beginning of this spiritual battle, this young girl seemed as close to a truly possessed person as I have ever prayed for. But greater is He who is in us than he who is in the world; and the gates of hell cannot prevail against Christ and His church when we persevere in faith and the power of His name.

We kept applying the blood of Jesus, by bringing every area of her life under the Lordship of Jesus Christ—not just in general, but also in these specific areas that were still giving ground to the enemy to torment her. I kept speaking to her human will to join with me in prayers of generational confession and renouncing the unholy dedication, while affirming her dedication to Jesus.

We stood against any witchcraft and curses, declaring and praying God's will from His Word and applying His spiritual principles in Jesus' name.

Jesus was made to be a curse for us through the cross, so that every curse against us is broken. "Christ redeemed us from the curse of the law by becoming a curse for us—for it is written, "Cursed is everyone who hangs on a tree" (Galatians 3:13). As God revealed through Balaam, no one can curse those whom God has blessed (Numbers 23:8). "Like a sparrow in its flitting, like a swallow in its flying, an undeserved curse goes nowhere" (Proverbs 26:2). By bringing these areas under the blood of Jesus, the enemy's power was being weakened and broken, as we overcame him by the blood of the Lamb and the word of our testimony (Revelation 12:11).

At one level, witchcraft and curses are the manipulation of spiritual forces for our fleshly, selfish purposes. There is power in the prayer of agreement, for good or for evil (Matthew 18:19; Genesis 11:6). As we agree with God's Word in the nature of His name for one another, we come into agreement with His will for them, releasing the Holy Spirit to move in their lives. The enemy uses that same principle against us in the opposite way. As one agrees with the enemy's nature to kill, steal, and destroy in someone's life, they come into agreement with his will for in a victim's life, releasing his unholy spirits to move in evil ways.

We Confront the People Differently than the Demons

God calls us to deal with the human beings who harm us differently than the spiritual beings who carry out their sinful desires. We are to confront the human beings by speaking the truth in love and releasing them to God.

> But I say to you that listen, Love your enemies, do good to those who hate you, bless those who curse you, pray for those who abuse you
> (Luke 6:27–28).

I often lead someone in prayer for those who have hurt them or are trying to hurt them, to bless them with the fear of God and His conviction for their sin that will lead to repentance that will then lead to mercy. This is a way, with God's grace, we can choose to bless those who curse us, pray for those who persecute us, and love those who hate us. But while we forgive the human beings, we are to war against the spiritual beings.

For our struggle is not against enemies of blood and flesh, but against the rulers, against the authorities, against the cosmic powers of this present darkness, against the spiritual forces of evil in the heavenly places (Ephesians 6:12).

I often pray passages from the Psalms and Old Testament war passages, applied to our spiritual "enemies," rather than human "enemies." When we see and pray these passages in light of spiritual warfare rather than human warfare, the Scriptures and the spiritual principles they are intended to convey come to life. We are to be unfailing in our release of mercy for the human beings involved, while at the same time unrelenting in our execution of judgment toward the spiritual beings involved.

For the Lord takes pleasure in his people. He adorns the humble with victory. Let the faithful exult in glory; let them sing for joy on their couches. Let the high praises of God be in their throats and two-edged swords in their hands, to execute vengeance on the nations and punishment on the peoples, to bind their kings with fetters and their nobles with chains of iron, to execute on them the judgment decreed. This is glory for all His faithful ones. Praise the Lord! (Psalm 149:4–9)

As we pray and take our stand in the name of Jesus and in the authority of Christ—the authority of Christ in us—God begins to move. In Scripture, the name speaks of the nature. To speak or pray in the name of Jesus is to speak or pray in the nature of Jesus—as one in perfect agreement with God's Word and God's will. Those are prayers we know God will answer because those are the prayers He is putting on our hearts through His Spirit in accordance with His will (Romans 8:26–27; 1 John 5:14–15).

The Lord sends His holy angels to execute His word in response to our words and prayers in accordance with His will (Daniel 10:10–12; Psalm 91:11 and 103:20). If we could see the angelic host fighting with us in the spiritual battles of that realm, as some are sometimes gifted to do, we would not fear. "For there are more with us than there are with them" (2 Kings 6:16). What we speak in the earthly realm is happening in the spiritual realm, as we speak in the name and nature of Jesus.

237

Truly I tell you, whatever you bind on earth will be bound in heaven, and whatever you loose on earth will be loosed in heaven. Again, truly I tell you, if two of you agree on earth about anything you ask, it will be done for you by My Father in heaven. For where two or three are gathered in My name, I am there among them (Matthew 18:18–20).

Victory in Jesus!

That night in India, we persisted in prayer and asserted our authority in Christ. We helped this young woman bring every area of her life under the Lordship of Christ, submitting to God, resisting the devil, and commanding him to flee. At last, she was completely set free by the power of the blood of Jesus. When I saw her the next morning, she was very peaceful, but very tired. So were we! But we all praised God for His victory in Jesus' name!

I recently asked Brother Ghuna Kumar about this young woman, since it's been several years now since this deliverance. With his broad smile, he said, "Praise the Lord! She is doing very well. She has much joy and peace in her heart." I know much of that is due to the steady discipleship that new Christians receive through the ministry of Gospel Friends. They not only bring new babes in Christ into the kingdom, but bring them into a loving, trusting relationship they are taught and helped to live out day by day. This is a very important principle to follow, especially following deliverance ministry. As Jesus taught, the spirits will be very angry to lose their home and will want to return.

When the unclean spirit has gone out of a person, it wanders through waterless regions looking for a resting place, but not finding any, it says, "I will return to my house from which I came." When it comes, it finds it swept and put in order. Then it goes and brings seven other spirits more evil than itself, and they enter and live there; and the last state of that person is worse than the first (Luke 11:24–26).

So healing and deliverance must always be seen in the broader context of sanctification and discipleship. In Christ, our bodies are the temples of the Holy Spirit. Our hearts are to be houses of prayer, surrendered and submitted to the Lord alone, filled with His Holy Spirit alone. God wants us to make room for Him and not make room for the devil. He wants to set us free, but that's not the end. He wants to transform us and conform us into the image of Christ and then send us in ministry for His glory. He wants to set us free to be like Jesus.

Deliverance from our "Enemies"

All of the stories of the Old Covenant Scriptures serve as examples and illustrations to teach us spiritual principles "for our instruction" (Romans 15:4). They point us to Christ, who fulfills the law and the prophets, and teach us spiritual principles for life in Christ under the New Covenant (Matthew 5:17; 2 Timothy 3:14–17). There are many passages of the Old Testament which speak of deliverance in the sense of being delivered or rescued from physical enemies, which speak to us of being delivered from our spiritual enemies.

David's Psalms often cry out for the Lord's deliverance. I often pray Psalm 18 over a person during deliverance ministry. It lets them see the heart of Jesus for them, rushing in to destroy their spiritual enemies with a sword in His hand and fire in His eyes:

> *I love you, O Lord, my strength. The Lord is my rock, my fortress, and my deliverer, my God, my rock in whom I take refuge, my shield, and the horn of my salvation, my stronghold. I call upon the Lord, who is worthy to be praised, so I shall be saved from my enemies.*

> *The cords of death encompassed me; the torrents of perdition assailed me; the cords of Sheol entangled me; the snares of death confronted me. In my distress I called upon the Lord; to my God I cried for help. From His temple He heard my voice, and my cry to Him reached His ears.*

> *Then the earth reeled and rocked; the foundations also of the mountains trembled and quaked, because He was angry. Smoke went up from His nostrils, and devouring fire from His mouth; glowing coals flamed forth from Him. He bowed the heavens, and came down; thick darkness was under His feet. He rode on a cherub, and flew; He came swiftly upon the wings of the wind. He made darkness His covering around Him, His canopy thick clouds dark with water. Out of the brightness before Him there broke through His clouds hailstones and coals of fire. The Lord also thundered in*

the heavens, and the Most High uttered His voice. And He sent out His arrows, and scattered them; He flashed forth lightning, and routed them.

Then the channels of the sea were seen, and the foundations of the world were laid bare at Your rebuke, O Lord, at the blast of the breath of Your nostrils. He reached down from on high, He took me; He drew me out of mighty waters. He delivered me from my strong enemy, and from those who hated me; for they were too mighty for me. They confronted me in the day of my calamity; but the Lord was my support. He brought me out into a broad place; He delivered me, because He delighted in me (Psalm 18:1–19).

When I begin to personalize this Scripture and declare it over a person receiving prayer ministry, with the authority and power of Jesus' name, I can always sense the enemy trembling in fear at the coming of the glory of the Lord in power. "Let God rise up, let His enemies be scattered; let those who hate Him flee before Him" (Psalm 68:1).

We Have an Active Role in Deliverance

Psalm 18 also illustrates our role in our own deliverance and in the ministry of deliverance for others. David begins by calling upon the name of the Lord as his Deliverer, then he sees the Lord comes in power to deliver him from his enemies. But David also discusses his own role to agree with God and take an active stance in resisting the enemy. He gives all credit to God as the Deliverer, but at the same time, acknowledges that what God is doing in the spiritual realm, He is also doing through his people in the natural realm. We have a very active role, not a passive role, in God's ministry of deliverance:

He trains my hands for war, so that my arms can bend a bow of bronze. You have given me the shield of your salvation, and your right hand has supported me; Your help has made me great. You gave me a wide place for my steps under me, and my feet did not slip.

I pursued my enemies and overtook them; and did not turn back until they were consumed. I struck them down, so that they were not able to rise; they fell under my feet. For You girded me with strength for the battle; You made my assailants sink under me. You made my enemies turn their backs to me,

240

and those who hated me I destroyed. They cried for help, but there was no one to save them; they cried to the Lord, but He did not answer them. I beat them fine, like dust before the wind; I cast them out like the mire of the streets (Psalm 18:34–42).

This might seem like blasphemy if this were not the Scripture, and God's consistent plan to minister His love and His power through His people who submit to Him in humble obedience and trusting faith. We are called to receive and minister God's deliverance from our spiritual enemies. This is what the Lord means when He says through Paul:

The God of peace will shortly crush Satan under your feet. The grace of our Lord Jesus Christ be with you (Romans 16:20).

The Lord is the Deliverer. And in His sovereignty, He has chosen to minister His deliverance through His people. God is the One who crushes Satan; but at the same time, He has chosen to crush him under our feet—as we exercise our authority and faith in obedience to Christ.

*The Son of God was revealed for **this** purpose, to destroy the works of the devil* (1 John 3:8, emphasis added).

Jesus, the Son of God is continuing His ministry of destroying the works of the devil, the evil one, today—through His body, filled with His Spirit, obeying His commission. "As the Father has sent Me, so I send you" (John 20:21). He trains our hands for this war (Psalm 18:34). And He rejoices when He sees us return to Him with joy, saying, "Lord, in Your name even the demons submit to us!" (Luke 10:17)

Chapter 14

Renewed and Restored in Christ

The "New Self" — "Renewed in the Spirit"

> *Truth is in Jesus. You were taught to put away your former way of life, your old self, corrupt and deluded by its lusts, and to be renewed in the spirit of your minds, and to clothe yourselves with the new self, created according to the likeness of God in true righteousness and holiness* (Ephesians 4:20–24).

The "new self" is that part of us that is whole and free, surrendered and submitted to the Lordship of Jesus Christ, and sanctified by the Holy Spirit into "the likeness of God in true righteousness and holiness." The "old self" is the flesh, the unsanctified area of the soul that is not yet like Jesus. The old self is what is to be crucified and buried, but the old self does not die easily and it does not die instantaneously the moment we pray the sinner's prayer.

At home, I have an old, handmade rocking chair where I come to meet the Lord morning by morning in the communion of prayer. It used to be painted white when it was sitting in the living room of dear friends, Greg and Connie Gallaher. Greg was one of the pastors at our home church before the Lord called them to ministry in Cambodia. Before they left, they gave away most of what they owned. This old rocker seemed to fit me just right, so it's where I always sat when we went to their home.

A few days before they left for Cambodia, they brought it over and gave it to me. But it wasn't painted white anymore. Greg had stripped away all the layers of paint, sanded it down, varnished it, and restored it to its natural beauty of solid oak. Connie said it took Greg a long time, especially sanding away all the tight places around the carved spindles on the back. But he said it was a labor of love and we were all thrilled to see what beauty was hidden beneath all that paint. What a gift! That's how the Lord is with us in His labor of love. It hurts at times, as He strips away all the layers of the old self that people have put on us and we have received onto ourselves—our pride, ego, insecurities, fears, and all the other ways we've allowed ourselves to become somebody different than who we really are inside. But God patiently and lovingly takes His time with us, even in the places where we make it the hardest for Him to reach us. He renews us, restoring us into the true self that He created us to be—according to His likeness, but in a uniqueness of beauty made by His hands, like no one else in the world. What a gift!

God wants to renew us in our spirits of our minds—in our spirit and soul and body; in our mind and will and emotions. He wants to clothe us with the nature of Christ, to transform us and sanctify us into His likeness in true righteousness and holiness. That's a process; and He is faithful to bring to completion all that He has begun—step by step, layer by layer, and little by little. But He will not force us to embrace the process of sanctification. It always seems to come back to this key principle: God is love; He has created us for a relationship of love; and to have a true relationship of love, we must always have the freedom to love Him or not, to trust Him or not, to go on with Him or not. He will not override our freedom to choose, because if He did, it would take away the potential for a true relationship of love.

So God allows His spiritual principles to have their full effect in our lives. He allows us to reap what we sow, to receive by the measure we give, to be forgiven as we forgive others, and so forth. He allows the circumstances and struggles of our lives to expose those things in us that need to change. He'll let us get miserable enough in our flesh that we're finally ready to come out of our flesh. He'll keep putting His finger in the tender areas until we finally cry out to Him for healing. And He will allow our pockets of resistance be exposed until we become desperate enough to seek deliverance from the insurgents who use them as their base of operations to steal and kill and destroy in those areas of our lives.

Set Free from Our Strongholds

The answer to getting free from the enemy's strongholds built up through the pockets of resistance in our flesh is this key verse:

> *Submit yourselves to God, resist the enemy and he will flee*
> (James 4:7).

244

This is the heart of deliverance ministry, which we will discuss in more detail in the following section. As we submit these pockets of resistance to God—the ungodly, unsanctified areas of our flesh—then we can arise. We can resist the devil and push him out while the Holy Spirit begins to rise up within us, increasing as we decrease, as we are filled with the fullness of God. That's this journey that will bring us into wholeness and freedom. This is God's plan: He wants us to be healed and delivered. He wants us to be whole and free. (1 Thessalonians 5:23).

So that's the big picture. Even though we start off this life as a diamond in the rough, God wants to call forth the diamond, call forth who He created us to be, call forth our gifting, anointing, and purpose as He chisels off the rough. Cleanse us from all the defilement, free us from everything that is unholy, and impure. We are the priests of God, and we are ministers of our God (Revelation 1:6), and He wants us to minister to Him in holiness and purity. He wants to welcome us into the very Holy of Holies in complete, unhindered freedom. He's inviting us to enter in to the fullness of His presence to minister to Him, and He sends us forth in His power to minister to others. We are His vessels who are so pure, holy, and clean, that the anointing that flows through us with a holy intensity is released in power to accomplish His purposes upon the earth. He is sanctifying us in spirit, soul, and body.

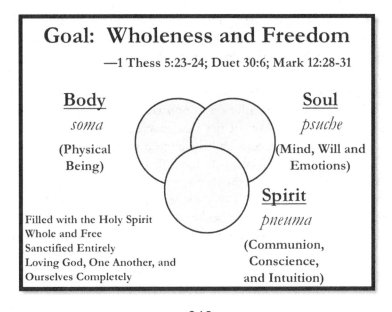

Goal: Wholeness and Freedom
—1 Thess 5:23-24; Duet 30:6; Mark 12:28-31

Body
soma

(Physical Being)

Soul
psuche

(Mind, Will and Emotions)

Spirit
pneuma

(Communion, Conscience, and Intuition)

Filled with the Holy Spirit
Whole and Free
Sanctified Entirely
Loving God, One Another, and
Ourselves Completely

Whole and Free in Christ

When we yield ourselves to the Lordship of Christ in every area of our lives—as best as we can by God's grace—He heals us, delivers us, and fills us with His Holy Spirit. We're able to love God and love one another. Then He sends us forth and frees us to be like Jesus.

One of my great joys in ministry is the chance to sow into the lives of God's servants. And I'm so thankful for the way the Lord has used His servants to sow into mine. It works both ways so often. One who has become a great friend of our ministry and family is Rev. Heather Butler of Wales. The Lord has gifted her with the heart of a prophetic psalmist, as she sings the song of Lord prophetically over people to release His healing love and freedom. The Lord often sends her to the nations to speak the messages he puts in her heart. On her first ministry visit to Kentucky, we invited her to minister at one of our ministry's city-wide gatherings called The Fountain, and joined her and another prophetic minister, Mary, from Wales. Along the way, Heather received another level of healing in her own life and she's graciously agreed to let us hear her story.

Heather's Story of Healing Prayer Ministry

Heather: Have you ever had one of those moments when the world suddenly seemed to stand still, as you tried to work out what happened in your life to make you the person that you are?

I had many unresolved issues in my life. I'd been through seven years of psychotherapy after the death of my son Eric, the abuse that I'd suffered as a child, and the breakup of my first marriage. Emotionally, I was a wreck. I trusted no one and had developed a mask that I wore really well. To most people I looked in control. I was a woman in ministry who travelled abroad alone, the ministry was doing great, and for those looking from the outside, I was a successful woman in control or her life. In all honesty, though, the reality was that my life was falling apart on the inside and I was spiralling out of control emotionally. You see, the psychiatrist could lead me to a place where I could see what the issues were, but he could not seem to set me completely free!

246

I remember crying out in the midnight hours for the Lord to help me. I was desperate to change, but didn't know how it was ever going to happen. My life was anything but happy. I was out of control, and that made me feel insecure and uncertain of my future.

One of my greatest fears was of abandonment—being left alone, tossed aside, not wanted anymore. My father is still alive, but he was never there for me. He said he loved me but his actions belied the truth. During the most painful times of my life, he had abandoned me. He simply didn't visit or even check to see how I was. I pretended that I didn't care, but I did care. I needed the reassurance of an arm around me, words of comfort, someone to tell me that everything was going to be alright. The rejection that I felt was all consuming, and I was fast falling into an abyss from which I didn't know how to escape.

I also had scars left from sexual abuse as a child, and the deep mistrust that they brought into my life. It had meant that I was very careful about not getting into a car with a man that I didn't know well, and I constantly made sure that my children were safe and that no one had access to them unless I knew them well. I kept people at arm's length, desperately wanting to be loved, yet pushing people away and rejecting them before they could reject me.

I met Rev. Tommy Hays of Messiah Ministries in May 2004. I was the speaker for the night at The Fountain, his ministry's monthly gathering of people from various churches in the area. I was very excited to be running with a message into Kentucky. I had flown in from Wales full of expectation, the meeting went really well, and many friendships that last even today were birthed and have grown.

No one would ever have known the mess that I was in except for my husband. He was a constant supply of support and love, but he simply didn't know what to do with me, and despaired of having a wife who felt so insecure, and all that it meant in our relationship—the constant questions about his fidelity, about his love for me, it was a nightmare. I constantly worried about losing him—that he would leave the house one day and not come home because he'd had an accident and died.

It was during this visit that Tommy spoke to me about having some personal prayer ministry for myself. I was shocked that he had seen through the mask, and I felt concerned that others would have seen me as I truly was. He reassured me, and told me that he felt that the Lord had some very specific things that He wanted to deal with in my life, and I agreed to go and meet with him and his prayer partner for healing prayer ministry.

I sat there dazed, not knowing where to start, concerned that if they saw me as I really was that they would reject me. I tried to compose myself, but during the prayer time something happened to me.

As Tommy prayed, he asked the Lord to reveal to me areas of my life that needed healing, and he prayed that I would see what it was that the Lord wanted to touch upon that day. You must understand that Tommy has a wonderful father's heart, and that even the tone of his voice is reassuring. He is a man of real compassion, and wanted to see me set free from the bondage of the life that I was living. I didn't know this man, yet everything within me felt that I could trust him and that I could pour out my heart, knowing that I was in a safe place.

As we went through many issues, Tommy would ask simple questions; questions that made me look at how I had felt about those things that had brought such hurt and pain into my life. His prayer partner would interject at times and ask me what this picture was that they could see, as the Lord revealed things, giving Tommy the opportunity to lead me through those things one by one.

I was shocked as I began to cry uncontrollably. I shook with emotion as I was led into the realization that I mourned the loss of my innocence. Because of the abuse, I had grown up feeling dirty, tainted, and unclean, and because other men throughout the years had come and defiled me, I'd felt that it was my fault, and that I had done something to invite them to treat me in that way.

Tommy explained to me, as a good father would, that the abuse was *not* my fault, and that Jesus wanted to bring healing into that area of my life. He went on to explain that as I grieved my loss, that Jesus was able to restore that innocence and purity to me, and he asked Jesus to come into

248

the midst of those memories to heal and cleanse me. The abuse had affected me mentally, physically and spiritually, but now was the time to come out of the cocoon of darkness and entrapment and out into a world of freedom and hope.

As Tommy prayed over me, I began to feel an anger rise within me, and suddenly I could see that there was a big problem. I wasn't afraid by what I saw, but I was taken aback by the two things that began to happen to me as Tommy prayed for release. I could clearly see myself as a small child, yet here I was as an adult looking in on my own life. I saw a dark shadow leaning over me. I knew that it was the tormentor, and he stood over me, trying to stop me from receiving the truth, telling me that I was no good, that I wasn't worthy to be in that place, and that freedom could not come because I'd allowed the abuse to continue in many forms over the years.

But it was a lie, and as I spoke these things out to Tommy, he bound the voice of the tormentor in the name of Jesus, and released me from the bondage of the lies—those words spoken over me. He took authority over every demonic influence, one by one, and rendered the influence of it over my life null and void! One by one, he cancelled in the name of Jesus the lie of the enemy, decimating every act of him against me until I was totally set free.

Tommy showed me the reality of a loving Father, a Father who had seen it all, and who had made provision for me to come and be ministered to so that I would be made whole.

We prayed about the abuse, the emotional turmoil of guilt and pain, over lost relationships, cutting the ties to all that had oppressed me due to them. I was released from the pain of losing my son, of my broken marriage, the anger that I felt at not having a father who was there for me, and the sadness that had caused me.

Jesus had come! He had come and taken part in every aspect of that meeting. He had made himself known to me in every situation as Tommy prayed, and gently led me into forgiveness of others and myself, leading me into a place of repentance before the Lord, as one by one I was able to release those who hurt me over the years.

249

One of the biggest triumphs was coming to a place where I was able to minister not only to the abused myself, but I was even able to come alongside and pray for someone who had been an abuser, who was now totally shattered by what he had done. Confronted by this man who was broken and remorseful, all I felt for him was compassion, and a deep, deep sense of the love of Jesus for him. I knew at that moment, that the healing I received was real, and not only that but that it had become an active force within me that enabled me to break the power of suffering in his own life, and be part of breakthrough in him.

I have been to see Tommy and his ministry on three occasions for prayer over the last few years, and each time I feel the change in my life—the freedom. Something happened to me in that first meeting with Tommy Hays that changed my life forever; I met with a Father, a heavenly Father who wanted to deal with every thought, every emotion, every physical sickness, and reach into the depths of me in healing on every level. I had an encounter with the love of Jesus poured into every area that brought restoration and healing on such a scale that my life was completely changed.

You know what? After that prayer ministry time, my whole appearance changed as the guilt and shame fell off of me, and as forgiveness entered into me. I not only felt brand new inside, but I looked a picture of health! There was something different about me. There was a cleansing that was recognizable in my face, and I felt so clean that I shone with the glory of God.

Today, I have put those same principles into practice. I now run / lead a healing rooms ministry on our island of Anglesey here in Wales. We visit people in their own homes to pray and break the bondage of sickness, sin, and oppression from over their lives. The treasure I received, I am now able to pour into others. We have seen some wonderful miracles of the Lord as He has brought healing on every level into the lives of others. And I feel so privileged to have been brought in the first instance into a place of safety, to a person with the Father's heart in whom the lord had invested great compassion and love for those who were suffering.

Messiah Ministries is what it says it is—a ministry of the Father to heal the broken hearted and set the captives free, by and through the love and grace of our Messiah, our Lord Jesus Christ. All in the power of the Holy Spirit! I praise God every day for the change the Lord made in my life through this ministry, and for the joy of being able to minister in the same way into the lives of others. God bless you as you hear my story, and may the freedom and healing love of God become a great part of your story!

Part 4 – Seven Potential Barriers to Healing

God's will is to heal us and make us whole. He has made provision for our healing through the blood of Jesus Christ. But we are not always experiencing the fullness of our salvation on this side of heaven. Sometimes there are barriers to our healing of spirit, soul, or body. At times, it may have something to do with us—our heart, our faith, our sin. But at other times, it may have absolutely nothing to do with us at all. It may involve our response to the sins of others or it may not have anything to do with sin at all. It may involve the sins and curses of the generations before us or the sins and curses of those around us in our culture, affecting our land and our lives. It may involve—more than anything—the fact that we live our lives in a broken, fallen world, where we are all affected by one another, now and throughout all generations.

The kingdom of God has come, but it has not yet fully come. It is not yet fully manifested on earth as it is in heaven. There is still brokenness and bondage in our lives and in all creation, as we long for God's redemption of all things. We live in the time between the coming of the kingdom of God in Christ and the ultimate fulfillment and consummation of the kingdom of God when Christ comes again in final victory.

We each have a personal journey of healing and wholeness with the Lord, but at the same time, we are not alone in this journey. We are affected by one another, the generations before us, and the cultures and communities around us. In addition, we're affected by a spiritual enemy who is doing everything in his power to steal, kill, and destroy, so that we do not experience the fullness of God's will for our lives.

In our own lives and in the lives of others, we sometimes don't know why healing and deliverance doesn't come. Sometimes the best response to someone asking why is simply, "I just don't know." At the same time, there are spiritual principles affecting our healing and wholeness which God has revealed to us in His Word. He wants us to know His Word and seek out those things that He desires to teach us so that may be breakthroughs of the barriers to our healing and wholeness. "It is the glory of God to conceal things, but the glory of kings is to search things out" (Proverbs 25:2). Also, we are to "grow in wisdom" (Psalm 90:12 NLT).

I would like to highlight seven key barriers to healing that I have noticed as I have learned from others and learned from the experiences of my ministry. There are, of course, other areas and categories, but I have come to use these seven because these are general enough to cover most areas, they are fairly easy to remember, and they help focus our times of prayer ministry. My seven categories for prayer ministry are:

(1) Personal Sin
(2) Generational Sins, Cycles, and Curses
(3) Unholy Responses
(4) Words and Attitudes
(5) False Spirituality
(6) Unholy Ties
(7) Brokenness of Unresolved Trauma

Each area can be a barrier or blockage to our healing and wholeness. Likewise, each area can be a potential means the enemy may use to gain access and influence to oppress us and block the plans and purposes of God in and through our lives. Within each of these general categories, there are often subcategories as well, such as unforgiveness, judgments, word curses, inner vows, etc. We will discuss these all in some detail, along with sample prayers for healing and deliverance using these biblical, spiritual principles of prayer ministry.

In a sense, each one of these barriers and blockages is the opposite of the freedom and blessings the Lord wants to bring into our lives. They are Satan's perversions of God's promises. For example, God wants to forgive us for every specific personal sin, but the enemy wants to condemn us for every specific personal sin. God wants to bring generational blessings, but the enemy wants to bring generational curses. God wants us to receive His Word and believe His truth, but the enemy wants us to receive his thoughts, often accepting them to be our own, and believe his lies. God wants to strengthen our holy ties and bonds for one another, but the enemy wants to break our holy bonds and form unholy ties and bonds with one another, and further examples could be given.

254

Satan is a created being, now fallen and in rebellion, who can't create anything on his own. Instead, he has to try to use what God has created for our good against us, perverting God's principles by drawing us into sin against God, ourselves, and others so he can accuse us and condemn us. He is the accuser and the deceiver who perverts the truth and principles of God and uses them against us. His tactics heap embers of condemnation on us, which are designed to engulf us in flames of destruction that divide us from intimacy with God. And He doesn't play fair, often attacking when we are the most vulnerable.

To understand these seven categories is to understand many of the enemy's devices and strategies, "so that we may not be outwitted by Satan; for we are not ignorant of his designs" (2 Corinthians 2:11). And in the process, we also understand more of the ways we often "make room for the devil" through indulging the unholy desires of our flesh in sin, embracing the thoughts he sends, and often becoming vulnerable through the sins of others and our responses
(Ephesians 4:27).

Chapter 15

Personal Sin

In a broad sense, sin is disobedience to the perfect will of God. We are responsible for our choices before God. And our choices have consequences, based upon God's spiritual principles. He spoke these principles into existence and set them in motion to help us and encourage us to bring our lives into alignment with His will and ways. One of His spiritual principles is that obedience brings blessings. But by that same principle, the opposite is also true. Disobedience brings curses. "For the wages of sin is death, but the free gift of God is eternal life in Christ Jesus our Lord" (Romans 6:23).

We need not fear the broadest possible definition of sin, because God gives us the broadest possible definition of grace. There's no sin He will not forgive if we'll admit it and bring it to the foot of the cross and under the Blood of Jesus. His loving desire for us is to, "forgive us our sins and cleanse us of all unrighteousness" (1 John 1:9). "For the Lord is good; His steadfast love endures forever, and His faithfulness to all generations" (Psalm 100:5).

Freedom to Choose

God gives us the freedom to choose. Our choices of submission to the obedience of God open the door for blessings into our lives. By the same token, our choices of rebellion in disobedience to God open the door for curses in our lives. Just because a door is open does not necessarily mean something will come in, but it does prepare the way and make room; increasing the potential at the very least.

> *You must therefore be careful to do as the Lord your God has commanded you; you shall not turn to the right or to the left. You must follow exactly the path that the Lord your God has commanded you, so that you may live, and that it may go well with you, and that you may live long in the land that you are to possess* (Deuteronomy 5:32–33).

Our choices not only affect our lives, they affect the lives of everyone else. Further, they not only affect our lives in our generation, but also

257

the lives of our descendants to follow, as we will cover in more detail in the section on generational sin, cycles, and curses in another chapter.

> *I call heaven and earth to witness against you today that I have set before you life and death, blessings and curses. Choose life so that you and your descendants may live, loving the Lord your God, obeying Him, and holding fast to Him; for that means life to you and length of days, so that you may live in the land that the Lord swore to give to your ancestors, to Abraham, to Isaac, and to Jacob* (Deuteronomy 30:19–20).

Some say sin is old-fashioned. And I guess it is, because it's been around forever—at least since the first choice of disobedience made by Adam and Eve. Some say obedience is Old Testament, and that we're under grace in the New Testament. But God's commands of obedience are just as much New Testament as Old Testament. He calls us to holiness of heart and life in both: "Be holy, for I am holy" (Leviticus 11:44; 1 Peter 1:16).

The Dominion of Sin

I often teach that "Sin" stands for "Self-Ish-Ness"—my ways, rather than God's ways; my will, rather than God's will. Sin is a choice of agreement with the world, the flesh, and the devil instead of choosing to agree with God, His will, and His ways for our lives.

> *So you also must consider yourselves dead to sin and alive to God in Christ Jesus. Therefore, do not let sin exercise dominion in your mortal bodies, to make you obey their passions. No longer present your members to sin as instruments of wickedness, but present yourselves to God as those who have been brought from death to life, and present your members to God as instruments of righteousness. For sin will have no dominion over you, since you are not under law but under grace* (Romans 6:11–14).

Our personal sin can be a barrier to our healing and an open door to the enemy of our souls. Paul gives us a classic example in addressing the emotion of anger expressed in an unholy way: "Be angry but do not sin; do not let the sun go down on your anger, and do not make room for the devil" (Ephesians 4:26–27). As we discussed earlier, the emotion of anger itself is not sin, just an emotion. And there are times when we

258

actually should be angry as this Scripture literally commands. But we can express that anger in ways that are sinful, such as violence, retaliation, hatred, bitterness or in the opposite way by burying it, denying it, letting it seethe and simmer, waiting to erupt when finally triggered.

And if we sin in our anger, we "make room for the devil." We give him a "foothold," as some versions translate this passage of Scripture. I say "we" because Paul is speaking to the believers of the church at Ephesus in this passage—believers in Christ can make room for the devil in the unsanctified, sinful areas of our soul. Sin separates us from God and gives access to Satan. It's a potential barrier to our healing and a means of bondage to the enemy of our souls.

Bonds Formed through Agreement and Submission

We are bound to the one to whom we submit—either God and His ways or Satan and his ways. As the famous populist prophet Bob Dylan sang for his generation, "It might be the devil or it might be the Lord, but you're gonna have to serve somebody." This is simply an expression of the spiritual principle that we become slaves to the one we serve:

> *Do you not know that if you present yourselves to anyone as obedient slaves, you are slaves of the one whom you obey, either of sin, which leads to death, or of obedience, which leads to righteousness? But thanks be to God that you, having once been slaves of sin, have become obedient from the heart to the form of teaching to which you were entrusted, and that you, having been set free from sin, have become slaves of righteousness* (Romans 6:16–18).

Idolatry of Serving False Gods

Anything or anyone we serve instead of God or in place of God is an idol and a false god—the object represents the sin of our idolatry. Whatever we hold more dear in our hearts than Jesus is what we are truly worshipping, and the enemy can gain access to our soul because of our inappropriate high regard for that person or thing. Our sin separates us from God and the intimacy of relationship He longs for us to have. And our sin has consequences for the other relationships in our lives, in our generation, and those to come.

259

I am the Lord your God, who brought you out of the land of Egypt, out of the house of slavery; you shall have no other gods before Me. You shall not make for yourself an idol, whether in the form of anything that is in heaven above, or that is on the earth beneath, or that is in the water under the earth. You shall not bow down to them or worship them; for I the Lord your God am a jealous God, punishing children for the iniquity of parents, to the third and the fourth generation of those who reject Me, but showing steadfast love to the thousandth generation of those who love Me and keep My commandments (Exodus 20:2–6).

Cleansing of Sin through Confession and Repentance

The answer to getting free from the bonds of sin is confession and repentance. To confess is to agree with God that what we have done is wrong. To repent is to turn away from our sin and turn to God. Out of the goodness of God's grace, He convicts us of our sins of disobedience so that we will turn to Him in confession and repentance, and receive the cleansing and peace of His forgiveness.

If we say that we have fellowship with Him while we are walking in darkness, we lie and do not do what is true; but if we walk in the light as He himself is in the light, we have fellowship with one another, and the blood of Jesus His Son cleanses us from all sin. If we say that we have no sin, we deceive ourselves, and the truth is not in us. If we confess our sins, He who is faithful and just will forgive us our sins and cleanse us from all unrighteousness. If we say that we have not sinned, we make Him a liar, and His word is not in us (1 John 1:6–10).

God immediately forgives us of our sin the moment we truly confess and repent of our sin (1 John 1:9). And at the same time, it is also equally true that there are times we need to confess our sins to one another—not to be *forgiven*, but to be *healed* of the shame and condemnation we may still be carrying despite God's forgiveness.

The prayer of faith will save the sick, and the Lord will raise them up; and anyone who has committed sins will be forgiven. Therefore confess your sins to one another, and pray for one another, so that you may be healed. The prayer of the righteous is powerful and effective (James 5:15–16).

This spiritual principle and biblical truth from James 5:16 does not take away anything from the spiritual principle and biblical truth of 1 John 1:9. Both are true at the same time. God forgives us when we confess and repent whether anyone "hears our confession" or not. But sometimes we need to speak out our confession to another human being in order to truly receive healing, God's forgiveness, freedom from the guilt, shame, condemnation, and to silence the voice of the accuser and enemy of our souls. Another reason that we may need to do this is so that we are able to forgive ourselves.

Often times, one of the most powerful and healing moments of prayer ministry occurs when someone speaks out loud something they've never told anyone before. It's often something they have not ever been able to fully release to God, though they have often tried. God has long since forgiven, but often they have not yet forgiven themselves.

Voicing God's Forgiveness of All Sin

As they speak out loud their confession in repentance and faith, we can look them in the eye with the authority we have as disciples of Christ in response to their choice of confession and repentance and proclaim, "In the name of Jesus, your sins are forgiven." Sometimes it's really good to be just as specific in speaking the words of forgiveness as they were in speaking the words of confession, so they can truly release it to the Lord.

> *Jesus said to them again, "Peace be with you. As the Father has sent Me, so I send you." When He had said this, He breathed on them and said to them, "Receive the Holy Spirit. If you forgive the sins of any, they are forgiven them; if you retain the sins of any, they are retained"*
> (John 20:21–23).

Some in the Protestant traditions protest that this is a practice from the Catholic traditions rather than Scripture. But according to James 5:16 and John 20:23, it's not just "a Catholic thing," it's "a Bible thing." And from the experience of seeing many set free from years of shame in the moment they truly receive the forgiveness and grace of God He longs to release, despite years and layers of resistance, it's a powerful thing. This is part of our inheritance, authority, and responsibility in Christ—to speak forgiveness in the name and authority of Jesus.

All that Jesus did on earth, He did as Son of Man by the power of the Holy Spirit in obedience to the Father. And He often releases His words of forgiveness through us to one another—"The Son of Man has authority on earth to forgive sins" (Matthew 9:6). We are sons and daughters of man just as we are sons and daughters of God. And there are times when we need to respond in the love and mercy of God, in the authority of the name of Jesus in accordance with the Word of God when someone confesses their sins, so that they may be healed.

There is no sin that that God will not forgive. If we will confess our sin to Him with a repentant heart, trusting in Him as best as we can, He will be faithful to forgive us. (1 John 1:9). Some think that their sin is "the unpardonable sin," the blasphemy of the Holy Spirit (Mark 3:28–29). But the only sin that cannot be forgiven is the sin that we will not turn over to God in response to the conviction of the Holy Spirit. When we respond to God's unconditional offer of love and grace, God will be mercifully "patient with (us), not wanting any to perish, but all to come to repentance" (2 Peter 3:9).

Chapter 16

Generational Sins, Cycles & Curses

When we go to see the doctor, the first thing they do is take our medical history. They want to know the problems we are having now and the problems we have had in the past. But they also want to know the history of problems in our family line as well. Medical science has discovered God's truth that we are affected by the lives of those who have lived before us. We are affected by the acts of our forefathers (and "foremothers"), our ancestors before us— like it or not, whether we think it is fair or not. Sin affects and infects everything and everyone around us, in our generation and in the generations to follow.

A Community Dimension of Our Relationship with God

We tend to think of our relationship with God as deeply personal, and it is. But there is also a community dimension of our relationship, as well as the individual dimension. As they say, "We're in this thing together." We are created to not only love God, but to also love one another. The spiritual principles of generational sin, generational blessings, and generational curses are a reflection of the vertical dimension of our relationships with one another—going up and down the generational lines. When we discuss the category for prayer ministry of holy and unholy ties, we will also be discussing the horizontal dimension of our relationships—going out from side to side in our mutual relationships.

In both the vertical and horizontal dimensions of our relationships with others, our choices and actions affect one another, for good or for bad. God intends it that way. This is one of the ways He keeps us from becoming too self-centered and self-focused. It's also one of the ways He teaches us and manifests the nature of His love to us and through us to one another. God has designed life to keep us turning to Him and turning to one another, to keep looking outwardly in love instead of only inwardly in selfishness.

Generational Inheritance and Legacy

Strengths and weaknesses, sensitivities and vulnerabilities are passed down the generational line like an inheritance or legacy. As they say, "It's in our blood" or "It's in our genes." Who hasn't heard, "The apple doesn't fall far from the tree?" Or "Like father, like son?" The scientific field of genetics is a field dedicated to the reality that we are affected by the generations of our past, and that our generation will affect those of the future. Our physical DNA reflects the influences of our parents' DNA and that of their parents' on up through the branches of our ancestral tree. If my Father and his Father suffered from heart disease or diabetes or alcoholism, there may be more of a propensity—more of a likelihood, potential, and pressure that I will have a vulnerability to suffer or struggle in those same ways.

If I have inherited these vulnerabilities from before birth, these become challenges and struggles that I may have in my life. These may be battles set up for me to have to fight even before I ever make my first decision to eat fried chicken that may lead to heart disease or drink hard liquor that may lead to alcoholism or any of the other choices that may lead to my receiving the "inheritance" of these generational traits. The choices of the generations of my ancestors in their lives before me affect the kinds of struggles and challenges that I will face as part of my life. It doesn't seem fair, but it is a medically proven fact of life. But at the same time, if my parents and ancestors were really fun or really fast or really fit, there is also a propensity for those good things to pass down the generational line as well. That's God's purpose in the principle of generational blessing. He wants the good things of life to be passed down as a legacy and blessing throughout our generations.

Like Spiritual DNA

What is true of our natural DNA is also true of our spiritual DNA, so to speak. We are affected by the generations of our past. As David said, "Indeed, I was born guilty, a sinner when my mother conceived me" (Psalm 51:5). Before David committed his first sin, he was a sinner— one who is drawn to sin—because of the spiritual influences of his Mother and Father and their generations, all the way back to Adam and Eve. What was true of David is true of each of us. We all have need of a Savior to redeem us from the moment of conception, not just from the moment of our first sin.

The choices our ancestors made— good or bad, in line with life or in line with death, whether in obedience or rebellion to the will of God— influence the lives of their descendants in the generations to follow.

> *I call heaven and earth to witness against you today that I have set before you life and death, blessings and curses. Choose life so that you and your descendants may live, loving the Lord your God, obeying him, and holding fast to him; for that means life to you and length of days, so that you may live in the land that the Lord swore to give to your ancestors, to Abraham, to Isaac, and to Jacob* (Deuteronomy 30:19–20).

God wants His blessings to pass down through the generations. In fact, He even wants those blessings to increase through the generations, as we'll discuss in a moment. But the enemy of our souls tries to turn those generational blessings into generational curses. God intends cycles of godliness, but our enemy wants cycles of ungodliness. God intends cycles of health and prosperity, but our enemy wants cycles of infirmity and poverty. God intends cycles of blessings, but our enemy wants cycles of curses.

> *I am the Lord your God, who brought you out of the land of Egypt, out of the house of slavery; you shall have no other gods before Me. You shall not make for yourself an idol, whether in the form of anything that is in heaven above, or that is on the earth beneath, or that is in the water under the earth. You shall not bow down to them or worship them; for I the Lord your God am a jealous God, punishing children for the iniquity of parents, to the third and the fourth generation of those who reject Me, but showing steadfast love to the thousandth generation of those who love Me and keep My commandments* (Exodus 20:2–6).

The Blessings of Obedience

God is always trying to draw us into obedience so that our lives will be covered by His protection and showered with His blessings. And at the same time, our enemy is always trying to draw us into disobedience so that our lives will be exposed to destruction and pelted with curses.

According to God's spiritual laws, ultimately designed for our benefit, obedience brings blessings and life, while disobedience blocks the blessings and brings curses and death. So the enemy, our accuser, tries to draw us and our generations into disobedience and sin to open the door for curses instead of blessings—to block the blessings and release the curses if he can—by using God's laws and principles against us.

Our enemy knows God's law and tries to use it against us. That's what Satan (his name literally means "the accuser") does. He accuses us before God that we are in violation of God's own laws and deserving of His just sentence, which is carried out by God's spiritual principles, as we reap what we sow in our personal lives and throughout the generations. In a sense, the unconfessed sin of the generations gives Satan and his kingdom legal right to attack and attach to the lives in each generation. There is agreement with sin instead of agreement with God, giving permission, access, and influence to the enemy and everything associated with the sin. The cycle and patterns continue down the generational line until there is confession and repentance through the blood of Jesus.

Generational Curse of Original Sin

Original sin is the ultimate example of spiritual DNA being passed down through the generations. Adam and Eve sinned against God way back when, and we are still paying the price for it. From the beginning it has been true that the consequences of our sins influence others far beyond our own lives.

Adam and Eve's sin of disobedience brought all of creation under the curse of sin (Genesis 3:14–19). And the curse of sin is death—death to God's perfection and defilement of His created order (Genesis 2:17; Romans 6:23). The sin of Adam became a generational curse of sin throughout all the generations of Adam. The personal sins of each generation then reinforce the dominion of the curse of sin.

> *Therefore, just as sin came into the world through one man, and death came through sin, and so death spread to all because all have sinned—sin was indeed in the world before the law, but sin is not reckoned when there is no law. Yet death exercised dominion from Adam to Moses, even over those*

266

whose sins were not like the transgression of Adam, who is a type of the One who was to come (Romans 5:12–14).

Generational Blessings through the Righteousness of Christ

But God has known from the beginning that love requires freedom to choose to accept that love or not, to obey God or not. And that freedom allows the potential for sin and all its deadly consequences to affect us and one another—even throughout all generations. So God had a plan from before the foundations of the earth for our redemption—to break the power of the curse of sin through the obedience and sacrifice of Jesus the Christ (Ephesians 1:3–14).

> *If, because of the one man's trespass, death exercised dominion through that one, much more surely will those who receive the abundance of grace and the free gift of righteousness exercise dominion in life through the one Man, Jesus Christ. Therefore just as one man's trespass led to condemnation for all, so one Man's act of righteousness leads to justification and life for all. For just as by the one man's disobedience the many were made sinners, so by the one Man's obedience the many will be made righteous* (Romans 5:17–19).

> *For since death came through a human being, the resurrection of the dead has also come through a human being; for as all die in Adam, so all will be made alive in Christ* (1 Corinthians 15:21–22).

God's will is for generational blessings to pass down through the generations. He desires for the blessings to extend even "to the thousandth generation" (Exodus 20:6). One of His spiritual principles is that obedience brings blessings. But by that same principle, the opposite is also true. Disobedience brings curses. God gives us the freedom to choose. Our choices of submission to the obedience of God opens the door for blessings into our lives; but our choices of rebellion and disobedience to God are choices that open the door for curses in our lives. These choices affect our lives and the lives of our descendants.

> *I call heaven and earth to witness against you today that I have set before you, life and death, blessings and curses. Choose life so that you and **your descendants** may live, loving the Lord your God, obeying Him, and holding fast to Him; for that means life to you and length of days, so that*

267

you may live in the land that the Lord swore to give to your ancestors, to Abraham, to Isaac, and to Jacob (Deuteronomy 30:19–20, emphasis added).

Specific Sins Bring Specific Generational Curses

The Scripture identifies several categories of particular sins that carry the consequences of specific generational curses. The first of the Ten Commandments speaks of generational blessings for our obedience and generational curses to four generations for our disobedience through the sin of idolatry.

> *You shall not make for yourself an idol, whether in the form of anything that is in heaven above, or that is on the earth beneath, or that is in the water under the earth. You shall not bow down to them or worship them; for I the Lord your God am a jealous God, punishing children for the iniquity of parents, to the third and the fourth generation of those who reject Me, but showing steadfast love to the thousandth generation of those who love Me and keep My commandments* (Exodus 20:4–6).

Under the law, certain sins carry of the judgment of a generational curse to ten generations. For example:

> *Those born of an illicit union shall not be admitted to the assembly of the Lord. Even to the tenth generation, none of their descendants shall be admitted to the assembly of the Lord* (Deuteronomy 23:2).

And the nations who refused to assist the Hebrew people on their journey out of Egypt and into their promised land and who hired Balaam to curse them were punished by a curse to "the tenth generation" as well (Deuteronomy 23:3–4).

Left to ourselves, each generation sins and the patterns and propensity for sin and judgment continue down through the generational lines. Like the Psalmist, we cry out, "Will You be angry with us forever? Will You prolong Your anger to all generations?" (Psalm 85:5). We see the consequences of our actions and the actions of those who have gone before us. We sense the pull toward sin and disobedience to the will and ways of God, drawing us into rebellion and under the condemnation of our accuser and the curse of God's righteous judgment.

Spiritual Principle of Reaping and Sowing through the Generations

The spiritual principle of reaping and sowing applies in our lives and through our lives down through the generations to come. God wants us to sow good seed to bring a good harvest, increasing in its yield and blessing in our lives generation after generation. The seeds that are sown—whether good or bad—will grow into maturity through the generations until they produce a harvest to be reaped "at the end of the age" (Matthew 13:36–43).

> *Do not be deceived; God is not mocked, for you reap whatever you sow. If you sow to your own flesh, you will reap corruption from the flesh; but if you sow to the Spirit, you will reap eternal life from the Spirit. So let us not grow weary in doing what is right, for we will reap at harvest time, if we do not give up. So then, whenever we have an opportunity, let us work for the good of all, and especially for those of the family of faith* (Galatians 6:7–10).

Spiritual Principle of Increase through the Generations

This is all part of the Lord's principles and plans of increase for His people and all His creation.

> *The Lord your God has multiplied you, so that today you are as numerous as the stars of heaven. May the Lord, the God of your ancestors, increase you a thousand times more and bless you, as He has promised you!* (Deuteronomy 1:10–11).

> *May the Lord give you increase, both you and your children. May you be blessed by the Lord, who made heaven and earth* (Psalm 115:14–15).

> *He who supplies seed to the sower and bread for food will supply and multiply your seed for sowing and increase the harvest of your righteousness* (2 Corinthians 9:10).

The Spiritual Principle of Increase is expressed throughout Scripture in many ways: God's command from the beginning to be fruitful and multiply; Abraham being the father of many nations; Joshua going farther than Moses; Elisha receiving a double portion of Elijah's anointing; the glory of the latter temple being greater than the glory of the former; saving the best wine for last; all the parables of the kingdom of God that begin small and grow into maturity such as the yeast, the ears of corn, the mustard seed, the wheat and tares growing into the full maturity of the harvest; and Jesus' promise to His disciples to come that even greater works would be done than even His. Sin and darkness will increase until the end of the age, but at the same time, the light and glory of God upon His people will shine with ever-increasing brightness in the midst of the darkness until the King of Glory returns (Isaiah 60; Psalm 24). "But where sin increased, grace abounded all the more" (Romans 5:20).

Now the enemy of our souls wants to do just the opposite. And he uses these same principles against us. Our sin and the sins of our generations can separate us from fully abiding in the presence of God and stifle us from fully abounding in the blessings of God. Just as the light will increase, so will the darkness (Isaiah 60:1–2). And just as good will increase, so will evil.

> *Many of those who sleep in the dust of the earth shall awake, some to everlasting life, and some to shame and everlasting contempt. Those who are wise shall shine like the brightness of the sky, and those who lead many to righteousness, like the stars forever and ever. But you, Daniel, keep the words secret and the book sealed until the time of the end. Many shall be running back and forth, and evil shall increase*
> (Daniel 12:2–4).

> *And because of the increase of lawlessness, the love of many will grow cold. But the one who endures to the end will be saved. And this good news of the kingdom will be proclaimed throughout the world, as a testimony to all the nations; and then the end will come* (Matthew 24:12–14).

Breaking the Power of Generational Sin and Curses

So we have need of a Savior to deliver us from this bondage and break the power and the curse of the law of sin and death. We need a Savior who will free us from the curses and release the blessings. We cry out, "Will You not revive us again, so that Your people may rejoice in You? Show us Your steadfast love, O Lord, and grant us Your salvation" (Psalm 85:6–7).

God heard the humble cry of His people for salvation and freedom. He made promise of provision to break the generational curse for generational sins. The same prophets that declare God's judgment also declare the hope of God's redemption. For example, through Jeremiah, God prophecies of a time to come:

> *The days are surely coming, says the Lord, when I will sow the house of Israel and the house of Judah with the seed of humans and the seed of animals. And just as I have watched over them to pluck up and break down, to overthrow, destroy, and bring evil, so I will watch over them to build and to plant, says the Lord. In those days they shall no longer say: "The parents have eaten sour grapes, and the children's teeth are set on edge." But all shall die for their own sins; the teeth of everyone who eats sour grapes shall be set on edge* (Jeremiah 31:27–30).

The "days to come" are the days of the "new covenant" (Jeremiah 31:31). This speaks of the new covenant to come through the blood of Christ. It is His blood that forgives us of our sins and the sins of our generations. He is our salvation and the revelation of the steadfast love of the Lord. Through the sacrifice of His blood, He took upon Himself all of our sins, "wounded for our transgressions, and crushed for our iniquities, upon Him was the punishment that made us whole, and by His bruises we are healed" (Isaiah 53:5–6; 1 Peter 2:24). "For our sake He made Him to be sin who knew no sin, so that in Him we might become the righteousness of God" (2 Corinthians 5:21).

> *But now, apart from law, the righteousness of God has been disclosed, and is attested by the law and the prophets, the righteousness of God through faith in Jesus Christ for all who believe. For there is no distinction, since all have sinned and fall short of the glory of God; they are now justified by His*

271

grace as a gift, through the redemption that is in Christ Jesus, whom God put forward as a sacrifice of atonement by His blood, effective through faith. He did this to show His righteousness, because in His divine forbearance He had passed over the sins previously committed; it was to prove at the present time that He himself is righteous and that He justifies the one who has faith in Jesus (Romans 3:21–26).

Just as Jesus took on our sin, so He took on our curse. By the steadfast love and unfailing mercy of God, He became a curse so that every curse against us, including every generational curse, could be broken:

Christ redeemed us from the curse of the law by becoming a curse for us— for it is written, "Cursed is everyone who hangs on a tree"— in order that in Christ Jesus the blessing of Abraham might come to the Gentiles, so that we might receive the promise of the Spirit through faith (Galatians 3:13–14).

Just as the blood of Jesus is available to cleanse us of our personal sins, so the blood of Jesus is available to cleanse us of our generational sins. Just as it is available to break the power of the curse of the law of sin and death upon our lives for our personal actions, so the blood of Jesus is available to break the power of the generational curses upon our lives for the actions of our ancestors before us.

You know that you were ransomed from the futile ways inherited from your ancestors, not with perishable things like silver or gold, but with the precious blood of Christ, like that of a lamb without defect or blemish. He was destined before the foundation of the world, but was revealed at the end of the ages for your sake (1 Peter 1:18–20).

Nothing but the blood of Jesus can break the power of sin and cancel the consequences of the resulting curse upon our lives from our ways and the "ways inherited from (our) ancestors." The blood is available through the sacrifice of His love for each of us at the cross. But we each have the responsibility to respond to His sacrifice, to respond to the offer of His grace, which He extends to all from His heart of steadfast love. We have to choose to apply the blood of the Lamb to our sins and to the sins of our ancestors to be forgiven of our sins and freed from the curse.

Applying the Blood of the Lamb

As we discussed earlier, the blood of the Lamb is available to all through the sacrifice of Christ for all to be saved. But are all saved? No. Only those who willingly choose to humbly avail themselves of the sacrifice of Jesus by the blood of the cross. Though it has been available to all for over two thousand years, salvation comes as we specifically, intentionally apply His blood to our heart. That's the meaning of the Old Testament story of the deliverance from the bondage of Egypt. They had to obediently apply the blood of the Lamb in order for the spirit of death to pass over their houses
(Exodus 12:1–14)

Today, Jesus is our Savior, the Salvation of God, "the Lamb of God who takes away the sin of the world" (John 1:29). "But if anyone does sin, we have an advocate with the Father, Jesus Christ the righteous; and He is the atoning sacrifice for our sins, and not for ours only but also for the sins of the whole world" (1 John 2:1–2). The blood of Jesus is available, but we must apply the blood of the Lamb. We apply the blood of the Lamb to our own sins to break the curse of the judgment of God upon our personal lives by turning to God in faith, through confession and repentance of our sins. "*If we confess our sins*, He who is faithful and just will forgive us our sins and cleanse us from all unrighteousness" (1 John 1:9).

Identificational Repentance and Standing in the Gap

How do we apply the blood of the Lamb for the generational sins of our ancestors and break the generational curses from the sins of our ancestors? Through the biblical models of confessing the sins of the generations before us. This is called "identificational repentance" or "standing in the gap" on behalf of our generations. It's God's way of giving us the grace to bring the unconfessed sin of our former generations to the foot of the cross and before His throne of grace to apply the blood of the Lamb.

We see examples of this model of generational confession and repentance in prayer through the ministry of Nehemiah and Ezra:

273

Now on the twenty-fourth day of this month the people of Israel were assembled with fasting and in sackcloth, and with earth on their heads. Then those of Israelite descent separated themselves from all foreigners, and stood and confessed their sins and the iniquities of their ancestors (Nehemiah 9:1–2).

We also see it in God's warnings to Moses and the provision the Lord makes for confession of generational sin on behalf of the people and their ancestors who sin against Him.

But if they confess their iniquity and the iniquity of their ancestors, in that they committed treachery against me and, moreover, that they continued hostile to me— so that I, in turn, continued hostile to them and brought them into the land of their enemies; if then their uncircumcised heart is humbled and they make amends for their iniquity, then will I remember my covenant with Jacob; I will remember also my covenant with Isaac and also my covenant with Abraham, and I will remember the land (Leviticus 26:40–42).

And we see it in the prayer of Daniel on behalf of the Hebrew people exiled to Babylon, so that God could forgive them of their sins and the sins of the former generations and return them to their promised land.

Then I turned to the Lord God, to seek an answer by prayer and supplication with fasting and sackcloth and ashes. I prayed to the Lord my God and made confession, saying, "Ah, Lord, great and awesome God, keeping covenant and steadfast love with those who love You and keep Your commandments, we have sinned and done wrong, acted wickedly and rebelled, turning aside from Your commandments and ordinances. We have not listened to Your servants the prophets, who spoke in Your name to our kings, our princes, and our ancestors, and to all the people of the land. Righteousness is on your side, O Lord, but open shame, as at this day, falls on us, the people of Judah, the inhabitants of Jerusalem, and all Israel, those who are near and those who are far away, in all the lands to which You have driven them, because of the treachery that they have committed against You. Open shame, O Lord, falls on us, our kings, our officials, and our ancestors, because we have sinned against You"
(Daniel 9:3–8).

Though Daniel was a righteous man, even willing to be thrown into the lion's den because of His faith in God and refusal to disobey God's law, he was still willing to identify in confession and repentance on behalf of the people of Israel and their ancestors. Daniel recognized that it was the sins of his nation that caused God's judgment of exile to come upon them. Therefore, he did not pray, "*I* have sinned against you" in personal confession and repentance alone. Instead, he prayed on behalf of *all*, confessing, "*We* have sinned against You." Then, having identified with the people of Israel and the generations of their ancestors in confession and repentance, Daniel then identifies with them in intercession for God's mercy:

> *And now, O Lord our God, who brought Your people out of the land of Egypt with a mighty hand and made Your name renowned even to this day—we have sinned, we have done wickedly. O Lord, in view of all Your righteous acts, let Your anger and wrath, we pray, turn away from Your city Jerusalem, Your holy mountain; because of our sins and the iniquities of our ancestors, Jerusalem and Your people have become a disgrace among all our neighbors. Now therefore, O our God, listen to the prayer of Your servant and to his supplication, and for Your own sake, Lord, let Your face shine upon Your desolated sanctuary. Incline Your ear, O my God, and hear. Open Your eyes and look at our desolation and the city that bears Your name. We do not present our supplication before You on the ground of our righteousness, but on the ground of Your great mercies. O Lord, hear; O Lord, forgive; O Lord, listen and act and do not delay! For Your own sake, O my God, because Your city and Your people bear Your name!* (Daniel 9:15–19).

God was allowing Daniel to "stand in the gap," to intercede, to pray on behalf of those who had not been willing to "stand in the gap" for their own sins in their own generation.

> *And I sought for anyone among them who would repair the wall and stand in the breach before me on behalf of the land, so that I would not destroy it; but I found no one. Therefore I have poured out my indignation upon them; I have consumed them with the fire of my wrath; I have returned their conduct upon their heads, says the Lord God.*
> (Ezekiel 22:30–31).

God looks for someone willing to intercede before Him on behalf of those who have sinned and allowed the land and the people to be defiled. Sin opens the door to the devil. It also opens the gates of hell to the hordes of darkness who are ready to come rushing in like a flood where there is no resistance by the gates of righteousness. Its polluted waves give permission to the putrid spirits associated with that sin to have access and influence in the lives of those touched by it— personally, corporately, and generationally.

So God looks for someone to shut the door and close the gate. He looks for someone who will "lift up a standard" when "the enemy comes in like a flood" (Isaiah 59:19 NKJV). The doors are shut and the gates are closed by admitting the sins that have never been confessed and by bringing them to the foot of the cross and under the blood of Jesus through humble repentance and trusting faith.

Transformation of the Land through Generational Prayers

When we "stand in the gap" through "identificational repentance" and intercession for ourselves and our generations, we not only have an affect upon our personal lives, we also have an affect upon the land in which we live. Just as God broke the curse upon the land of Israel through the prayers of Daniel and Nehemiah so He could bring mercy instead of judgment and blessing instead of curses, He wants to heal our land as well. He wants to push back the forces of darkness and open up the windows of heaven to heal our land when He moves us to pray:

> *If My people who are called by My name humble themselves, pray, seek My face, and turn from their wicked ways, then I will hear from heaven, and will forgive their sin and heal their land* (2 Chronicles 7:14).

Some call this powerful passage God's Covenant for Revival. He wants to revive our hearts and revive our land to display His glory. So He moves in the hearts of His people to pray, repenting of the sins of the generations to displace the enemy and break the curses, then embracing the blessings of God and declaring them by faith.

> *For the creation waits with eager longing for the revealing of the children of God; for the creation was subjected to futility, not of its own will but by the*

276

will of the one who subjected it, in hope that the creation itself will be set free from its bondage to decay and will obtain the freedom of the glory of the children of God (Romans 8:19–21).

Since the beginning of my ministry, I've always sensed the leading of the Holy Spirit to join with the intercessors and spiritual leaders from across the broad spectrum of the streams of the Body of Christ in the unity of the Holy Spirit to pray for the land, for the city, for the state, for the region, for the nation, and for the earth. I've learned that these same principles of healing and deliverance for a person's healing and freedom also apply to the larger levels of the geographical regions where we live. Generational prayers, in the unity of the Spirit of the larger Body of Christ in a region have tremendous power, as led by the Lord, to impact the people and the land in the spiritual realm at the territorial level.

Many times I've been honored to have opportunities to teach and minister on this topic of the transformation of the land and territorial intercession, praying at state capitols, city courthouses, at the Washington Mall, the prayer gathering on 7-7-7 at Titan Stadium in Nashville and on 8-8-8 at the Rose Bowl, and many other city-wide, state-wide, and regional prayer gatherings. I believe in the power of prayer to change our lives, to change our nations, and to change history. God invites us to pray so He can act on the basis of our prayers (2 Chronicles 7:14). In this sense, I completely agree with the famous declaration, "History belongs to the intercessors!"

An in-depth teaching on territorial-level spiritual warfare and prophetic intercession is a topic for a book on another day, but I do want to share one experience I had that encouraged me so much.[34] Early in my ministry, Pastors Jeff Bealmear and Tim Johnson, who have turned out to be life-long friends and ministry colleagues, along with the other pastors in a community in northern Kentucky out in the middle of the rolling hills and tobacco fields, invited me to come preach an old-fashioned, community-wide tent revival.

---

[34] In part, I must confess, I'm mainly including this story in this revision of my book because every time Pastor Jeff Bealmear invites me to come preach and minister at his church, he teases me that he begged me to include his name in my book and I didn't. So I'm fixing that forever at this time.

The region had been in a severe drought for a long time. And on the last night of the revival, I felt the Holy Spirit was leading me to lead the pastors, city leaders, and people in prayers of repentance on behalf of the sins and generational sins of the people and the land (see Isaiah 24:5–6; Leviticus 18:25; Jeremiah 23:10; Romans 8:19–21; 2 Chronicles 7:14). We prayed for the Lord to cleanse the land of defilement, break the drought, and heal the land.

At the end of our prayer, I cried out to God at the close of the revival, "Lord, if You've been in this, if You've been moving our hearts and leading our prayers, would you show us a sign? Lord, would You send Your rain?" We finished our revival and went home to bed.

The next morning, I was having breakfast at a little café and I could hardly believe my eyes when it started to rain! My cell phone rang right then and it was Pastor Jeff telling me the same exciting news! We both laugh to this day that it was the tiniest drizzle of rain, maybe about the size of a light shower that might come out of a cloud about the size of a man's hand, but it was rain, praise God!

Joining Jesus in His Ministry of Intercession

To intercede in prayer is to come before God on behalf of another. "If one person sins against another, someone can intercede for the sinner with the Lord..." (1 Samuel 2:25). To join in the ministry of intercession is to join in the present ministry of Jesus, who "always lives to make intercession" in order "to save those who approach God through Him" (Hebrews 7:25). "Who is to condemn? It is Christ Jesus, who died, yes, who was raised, and who is at the right hand of God, who indeed intercedes for us" (Romans 8:34). In a sense, we might even say we are never more like Jesus than when we are interceding for another in prayer.

In the intercession of Jesus, He not only comes before God the Father as God the Son on our behalf, He actually takes on our sin so that we can come into the presence of God, cleansed from unrighteousness, and clothed in the righteousness of Christ (2 Corinthians 5:21). As the Father prophesied through Isaiah of His Son, the Suffering Servant to come:

Yet it was the will of the Lord to crush Him with pain. When You make His life an offering for sin, He shall see His offspring, and shall prolong His days; through Him the will of the Lord shall prosper. Out of His anguish He shall see light; He shall find satisfaction through His knowledge. The Righteous One, My servant, shall make many righteous, and He shall bear their iniquities. Therefore I will allot Him a portion with the great, and He shall divide the spoil with the strong; because He poured out Himself to death, and was numbered with the transgressors; yet He bore the sin of many, and made intercession for the transgressors (Isaiah 53:10–12).*

In a sense, Jesus "made intercession for the transgressors" by "standing in the gap" on their behalf. On the cross, He was standing in the gap between earth and heaven, between death and life, between our unrighteousness and God's righteousness, between our sin and His salvation, between how things are and how things are to be, between who we are in our flesh and who we are in His Spirit. "For in Him all the fullness of God was pleased to dwell, and through Him God was pleased to reconcile to Himself all things, whether on earth or in heaven, by making peace through the blood of the cross" (Colossians 1:19-20).

By the grace of God, we are in Christ and Christ is in us. Through His mercy, we can be "dead to sin and alive to God in Christ Jesus" (Romans 6:11). "There is therefore now no condemnation for those who are in Christ Jesus" (Romans 8:1). In Him, we have "become the righteousness of God" (2 Corinthians 5:21). And from that place in Christ of forgiveness and righteousness and intimacy with God, we are called to join with Christ in His ministry of intercession for others, as He abides in us and we abide in Him.

If you abide in Me, and My words abide in you, ask for whatever you wish, and it will be done for you. My Father is glorified by this, that you bear much fruit and become My disciples. As the Father has loved Me, so I have loved you; abide in My love. If you keep My commandments, you will abide in My love, just as I have kept My Father's commandments and abide in His love. I have said these things to you so that My joy may be in you, and that your joy may be complete (John 15:7–11).

When we ask for whatever we wish on behalf of another, we are joining Jesus in the ministry of intercession if we are allowing Him to abide in us and we are abiding in Him. God can freely give us the desires of our heart because we have allowed Him to shape our heart with His desires (Psalm 37:4). And His heart is for people to be saved and sanctified, healed and whole, forgiven and free, living with Him now and forever in the intimacy of a relationship of love for which we were created with Him and with one another (1 John 4:7–12).

When we intercede by standing in the gap, we are standing in Christ and Christ is standing in us. We pray for the Father's kingdom to come and His will to be done on earth as it is in heaven (Matthew 6:10). And in heaven, there isn't any sin, sickness, or sorrow, nor is Satan permitted. Bondages and curses are gone. Heaven exists as God desires. So He places those desires on our hearts by His Spirit, the Spirit of Christ in us, interceding through us (Romans 8:9). And we begin to intercede for His kingdom to come and His will to be done, as He leads our hearts to pray for ourselves and for one another according to His will.

> *Likewise the Spirit helps us in our weakness; for we do not know how to pray as we ought, but that very Spirit intercedes with sighs too deep for words. And God, who searches the heart, knows what is the mind of the Spirit, because the Spirit intercedes for the saints according to the will of God (Romans 8:26–27).*

Intercession and Intimacy with God Through Prayer

So intercession is not begging God to do something that He doesn't want to do. In fact, the heart of prayer is actually intimacy with God, abiding in Him as He abides in us, coming into agreement with His will and His desires. *With our human spirit in communion with God's Holy Spirit through prayer, God puts His thoughts in our minds and His desires in our hearts to pray according to His will on earth as it is in heaven.* This is one of the ways we become "co-workers for the kingdom of God" (Colossians 4:11). We participate in the plans and purposes of God as He leads us in prayer and intercession as "participants of the divine nature" because He is forming His nature and His desires in ours for His purposes (2 Peter 1:4).

280

Through the communion of prayer and the ministry of intercession, we are abiding in God, and truly united with the Lord and the love of God in an intimate way. And "anyone united with the Lord becomes one spirit with Him" (1 Corinthians 6:17). Being one with Him, we then intercede from His vantage point and with His perspective. Christ is now at the right hand of the Father, interceding from the place of victory and the position of authority. And since we are in Christ and Christ is in us, we get to intercede in partnership with Him from the place of victory and the position of authority.

> *God put this power to work in Christ when He raised Him from the dead and seated Him at His right hand in the heavenly places, far above all rule and authority and power and dominion, and above every name that is named, not only in this age but also in the age to come. And He has put all things under His feet and has made Him the head over all things for the church, which is His body, the fullness of Him who fills all in all* (Ephesians 1:20–23).

> *But God, who is rich in mercy, out of the great love with which He loved us even when we were dead through our trespasses, made us alive together with Christ—by grace you have been saved—and raised us up with Him and seated us with Him in the heavenly places in Christ Jesus, so that in the ages to come He might show the immeasurable riches of His grace in kindness toward us in Christ Jesus* (Ephesians 2:4-7).

This is not only for ourselves, but also for the lives of others the Lord will touch through our intercession by the moving of His Spirit in our hearts and prayers. God has placed us in such a position of authority in Christ for a purpose—so we can join in the ministry of Christ. Jesus has already taken all the sins of the world upon Himself, so we do not have to bear them ourselves.

Bearing One Another's Burdens

When we intercede for another, we are bearing one another's burdens. "Bear one another's burdens, and in this way you will fulfill the law of Christ." (Galatians 6:2). But we are not bearing that person's sins or burdens into ourselves. We are not called to "absorb" them into ourselves as some kind of act of selfless sacrifice. We are bearing them

281

to Jesus, who bears them into Himself.[35] Each person is responsible for their sin through their own choices and actions, things done and things left undone. But our prayers make a difference in their lives. I think of it like opening a window of heaven and pushing back the darkness over their lives through our prayers. Then they are better able to hear the truth of Christ, receive the conviction of the Holy Spirit, and turn to the embrace of God our Father.

Prayer changes things because prayer brings us into communion with the One who has the power to change things. This is true not only in our lives, but in all lives of everyone, not only in our generation, but in all generations. God is not limited by time or space. "Jesus Christ is the same yesterday and today and forever" (Hebrews 13:8). That's how far His grace will go, that's how far the power of His blood will reach, as He intercedes for us and as He intercedes through us.

Generational Influence of Intercession

This ministry of intercession for others is not only for those of our generation, but also on behalf of all generations—past, present, and future. We are called to do our part in our generation for His glory. And both the mistakes and the ministry of each generation affect the others before it and after it.

One of the interesting passages of Scripture which makes this principle of the generations affecting one another clear is the connection between

---

[35] I have often prayed for intercessors in personal prayer ministry appointments because they seemed discouraged or depressed, sometimes sick and really tired. Often, when the Lord leads us to the root of the issue, we find that they have sometimes misunderstood the nature of "bearing one another's burdens" in a way that they were subconsciously (and even sometimes consciously) taking on the burdens of those for whom they were praying. Sometimes they would even begin to take on the illnesses or struggles of the person for whom they were interceding. There can be a fine line between empathy and compassion for the person and taking their burdens onto ourselves. Healing and freedom comes as they confess this as sin, even though they didn't mean to sin, by subtly taking the place of Christ, the place that He alone has as our ultimate burden-bearer. Then we pray to release to Him all the undue burdens ever taken on or absorbed, cutting any unholy ties between the intercessor and the people prayed for (as we discuss later). Then, having submitted these areas to God, we can command the devil to flee, along with any spirits of infirmity, depression, discouragement, deception, etcetera (James 4:7).

Hebrews chapters 11 and 12. The "Hall of Faith" of Hebrews chapter 11 names one saint after another who walked "by faith" and not by sight for the glory of God to shine through their lives in their generation. They were, "those of whom the world was not worthy" (Hebrews 11:38). But the fruit of their labors was not fully manifested in their lives, and cannot be fully realized without faithfulness in our lives:

> *Yet all these, though they were commended for their faith, did not receive what was promised, since God had provided something better so that **they would not, apart from us, be made perfect.** Therefore, since we are surrounded by so great a cloud of witnesses, let us also lay aside every weight and the sin that clings so closely, and let us run with perseverance the race that is set before us, looking to Jesus the pioneer and perfecter of our faith, who for the sake of the joy that was set before Him endured the cross, disregarding its shame, and has taken His seat at the right hand of the throne of God* (Hebrews 11:39–12:2, emphasis added).

"...They would not, apart from us, be made perfect." Our actions affect the destiny of others, just like their actions affect our destiny. We're in this thing together. There is much more of a community dimension to our faith than we realize in our often individualistic perspective of faith. Those who are now part of "so great a cloud of witnesses" who have run their race and finished their course are now cheering us on. I think of them now seeing Jesus face to face in heaven, praying perfect prayers for us, as they join in His ministry of intercession, no longer hindered by the human limitations and tainting of self-focused flesh and self-centered pride.

So each generation will pass along a legacy of blessings, curses, mistakes, and ministries that the generations will follow. We want to do our part in our generation to pass on the blessings and break the curses. We want to see the next generation go further than we could go, be more faithful than we could be, and bear more fruit than we could bear. We are created to abide and abound. By "the power at work within us (God) is able to accomplish abundantly far more than all we can ask or imagine" (Ephesians 3:20).

Chapter 17

Unholy Responses

We can't always control the actions of others, but we can control our responses. Even when we are the victim, not the victimizer, even when we have not sinned, but have been sinned against, our reactions can become unholy responses. And those unholy responses then become our own sin—not taking away or replacing or justifying the sin of the one who has hurt us—but becoming a basis for our own sin, in and of itself. These unholy responses can be barriers to our healing and footholds for the enemy.

In prayer ministry, I generally think of this category of unholy responses in terms of two different sub-categories: (1) Unforgiveness, and (2) Unrighteous Judgments. These are most often interrelated and obviously overlap with our earlier discussion of the root of bitterness.

1. Unforgiveness

As I mentioned in the earlier section on Roots of Resistance, the root of bitterness and unforgiveness is incredibly destructive when we allow it fester and grow. And it's a potential barrier to healing. Many people in prayer ministry believe, as I do, that unforgiveness is probably the most significant barrier to healing and a primary foothold that opens the door to the enemy's influence in our lives.

God commands us in His Word to forgiven one another because He loves us and wants us free from all the destructive and often devastating affects of the sin of unforgiveness (Ephesians 4:32; Colossians 3:13; Matthew 18:35). The destructive, bitter root of unforgiveness begins to bear bad fruit in all the relationships of our lives, not only in the particular relationship of the one we are unforgiving towards, but also in our relationship with God.

> *Pursue peace with everyone, and the holiness without which no one will see the Lord. See to it that no one fails to obtain the grace of God; that no root of bitterness springs up and causes trouble, and through it many become defiled* (Hebrews 12:14–15).

Paul names "enmities, strife, jealousy, anger, quarrels dissensions, factions, envy" as some of the "works of the flesh" (Galatians 5:19–21). These are all potential fruit from the root of bitterness and unforgiveness. Helping someone see that and see the negative and often devastating effects of their unforgiveness helps bring them to a place of willingness to forgive once you show them why and how. Sometimes they may need to forgive others, forgive themselves, or "forgive God" in the sense of releasing Him from their judgments against Him.

These deep-seated feelings of bitterness, resentment, anger, or even vengeance will be very real and very understandable in light of the circumstances that led to those feelings. But to acknowledge and remove this barrier to healing, we must understand the nature of unforgiveness: Unforgiveness is a choice; unforgiveness is a sin; and healing from unforgiveness is often a process. Please review the in-depth discussion of the Scriptures and spiritual principles concerning unforgiveness and the healing power of forgiveness in the chapter on Roots of Resistance.

Prayers to Release Our Unforgiveness

The Seven Steps of Forgiveness discussed in detail in the earlier section on Roots of Bitterness and Unforgiveness is a good pattern for prayer in letting it all go to God. Remember that the Seven Steps are:

(1) Admit the wrong
(2) Admit the hurt
(3) Release the person to God[36]
(4) Release the hurt to God
(5) Repent of our sinful responses
(6) Bless the person who hurt us
(7) Receive God's blessing for us

---

[36] In our ministry, we generally lead people to release the person and the hurt to Jesus, but sometimes people are more comfortable praying and speaking to the Father or the Holy Spirit. Of course, God is One and God has revealed Himself in the three persons and dimensions of His Being as God the Father, God the Son, and God the Holy Spirit. In prayer ministry, the main thing is to help the person connect with God however best they can.

Following the principles and pattern of the Seven Steps of Forgiveness, we might pray along these the following lines to release our unforgiveness to God or lead someone else to do the same. Remember that we want to go slowly and deeply, being fairly specific with the wrongs and the hurt, to let it all come up and come out, to allow a kind of cathartic release of all that's been buried inside:

"Lord Jesus, thank You for revealing this area in my heart and letting me see that I've still been holding on to bitterness and unforgiveness toward _____. From those places in my heart where they hurt me, from those ages and moments of my life and also from every moment since then when I've thought back on it, help me to let it go. As best as I can and all by Your grace, I want to give it all to You.

What _____ did to me was wrong. It was less than Your perfect will and it was sin. I make no excuses for them. I don't try to justify what they did. It was wrong when they _____ and when they _____. It was wrong when they failed to _____ and when they failed to _____.

And that hurt me. I don't deny the hurt; I don't try to press it down or pretend it's not there or play like it didn't hurt me. It did. When they did that (or didn't do that) I felt so _____. And I felt so _____.

But even so, even though what they did was wrong and even what they did hurt me, I make a choice. As best as I can and all by God's grace, I choose to release _____ to You. I choose to give him/her a gift they don't deserve, just like You've given me a gift I don't deserve—forgiveness, mercy, release from my judgments against them. And I cancel their debts, every debt I feel they owe me. So that even if they never admit they were wrong, I still choose to forgive them; even if they never admit how much they hurt me, I still choose to forgive them; even if they never say they're sorry or ask me to forgive them, I still choose to forgive them. I release them; I forgive them in the name of Jesus. Let every holy and unhealthy entanglement or tie between us be broken. Strengthen every bond and tie that's of You but break everything that's not. Set me free from them and set them free from me. I release them to You, in the name of Jesus.

And now, Lord Jesus, I release this hurt to You. I release all the _____ and the _____ and the _____ to You. Come take it out of me. Draw it out of my muscles and nerves and joints, out of my immune system, out of every organ and cell of my body. Lift it all off of my spirit and out of my heart and my mind. Free me and cleanse me and release me in the name of Jesus.

Lord Jesus, I also admit that I have been holding on to this, maybe even deep down inside where I didn't even know it was there. But even though they have responsibility for what they did, I admit I have to take responsibility for my unholy response to their actions. When I held on to bitterness and unforgiveness, to resentment and judgment and hardness of heart against them, when I held on to any desire for retaliation or vengeance, that part was my sin. And I repent of my sin of bitterness and unforgiveness in the name of Jesus. I ask You to forgive me, and I receive Your forgiveness now in the name of Jesus.[37]

Now, Lord Jesus, would You give me Your heart for _____ (this person that hurt me). Help me see them as You see them, not just for what they've done and also for who You created them to be. By the power of Your grace, help me pray for them with Your heart. Let the fear of the Lord come upon them. Show them the truth of what they've done and the hurt they've caused. Convict them of their sin. But let Your conviction lead them to repentance and let their repentance lead them to Your mercy. Have mercy upon _____, Lord. May they know the fullness of Your salvation through Jesus Christ as Lord and Savior, Healer and Deliverer, in every way they need, as far as Your grace will go. I'm no longer their judge; I release them to You as the judge of the living and the dead, praying Your mercy for them, as You've had mercy for me, in Jesus' name.

And having released _____ to You and having prayed Your blessings for them, I pray to now receive any blessings You desire for me, as You

---

[37] As you can see, I use the name of Jesus often in prayer. There's power in the name of Jesus (Philippians 2:10; Acts 4:10; John 14:13). That's one reason why the enemy tries to make us feel embarrassed or intimidated to specifically speak the name of Jesus, even trying to get us to use other, more general references to God or titles for Jesus, because of the power of His name. You can't use the name of Jesus too often. And perhaps the greatest prayer of all is to simply call on His mighty name, "Jesus!"

replace in me all You have revealed and removed. Lord, open the eyes of my heart to see what You're doing, to hear what You're saying, to sense Your Presence in any way You would reveal Yourself to me in this moment, in the name of Jesus."

We may want to join with them speaking out agreement in prayer with them, also joining with them to take authority over any spirits of bitterness, unforgiveness, resentment, judgment, rage, anger, hardness of heart, retaliation, vengeance, sickness, infirmity, or others the Holy Spirit discloses in prayer or by word of knowledge and cast them out to the feet of Jesus (James 4:7).

We will want to leave lots of room all along the way for the person to see, hear, sense the Presence of God and anything He may be communicating all along the way in this process of reveal, remove and replace.

2. Unrighteous Judgments

Another sub-category of our unholy responses, along with unforgiveness, that can hinder the healing grace of God in our lives is the area of unrighteous judgments. "There is no one who is righteous, not even one" (Romans 3:10). But nevertheless, we can often act in our self-righteousness as if we were the "righteous judge" who needs to help God with our self-righteous judgments (Psalm 7:11).

There are "righteous judgments" and there are "unrighteous judgments." I think of "righteous judgment" being akin to good discernment, seeking the wisdom and ways of God and applying them justly in our lives. Some say that we are not to judge at all, but actually we are to "judge with right judgment," according to Jesus (John 7:24).

Speak out, judge righteously, defend the rights of the poor and needy (Proverbs 31:9).

You shall not render an unjust judgment; you shall not be partial to the poor or defer to the great: with justice you shall judge your neighbor (Leviticus 19:15).

289

Do you not know that the saints will judge the world? And if the world is to be judged by you, are you incompetent to try trivial cases? Do you not know that we are to judge angels—to say nothing of ordinary matters? (1 Corinthians 6:2–3).

It's when we judge with wrong judgment, with the wrong heart, that we have committed the sin of judgment. This is what Jesus means by His command, "Do not judge, and you will not be judged; do not condemn, and you will not be condemned. Forgive, and you will be forgiven" (Luke 6:37).

Rightly Judging with the Wrong Heart

Sometimes we may rightly judge something as truth with godly discernment. For example, someone may really be a big jerk and we have rightly discerned it with righteous judgment. We should take that into account in our actions and our relationship with that person with godly wisdom, according to the leading of the Holy Spirit. But where that righteous judgment becomes the sin of unrighteous judgment, I believe, is when we harden our hearts against that person as if to say, "That's how you are and that's how you will always be. You're a jerk now and you'll always be a jerk."

In these cases, we are coming into agreement with the accuser instead of coming into agreement with the redeemer. It's like saying here's someone or some situation that God cannot change. It's like shutting a window of God's grace over someone's life. And that's not the heart of God, for our God is a forgiving, redeeming God. "For mortals it is impossible, but for God all things are possible" (Matthew 19:26). We are to respond to one another with His heart of forgiveness and mercy, desiring redemption rather than judgment, and transformation rather than stagnation.

Examples of Unrighteous Judgments

Some common examples of unrighteous judgments are: "He's a jerk." "He's no good." "She's worthless." "She'll never change." "They are just selfish and self-centered." "They don't care about anybody but themselves." All of these might be true and accurate discernment, but our discernment should lead us to intercession for that person. We want

290

to come into agreement with the redeemer instead of the accuser, not agreeing with how things are, but in agreement with how things should be. That's not wishful thinking or blind foolishness. That's the heart of God being released through prayer. If we harden our hearts against someone or some circumstance, we are being used by the enemy to block the grace of God in that person's life or in those circumstances. That's why we are to "pray for one another" instead of judge one another, because our prayers, by God's grace, "are powerful and effective" when prayed with a righteous heart (James 5:16). God wants us to "love one another," and we do that with our prayers, our words, and our attitudes toward one another. And these things make a difference, either for good or for evil. This is another way the enemy of our souls tries to pervert God's principles and use them against us, drawing us into sin against one another.

Judged as We Judge

But not only does the sin of judgment affect the one we judge. It also affects us. There is a spiritual principle of judgment:

> *Do not judge, so that you may not be judged. For with the judgment you make you will be judged, and the measure you give will be the measure you get* (Matthew 7:1–2).

As Jesus warns us, the measure we give will be the measure we get. "Do not be deceived; God is not mocked, for you reap whatever you sow" (Galatians 6:7). If we sow judgment, we will reap judgment. Another way of saying that is, "What goes around, comes around." For some reason, this always makes me think of Woodrow Call's line in Larry McMurtry's novel, *Lonesome Dove*, when he and fellow Texas Ranger Gus McCray have to hang their old friend Jake Spoon: "You ride with horse thieves, you die with horse thieves." He might as well have said, "You reap what you sow. The measure you give will be the measure you get."

One of the ways Satan uses this principle against us through our judgments is that we often become just like the one we judge and we often find ourselves doing the very thing we have condemned. He uses the opportunity to see to it that our attitude of prideful arrogance comes back to haunt us. "Pride goes before destruction, and a haughty spirit before a fall" (Proverbs 16:18). It's like a spiritual boomerang that comes back on us. "For judgment will be without mercy to anyone who has shown no mercy" (James 2:13).

That hardness of heart and lack of mercy against another also has a way of hardening our heart against God, blocking His grace where we may need it the most. "God opposes the proud, but gives grace to the humble" (James 4:6). This sin of prideful judgment is like wearing a sign to the Satan that says, "Kick me. I'm making myself really vulnerable in this area, setting myself up for a big fall." Instead, we should be living our lives as a sign of humility before God that says, "Help me. But for the grace of God, go I."

I find over and over again that we are the most judging and condemning of others for the very things we secretly detest about ourselves. Though the enemy may be at work to destroy us, God will use the opportunity to convict us so He can cleanse us and use us positively, instead of destructively, in the lives of others. God has a way of exposing and confronting our hypocrisy. He'll bring His judgment against our unrighteous judgments, and His light to bear on the dark places we think are hidden. "For the time has come for judgment to begin with the household of God" (1 Peter 4:17).

> *Woe to you, scribes and Pharisees, hypocrites! For you clean the outside of the cup and of the plate, but inside they are full of greed and self-indulgence. You blind Pharisee! First clean the inside of the cup, so that the outside also may become clean. Woe to you, scribes and Pharisees, hypocrites! For you are like whitewashed tombs, which on the outside look beautiful, but inside they are full of the bones of the dead and of all kinds of filth. So you also on the outside look righteous to others, but inside you are full of hypocrisy and lawlessness* (Matthew 23:25–28).

Prayers to Release Our Judgments

When the Lord reveals places of judgment in someone's heart, I usually lead them in prayers to confess their judgment as sin, asking God for forgiveness. Then we pray to release those who have been judged and pray for their redemption and blessing. And finally we declare the enemy's assignments to bring negative consequences against that person's life are now broken can cancelled:

"Father, in the name of Jesus, I confess to You that I have judged _____. I see now that I have hardened my heart against (him) that (he) is _____. While that may be true or not, I know that is not Your will for (him). Forgive me for coming into agreement with the accuser instead of coming into agreement with the Redeemer. I repent of my sin of judgment. I turn away from that and I turn to You. I ask You to forgive me and I receive Your forgiveness now."

"And in the name of Jesus, I now release _____ from my judgments against (him). I pray You would show (him) Your truth and lead (him) in Your ways. Show (him) how much You love (him) and want (him) to be like You. I pray that (he) will by Your grace. In Jesus' name bless (him) with Your mercy and release (him) from my judgment. And I thank You for releasing me from Your judgments and breaking the enemy's assignments of destruction against me. Thank You that Your mercy triumphs over judgment as I repent of sin and turn to You in trusting faith by the power of the blood of Jesus. Amen."

Here, we might pray a prayer and take authority in Jesus' name over the assignments and unholy spirits. Then we might pray for healing, cleansing, and freedom, declaring the mercy of God over this person. By applying the blood of Jesus to our sins, including our sins of pride and judgment of others, God's "mercy triumphs over judgment" in our lives and in the lives of those we had judged (James 2:13).

Chapter 18

Words and Attitudes

Our words have power. This is one of the ways in which we are created in the image of God (Genesis 1:27). According to God's Word, "Death and life are in the power of the tongue, and those who love it will eat its fruits" (Proverbs 18:21). This is another spiritual principle which God intends to use as a blessing to us and for us to be a blessing to one another. Likewise, our thoughts and attitudes about ourselves, about others, about God, and about all of life have tremendous impact on every dimension of our lives. "For as he thinks in his heart, so is he" (Proverbs 23:7 NKJV).

In addressing these areas of the words we have spoken and the words others have spoken over us, along with our thoughts and attitudes, I break this category down into three sub-categories:

1. Blessings and Curses
2. Inner Vows
3. False Beliefs

Sometimes these areas involve our own sin and sometimes they involve the sins of others against us. We'll now look at each area and how they can be barriers to our healing.

1. Blessings and Curses

Perhaps the most common idea that comes to mind about curses is the image of someone involved in witchcraft putting a curse on someone. That is a type of curse, but that's not the focus of this section. More broadly speaking, curses, as well as blessings, have to do with our words. Words are powerful, and God intends them to be. He wants us to speak words of encouragement, honor, and blessing into one another's lives, "speaking the truth in love" (Ephesians 4:15).

The Lord wants us to hear His heart and speak His words over one another and into one another's lives. "Pursue love and strive for the spiritual gifts, and especially that you may prophesy.... those who prophesy speak to other people for their upbuilding and encouragement and consolation." (1 Corinthians 14:1–3). These are ways God blesses us and intends to bless through us with the power of words He entrusted to us.

God spoke the world into existence in the beginning and now God has also entrusted "the power of death and life" to our tongues (Proverbs 18:21). "You will also declare a thing, and it will be established for you" (Job 22:28 NKJV). So our words can be in agreement with God's words and God's will to declare life, or in agreement with the enemy's words and his will to declare death. Jesus said He brings life and the enemy brings death, only coming "to steal, and to kill, and to destroy" (John 10:10).

Some think of blessings and curses as being limited to the Old Testament, such as the story of Balaam being hired to curse God's people (Numbers 22:5–6). But the principles and practices of blessings and curses are seen throughout Scripture. In the New Testament, James warns of both the power and the danger of the words released with the tongue:

> *And the tongue is a fire. The tongue is placed among our members as a world of iniquity; it stains the whole body, sets on fire the cycle of nature, and is itself set on fire by hell. For every species of beast and bird, of reptile and sea creature, can be tamed and has been tamed by the human species, but no one can tame the tongue—a restless evil, full of deadly poison. With it we bless the Lord and Father, and with it we curse those who are made in the likeness of God. From the same mouth come blessing and cursing. My brothers and sisters, this ought not to be so* (James 3:6–10).

Curses are especially powerful to the degree that we come into agreement with them. The old adage, "sticks and stones may break my bones, but words will never hurt me," is just not true, and it's just not biblical. But by the grace of God, curses can be broken by renouncing them and their power in the name of Jesus and choosing to no longer coming into agreement with them.

Some Examples of Curses

Many common curses are words we heard when we were very young when parents or authority figures were angry or disappointed with us. Others came as people formed judgments about us, our character, or our abilities. Some were spoken intentionally to wound, shame, or control. Others were spoken in a moment of anger or frustration without the person even really meaning it, or just because it's a common practice or life-style of that family, group, or culture. Most heart-breaking of all, many of them we spoke over ourselves. And these words have power to influence our lives—at the time they were spoken and until the time they are broken.

Here are some common word curses that often come up in prayer ministry:

- You're no good.
- You'll never amount to anything.
- You can't do anything right.
- You're stupid.
- She's just like her mother.
- She'll never get over it.
- His career is over.
- He's such a loser.
- I'm such an idiot.
- I just can't think straight.

Of course, we can go overboard with anything. And while we should be more careful with the words we speak going forward, we must not be consumed with fear of our words either. But when we see negative patterns in our lives, sometimes it's wise to ask the Holy Spirit to show us if part of the problem is a pattern of curses that were spoken and that we received through our agreement. If we've done it to others or ourselves, we should welcome the Lord's conviction, repent of our sin, renounce the curse, and speak a blessing in line with the heart and will of God in its place.

Some Examples of Blessings

Instead of speaking curses, we should speak blessings. And when curses are broken, we should replace them with blessings. Here are some powerful blessings we can speak:

You're really good at that.

- You're such a blessing and encouragement.
- You're very thoughtful.
- She is so kind.
- She's a real gift.
- He is so brave.
- He really has a Father's heart.
- I'm really proud of you.
- That a boy! Way to go!
- I am a blessed man.
- I can do all things through Christ who strengthens me.
- I will not fear; God is with me.

Speaking words over others and ourselves from God's Word for the purpose of agreeing with God's will for our lives is especially powerful. This is one of the ways that we are transformed by the renewing of our minds—when we choose to bring our minds into agreement with how God sees us and wants us to be according to His word and the power of His grace (Romans 12:1–2).

Prayers to Break Curses and Release Blessings

When the Lord shows us curses that may be in place to block God's blessings and allow the enemy to enforce curses, here is an example of a prayer we might pray:

"Lord, thank You for showing us these words that have been spoken over Julie that are not in line with Your Word and Your will over Julie's life. When her ex-husband would say to her, 'You're worthless. You're good for nothing. I'm better off without you and all your problems,' that was wrong. It was sin against You and it hurt her. But we choose to forgive him this day and release him to You." (Walk her though the steps of forgiveness.)

"And now we break those words and any power they've had over Julie's life. Lord Jesus, when You hung upon the tree of the cross, You were made to be a curse so that every curse against Julie would be broken (Galatians 3:13–14). By the sacrifice of Your life and the power of Your blood, You take all of this onto Yourself so that Julie won't have to (Isaiah 53:4–6; 1 Peter 2:24). In the name of Jesus and by the power of the blood of the Lamb, we break and renounce every one of those curses and every curse and word spoken over Julie's life that is less than the perfect will of God for her."

Throughout this prayer or at any time through it, we can lead Julie to speak out these prayers as we lead her phrase by phrase, or just pray over her. This is true of any area of prayer ministry. When possible, I like to guide the person in prayers so that they are speaking out their words from their heart to help them own the prayers we are praying. So here, we might lead Julie to speak out these words as we lead her phrase by phrase, reminding her to let this be her prayer and declaration to God, to herself, and to all the spiritual realm:

"In the name of Jesus, I reject those words that _____ said over me, that, 'I'm worthless; I'm good for nothing; that he was better off without me,' and everything else that was less than God's will for me. I renounce those words and that way of thinking. That's not how God sees me. That's not the truth. The truth is, I'm a child of God. I have incredible value and significance and worth. I have a gifting and calling and purpose and destiny. I am the righteousness of God in Christ Jesus as God's word says in 2 Corinthians 5:21. I come into agreement with God's vision and God's word for my life; and I reject and renounce the enemy's vision and his word for my life, whether sent to me in my thoughts or spoken over me through the sinful words of others. By the power of the blood of Jesus, I am free of these curses and mindsets, and I receive and embrace the truth and fullness of God's blessings for my life. In Jesus' name I pray, Amen."

At this point we might take authority over any spirits that had claimed ground in Julie's life, and command them to come out of her, off of her, to lose her mind and her self-mage in the name of Jesus as we have modeled before. We might declare that we are binding God's truth to her mind and declare God's blessings over her life as the Holy Spirit leads. We can follow this same kind of pattern in all areas of prayer ministry "destroy the works of the devil" and release the blessings of God in a person's life in name of Jesus and power of the Holy Spirit (1 John 3:8; John 20:21; Matthew 16:19; Acts 1:8; etcetera).

There is never any set formula for these prayers of healing and deliverance, even though it's very helpful to learn from the patterns of others and the spiritual principles of God's Word. We always want to seek to be led in deep humility by the Holy Spirit; pray in great faith as we trust the Lord's leading; and speak with the boldness and authority the Lord gives us as His disciples and ambassadors.

> *Then Jesus called the twelve together and gave them power and authority over all demons and to cure diseases* (Luke 9:1).

> *So we are ambassadors for Christ, since God is making His appeal through us; we entreat you on behalf of Christ, be reconciled to God*
> (2 Corinthians 5:20).

> *Like good stewards of the manifold grace of God, serve one another with whatever gift each of you has received. Whoever speaks must do so as one speaking the very words of God; whoever serves must do so with the strength that God supplies, so that God may be glorified in all things through Jesus Christ. To Him belong the glory and the power forever and ever. Amen* (1 Peter 4:10–11).

2. Inner Vows

An inner vow is a form of self-protective defense mechanism—a vow we've made inside to ourselves to protect ourselves in the way we have determined best. For example, "I'll never let them see me cry," or "I'll never trust anybody again." In a way, this seems reasonable and even healthy to take care of ourselves. Many times this is because we've been deeply hurt, abused, rejected, taken advantage of, betrayed, had our weaknesses, vulnerabilities, and trust used against us, etcetera.

300

So down inside, we decide that's not going to happen anymore. And we make choices within our heart and mind that become walls of self-protection, which also become walls of self-isolation and self-restriction. An image the Lord showed me one time is that it's like setting the margins on a page of your typewriter or computer. Our lives were intended to flow freely and expressively across the experiences and encounters of our days, while we allow the Lord to lead our choices and guide our steps. But when we make these self-determined inner vows, it's like setting margins that restrict the fullness of our lives. We may think we are just being wise or responsible and just taking care of ourselves. Maybe we're doing this because something has happened and we feel like if we don't do it, nobody else will, not even God. We may feel like we've got to "watch out for number one." I've heard people say things like, "Fool me once, shame on you. Fool me twice, shame on me." These are all thoughts and attitudes that lead us to take the control ourselves, instead of submitting control to the Lord to lead our thoughts and guide our decisions.

There are some "vows" or decisions of our will that are godly and healthy. Where a vow becomes an inner vow that is unhealthy is when we make that vow out of our own will instead of seeking the leading of God's will. It's a form of pride that manifests in control. It's saying, "I'm going to do what I think I need to do to take care of myself." It's another way where we are tempted to take control, instead of letting the Lord be in control, and where we are being lord instead of letting Jesus be Lord over that area of our lives. The enemy of our souls will tempt us to take control and assert our own "lordship" over areas of our lives so he can then use God's spiritual principles against us. One of those key principles that comes up over and over again in healing prayer ministry is this: "God opposes the proud, but give grace to the humble" (James 4:6; 1 Peter 5:5).

Pride is the opposite of humility that says, "Lord, I was really hurt and I want to release that hurt to You. Give me Your wisdom and show me how to be wise in Your ways by Your leading. I'm willing to be fully alive to the painful emotions of things that happen in this broken, fallen world, but I want to release that pain to You and be unrestricted and unrestrained in the experiences of life."

Sometimes we don't even realize that we've done it or that we're continuing to do it. Other times, it's a conscious, deliberate choice of our free will. But many times, it's a much more subtle choice made out of the subconscious realm of our mind. It's rooted in a learned behavior from the first choice, which has been reinforced through habit with every subsequent choice—whether we even know we are continuing to make that choice or not. Sometimes, it's even a decision made in a broken, detached, dissociated part of our soul (mind, will, and emotions) and now hidden and buried deep down in the unconscious realm of our being, stuck at that age and moment of our life.[38]

In any event, when we've made inner vows, we have chosen to take control of that area of our life. And there are consequences for those choices. In essence, we find ourselves resisting God and opposing the power of His grace that He wants to release to us to help us. But our pride, manifested in our own control, pushes back the grace of God in areas where we need it the most. And then the vows we have made continue to be fulfilled, but at great cost. They limit the fullness of our lives in a self-imposed, self-protection pocket of resistance (a stronghold). We then function out of our own strength and will (the soul) and that becomes emotionally, spiritually, *and* physically exhausting.

Some Common Inner Vows

Common inner vows we often see in prayer ministry are:

- I'll never trust anybody again.
- I'll never let them see me cry.
- I'll never let anybody get that close to me again.
- I'll never be like my Dad.
- I can only count on myself: I can't ever count on anybody else.
- I'll show them I'm somebody worth their attention and respect.
- I'll always show my strengths and never my weaknesses

---

[38] We'll cover this concept of deep level detachment and dissociation of the soul in our section on Brokenness and Unresolved Traumas.

These can often seem like godly aspirations, but how we get there makes all the difference. Trouble comes when we choose to accomplish them in our own strength and out of our own self-will and self-determination. We need to choose to depend on God, entrusting ourselves to Him and His wisdom and power. Pride is depending on ourselves; humility is depending on God. "God opposes the proud, but gives grace to the humble" (James 4:6). None of us can afford to oppose the grace of God; we need all we can get! And we have a loving God who loves to give it if we will only humble ourselves to admit we need it and choose to receive it.

Prayers to Break Inner Vows

When we discover that inner vows may be a barrier to healing, and they're a barrier that prevents us from experiencing the full range of emotions and freedom in life, we might pray a prayer for ourselves or lead someone in a prayer like this:

"Father, forgive me. I realize now that I have made some inner vows. I have taken charge and taken control over some areas of my life instead of letting You be in charge and entrusting control to You. When I said in my heart, 'I'll never _____,' that was the sin of pride. That was me trying to take care of myself in my power and in my way, instead of turning to You and depending on You for Your wisdom and Your power to help me. But I confess that and repent of that as sin. I turn away from that way of thinking and living, and I turn to You. I renounce that vow in the name of Jesus. I choose, by Your grace, to be fully alive to the full range of emotions and the experiences of life, unrestricted and unrestrained by my own defense mechanisms.

Lord Jesus, I'm asking You to be my protector and defender, my healer and redeemer. As best as I can, I willingly humble myself in Your sight and ask for the fullness of Your grace. By the power of the blood of Jesus, I am free from these vows. As Your Word says, "For freedom Christ has set us free. Stand firm, therefore, and do not submit again to a yoke of slavery" (Galatians 5:1). I stand firm in the power of Your grace, no longer choosing to submit to my self-imposed yokes of slavery.

Come, Holy Spirit. Empower me to trust in God and depend upon You. Heal me from the hurts of my past and release me to move on in the grace of God. Give me wisdom and grace to live as Your Word says: "Trust in the Lord with all your heart, and lean not on your own understanding. In all your ways acknowledge Him, and He shall direct your paths. Do not be wise in your own eyes; fear the Lord and depart from evil. It will be health to your flesh, and strength to your bones" (Proverbs 3:5–8 NKJV). In Jesus' name I pray, Amen."

Then we might pray for deliverance and cleansing from anything unholy that's attached to this person through any of these areas, as we've discussed before. It's good to always fill the places where there was darkness with the light of God's Spirit and Truth, as His Holy Spirit leads.

A Few Prayer Ministry Pointers

These kinds of prayers can be very short and simple. Here, I'm adding a little more detail to emphasis the principles. I often do this in prayer ministry as well when I feel led by the Lord. Short prayers are just as powerful as long prayers. Jesus reminded us that it's not by our "many words" that we are heard and answered by God through prayer (Matthew 6:7). However, sometimes praying a longer prayer for ourselves or others helps us grasp more or the depth of what we are praying as God transforms us by the renewing of our minds (Romans 12:1–2).

As you can see, I often weave in Scripture into my prayers, either reading them from the Bible or quoting them or paraphrasing them as I pray. *Getting the exact chapter and verse is not really as important as releasing the power of the Word of God into someone's life through our prayers.* We can always look up the exact reference later to help them keep living it out, so we should not be intimidated to use the key gist of Scripture in our prayers as we believe the Lord is leading, even if we don't have it perfectly memorized. God hears our hearts and sees our desire to seek Him and the power of His Word and Spirit in our lives. His abundant grace covers our shortcomings and failures in ways we would be astonished to believe.

304

And God is able to provide you with every blessing in abundance, so that by always having enough of everything, you may share abundantly in every good work (2 Corinthians 9:8).

But law came in, with the result that the trespass multiplied; but where sin increased, grace abounded all the more (Romans 5:20).

3. False Beliefs

The last sub-category of Word and Attitudes that can be barriers to healing is False Beliefs. The things we believe about ourselves, about others, about God, about life—right or wrong—affect every area of our lives. Our worldview determines and defines our world in many ways. In a simple sense, our belief systems are the ways we process and filter the information and events of life through our minds.

Key Scriptures and Principles

Some key Scriptures and guiding spiritual principles for this area of ministry are:

For as he thinks in his heart, so is he (Proverbs 23:7 NKJV); and

According to your faith, let it be done to you (Matthew 9:29).

It matters what we think and what we believe. There is absolute truth, which is objective and true whether we believe it, embrace it, obey it, or not. And at the same time, what we believe and embrace as "our truth" in the belief systems of our minds determines, in large part, how we perceive and experience life. God wants those belief systems to be based upon His Word and His Truth. His Word and Truth is personified in Jesus Christ our Lord. He is the Word made flesh (John 1:1, 14). He is the Truth (John 14:6).

God wants to conform our thoughts to His thoughts and our mind to His mind, as He conforms our nature to His nature (Romans 8:29). He does not want us or our belief systems "conformed to this world" but wants us "transformed by the renewing of (our) minds" (Romans 12:2). His Word inspires us and even commands us: "Let the same mind be in you that was in Christ Jesus" (Philippians 2:5). Growing the grace of

God and the knowledge of His truth, "we have the mind of Christ" (1 Corinthians 2:16).

Battlefield of the Mind

This is why the mind is such a battlefield—such a war zone between our flesh and God's Spirit, between the enemy of our souls and the Redeemer of our souls. As Paul observed in his own life what is true in each of our lives:

> For I delight in the law of God in my inmost self, but I see in my members another law at war with the law of my mind, making me captive to the law of sin that dwells in my members. Wretched man that I am! Who will rescue me from this body of death? Thanks be to God through Jesus Christ our Lord! So then, with my mind I am a slave to the law of God, but with my flesh I am a slave to the law of sin
> (Romans 7:22–25).

The "law of God" is His Word and His Truth. The "law of sin" is everything that is false and opposed to the Word and Truth of God, personified and perfectly revealed in the person and nature of Jesus Christ our Lord. We can thank God for exposing our flesh, the unsanctified areas of the mind, will, and emotions of our soul that are not yet conformed to the mind of Christ. He rescues us and sets us free from sin and death by exposing the lies of our false belief systems. Then in the steadfast mercy of His healing love, He reveals the truth, and giving us grace to embrace it, He reveals Christ as Truth and gives us grace to embrace Him.

The Spirit of Truth

This is all part of the ministry of the Holy Spirit, who is "the Spirit of Truth" (John 14:17 and 15:26). "When the Spirit of Truth comes, He will guide (us) into all truth," just as Jesus promised (John 16:13). The Holy Spirit is always leading us to Christ; therefore, He is always leading us to Truth (John 16:14). In healing prayer ministry, He is exposing the lies and replacing them with truth. He is exposing our false belief systems so we can recognize them and replace them with true belief systems in the power of God's grace.

306

Then Jesus said to the Jews who had believed in Him, "If you continue in My word, you are truly My disciples; and you will know the truth, and the truth will make you free" (John 8:31-32).

So if the Son makes you free, you will be free indeed (John 8:36).

Some Common False Beliefs

False beliefs and false belief systems are as endless as the lies we are tempted to believe from "the father of lies" (John 8:44). He uses these lies to build "strongholds" of deception and "every proud obstacle raised up against the knowledge of God" (2 Corinthians 10:3-5). So many of these false belief systems are false ideas, false teachings, false doctrines, false mindsets calculated to distort our image of God and get us to mistrust Him, His goodness, and His Word.[39]

This has been a key strategy of Satan's warfare from the beginning, when the serpent questioned the truth of God's words and tempted Eve to reject God's truth and embrace Satan's lies (Genesis 3:1–5). He questioned God's integrity: "Did God say..." Then he questioned God's consequences: "You will not die..." In a sense, then, from that first encounter with the kingdom of darkness, the most ancient false belief system of all is, "God cannot be trusted." And close behind that one is, "I can sin without consequences."

From the enemy's attempts to deceive us and confuse, to divide us from God and get us angry with Him instead of at the one who comes "to steal and kill and destroy," these are some common false belief systems that form strongholds of the enemy in our minds:

- God cannot be trusted.
- I can sin without consequence.
- God doesn't love me or care about me.
- I'm not worthy of God's love or anybody else's.
- God will help or heal others, but not me.

---

[39] Mike Chaille, a good friend of mine with a powerful prayer ministry who has prayed for me, calls this "stinking thinking." But you'd have to hear it in his southern accent and dry sense of humor to get the full flavor of his wit and wisdom.

- I can't be forgiven for the things I've done.
- My future will be just like my past; things will never change.
- People don't ever change, and I can't ever change.
- Evil is greater than good; the wicked always prosper.
- You have to go along with the world to get along in the world.
- The Bible is not always true, or not true for today, or not true for me.
- Everything that happens is God's will.[40]

Many false beliefs are rooted in a fatalistic, hopeless mindset, devoid of the will and power of God to redeem. No wonder the fruit of these roots is so often discouragement, depression, and despair. When the truth is, "For God all things are possible" (Mark 10:27). And when we choose to believe God, trust in the truth of His Word, and embrace His will and power to redeem, "All things can be done for the one who believes" (Mark 9:23).

---

[40] This is such a critical area that almost always comes up in one way or another where either consciously or subconsciously a person is so angry at God down deep inside for something God never did or willed. It's a mistaken understanding of the sovereignty of God. As explained in depth before, God is love and in His sovereignty He created us for a relationship of love. To have true love, we must have the freedom to love Him or not, obey Him or not, worship Him or not. So when He created us in His nature for a true relationship of love, freedom to refuse to love Him or obey Him was necessary. Out of that freedom to choose, which all human beings and spiritual beings have, as created by God, evil choices are often made by humans and spirits that are absolutely contrary to God's will, despite His sovereignty. It breaks God's heart when it happens and He is fiercely angry at the enemy of our souls, but He comes in power to redeem what's been done when we entrust it to Him and call on His name (See, for example, the heart of God to liberate us and destroy our spiritual enemies revealed and personified in Psalm 18 and Revelation 19).

I know many of my Calvinist-oriented brothers and sisters in Christ have a different perspective, but one day we will all see how all this fits together in God's perfect harmony, even the paradox of God's sovereignty and free will (1 Corinthians 13:9). In the meantime, from my perspective, I often find this misunderstanding to be at the heart of deep-seated anger and mistrust toward God for something that God didn't do and God didn't will. When people begin to renounce the lie that God did this evil thing to them or to the one they loved and turn their anger toward the true enemy, "the spiritual forces of evil," and release God of their judgments against Him, they can trust God again at a deeper level than ever before (Ephesians 6:12). They shall will the truth and the truth will set them free (John 8:32).

So the path to victory in the battlefield of our mind is to allow God to expose the lies and replace them with truth. We pray for discernment and expect by faith to receive it as God begins to answer our prayers in line with His will revealed His Word to renew our minds and transform our ways.

> *Do not be conformed to this world, but be transformed by the renewing of your minds, so that you may discern what is the will of God—what is good and acceptable and perfect* (Romans 12:2).

As we allow the Lord to search our hearts and minds to expose where we have embraced lies instead of truth, where we are living under false belief systems instead of a true belief system, where we have "exchanged the truth about God for a lie and worshipped and served the creature rather than the Creator," God begins to free us from the captivity of deception and confusion (Romans 1:25). But we are not merely passive in this process, not merely spectators in the warfare of our minds. By the power of God's grace, we renounce the lies we've embraced and we choose to believe God's truth.

> *Indeed, we live as human beings, but we do not wage war according to human standards; for the weapons of our warfare are not merely human, but they have divine power to destroy strongholds. We destroy arguments and every proud obstacle raised up against the knowledge of God, and we take every thought captive to obey Christ* (2 Corinthians 10:3–5).

Going forward in the freedom that we find in Christ, we have greater discernment, no longer tainted by the deception and confusion of the enemy and his strongholds of false belief systems. We can more easily recognize the lies as they come like "flaming arrows of the evil one" (Ephesians 6:16). Instead we can "take every thought captive" and bring them into submission to the obedience of Christ by rejecting them before we ever receive them and allow them to poison our minds and hearts against the truth.

Prayer for Freedom from False Belief Systems

However the Holy Spirit would lead us, we want to come to a place of renouncing the lies and embracing the truth when a false belief system

309

is exposed. We want them to stop agreeing with the lie and start agreeing with the truth. Getting to the lie that a person first believed is often the heart of a mighty fortress that's been built up and reinforced to fortify that lie through many years of thinking that way. Sometimes this is discovered in the person's attitudes, comments, and perspective about other things that are more superficial or immediate. But it's good to let the Holy Spirit lead us back to the place that the lie first entered in, which is usually some traumatic, painful, or shameful experience. And sometimes it's more a matter of embracing a teaching, understanding, or doctrine that is not fully in line with the Word of God or the whole counsel of God.

A prophetic picture[41] the Lord showed me once in this area was a picture of a medieval castle with thick walls and a heavy wooden gate, protected by metal bars. This is a stronghold of the mind, holding the person captive to deception and often isolated and surrounded by walls of bitterness, resentment, judgment, and prideful control. Some people are like a damsel in distress, crying for help, because they've come to know from the misery of their lives that they need to be set free but don't know how. Others are more like the black knight standing guard at the gate or eternally patrolling the walls to make sure nobody gets in and pouring down hot oil on the heads of any who try.[42]

Still others are like the king of their castle, constantly surveying their domain and the kingdom they've built with their own hands. They are never asking for nor willing to receive help until all they've built and sustained by their own power and might, rather than the Spirit of the

---

[41] See Acts 2:17. Since old men dream dreams and young men see visions, the Lord is gracious to continue to affirm me that I'm still a young man.

[42] I just have to say, it's more fun to pray for the damsels in distress than the black knights, but often the damsels turn into the knights when you start getting close to the most sensitive areas of pain and confusion. Either way, you often get a little hot oil poured on your head before Jesus comes in to save the day, riding on His white horse with fire in His eyes and a sword in His hand (see Revelation 19). But it's all worth it in the end. After all, our true treasure is stored up in heaven, where we will receive our true thanks (Matthew 6:19-20). [Special note to the reader: At this point in my writing, I've just returned from a renewal conference, filled afresh with the Holy Spirit and the joy of the Lord, so if my writing style seems a little too irreligious or offensive to you, blame God].

Lord, begins to crumble and fall like castles made of sand. But brokenness is always a good place for healing to begin. "The Lord is near to the brokenhearted, and saves the crushed in spirit" (Psalm 34:18). If we will humble ourselves in the sight of the Lord, He will lift us up (James 4:10).

But no matter how thick the walls, how heavy the gates, how sturdy the bars, Jesus taught us to be aggressive in the authority of His name as His disciples and His church. Truth is a key of the kingdom of heaven. The power of His name and the Blood of the Lamb are mighty weapons of our warfare. And those gates will not prevail and those strongholds must come down if that person is willing to agree with God, the Redeemer, and quit agreeing with Satan, the deceiver.

> *And I tell you, you are Peter, and on this rock I will build My church, and the gates of Hades will not prevail against it. I will give you the keys of the kingdom of heaven, and whatever you bind on earth will be bound in heaven, and whatever you loose on earth will be loosed in heaven* (Matthew 16:18–19).

> *Indeed, we live as human beings, but we do not wage war according to human standards; for the weapons of our warfare are not merely human, but they have divine power to destroy strongholds. We destroy arguments and every proud obstacle raised up against the knowledge of God, and we take every thought captive to obey Christ. We are ready to punish every disobedience when your obedience is complete* (2 Corinthians 10:3–6).

Jesus rejoices when we go in the authority He has given us to minister healing and deliverance in the lives and places where He sends us:

> *The seventy returned with joy, saying, "Lord, in Your name even the demons submit to us!" He said to them, "I watched Satan fall from heaven like a flash of lightning. See, I have given you authority to tread on snakes and scorpions, and over all the power of the enemy; and nothing will hurt you. Nevertheless, do not rejoice at this, that the spirits submit to you, but rejoice that your names are written in heaven." At that same hour Jesus rejoiced in the Holy Spirit and said, "I thank you, Father, Lord of heaven and earth, because You have hidden these things from the wise and the intelligent and*

have revealed them to infants; yes, Father, for such was Your gracious will"
(Luke 10:17–21).

So by the leading of the Holy Spirit, we might lead the person in a prayer
of freedom and healing in this area with something like this:

"Lord Jesus, You are the Way, the Truth, and the Life. And You have
been revealing Your truth to me. I see now that I have been confused
and deceived into believing that _____. And I see now that what I have
been believing about You (or about myself, or about that situation, etc.)
is not true. The truth is _____ (the scriptural opposite of that lie or
whatever the Lord shows).

So right now, in the name of Jesus, I renounce that lie and I embrace
the truth. I renounce every spirit that's claimed any ground in my life
and that's confused my thinking. I give them no permission to remain,
no access point or hold to claim. I bind them up, with all their lies and
means of access and influence, and I overcome them by the Blood of
the Lamb and the word of my testimony. I submit this area and every
area of my life to God, under the Lordship of Jesus Christ, and
command them to go now, defeated, to the feet of Jesus, to be judged
by Him, and never to return. I know the Truth and the Truth is setting
me free.

Come, Holy Spirit. Come and fill me afresh with Your truth and Your
life. Empower me to walk in the ways of Christ. Bind the mind of Christ
to my mind and loose away from my mind all deception and confusion.
Sanctify me entirely in my spirit and soul and body, and cleanse me, fill
me, and empower me to be sound and blameless at the coming of Christ.

Thank You, heavenly Father. I am Your son, a child of God. Thank You
for the gift of Your Spirit living in me, leading me into all truth, and
filling me with all the fullness of God. What I have asked for is already
done in heaven and it's being done here on earth as it is in heaven. And
I know You will be faithful to bring to completion all that You have
begun. I praise You and thank You for who You are and all You have
done. In Jesus' name I pray, Amen."

At this point, we might just pray a prayer of blessing over the person, as the Lord leads or share any Scriptures or images that came to mind during the prayer. If led, we might speak words in affirmation and agreement of what's been prayed. Sometimes we might identify any specific spirits that came to mind or that were revealed in any way, commanding them something like this:

"In the name Jesus, I command every spirit that's claimed any ground in any of these areas to be bound. I bind every spirit of deception, confusion, false teaching, bitterness, judgment, and pride to be bound. I overcome you by the Blood of the Lamb and agree with my brother, _____, that you must go now, defeated to the feet of Jesus.[43] Thank You, Jesus, that You came to destroy the works of the devil, to bind up the brokenhearted, and to set the captives free. Thank You for this breakthrough in _____'s life and all the breakthroughs to come as he continues to trust in You, submit every area of his life to Your Lordship, resisting the devil and commanding him to flee. Come, Holy Spirit, and fill ____ with the righteousness, peace, and joy of the kingdom of God. In Jesus' name I pray, Amen."

In these prayers, as in all prayers, we want to just follow the leading of the Spirit, as I have tried to do even in writing these prayers here as one possible flow of healing prayer ministry. But God is infinitely creative and so are the prayers He moves on our hearts to pray for one another.

---

[43] Some very powerful and effective prayer ministries teach that you should not speak directly to the spirits, that embracing the truth is enough, and that sooner or later, the spirits feeding on the lies will go. I'm sure that's true, but at the same time, Jesus often spoke directly to the spirits and commanded them to go. He is our model, in the authority of His name. But He rarely ministered healing and deliverance in the same way. So we just all give much grace to one another in how the Lord uses all parts of His body for the purposes of His kingdom. We can all learn from one another because we are learning from Him through one another.

By the same token, some teach that the spirits do not have specific names or functions or identities and we should not identify specific spirits (demons) in ministry. But Scripture does identify many spirits by specific identity, such as fear, infirmity, Python, etcetera. So, once again, we should seek the Lord's leading, and follow His leading for how He chooses to use us personally in ministry, testing all things against His Word, and giving much grace to one another since none of us fully understand all of His Word on this side of heaven. Much of this discussion is included in more detail in my section on deliverance.

So we can learn the principles of His Word, learn from the ministries and prayer patterns of others, but we should always seek to be led by the Holy Spirit at every particular moment of prayer ministry. I find myself praying the gist of this Scripture at the beginning of many prayer ministry times, which always helps keep me humble and desperately dependent upon the Lord's leading:

> *Likewise the Spirit helps us in our weakness; for we do not know how to pray as we ought, but that very Spirit intercedes with sighs too deep for words. And God, who searches the heart, knows what is the mind of the Spirit, because the Spirit intercedes for the saints according to the will of God* (Romans 8:26–27).

And while we come to God in deep humility, we also want to come to Him with bold faith. It's not either/or, but rather both/and. Both humility and faith honor and please God.

> *And this is the boldness we have in Him, that if we ask anything according to His will, He hears us. And if we know that He hears us in whatever we ask, we know that we have obtained the requests made of Him* (1 John 5:14–15).

> *And without faith it is impossible to please God, for whoever would approach Him must believe that He exists and that He rewards those who seek him* (Hebrews 11:6).

Chapter 19

False Spirituality

"God is Spirit" (John 4:24). And He has created us to desire Him and worship Him spiritually. This is our true spirituality, which is a gift of God: to know Him and worship Him in spirit and in truth.

> *But the hour is coming, and is now here, when the true worshipers will worship the Father in spirit and truth, for the Father seeks such as these to worship Him. God is Spirit, and those who worship Him must worship in spirit and truth* (John 4:23–24).

"By the mercies of God" we are invited "to present [our] bodies as a living sacrifice, holy and acceptable to God, which is [our] spiritual worship" (Romans 12:1). We choose whether to present ourselves to Him or not—true worship must be freely given.

To worship God is to honor Him and reverence Him as our Creator and Sustainer of life. "O Come, let us worship and bow down, let us kneel before the Lord, our Maker! For He is our God, and we are the people of His pasture, and the sheep of His hand" (Psalm 95:6–7). To bow before Him is to humble ourselves before Him and submit to His rule and reign in our lives.

We worship God because He alone is worthy of our worship. And though He calls us and commands us to worship Him alone, even His commandment is not out of some sense of ego or pride. He calls us to worship Him as means of His grace to change us into His nature. It is His spiritual principle that we become like the One we worship.

> *Now the Lord is the Spirit, and where the Spirit of the Lord is, there is freedom. And all of us, with unveiled faces, seeing the glory of the Lord as though reflected in a mirror, are being transformed into the same image from one degree of glory to another; for this comes from the Lord, the Spirit* (2 Corinthians 3:17–18).

Through worship, God transforms us into His image. In the culture of the world, people worship their heroes and idolize their gods, wanting to be just like them. Idols and gods are the things to which they give priority and authority in their lives in the place that only God deserves. "Those who worship vain idols forsake their true loyalty" (Jonah 2:8). And they become transformed into the image of the idols that they worship and the gods to which they bow down.

You become like what (or whom) you worship. So God wants us to worship Him alone, so that we become like Him, "from one degree of glory to another" (2 Corinthians 3:17). That's why Jesus boldly confirmed this spiritual principle in the face of Satan's temptation to worship him rather than God: "It is written, 'Worship the Lord your God, and serve Him only' " (Luke 4:8). God declares, "You shall worship no other god, because the Lord whose name is Jealous, is a jealous God" (Exodus 34:14). This is not a human jealousy like envy or insecurity. This is a holy jealousy that is unwilling to settle for anything less than our love for Him with all our heart, all our mind, all our soul, and all our strength (Mark 12:20). To love Him is to worship Him, to know Him, and become like Him, for He is love.

> *Whoever does not love does not know God, for God is love.... By this we know that we abide in Him and He in us, because He has given us of His Spirit.... So we have known and believe the love that God has for us. God is love, and those who abide in love abide in God, and God abides in them* (1 John 4:8–16).

Worship as Intimacy with God

He calls us and longs for us to come into the bond of fellowship and communion with Him, but He does not force us. "God is faithful; by Him you were called into the fellowship of His Son, Jesus Christ our Lord" (1 Corinthians 1:9). When we respond to His call by His grace through our spiritual worship, we share in "the communion of the Holy Spirit" (2 Corinthians 13:13). And "anyone united to the Lord becomes one spirit with Him" (1 Corinthians 6:17).

Through the abiding presence of God's Holy Spirit living within us, we come to know Him. This spiritual bond of "the communion of the Holy Spirit" is the deeply intimate fellowship of our trusting relationship with God in every dimension of His Being with every dimension of our being.

316

By the Holy Spirit, the Father and the Son come and abide within us in the spiritual intimacy and bond of God's love for us.

> *If you love Me, you will keep My commandments. And I will ask the Father, and He will give you another Advocate, to be with you forever. This is the Spirit of Truth, whom the world cannot receive, because it neither sees Him nor knows Him. You know Him, because He abides with you, and He will be in you. I will not leave you orphaned; I am coming to you. In a little while the world will no longer see Me, but you will see Me; because I live, you also will live. On that day you will know that I am in My Father, and you in Me, and I in you. They who have my commandments and keep them are those who love Me; and those who love Me will be loved by My Father, and I will love them and reveal Myself to them.... Those who love Me will keep My word, and My Father will love them, and we will come to them and make Our home with them*
> (John 14:15–23).

Satan's Counterfeit of False Spirituality for True Spirituality

The enemy of our souls hates the intimacy we have with God. He's insanely jealous of the relationship and place of honor and love we have with God. And he jealously craves the worship that only God is due. He exposed his true heart and dark strategy as he tempted Jesus, when the Son of God lived out His life in the flesh on earth as the Son of Man:

> *Jesus, full of the Holy Spirit, returned from the Jordan and was led by the Spirit in the wilderness, where for forty days He was tempted by the devil.... Then the devil led Him up and showed Him in an instant all the kingdoms of the world. And the devil said to Him, "To You I will give their glory and all this authority; for it has been given over to me, and I give it to anyone I please. If You, then, will worship me, it will all be Yours." Jesus answered him, "It is written, 'Worship the Lord your God, and serve only Him'"*
> (Luke 4:1–8).

Satan boasts, "I will ascend to heaven; I will raise my throne above the stars of God; ... I will ascend to the tops of the clouds, I will make myself like the Most High" (Isaiah 14:13–14). The Lord is enthroned on our worship and praise (Psalm 22:3). When He is high and lifted up, He draws all people to Himself (John 12:32). That's just what Satan wants—

to be high and lifted up, enthroned on our worship, like the Most High, with all people and all creation in submission to him. He is filled with arrogance and pride (Ezekiel 28:17). And he wants all the world to turn from God and turn to him, to submit to him, to bow down and worship him.

But *worship is a choice*. We have the freedom to choose to worship or not, and the freedom to choose who or what we worship. Some worship the living God. Some worship nature or other elements of creation such as the stars, moon, sun, earth, animals, etcetera. Some worship idols of wood and stone, created as graven images with human hands. Some worship out of love and reverence. Others worship out of deception, confusion, control, intimidation, or fear.

King Nebuchadnezzar of Babylon demanded forced worship of his golden image. The people had a choice to worship or not, but there were consequences for their choice to refuse—the fiery furnace (Daniel 3:1–7). When King Darius took over the kingdom, he issued a decree that only he could be worshipped (Daniel 6:6–9). This was also prophetic of days to come at the end of this age. One day, "the earth and its inhabitants" will be forced to worship a blasphemous "beast" and take its mark or be killed (Revelation 13:11–18). All of these are manifestations of Satan's spirit of arrogant pride to exalt himself in the place of God, through whatever means of worship he can receive—forced or otherwise.

Some even choose to bow down and directly worship Satan. This is the occult, which means "hidden." These are the teachings and practices of "the deep things of Satan" (Revelation 2:24). Engaging the occult is active participation in the kingdom of "darkness," and willingly submitting to the "power of Satan" (Acts 26:18).

Others worship out of fear, control, and intimidation. But most are deceived and confused into thinking they are worshiping God or a god or some being greater than themselves. In any event, worship of any being besides the Lord our God is the sin of idolatry, a blasphemy of God, and in effect, the worship of Satan (Exodus 20:1–6). *Broadly speaking, then, false spirituality is seeking power, protection, insight, or benefits of* **any** *kind by means of* **any** *spiritual source besides the One True God.*

318

So Satan will try to deceive us into worshipping him—whether directly or indirectly—in any way that he can. The enemy of our souls knows that whatever we worship or idolize besides God "will surely be a snare to [us]" and will become a means of his power to deceive us and enslave us (Exodus 23:33).

Let no one deceive you in any way; for that day will not come unless the rebellion comes first and the lawless one is revealed, the one destined for destruction. He opposes and exalts himself above every so-called god or object of worship, so that he takes his seat in the temple of God, declaring himself to be God.... The coming of the lawless one is apparent in the working of Satan, who uses all power, signs, lying wonders, and every kind of wicked deception for those who are perishing, because they refused to love the truth and so be saved (2 Thessalonians 2:3–10).

False spirituality is false worship—worship of a false spirit trying to usurp the place of the one, true God in our lives. "There is no God but one" (1 Corinthians 8:4). False spirituality is a perverted, distorted intimacy with a false god. God wants true intimacy with us through the communion of worship, as He fills us with His Holy Spirit. Satan wants a false intimacy with us though the communion of false worship, as he seeks to fill us with his unholy spirits. True worship and spirituality frees us to worship God with all our heart in spirit and truth. False worship and spirituality enslaves us to the things we are deceived into worshipping.

> *Formerly, when you did not know God, you were enslaved to beings that by nature are not gods. Now, however, that you have come to know God, or rather to be known by God, how can you turn back again to the weak and beggarly elemental spirits? How can you want to be enslaved to them again?* (Galatians 4:8–9).

Perhaps the most extreme example of false spirituality is the false worship of a satanic ritual. At times, I have prayed for healing and deliverance for people who were subjected to these rituals. In seeing them come to freedom in Christ as their bondages were broken, I came to see how the enemy of our souls wants to mimic and counterfeit all that is true. For example, the false communion of a satanic ritual is just that—perverted. In addition, it's a distorted counterfeit of true communion with the One True God, and is intended to bring a false

319

communion with Satan's spirits to conform human beings into Satan's evil nature. It's the opposite and counterfeit of all God desires for us— to experience the communion of the Holy Spirit and to be conformed into the image of His Son, Jesus Christ (2 Corinthians 13:13; Romans 8:29). But there are many forms and degrees of false spirituality on the continuum between the deliberate worship of Satan and the deliberate worship of the One True God.

False Spirituality of False Religions

Another form of false spirituality is the worship of the false gods of false religions. God is the Creator of heaven and earth. And He has revealed Himself to us in the written Word of His Scriptures and in the Living Word of Jesus Christ. "There is salvation in no one else, for there is no other name under heaven given among mortals by which we must be saved" (Acts 4:12). "There is no God but one" (1 Corinthians 8:4). The One True God reveals Himself to us in three Persons and Dimensions of His Being—Father, Son, and Holy Spirit. God the Holy Spirit draws us to God our Father through God the Son, as we entrust our hearts and lives to Jesus Christ as Savior and Lord. "Jesus said to him, 'I am the way, and the truth, and the life. No one comes to the Father except through Me. If you know Me, you will know My Father also. From now on you do know Him and have seen Him'" (John 14:6–7).

But "Satan disguises himself as an angel of light" in many forms and in various religions and spiritual practices, deceiving people into thinking that he is a way to heaven (2 Corinthians 11:14). One of his deceptions is the false belief system that "all roads lead to heaven," that "all religions worship one god," and that anybody who believes the Bible and disagrees is unenlightened, self-righteous, shallow, naïve, and narrow-minded. But as Jesus dared to teach and declare:

> *Enter through the narrow gate; for the gate is wide and the road is easy that leads to destruction, and there are many who take it. For the gate is narrow and the road is hard that leads to life, and there are few who find it* (Matthew 7:13–14).

> *Do not let your hearts be troubled. Believe in God, believe also in Me. In My Father's house there are many dwelling places. If it were not so, would*

I have told you that I go to prepare a place for you? And if I go and prepare a place for you, I will come again and will take you to Myself, so that where I am, there you may be also. And you know the way to the place where I am going.

Thomas said to Him, "Lord, we do not know where you are going. How can we know the way?"

Jesus said to him, "I am the way, and the truth, and the life. No one comes to the Father except through Me. If you know Me, you will know My Father also. From now on you do know Him and have seen Him" (John 14:1–7).

The Father and I are One (John 10:30).

True religion is a personal relationship with Jesus Christ. Anything less than that or other than that is a deception, according to the Word of God. But God is faithful and merciful to meet us where we are and lead us to Himself. "He has not left Himself without a witness" in all nations, cultures, and generations—desiring for all to seek Him and turn away from every false image and idol that any may think represent Him (Acts 14:16–17). And though anyone may start off in a spiritual state of confusion from their culture or religion which they have believed to be true, in God's mercy and love, He promises us this:

When you search for Me, you will find Me; if you seek Me with all your heart, I will let you find Me, says the Lord. (Jeremiah 29:13–14).

False religions are a scheme of Satan to take advantage of our God-given desire for a spiritual relationship with the One True God. And the enemy is there to provide false images of false gods to lead us away from true worship of the One True God. But idols and gods of false religions are not really "gods" at all; these are "the elemental spirits" confronted by the truth of the gospel of Jesus Christ (Galatians 4:8–10; Colossians 2:8). They are a means of the enemy of our souls to deceive people by misrepresenting and counterfeiting the true identity and nature of our loving and merciful God who seeks, above all, an eternal relationship of love with each of us.

Hence, as to the eating of food offered to idols, we know that "no idol in the world really exists," and that "there is no God but one." Indeed, even though there may be so-called gods in heaven or on earth—as in fact there are **many gods and many lords**—*yet for us there is one God, the Father, from whom are all things and for whom we exist, and one Lord, Jesus Christ, through whom are all things and through whom we exist."*
(1 Corinthians 8:4–6, emphasis added).

The "many gods and many lords" are merely the means Satan uses to try to deceive us and enslave us through our submission to false gods and false lords over our lives. In the end, it's not the "so-called gods in heaven or on earth" that are worshipped, but Satan himself, who is jealously stealing the worship due God alone.

False Spiritual Practices

Not all spiritual practices are holy spiritual practices. Just because something is "spiritual" doesn't mean it's godly. Just as there are false gods and false religions, there are false religious and false spiritual practices. Many spiritual activities are a distorted counterfeit and deception of the true spiritual means of drawing nearer to God. They are calculated by the enemy of our souls to confuse us, deceiving us into drawing nearer to the false gods who masquerade as the One True God.

Many "New Age" practices, "spiritual disciplines" of false religions, and many forms of "prayer" and "meditation" that are not directed to the One True God are examples of false spiritual practices that lead to bondage rather than freedom. *The fruit of these practices is often confusion, depression, fear, and a growing distance from God.* When we follow the trail back to where these negative experiences began, the Holy Spirit often uses healing prayer ministry to reveal a person's participation in false spiritual practices as the door that gave access to the enemy to bring destruction into a person's life.

Christian ministries of healing and deliverance often provide checklists of various suspect spiritual activities that a person may have participated in along the journey of their life. Since most people have never heard of most of the things on most ministries lists, we just list a few things that are more common and ask the people to tell us about any particular spiritual practices in which they've been involved. The Holy Spirit often shows us things as well.

My purpose here will be to discuss some of the key spiritual principles to know and apply in discerning whether any particular activity is of the Lord or not. And even if we point something out to someone, I like to ask the Lord to show the person whether it's right or not. Some things may have been intentional and some inadvertent, some may have been taking it seriously and some may have just been playing around. But the enemy does not play fair and may take advantage of an open door, no matter how innocent or infrequent the activity may have been.

Spiritual Principle of Permission

As I said earlier, worship is a choice. God does not force Himself or force worship upon us. True worship must be freely given. In that sense, Satan can't force worship upon us either, though he does try to threaten, intimidate, and deceive us into worshipping him in one form or another. And when he gets us to participate in a religious or spiritual practice that is not directed to the One True God, he is gaining our permission to allow access of what we are worshipping into our lives.

We become like what we worship (2 Corinthians 3:18). Any spirit associated with the idol or alter or object of our worship then has legal right and permission in the spiritual realm to have access to us and to conform us into its nature. This is the opposite of God's plan for us, but uses the same spiritual principle God has created to help conform us and transform us into His nature (Romans 8:29).

> *I appeal to you therefore, brothers and sisters, by the mercies of God, to present your bodies as a living sacrifice, holy and acceptable to God, which is your spiritual worship. Do not be conformed to this world, but be transformed by the renewing of your minds, so that you may discern what is the will of God—what is good and acceptable and perfect*
> (Romans 12:1–2).

When we willingly present our bodies, our souls, or our spirits to false gods by participating in false religious or spiritual practices, we sin against God and open ourselves up to evil. Out of God's love for us and

His wisdom of knowing the enslaving power and bondages of unholy or occult false spirituality, He forbids us from it.

> *When you come into the land that the Lord your God is giving you, you must not learn to imitate the abhorrent practices of those nations. No one shall be found among you who makes a son or daughter pass through fire, or who practices divination, or is a soothsayer, or an augur, or a sorcerer, or one who casts spells, or who consults ghosts or spirits, or who seeks oracles from the dead. For whoever does these things is abhorrent to the Lord; it is because of such abhorrent practices that the Lord your God is driving them out before you. You must remain completely loyal to the Lord your God. Although these nations that you are about to dispossess do give heed to soothsayers and diviners, as for you, the Lord your God does not permit you to do so* (Deuteronomy 18:9–14).

"Idolatry" and "sorcery" or "witchcraft" are sinful "works of the flesh" in opposition to the fruit of the Holy Spirit (Galatians 5:20). These are acts of "participation in demonic activities" (v. 20 NLT). God forbids them because they can ensnare us and enslave us in bondage to the evil they invite and invoke. And there are many "New Age" versions of these ancient practices of every age.

When we've participated in false religions or false spiritual practices, we need to confess it as sin and renounce any spirits associated with those practices. As such, we revoke any permission given to those spirits to have influence in our lives, and we reject them from gaining any access into our lives. As we willingly submit ourselves to God, we can then actively resist Satan and the spirits of his kingdom who have claimed permission or access in our lives, and command them to flee (James 4:7).

Spiritual Principle of Passivity

In Christian prayer and meditation, we actively engage our spirits with God's Spirit. Even in contemplative prayer, where we try to be still and quiet and wait on the Lord, we still seek to actively, though simply, lift our hearts to the Lord in a specific, deliberate way. This is an active spirituality, rather than a passive spirituality. It's a simple, but deliberately active choice to respond to the Lord's invitation to "be still and know that I am God" (Psalm 46:10). To "wait on the Lord" is a conscious choice and act of our free will (Isaiah 40:31).

This is in stark contrast to many spiritual practices of the New Age movement or other religions where the person tries to become as passive as possible. Chants or mantras are often spoken or intoned in order to be numbed into nothingness to effect a peace and oneness with the universe. Part of the idea is that you are moving toward a state of being that is indistinct from all other beings in a type of transcending uniformity, and from there a person can either "contact" their "spirit guide" or they may choose to "astral project." Astral projection is when a person seeks to cause their spirit to leave their body while they are in this passive state.

Christian prayer and meditation, on the other hand, leads us toward unity, not uniformity. God created each one of us with great diversity, never intending to extinguish our individuality, but instead, intending to sanctify and release our unique personalities and gifts of God into their full expression. So any spiritual practice that offers a peace at the expense of our personhood is ultimately a dangerous journey into a false peace and spiritual confusion.

In a passive state of the mind or spirit, we are opening the door to the entrance of spirits associated with that practice. Like opening the front door of our house and going to sleep, we are opening the door of our soul to anything that may choose to enter in. In prayer ministry, we often find that these passive spiritual practices were the open door for occult spirits to enter in and bring spiritual deception and confusion, often followed by deep darkness, depression, spiritual dullness, and worse.

Occult objects, idols, altars, and any physical means of honoring or worshipping false gods or spirits should be destroyed (for example, 2 Kings 23:4–14). It's my perspective that the unholy spirits do no inhabit those objects, as in animism, but that the possession of these objects gives permission to the spirits associated with these objects to have access to the area and people who tolerate their presence. Another way of saying that is that the spirit is "attached" to the object, or it follows the object, the owner of the object, and can even influence the owner of the object.

Also many of those who became believers confessed and disclosed their practices. A number of those who practiced magic collected their books and burned them publicly; when the value of these books was calculated, it was found to come to fifty thousand silver coins. So the word of the Lord grew mightily and prevailed (Acts 19:18–20).

In all of our spiritual practices, we need to look at the root and source of the practice. Bad roots produce bad fruit (Matthew 7:17). Because these forms of false spirituality are so common in our culture today, often imported in whole or in part from false religions or occult practices and often relabeled as new age or enlightened spirituality, we need to know the basis of what we are practicing. We need to honestly and humbly bring them before the Lord, asking for discernment and correction when needed. Even if unintended, the answer is to confess and repent the sin of passivity, then rejecting and renouncing anything unholy that has entered in.

I mentioned before that the enemy is a created being and is not able to create anything on his own, therefore he perverts and defiles what God has created. The so-called gifts and benefits that we think we receive from the New Age movement, eastern mysticism or other false spiritual practices are counterfeits of God's gifts of His Holy Spirit (1 Corinthians 12:7–11).

Spiritual Discernment of Truth

As we can see from the previous section, all things that are spiritual are not of the Holy Spirit. All things that are supernatural are not of God. But at the same time, "God is Spirit"; and He created us to experience our relationship with Him "in spirit and in truth" (John 4:24). So we have need of great discernment—to discern what is true and what is false; what is real and what is counterfeit; what is of the Holy Spirit and what is of the unholy spirits; or merely the spirit of human will apart from the will of God. We need to grow in the gifts and graces of "the discernment of spirits" (1 Corinthians 12:10).

Jesus has warned us that in these last days, "false christs and false prophets would appear and produce great signs and omens, to lead astray, if possible, even the elect" (Matthew 24:24). "Beloved, do not

326

believe every spirit, but test the spirits to see whether they are from God; for many false prophets have gone out into the world" (1 John 4:1). And at the same time, the true nature of the true Christ will arise and shine in the body of Christ to display His character and power through His people, adding His "testimony by signs and wonders and various miracles and by gifts of the Holy Spirit, distributed according to (His) will" (Hebrews 2:4). As He declared long ago, "Very truly, I tell you, the one who believes in Me will also do the works that I do, and in fact, will do even greater works than these" (John 14:12). Your Word calls all Christians to "strive for spiritual gifts, and especially that you may prophesy" (1 Corinthians 14:1).

So as we hear prophetic words, as we're offered the wisdom that comes from God, as we observe signs, wonders, and miracles, we must discern the source and discern what is true. God's Word commands us to "test everything; hold fast to what is good" (1 Thessalonians 5:21). If we think we've heard from God, either directly or through another in the body of Christ, His Word commands us to "weigh what is said" (1 Corinthians 14:29). We are to "test the spirits" (1 John 4:1). So, as we "test everything," "weigh what is said," and "test the spirits" to fulfill our responsibility to discern the source and the truth, how do we do it? How do we "take the meat and leave the bone" so to speak? What tests or standards should we apply? How do we faithfully and accurately "discern all things" (1 Corinthians 2:15)?

Steps of Spiritual Discernment

Scripture gives us biblical, guiding principles for spiritual discernment:

1) Does it conform to the written Word of God?

"All scripture is inspired by God and is useful for teaching, for reproof, for correction, and for training in righteousness, so that everyone who belongs to God may be proficient, equipped for every good work" (2 Timothy 3:16–17). Nothing spoken through a prophetic word will contradict the written Word; nothing done in the name of God will contradict the Word of God. Yet, not everything we hear or see in our everyday lives is specifically addressed in Scripture. So this part of the testing is not solely whether something is contained in the Word of God, but whether it contradicts the Word of God. We can't look up by chapter and verse every circumstance of life, but we can seek to apply the statements and principles of God's Word to every circumstance.

2) Does it conform to the character of God?

"Beloved, let us love one another, because love is from God; everyone who loves is born of God and knows God. Whoever does not love does not know God, for God is love" (1 John 4:7–8). Does it seem to have the Father heart of God, the mind of Christ, the holy nature of the Holy Spirit? Jesus only said and did what He saw the Father do and say by the power and in the nature of the Holy Spirit (John 5:19). And a "disciple is not above his master, nor the servant above his lord" (Matthew 10:24 KJV). Is what is done or said something Jesus would do or say?

3) Does it bear witnesses with our spirit?

"For all who are led by the Spirit of God are children of God" (Romans 8:14). "We have the mind of Christ" (1 Corinthians 2:16). When we hear what is said or see what is done, do we have a sense in our spirit that this is true and of the Lord? Does it seem to "ring true"? Or do we have a check in our spirit that this may not be completely or at all from the Lord? Does it seem to bring "edification and exhortation and comfort" (1 Corinthians 14:3)? Does it seem to bring correction out of conviction that leads us to God for redemption or bring condemnation, guilt, or shame that seems to lead to despair and no hope of change? Does it bring clarity or confusion, turn us to God or turn us to another?

4) Does it bear witness to the council of others?

"In the abundance of counselors there is safety" (Proverbs 11:14). "Fools think their own way is right, but the wise listen to advice" (Proverbs 12:15). As others we trust and respect seek to discern it, what do they sense? "We know only in part, and we prophesy only in part," but when we put our parts together and seek to discern the truth in humble submission to God, do we come to a consensus and peace within ourselves and with one another? "Can two walk together unless they are agreed" (Amos 3:3)?

5) What is the fruit? "You shall know them by their fruits ... every good tree bears good fruit, but the bad tree bears bad fruit. A good tree cannot bear bad fruit, nor can a bad tree bear good fruit" (Matthew 7:16–18). Does the word or act seem to display the fruit of the Spirit or the fruit of the flesh (Galatians 5:16–26)? Does the life of the person sharing the word or doing the act seem to display the character of Christ, seeking to "follow in His steps" (1 Peter 2:21)? At the same time we must humbly remember that "there is no one who is righteous, no not even one" and "all have sinned and fall short of the glory of God," leaving a mixture of flesh and spirit, the wheat and the tares, within us all so that no one always says and does everything perfectly in line with the perfect will of God (Romans 3:10, 23).

These basic guidelines from God's Word can help us to navigate the waters of these days of both increasing darkness and increasing light (Isaiah 60:1–3). As we learn to listen to God's Spirit and to one another, affirming the gifts and graces of God speaking and moving through one another, discerning what is true, we will grow up into spiritual maturity. We will move forward in the advance of the kingdom of God within us and within our world, "until all of us come to the unity of the faith and of the knowledge of the Son of God, to maturity, to the full measure of the stature of Christ. We must no longer be children, tossed to and fro and blown about by every wind of doctrine, by people's trickery, by their craftiness in deceitful scheming. But speaking the truth in love, we must grow up in every way into Him who is the head, into Christ, from whom the whole body, joined and knit together by every ligament with which it is equipped, as each part is working properly, promotes the body's growth in building itself up in love" (Ephesians 4:13–16).

Receiving His True Spirit, not a False Spirit

There can be a danger of receiving another spirit besides the Holy Spirit (2 Corinthians 11:3–4). We must actively look to the Lord—not passively waiting on anything that may come along, but actively looking to Him alone. There is no vacuum in nature, and the emptiness will be filled with something. Unless the Lord is that something we are seeking, something else will seek to fill the void—possibly a false religious spirit, assigned to make us think we are embracing the Holy Spirit when we are embracing the false nature of an unholy spirit. Our lives will begin to manifest the fruit of the spirit we have received. We are not to become one with nature or one with any spirit but God's Holy Spirit—the Spirit of Christ in us, the hope of glory (Colossians 1:27). We are to become one with God as we abide in Him and He abides in us, as He conforms us and transforms us into the image of Son of God (John 15:4)

He is the peace we are called to seek—He who is the Prince of Peace—not the false nirvana of nothingness. We are on a journey of spiritual maturity to become fulfilled in who God created each of us to become in the uniqueness and glory of His infinite creativity. We are not on a journey to become nothing as our being is dispersed into the unity of identical conformity until there is finally nothing left of us after infinite cycles of reincarnation, as the false religions and philosophies teach.

Prayer for Freedom from False Spirituality

If we become convicted of participation in unholy spiritual practices of false spirituality, we might pray or lead others in prayers like this:

Lord Jesus, You are the way, the truth, and the life. You are the way to the Father, and I want to welcome Your Holy Spirit and not any other spirit into any area of my life. Forgive me for my participation in the false religion of _____. Forgive me for my participation in the false spiritual practices of _____. I confess that was wrong and that was sin against You. I receive Your forgiveness now through the cleansing of the blood of Jesus. Purify me in the holy fire of Your Holy Spirit. Deliver me from evil. I reject and renounce any unholy spirit that has entered in or claimed any ground in any area of my life. I reject any so-called gifts or benefits provided by any unholy spirit. I command them to be bound and I overcome them now by the blood of the Lamb and the word of my testimony. I command them to go now, defeated, to the feet of Jesus, to be judged by Him and never to return. Come, Holy Spirit. Come and fill me now with Your love and Your light as I am embraced by my Father in heaven, the One True God, my Creator, the Creator of heaven and earth.

Wherever or whenever I have used unholy powers or practices to influence the lives of others, I confess that as sin. I ask You to forgive me and I receive Your forgiveness. In the name of Jesus, I release them from every curse and effect of every unholy spiritual practice. I pray for their freedom and Your blessing of the fullness of Your salvation in their lives. I renounce and break any unholy ties between us in the name of Jesus.

Lord, reveal to me any unholy objects or possessions in my home or my life. Lead me to destroy them, as I bind up and cast out any unholy spirits associated with those things in the name of Jesus. Cleanse my home and every area of my life with the blood of Jesus and the purifying fire of the Holy Spirit. Replace them with Your peace and Your presence, in Jesus' name. Amen.

Chapter 20

Unholy Ties

God intends our relationships to be a means of His blessing in our lives—both our relationship with Him and our relationships with one another. Blessed are the ties that bind us together in love to God and to one another. "Above all, clothe yourselves with love, which binds everything together in perfect harmony." (Colossians 3:14). God desires to unite us to Himself and to one another in holy and godly ways. "Anyone united to the Lord becomes one spirit with Him" (1 Corinthians 6:17). Being bound together in godly love is at the heart of the purpose of our creation and the good news of the gospel of the kingdom of God—to love God and love one another.

> *"You shall love the Lord your God with all your heart, and with all your soul, and with all your mind." This is the greatest and first commandment. And a second is like it: "You shall love your neighbor as yourself." On these two commandments hang all the law and the prophets*
> (Matthew 22:37–40).

Synergy of Relationship

"Synergy" is the combined effect of two or more forces so that the sum is greater than the individual parts. This is a spiritual principle God uses to increase and multiply the expression of His love and power through His people.

> *Two are better than one, because they have a good reward for their toil. For if they fall, one will lift up the other; but woe to one who is alone and falls and does not have another to help. Again, if two lie together, they keep warm; but how can one keep warm alone? And though one might prevail against another, two will withstand one. A threefold cord is not quickly broken* (Ecclesiastes 4:9–12).

A significant part of the purpose of marriage, for example, is the synergy of relationship when the Lord bonds two hearts and lives together in covenant with God and with one another. Their gifts and graces

333

combine to complement one another, so that the whole is greater than the parts. While the man remains an individual person with his own personality, and the woman remains an individual person with her own personality, at the same time, the two also become one. A new entity is created through the covenant and bond of marriage in a holy tie.

> *Therefore a man leaves his father and his mother and clings to his wife, and they become one flesh* (Genesis 2:24).

> *He answered, "Have you not read that the one who made them at the beginning 'made them male and female,'" and said, 'For this reason a man shall leave his father and mother and be joined to his wife, and the two shall become one flesh.' So they are no longer two, but one flesh. Therefore what God has joined together, let no one separate"* (Matthew 19:4–6).

Holy Ties and Unholy Ties

When the two become one in marriage, a holy tie and spiritual bond is formed. Likewise, a holy tie is formed in other godly relationships as well. There is a "unity of the Spirit in the bond of peace" (Ephesians 4:3). For example, David and Jonathan were close friends who honored one another and honored God through their relationship. And "the soul of Jonathan was bound to the soul of David, and Jonathan loved him as his own soul. Then Jonathan made a covenant with David, because he loved him as his own soul" (1 Samuel 18:1;
1 Samuel 18:3).

In prayer ministry, we often refer to these kinds of godly bonds as holy ties or holy soul ties. But by the same token, there can be unholy relationships and ungodly bonds than can form unholy spiritual ties or soul ties as well. For example, just as the two can become one in a holy way within the bond of the covenant of marriage, the same spiritual principle also applies when the two become one in an unholy way outside of the covenant of marriage. Paul expresses the working of this spiritual principle when a man joins himself to a prostitute through sexual relations outside of the covenant of marriage:

> *Do you not know that your bodies are members of Christ? Should I therefore take the members of Christ and make them members of a prostitute? Never!*

334

Do you not know that whoever is united to a prostitute becomes one body with her? For it is said, "The two shall be one flesh." But anyone united to the Lord becomes one spirit with Him.
(1 Corinthians 6:15–17).

Practical and Spiritual Effects of Soul Ties

Being bound together with another is a means of access and influence to become like the other. For example, when we are bound to Christ, we become more like Christ (1 Corinthians 6:17). When we are bound to another person, we can become more like that person. And when we are bound to a spirit, we can become more like that spirit. It goes back to the principle of permission—we are giving permission to whatever is associated with that person or that spirit to have access and influence in our lives.

There is a practical sense of identity by association—whether guilt by association or innocence by association. Sometimes the association or the identity is real and sometimes it is only perceived. But either way, a bond of association carries a high potential of unity and influence, whether good or bad, whether desired or undesired. That's part of the innate wisdom of our mothers who tell us, "Don't you hang around with those kids or you'll grow up to be just them." That's part of the practical truth of the old adages, "Birds of a feather flock together," "Two peas in a pod," "The apple doesn't fall far from the tree," "Like father, like son," and "One bad apple spoils the whole bunch." Our bonds of relationship matter. And our bonds of relationship matter in every dimension—spiritually, mentally, emotionally, and physically. They even matter legally and financially. For example, the debts of a spouse or a business partner attach to one even if it was the other who incurred the debt or received the benefits. Through holy or unholy ties, what identifies with one person identifies with the other person; and what has access to the one person has access to the other person.

Example of Sexual Soul Ties

A classic example of how an unholy tie can affect two people is a sexually transmitted disease. One person with an STD has sex with a second person, and the second person receives the first person's disease. What had access and influence in the first person's life now has access and influence in the second person's life. And it doesn't stop there. If the second person has sex with a third person, the third person can receive the disease from the first person, even though they've never met, let alone had sexual contact. The disease that tormented the first person has access and influence in the third person's life through a series of unholy physical ties.

What happens in the physical realm, through an unholy physical tie, is a picture of what happens in the spiritual realm, through an unholy spiritual tie. This is another way the enemy of our souls, who can't create anything himself, takes one of God's principles that God created for our good and twists it and perverts it to use it against us, if we give in to his temptations and deceptions through sin. Whatever spirits were associated with that sin or stronghold can now have access and influence over every person who becomes tied or bonded to that person through relationship or through a series of relationships. It doesn't always necessarily happen, but the potential for it to happen is there.

Other Examples of Unholy Ties

And what happens through sin in the sexual realm can also happen through sin in any other realm. Forming unholy bonds and ties allows the access and influence of sin and its associated spirits to be passed on from one to another and beyond. For example, if two people steal something together, or join in a lie together, or otherwise engage in unholy actions together, an unholy tie can be formed. There can be a flow of access and influence that continues until the tie is broken through confession, repentance, and prayer. And that's always the good news—that sin can be cleansed and the access and influence it allows can be broken through the power of the blood of Jesus. We just have to learn how to apply the blood of Jesus, as the Holy Spirit leads, according to God's Word and spiritual principles, as we grow by God's grace in spiritual maturity, freedom, and health.

Here are some other common examples of unholy ties that often come up in prayer ministry. One is when a young couple have sexual relations outside of the covenant of marriage. Later they go on to get married to other people. But they can't ever quite get away from the images, emotions, and desires they experienced with one another when they were younger. Countless times in healing prayer ministry, we find that divorces happened when a spouse went back to rekindle the old romance. Though there can be many other factors and this is not always the reason, an unholy soul tie that was never broken is often a key that leads to much destruction and pain.

Another example is when someone participates in occult activity and then has sexual relations with someone else. Even though the second person may have never participated in occult spiritual practices, the second person can begin to experience nightmares, spiritual confusion, depression, tormenting thoughts and all the other things that often follow the sin of false spirituality in the occult. These will often continue until the soul tie is broken.

One of the most common unholy ties is formed through unforgiveness. In a sense, unforgiveness is to continually participate in a sinful relationship with another person. Even if the relationship may be over in the physical realm, it can continue in the spiritual realm. As we discussed earlier, holding on to bitterness and unforgiveness towards a person is our sin, no matter how wrong that person may have been and no matter how right or innocent we may have been in the underlying event or offense. And there are consequences to that sin in our life, in that person's life, and in the lives of those around us. *Many* are defiled. "See to it that no one fails to obtain the grace of God; that no root of bitterness springs up and causes trouble, and through it many become defiled" (Hebrews 12:15).

In prayer ministry, it is amazing how many times something happens to the offending person when the offended person receiving prayer ministry forgives that other person. When the unholy tie is broken in the spiritual realm through confession, repentance of the sin of unforgiveness, and removal of the root of bitterness, the unholy tie can be broken. Often we hear reports of that relationship changing. Sometimes we even hear of sudden phone calls asking for forgiveness. These kinds of experiences help really convince me that the Bible is true and these spiritual principles are real. And when we apply the blood of Jesus by the leading of the Holy Spirit, freedom and healing comes in ways that can't be explained by the natural realm alone.

337

Prayer for Freedom from Unholy Ties

For prayer ministry in this area, we want to begin by repenting of any sin, followed by breaking any unholy ties. Then I like to pray a releasing of any part of that person that is bound up or has become one in any way with any person or anything else. We might also lead the person to "stand in the gap" through identificational repentance for the other person or people involved, similar to the prayers for cleansing of the generations. So we might lead them to pray something like this, followed by our commands in the name of Jesus for freedom and release:

The person receiving prayer could pray:

"Father, please forgive me for the sin of _____ and my participation in that sin with (John). I confess that it was wrong and against Your will. And by Your grace, I choose to repentant of it, turn away from it, and turn to You. I bring it to the foot of the cross and under the blood of Jesus. I ask for and I receive Your forgiveness and the cleansing of the blood of Jesus. I thank You, that I am forgiven now by Your tender mercies and Your steadfast love.

And Lord, I'm willing, as far as Your grace will go, to stand in the gap on behalf of (John) to bring our sin to You. Forgive us for every way we have sinned against You. Open our eyes to see You as You truly are, and turn to You for the fullness of Your salvation, healing, and deliverance in the name of Jesus. May we come to know You and fully receive all You have for each of us in Christ. I put not limitations on Your Word or Your grace, but ask for the fullness of Your mercy, as far as Your grace will go for (John) and for me."

The prayer minister could pray:

"Yes, Father. We agree with Your Word that You are faithful and just and when we confess our sins, You forgive us and cleanse us of all unrighteousness. And now according to the Word of God, (Jenny), You are forgiven of your sin of _____ with (John) in the name of Jesus. You are cleansed now of all unrighteousness in this area of your life. As you choose to hold nothing back from God, but bring all things out of the darkness and into His light, you are holy and pure through the blood of the Lamb.

And Lord, we pray the same for (John), as far as Your grace will go. That his mind and heart would be opened to You and to Your truth, that he would be convicted of his sin, that conviction would lead to repentance, and repentance would lead to the fullness of Your mercy, as far as Your grace will go, through the blood of Jesus.

Father, we ask You to now break every unholy tie of spirit, soul, or body between (Jenny and John). And in the authority of Jesus' name, we agree that every unholy tie is broken now. We call back any part of (Jenny) bound up with (John) in any dimension in any unholy way back to herself to where it belongs through the cross and blood of Jesus. And in Jesus' name, we release any part of (John) bound up with (Jenny) in any unholy way, and send it back to where it belongs, through the cross and blood of Jesus. Lord, make (Jenny) and (John) holy and whole, healed and free, filled with Your Holy Spirit to fulfill their destiny in You. We pray for healing of all the damage that's been done in their lives and in their relationships. Let their souls now be at peace in Christ, in the name of Jesus."

Chapter 21

Brokenness and Unresolved Traumas

We addressed the topic of unresolved traumas as a "root of resistance" in an earlier chapter. The concept of "brokenness" includes that concept of unresolved trauma, but also includes a deeper level of detachment and brokenness of the soul, requiring a deep level healing. Sometimes the traumatic experience is so traumatic that the memory is even completely blocked or repressed until later revealed, if ever. Here, we'll address the principles of ministry involved at a deeper level, without repeating most of what I've said earlier on this related topic.

Godly Brokenness and Ungodly Brokenness

When we hear the word "brokenness" in the spiritual sense, we often think of being broken before God. This is a godly brokenness that the Lord desires from us. "The sacrifice acceptable to God is a broken spirit; a broken and contrite heart, O God, you will not despise" (Psalm 51:17). This is an example of humility before God; being broken of our own will apart from His will; being broken of our old nature to take on more of His nature. Rather than being strong and proud in our own strength and power, we come to the place of choosing to be broken before God, desperately dependent upon His strength and power. Humility is positioning ourselves to acknowledge our need of the grace of God. "But He gives all the more grace; therefore it says, 'God opposes the proud, but gives grace to the humble' " (James 4:6). "For whenever I am week, then I am strong"
(2 Corinthians 12:10).

But there is also an ungodly brokenness. This is not the kind of brokenness God desires for us to feel; this is the brokenness God desires to heal. This is a brokenness of our soul, where we are less than whole in spirit, soul, and body. This often comes from one or more unresolved traumas in our lives. In understanding and encountering the healing love of God in this area, I find it helpful to think of this form of brokenness in two ways, using two biblical terms and concepts: Being brokenhearted and being "double-minded." The Lord wants to heal our broken-heartedness and free us of our double-mindedness.

341

Being Brokenhearted

Jesus came to bind up the brokenhearted and set the captives free (Luke 4:18, fulfilling Isaiah 61). The brokenhearted are more than those whose hearts are broken through torn relationships or shattered hopes and dreams, though these are certainly included as well. Sometimes the brokenhearted are those whose spirits, souls, or bodies have been broken, shattered, and unhealed through traumatic experiences. They are not whole, as God intends, but broken inside or outside from an unresolved trauma.

Sometimes these traumatic events happened long ago, and that person has moved on with life to a degree. But at the same time, to another degree, "a part of that person," so to speak, may still be stuck there in the experience of that trauma. These traumatic experiences are often very fearful, painful, or shameful experiences. And they often occur at very vulnerable times of our lives, such as when we are very young or exposed to dangerous circumstances beyond our control, where we are unprotected, rather than safe and secure. Some frequent examples in prayer ministry are traumatic experiences of sexual abuse, severe emotional turmoil, strong sense of rejection even while still in the womb, physical calamities or accidents, and many others.

In this sense, this form of brokenness is like a detachment from conscious reality. It can be like a defense mechanism to help us survive through the moment of that experience. For example, our soul can become broken and fragmented when a part of our mind, will, and emotions experiencing the traumatic event absorbs into itself all the pain, fear, rage, shame, bitterness, and other emotions and thoughts bound up with that event. It's like that part of the soul goes down into a dark room in the subconscious and sometimes unconscious realms of the mind, as our conscious mind detaches from the experience. It can be kind of like our conscious mind saying to itself, "This isn't real. This isn't happening to me. I'm not going to feel this. I'm going away from this. I'm out of here. I'm not going to ever think of this or remember this again."

In a way, that broken part goes away or goes down deep until there is no sense of pain, shame, fear, or other unwanted emotion. It's like that part of our soul at that age and moment of the traumatic event kind of breaks off and goes down into the unconscious realm so that we don't have to feel it or experience it. Sometimes it may be a conscious, deliberate choice of the will, but many times it's an unconscious choice, made involuntarily, but out of necessity in the face of overwhelming emotional and physical circumstances. I believe it's even likely that this is the mercy of God, many times, to allow this to happen, in that moment, in order to survive these kinds of experiences that we were never intended by God to have to experience or endure.

So brokenness of this form may help in the moment, but the problem is that our unhealed brokenness influences every area of our lives, whether we know it or not. That part of us down deep inside knows we are broken, and often is crying out for help in many ways that can seem irrational and even destructive. That "broken part" is still a very real part of us, but often feels isolated, alone, abandoned, rejected, forgotten, afraid, or ashamed. And that part often feels bitter, angry, resentful, and rebellious. These kinds of emotions and thoughts can lead to choices of the will that steal the peace and joy of life.

So one way of thinking of brokenness, in biblical terms, is being "brokenhearted." And Jesus comes to heal and "bind up the brokenhearted" in the mercy of His grace and the power of His love (Isaiah 61:3). "The Lord builds up Jerusalem; He gathers the outcasts of Israel. He heals the brokenhearted, and binds up their wounds" (Psalm 147:2–3). If we feel outcast, abandoned, rejected, unloved, or uncomforted deep down in our soul, He draws us near as we allow Him to draw near to us. He invites us to trust Him, as best as we can, with as much as we can. He takes that, never forcing more than we are allowing to give, and helps us trust Him more.

"The Lord is near to the brokenhearted, and saves the crushed in spirit." (Psalm 34:18). If we are broken, He longs for us to welcome Him into our brokenness so that He can heal us and make us whole. He wants us to allow Him to connect the memories and events and emotions that are detached or buried, so that He can draw up and out our pain and shame and fear to replace with His peace and love. Then He can cleanse us and heal us and grow us up into wholeness and maturity as one in Him and one within ourselves.

343

Being Double-Minded

Another way of thinking of brokenness, in biblical terms, is being double-minded. One part of our mind thinks one way, but another part of our mind thinks another way. Perhaps our conscious mind understands about trusting God and going on with Him in life, despite the pain and suffering of all we endure in a broken, fallen world. Our conscious mind may even learn about choosing to forgive those who trespass against us, blessing those who curse us, praying for those who persecute us, and loving those who hate us. In addition, our conscious mind may also understand that these things that break our hearts break God's heart as they happen, and that He never leaves us, never forsakes us, and even works to redeem all things for our good in His time and His way. But this "broken part" of us buried down in the unconscious realm of our mind probably doesn't think this way at all. And that affects every area of our lives.

Double-mindedness makes us unstable and insecure, full of doubt, resisting faith, and refusing to trust God, anyone else, or even ourselves. The biblical, spiritual principle of double-mindedness is expressed this way:

> If any of you is lacking in wisdom, ask God, who gives to all generously and ungrudgingly, and it will be given you. But ask in faith, never doubting, for the one who doubts is like a wave of the sea, driven and tossed by the wind; for the doubter, being double-minded and unstable in every way, must not expect to receive anything from the Lord
> (James 1:5–7).

In the original language of this passage, the Greek word translated "double-minded" is *dipsuchos* from the root word *psuche*, which means soul. So the expression literally means "two-souled."[44] A double-minded person is a two-souled person. Their soul is broken and fragmented. The soul is the mind, will, and emotions. And that part of the soul that is still bound up with experiences and emotions of the traumatic event has a mind of its own, a will of its own, and emotions of its own. The mind,

---

[44] *Vine's Complete Expository Dictionary of Old and New Testament Words* (Strong's Lexicon, 1374).

will, and emotion of this broken part of the soul are usually in great contradiction and resistance to the mind, will, and emotions of the person coming to receive prayer ministry and healing.

Healing the Brokenhearted, Freeing the Double-Minded

For healing of these roots of unresolved traumas, sometimes we just need to give permission to God to connect what is disconnected. We ask Him to connect every age and moment of our life with the memories and the events and the emotions that are buried down inside, bringing them together so that He can bring them up and out.

Now sometimes God almost lets us relive those moments, but it's not to hurt or punish us. It's so that we can release it to Him. And sometimes He deals sovereignly with many moments at once or in a short sequence, so that you do not even have to ever experience or remember anything in doing it. I find that just our willingness to ask God for the grace to trust Him is enough with regard to releasing our control of that part of the soul—the mind, will, and emotions, (relating to the event) into His control. Often it's just a willingness to pray something like, "God, I'm willing to give you every age and moment, every trauma of my life so that you can connect what is disconnected and draw it out, in Your timing and in Your way." And a great deal of healing comes from just being willing to do that.

The ways in which God chooses to do that vary from person to person. Sometimes a person doesn't sense or see or hear anything at all, but notices in the days to come that there is a deeper peace, and that things are different. Sometimes in the person's "mind's eye" or spirit, they see themselves in an earlier moment of life, either as that earlier version of themselves or something that represents that. Sometimes it's as if they feel and think as if they are that part of themselves again, and sometimes it's as if they are up above the scene looking down on all that is happening. Every time is different. I like to ask the Holy Spirit to guide the process and rather than suggesting what to see or think, just asking the person to pass along what *they* may sense or see or hear. Then I help them give it to Jesus—"Pain out, love in; Shame out, love in." Without pressuring their will or forcing the timing, I just try to help them trust

God enough to entrust their control to Him, so that He can take out what is buried inside that needs to be released.

In prayer ministry, it's often like Jesus steps into that moment, for example, when that little six year old girl was abused by her uncle. Since Jesus isn't limited by time and space, He reveals Himself in that moment when she was a six year old child, frees that little child of all that buried anger, shame and hurt; and releases that child from their uncle, along with the pain, shame, and the hurt. I often lead them in prayers of forgiveness or answer questions as the Lord leads. Often, we listen for what Jesus may say or bring to mind to the person. Or sometimes we just wait in the silence and trust that He's at work in His healing love. Then Jesus cleanses, purifies, and takes all of that away and he holds that little child, grows her up, and matures her into the full measure of the stature of Christ, making her whole.

Now that's one of the most beautiful things of the ministry that I get to do. Sometimes it works out where it is almost like I am speaking to that six year old part of that person. I am leading her to Jesus, because in a sense, they are holding on to control, and they need to release control and let Jesus be Lord. And He comes into the place where they are or into their heart, and sometimes the person actually sees Jesus in her mind or spirit very clearly. Often the Lord gives them a vision or impression of what He is doing or saying. People that don't even normally see or experience things in the Spirit might see and experience that, and when they do, it's a beautiful thing. It just makes my faith and my love for God go sky high every time it happens!

The goal is to receive the blessing of wholeness and holiness; to be sanctified entirely, spirit, soul and body. It comes when all things are brought back into God's created order, redeemed by the blood of Jesus. Our spirit, soul, and body are once again united as one in trusting faith and submission to the Lordship of Jesus. We are sanctified and filled with the Holy Spirit, restored into intimate relationship as children of God.

Sabrina's Story of Healing Prayer Ministry

Sabrina: God had been helping me to trust Him with going to some very deep and painful places of my past with Tommy in prayer ministry. I was asking the Holy Spirit to come into the ages and moments of my life where I seemed to be stuck in some unhealed parts of my soul. As I let go of my control and all the ways in which I had been trying to protect and defend myself, releasing to Him the instances where I had felt very out of control and unprotected, I was letting God have control. I was letting Him take out my hurt and pain to replace it with His love, as we prayed for God to heal my brokenness and make me whole. While waiting for the Holy Spirit to lead us after a time of this deep healing, God began to show me a vision of what He was doing:

I was sitting in the throne room on this beautiful and very big throne. I was about two years old and wore a white ruffled dress, ruffled socks and black sandals. I was so happy and I had a huge smile on my face. My legs were swinging back and forth, and in my mind I was saying, *Yep, this is my Daddy's chair!* Then I hopped down and ran around behind the throne; and when I came back out, I was older. I was around eleven or twelve years old. I was still very happy and smiling, skipping around the throne a couple of times. Then after about two times of going around the throne, the Father came in and I ran to Him, very excited to see Him. I jumped up on Him and wrapped myself around Him, hugging Him. I said to Him, "I don't want You to ever leave me!" And I kept hugging Him for dear life.

Then God gave me another picture. We were outside in a horse chariot. I was a little girl again, maybe seven years old. He looked over at me, smiling, and reached over and gave me His crown from His head. It was so big that it just dropped over my eyes, so I pushed it back so I could see. I felt like we were going somewhere together. It was just Him and me.

In the next picture, I was still in the chariot with Him, but I was about sixteen years old and I was wearing street clothes. I was hugging up to Him and then, in the blink of an eye, I was my current age, thirty years old. I was wrapped in beautiful white linen clothes and so was the Father. He was wearing a white robe and a beautiful gold crown. He was the

King and I was his Princess. I felt so at peace, holding onto Him. I felt like I had absolutely everything I ever wanted or needed in my life. He made me whole.

What Sabrina experienced is an example of a prayer ministry experience from just a few weeks ago. The Lord is infinitely creative in the ways He reveals Himself and His love to His children. In Sabrina's case, the Lord was letting her know how much He was the kind of Father that welcomes His little girl into His presence and that she belongs there. He was healing some deep wounds and brokenness from many traumatic experiences along the way. When she saw herself at different, increasing ages of her life until she was full grown to her current age, this is one of the ways the Holy Spirit shows us that healing, maturity, and integration of the "broken parts" of the person's soul is being healed and made whole. The deep peace and often joy that comes at the end of a prayer session is often a strong indication that the Lord has accomplished the healing He intended for that time. And He is faithful to bring to completion all that He begins.

A Prayer to Begin the Process of Healing from Brokenness

"God, I'm willing to give you every age and moment, every trauma of my life, so that you can connect what is disconnected and draw it out, in Your timing and in Your way. Wherever I am detached or dissociated in my mind, my will, my emotions, I'm giving You permission, as best as I can, to come into those places of the hurt, pain, anger, fear, shame, and distrust in my life. Help me trust You enough to allow You to come and help me entrust my control and defenses to You. Draw out the pain, the shame, the anger, the fear and all that is me that is not yet like You, and give me Your peace and love. Restore unto me the joy of my salvation. Come and make me whole. Come and help me know Your security, Your love, and Your Father's blessing. Help me trust You and love You and receive Your love for me. In Jesus' name I pray, Amen.

Part 5 – Empowered for Ministry

Let the wise also hear and gain in learning,
and the discerning acquire skill (Proverbs 1:5).

The Lord heals us and frees us because He has compassion for us to make us whole and wholly His. In our journey of healing and holiness, He is redeeming us and restoring us back into His created order, redeemed by the blood of Jesus and conforming into the nature of Christ. But He also heals and frees us because He wants to empower us to represent Him as His sons and daughters in the earth, having the nature of Christ and continuing the ministry of Christ.

We are healed for a purpose, freed for a destiny, and empowered for a ministry. We are to be as the hands and heart of Jesus in the earth. We are to teach the things He taught, to do the things He did, in the power that He had. "So we are ambassadors for Christ, since God is making His appeal through us" (2 Corinthians 5:20). In Christ, we are empowered for ministry to boldly and genuinely represent the nature of the One who sent us in the power and authority of His name. By the grace of God our calling and destiny is to be free to be like Jesus. Jesus Himself said it this way: "As the Father has sent Me, so I send you" (John 20:21).

As you've read the pages of this book, it has been my prayer that you would gain in learning and grow in wisdom of God's biblical, spiritual principles of healing and deliverance prayer ministry. It's been my prayer that these truths would help you come to a deeper place of trusting surrender and intimate communion with the Lord our God, embracing the fullness of His salvation in personally receiving healing, deliverance, and eternal life. But it's also my prayer that the Holy Spirit would set you ablaze with a burning passion for Jesus and a passion for people, and that you would receive a fresh anointing and impartation as you are clothed with power from on high to go forth into your calling and destiny—proclaiming the coming of the kingdom of God, binding up the brokenhearted, and setting the captives free. In this, may your joy be made complete, I pray.

Chapter 22

Blessed to be a Blessing

In this final chapter, I'd like to share with you the actual transcript of Linda's healing prayer ministry session from her testimony in Part 1. Rarely does someone ask to record our prayer sessions, but I believe that Lord had purpose in it. Linda says that every time she reads it the Lord continues to bring deeper levels of healing and freedom, as well as fresh passion for praying for others.

I share her ministry session here as a further testimony to the love and glory of our God who loves to heal us and free us. But I also share it so that you can literally see prayers based upon the principles of this book. Every ministry session is different and we should always try to be led by the Holy Spirit as best as we can with the tools that He's given us. So these prayers are not a formula or program for healing prayer ministry; they are examples of ways to pray and principles to follow, as the Lord develops your individual style in line with the unique gifts, personality, and experiences He has given you and redeemed for you. We purposefully made only technical edits to keep this transcript as authentic as possible.

Linda's Prayer Ministry Session with Tommy Hays and Team

Tommy: Lord, thank You for bringing us here together today. You have arranged this time and You've led us to guard this time on behalf of Your daughter that You've called; that You've drawn near to You Lord. We pray You'd just come now, focusing our eyes, attention, and spirits on what You're saying to Linda, Lord. We want to hear what You're saying, Father, we want to see what You're doing in her life, Lord. Just guide our thoughts; guide our hearts. Give us the Father heart of God for Linda, Lord. Give us Your compassion, give us Your love, give us a sensitivity to all that You desire to do.

We just say Lord, You are the healer, You are the deliverer, You are the Lord our God and Savior. We make ourselves available to You Lord, in any way that You would choose to use us in Linda's life today. We pray that You just guard and protect us. We put the cross and the blood of

Jesus between us, and we declare, Lord, that nothing that's not of You shall go forth, nothing that's of the flesh, nothing that's of the world, nothing that's of the devil, nothing that's out of Your timing and out of Your will. But everything that is of You will go forth; every prayer we pray, every decree we command, every word we speak shall go forth that is of You, Lord. And it shall bear fruit that will return a harvest, God. We just pray that protection for us. We break off any attachments or ties to any spiritual beings outside of us, in Jesus' name. Anything unholy or impure that would try to disrupt or block or shut down anything You're doing, we forbid that in the name of Jesus. We ask you, Father, to bind back all principalities and unholy beings from interfering in Jesus' Name.

We Command that nothing that is not of God will go forth; nothing that is of the flesh, the devil, ties to any other beings – only what is of God. We put on the Armor of God, the helmet of salvation; You are our salvation. We take up the breastplate of righteousness; You are our righteousness. We take up shield of faith; You are our faith, Lord. Give us the faith of God! We take up the shoes of peace; You are our peace— Prince of Peace! We take up the belt of truth; You are our truth. We take sword of Spirit; the very Word of God!

We ask for the mantle of humility as we humble ourselves in Your sight, Lord; as we're desperately dependent on You, Lord! Come in power, come in glory, come and release Your power and love through us to Linda today, Lord. Lord, we ask for all the gifts of Your Spirit. We thank You that the same Holy Spirit that raised Jesus from the dead is here! All Your gifts, all Your power, all that You would do is here right now Lord. We also ask that You'd manifest Your particular gifts through us in any way that You desire. We ask for words of wisdom and knowledge, gifts of miracles, healings, discernment of spirits, faith, tongues, interpretation of tongues. All the ways that You would move in us today, we pray You'd come. We exalt You here today Lord Jesus. We exalt You, Father God and Your Holy Spirit.

We bind in the name of Jesus and we command any strong man, any ruling spirit that is assigned to Linda; we bind you, we overcome you by the blood of Jesus. We command you to stand back! We issue these decrees to any demonic spirits: you will do nothing to cause any harm or embarrassment to any of us or Linda; you will speak only if you are spoken to; if you are commanded to speak, you will reveal only what the Lord Jesus Christ himself commands you to speak or reveal; otherwise you will be silent. We bind you, we gag you, and we command you to go! You must go immediately with all your forces and all your emissaries, your instruments, and devices. All the works of the enemy must be undone, and you must go defeated to the feet of Jesus, where you will be judged, never to return. There will be no shouting, no screaming, no unclean speech, no throwing up, you'll do nothing to cause any harm or pain or embarrassment to anybody.

In its place, we ask You to come Holy Spirit. Come and leave no voids, no empty places, Lord. Just fill us through and through forever with Your life, Your love, and Your purifying holy fire.

Now we just want to agree with Linda. Now Linda, if you'll just speak out a prayer in your words, just call upon the name of the Lord, and give Him permission to do in you all that He desires to do in you today. And we'll agree with you."

Linda: Oh You've been so good to me Lord! Father, You've healed me of so many things, Lord. You told me in coming down that I was to be totally healed, and that is my desire! Right now, Lord, I just surrender everything to You. I open my mind, my heart, my spirit, my soul, every part of my being to You. I ask you to reveal if there's any pockets of resistance, any brokenness, any trauma, anything that is blocking my freedom and keeping me from flowing with You, God, and using the gifts You've put in me, the gifts You're still awakening in me Lord. If there's any walls, any blocks Lord, anything that I'm not seeing that someone else could see, Lord, just reveal it now. I pray Your anointing upon Tommy, and Leslie, and Ave that You would use them as Your instruments of healing in my life. I trust You Lord!

Tommy: We agree, Lord, with Linda's prayer and the cry of her heart. Now we just wait on you Jesus. Lord, we're just asking you to strategically put your finger on what it is you wish to touch and everything you desire to do. We know You'll be magnifying and multiplying all that You do. We wait upon you, and we look simply, actively, deliberately to You alone, and as we do, we listen. Would you speak to Linda, Ave, Leslie, would You speak to me? Guide us Lord, as we wait on you Jesus.

Linda: I'm seeing a picture of myself when I was 8 months old, probably. I was sitting on the ground on a blanket all by myself. You know how little babies, when they're first learning to sit up by themselves, kind of fall forward? I was kind of leaning forward trying to hold myself up. I was a fat little baby. In the background is my Dad, who was standing behind me, holding my older sister in his arms.

Tommy: Thank you for bringing that up Lord, that's Your answer to our prayer. You're connecting memories, events, and emotions. And bring up any thought that entered into that baby's mind, whether rational, or not rational; whether it was intended or not; whatever thoughts entered into her mind about herself, her father, her sister, we bring all that to you Lord. We say to that part of Linda, it's okay to remember. It's okay to express your feelings and thoughts as we release them to God. Lord, just come and draw up and draw out what needs to be taken out and we release that, Lord, and replace that with Your truth and love and grace.

Linda: There was my Dad holding my sister, and I'm just trying to hold myself up—all alone. There's just 11 months between us, and Mom cried the whole time she was pregnant with me. She always said, "I'm not ready to have a baby!" My sister had this beautiful auburn hair, and I was just this fat little baby. Mom always said, "You look like your Aunt Maxine." She was kind of plump, sweet, but kind of plain. I just didn't want to look like her. I probably felt some rejection, I guess.

Tommy: Thanks for showing that, Lord. We believe this is You guiding our thoughts. We speak in the name of Jesus to that feeling of rejection, to any inner vow, any way inside that baby she formed a thought or choice, "My Daddy doesn't love me. He loves my sister more than me. He doesn't take time with me. I'm all alone. I wasn't wanted. I was a mistake. She'll never love me." Any of those thoughts of rejection, isolation, or hurt, we speak to those words and thoughts and vows, we call you up and out. Release her! Release this child of God—that baby— release her now in the name of Jesus.

We command that rejection to come out of her and off of her. Loose that part of her! Loose her! Free her in the name of Jesus! Loneliness, we command you to come out. Loneliness that's taken a root, trying to make her lonely, isolated, left aside, not valued, not honored – go! We loose you from her in the name of Jesus.

Now Lord, just pour into her. Pour into that part of Linda Your truth that You love her, You never left her, You've never forsaken her even though human beings—maybe there were times when they have (forsaken her). Maybe they had set her aside or didn't value her, but the truth is, You never did that. She was never left alone, You've always been there in ways she couldn't see, doing things she didn't know You were doing, trying to move on hearts and wills and choices and ways we could not see. Human beings have choices and there is a spiritual battle, but You are redeeming these things, and You're causing good to come out of it, Lord. You don't change the facts of history, but You change the effects of history. Right now, you're changing the effects of history! Right now, we're commanding that to come out of her. Loose and free her, Loneliness! Rejection, Isolation, come out! Come off!

Jesus, You are drawing out isolation, rejection, a hold of jealousy or envy, or other people who seem to have that—even if it wasn't intended, we break that power in the name of Jesus. We break the power of envy and jealousy in name of Jesus. Any way that brought offense or hardness of heart, or just a longing to be like that – a longing to be the one accepted, or nurtured, or cherished, or valued. We break that off. Loose and free her in name of Jesus. Replace that with a true and pure love— a longing for you, Lord! Just fill her up. Fill Linda up, Lord, with Your love. All those places that were left empty, all those places where she was not nurtured, not held Lord, hold her now. Comfort her now. Love her and hold her now.   Pour into her, Lord.

Linda: Dad was verbally abusive—controlling. My Mom didn't stick up for her kids. I was 14 yrs. old when a guy tried to rape me. I was walking through our little town – a safe little town. He yelled at my brother and sisters to go on home. He was a jock, an athlete. He threw me down a levy bank and almost raped me. I fought him so hard; finally he gave up. I walked home shaking, crying, in shock. I didn't tell anybody for a long time. When I finally told Mom, she said I had to tell Dad. He said it was my fault and he called me a whore and slut and said it was all my fault. I thought, *I'll never tell him anything ever again.*

<u>Tommy</u>: We connect this all together—the feelings, emotions, all that's been detached, broken, buried inside. You've brought this up to Linda, bring healing, Lord. Just draw it out. We just draw out right now the power of those words, the pain, the poison of those words, those are lies – in the name of Jesus. She is not any of those things: she doesn't desire those things. We command those things to come out of her! False identity, that curse over her, be broken off in the name of Jesus. We break that off, Lord. Be loosed now in the name of Jesus. Lord, go into that moment and draw out the fear, draw out the terror when it happened, the shock, being vulnerable, unprotected, nobody stood up for her, she couldn't go to anybody or tell anybody; release her of it in the name of Jesus. You're here now, and you were there then. All the things that could have happened, but didn't because You were there fighting and releasing angels and Your power.

Come and just draw it out. Any hardness of heart, resentment, anger, rage, bitterness, lack, disappointment; help her to release each person to you. What was done was wicked and wrong. What that boy did was wicked and wrong. What her father did was wicked, wrong and cruel. Having a mother and father in an atmosphere where the daughter couldn't tell them was wrong. It was less than your perfect will. And we don't make excuses, we're not blaming; just acknowledging the truth, Lord. There are things that were done that caused damage and pain, hurt and disappointment. That caused Linda to make vows where she is taking control, Lord. We bring it all to you.

We call that part of Linda, speak that out to the Lord, (repeat after me) Yes Lord, what was done to me was wrong. That boy raped me and that was wrong. He threw me down and scared me. I make no excuses for him. That hurt me, but I choose to forgive him. From that part of me that experienced that, I choose to release him to you, Lord. I release him in to the freedom of my forgiveness. I pray for him, for conviction of his sin, and for that conviction to lead in to godly sorrow, and repentance to turn to you, Lord. With this sin and all of his life, and I pray for Your mercy for him and the fullness of your salvation. I trust him to you, Lord. Now take this all from me; all the calamity, shock, terror, shame, the questions about it, rumors, all the words, accusations.

<u>Tommy</u>: Yes Lord, take all that. All the ways Linda internalized that or took that in, *They think I'm a whore, a slut, they think I did that, they think I'm that kind of a girl.* We release it all to You! Come off her identity, her spirit, her mind. Come off her! Be lifted off! We break off that label and identity—taken off in Jesus' name—released from her. It's not who she is! We call to that root of bitterness that ruined her life, her reputation, we take that off and we replace that with the cleansing of purity and identity, Lord. Thank you Lord. Now heal that part of Linda. Restore her being and make that part of her grow up into maturity. Thank You Lord!

Now we bring her (earthly) father to you. Use this moment to touch every area with her relationship with her earthly father—not shutting it down, "I don't need him, his love, protection, honor." We open all the places where Linda's quit feeling—quit wanting to feel. She's releasing control to You, entrusting control to You, Lord. We speak to every part of Linda that would represent anything that's been hurt or wounded by her (earthly) father.

Linda, just repeat after me: Yes Lord, I bring my father to you. He's hurt me in many ways. He's fallen short of Your will for my life. You wanted him to love me, honor me, spend time with me, and to see the good of God inside of me.

All the things that were never done, that she needed and longed for and never had, Lord. All the things that were done that were harsh, wicked and less than Your will, the curses, frustration, blame. We bring all the injustice, Lord, we don't hold any of it back, or make excuses. We open all the pain that's buried, all the lacking, needing—open that up, Lord, so You can draw it out in name of Jesus. Just release it now.

<u>Linda repeats after Tommy</u>: Lord, I do make a choice. What my father did was wrong and it's hurt me. I make a choice. I release him to You into the freedom of my forgiveness in the name of Jesus. I give him a gift he doesn't deserve, just like you've given me a gift I don't deserve. I cancel his debt. Every debt he owes me, like admitting he was wrong,

saying he's sorry, asking for my forgiveness; if he never does any of those things, I still forgive him. I release him. I pray for him and for the fullness of your salvation, that his eyes and heart would be open to You. Forgive him of his sins and hold him in Your arms. We release him to You and all that this represents, as far as Your grace will go.

Tommy: Every father figure, every authority figure, every person in Linda's life that was supposed to protect her and affirm her and walk with her and encourage her, but instead, condemned her and shamed her, judged her, left her, isolated her, ran her down instead of lifting her up, cursed her instead of blessing her (thereby) failing at being Your means of blessing; we bring every person and every figure that represents to You, Lord. We join with Linda from every age of her life, and we release them to You -- not holding anyone back. We break unholy ties between those people who have hurt her and sinned against her. We release the words and accusations, we release (it all) back to the cross and the blood of Jesus. We call back to Linda every part of her that's been bound up or attached to them – any faces or thoughts, we call it all back to her, to the cross, and blood of Jesus. We break off anything unholy. We take every unholy soul tie and we strengthen all that is holy, every bond that is of You in the name of Jesus. Grow her up. Grow up every part of her into maturity, to the full measure of the stature of Christ.

Any way her mother didn't nurture her, honor, make her feel welcome, Lord, that was sin. We acknowledge that.

Linda repeats after Tommy: Lord, what that did to me angered You. What the enemy did to me angered You. By Your grace I release my mother to You. I pray for her, Lord, repentance that leads to conviction, conviction that leads to Your mercy. We pray for the fullness of Your salvation, as far as Your grace will go. I pray the same (blessing) Lord, for all those in my life that were (supposed) to nurture me, comfort me, hold me, love me, be Your hands of grace and heart of love in my life. I release them all to you, and ask you to heal me.

Tommy: Lord, we agree with Linda. Thank You that You're releasing her from those unholy ties. You're pouring into her Your nurture, love,

358

a sense of stability and security. Lord, we pray right now You pour into Linda a mother's blessing and a father's blessing.

Tommy (prophesying): My daughter, my daughter, who I formed and made, who I love, I pour My love and heart into you! I pour My Spirit into you. I am pleased with you. I want to be near you. I am pleased that you walk with Me. I created you. You were not a mistake! You were not an accident. You were chosen by Me, says the Lord Your God. I have such plans for you – such purpose for you. I have been loving through you, touching through you, changing lives through you. And I will continue, My daughter. My daughter, My bride, says the Lord God Almighty, your Maker is your Husband, your Lord, your God is your Creator and your Husband.

Tommy: Thank you, O God. You are her constant and steady companion. You are her strength, You are her comfort, You are her protector, You are her Father's blessing, Lord. Just pour it in, Lord, pour it in, Lord - your comfort and peace in every way. Let Linda be steady. Steady and established—secure. We pray a blessing of security, a blessing of security! Secure, and stable and confident. Confident in the Lord, in His grace, confident in who He has created you to be!

Lord, we call forth those gifts of compassion. Lord, you've anointed Linda with compassion. You've anointed Linda with mercy and compassion and healing and love. You've anointed Linda with wisdom to walk in it, to bring it, to teach others to walk in that, to model it before them, Lord. Wisdom Lord, thank you God, let her grow up into maturity. Anoint her to share that, to impart that, to model that in the name of Jesus, as You are healing her – so You will use her to heal and comfort others Lord. We thank You, God! Now God, just speak to her Your words. Let her see and hear You the way You choose, Lord. We wait upon You, Lord. What do You say to your daughter, Your child, Your bride?

Linda: I heard Him say, "You are my beloved one. I am pleased with you." Thank You, Lord, that You see me in ways I don't see myself. Help me to see myself as You see me!"

(Linda: The Lord later led me to Romans 9:25. Thank you Father!)

<u>Tommy</u>: Yes Lord, open the eyes of her heart to see herself the way You see her, Lord. Thank You for speaking that. She is your beloved. You're well pleased in Your beloved child; Your beloved daughter. We release this word into her spirit in the name of Jesus: when we cry *Abba* Father, it is that very Spirit bearing witness with our spirit that we are children of God, and heirs of God, joint heirs with Jesus Christ. If we suffer with Him, so we may be glorified with Him.

Lord, we just pray right now, You take all the sufferings, all the pain, shame, longing, hurting, feelings of being rejected, isolated, not comforted, not held, not steadied, secure, abandoned, and rejected; Lord, take all that out (from) parents, accusations, abuse of men, (other) people in her life, take all that suffering and draw it out now. Through that suffering, may she be resurrected. May she be glorified with You and in You.

Linda is a child of God. She is a daughter of the King, a daughter of the King! She is your beloved! We seal that to Linda now. Where there were other words that were marked and sealing her, false words, Lord, those are released from her now in the name of Jesus.

In its place, Lord, the truth is Linda your Beloved. We just mark and seal that to Linda's spirit—to her now! We seal that to you, Linda. You are, "Beloved of the Lord!" He has changed your name! He has sealed His name to you, Beloved of the Lord! Beloved of the Lord! Beloved; sought after; loved!

Your God is passionate for you! Passionate to be with you, to walk with you, to hold you, to love you, to pour Himself into you! Thank you God! Protected! You are Protected! You are safe, you are secure! Protected and safe and secure in the arms of the Lord. He is your defender, He is your shield! He is your glory, He is your rock, your refuge, your mighty fortress. You are safe and secure in Him. He is your strong tower! You are mighty in Him! Beloved in Him!

Oh, we're waiting on You Lord. Speak into her spirit, Lord.

<u>Linda</u>: Abuse of Power. It seems like those who have had power over me—I seem to have a block or a clog from that abuse of authority or

360

abuse of power that's keeping me from flowing. I know what's in me! I know it's in me – I need it to come out!

Tommy: Yes Lord, You desire for all damage of abusive powers to come out—come off in the name of Jesus. We speak in the name of Jesus to every spirit and every assignment of abuse to crush her, to defile her, to defame her, to press down her spirit, to keep her from having her place and position of authority and honor and blessing.

(Linda was being physically pushed down and pressure was on her back, pressing her face down!)

Tommy: We speak to you in the name of Jesus. We command you (to) come out, come off, release and free her. We cancel that assignment against her; that assignment that draws that abuse; that assignment that allows abuse; that allows others where the enemy has targeted against her to hold her back; be broken off! You're exposed! You're uprooted! Be broken off in the Name of Jesus. Abuse, abuse of powers, go! False powers, go in name of Jesus! False father, go in name of Jesus! False authority figures, come off of her in name of Jesus. False submission, every false submission, every spirit that tries to make her bow into false submission, we command you come off of her in the name of Jesus!"

Now I just command all that that represents—that big tall boot—there's like a boot just pressing down on her neck! I command that to come off of her neck! Come off her neck (all) that's trying to press her to the ground—with her face to the ground—trying to defile her, shame her, crush her, that boot on her neck, we break that off! I command you come off of her! I break your leg in the name of Jesus! I break the leg of that spirit and release the judgment of God against that! You'll not do that to anyone else again in the name of Jesus! Release the angels! Execute that judgment now!

Now in the name of Jesus, Lord, come heal! Come and lift and place your daughter, place your child, Lord, in that place of authority! In that place of honor!

(Linda started sitting up straight and tall. The pressure and pain was released)

Tommy: We pray honor! You are honored! You are honored! Just as a mother is to teach her daughter to walk with poise and walk with stature and to lift her head up high; just as a father is to light up in his spirit, light up in his eyes when he sees his daughter walk into the room, I just release that; pour that into Linda. Honor – you are honored, you are beloved, you are grace! That's how your Father sees you. When you walk in, His eyes light up! His Spirit soars! He has everyone stop talking, everyone stop to listen and to see His love for you! His honor for you! We release that grace! We pray a blessing of honor and favor upon you, Linda. A hundred fold and more! Redeeming all the enemy has tried to steal from you, take from you, in the name of Jesus! You are honored and beloved in the name of Jesus.

Lord magnify this out to the Bride of Christ! We're praying big prayers, Lord! Your people, Your daughters will be filled with the Father's Blessing! Your daughters will be filled with the sense of honor and value and significance. Your daughters would walk with poise and with grace with their heads held high. They will not walk in haughtiness, they will not try to demand honor or attention or their rightful place; but it shall be given to them joyfully, gladly Lord! We release a blessing of honor over your daughters! Thank you God!"

Heal their necks, heal their shoulders, lift off of them every form of oppression, everything that would shut down the giftings of the women of God, everything that would not honor their value, their place. Every way the enemy has twisted words, twisted scriptures to silence them, to shut them down, to not let them be seen and welcomed and embraced, Lord, all the ways that the Body of Christ is anemic to this! Not nurtured, because we need to nurture the women, the mothers—we need what we can only receive by honoring them and honoring all that they have to give. We just repent of that as the body of Christ, we repent of that as men, we repent of that as leaders—forgive us Lord! We repent of that sin throughout the generations. We renounce it in the name of Jesus! We pray You pour in now, all the blessings, all the graces, nurture, all the growth and love we've needed and never been able to have because of the hardness of our hearts, Lord—the deceptions of our minds, Lord, we renounce all those things.

362

Now we receive the women in to their rightful positions—the mothers and the daughters and the sisters Lord. Now Lord, we receive them. May they be positioned, may they know they are honored, welcomed, cherished, and beloved, in the name of Jesus!"

Leslie: I pray for favor, incredible favor where Linda has experienced rejection. I renounce that (rejection) and pray the reverse, incredible favor with those in authority over her. I pray for incredible favor with those under her care. I pray that you will unstop their ears and open their eyes and hearts so that they are free to receive the bread of life that she is offering. The wine of the spirit—free to understand, and no longer walk in an infantile state; that they would just grow and be nourished and liberated and able to see her. I just pray for people to understand her, I just pray that you will anoint her to be understood. (I pray) That her heart would be obvious to others, that it would be visible to others, and that there would be no misunderstandings any more. That she would be seen for what you have made her to be. That her flock and those around her and even in authority over her would receive the truth about her – that the truth about her would be what is projected. Truth in Jesus Name.

Ave: Jesus, I pray for power, authority, and trust. I pray you would increase Your power in Linda!

Tommy: All the disappointments in Linda's life and all the disappointments in your Bride, we pray a freeing.

Tommy: (prophesying): All your disappointments shall be washed away and you shall find fulfillment in my promises. For My promises are being fulfilled, says Your Father in heaven.

Tommy: We thank you Lord that You are lifting from us all disappointment, all hurt feelings, all ways we've been let down, all that is being taken away. All of that for the sake of the joy that is to come, for the joy and the peace and fulfillment that is coming, Lord. Now wash away all disappointment, all grief and all sorrows, and replace with joy in Jesus' Name!

We pray now You just let Your peace arise within Linda. Fill her every cell in her body, every organ; body, soul and spirit, every dimension of her mind, will, emotions; every dimension of her place of communion with You, (her) intuition, conscious, sensibility Lord. Awaken in her every gifting and calling, anointing and destiny, Lord. Just let all the gifts be revealed. Unseal all the gifts and treasures, that You've given her, Lord. We awaken those treasures, awaken those gifts!

All that You've called her to, Lord. That hunger, that hunger You've given her Lord! Let her release that and impart that hunger wherever she goes. Fill her up! Fill her up with the new wine, new wine, new wine of Your Spirit! New wine! Fill her up! Fill her up in the name of Jesus, releasing your Spirit. Everywhere she goes she will impart Your Spirit, impart Your calling, impart that hunger, Lord! Rising up in her! She brings order where she goes. She brings hunger (for more of Jesus) where she goes. She brings healing where she goes. She brings new life! New life and new wine! New life, new life, new life! There shall be a bursting forth of new life when Linda speaks, when she preaches, when she prays, when she teaches—new life shall spring forth and blossom! Even as out of the desert places, out of desert places shall flow streams of living water. Wilderness places shall bring forth in name of Jesus. Release that impartation of new life to spring up and grow into the greenness and beauty of new life in the name of Jesus! Thank you Lord. And all that's needed for that! We just pray that into these hands!

Tommy (speaking to the other prayer ministers): Let's put our hands over hers.

Tommy (resumes praying for Linda): Hers are hands of authority, hands of healing, hands of compassion and mercy, hands of praise, glory. Pour that in Lord. Like hands that are like a gardeners hands, that gently tills the soil and plants the seed and nurtures and waters and brings forth, Lord. Thank you Lord, all that that speaks of; the nurture, the prayer, the healing going forth into maturity. Thank you for this anointing of new life. Dead things shall come to life—resurrection power! (Let) Resurrection power be released—calling life out of death—life out of dead places. Decay and darkness and death shall be broken off, cut away, stripped away, and the tenderness of new life shall come forth and it shall be protected and guarded and nurtured.

For all those ways that Linda didn't feel protected, Lord, You've redeemed all that. Now she is protected. Now she is a protector of others! She is protected and safe in You, and she will protect and guard the new life that You bring forth, Lord. She will protect them with her prayers, her leadership, her compassion, her mercy, with Your power of healing, Your miracles, Your Word of God being released. (We) Just pray impartation of all that is needed for her gifting and calling and destiny. In the name of Jesus! Give her grace to lay the burdens of others at your feet! Grace to not carry them herself, Jesus!

Linda: Forgive me Lord, for not walking completely in the authority that You've called me to. I will speak for You; I will stand up for You! I will serve You and walk with You always, Lord.

Tommy: Linda, in the name of Jesus, you are forgiven! Anytime you draw back, whether you intend to or not, you are forgiven. That is no hindrance to the authority you will walk in now and forever, in the name of Jesus, Amen!"

Tommy: We just bless and seal all that You've done in Linda, all that You're doing and all that You will continue to do. It is done in heaven and its being done here on earth as it is in heaven. To the glory of our Father, in the name of Jesus, Amen! Yes Lord, You're good Lord! Praise God!

Tommy (prompted by the Holy Spirit to continue praying): You need boldness! Lord God, we thank You for the mercy gifts—the compassion of God, the servant's spirit that You've given Linda to love You, to honor You, to serve You, and to be a servant of all. Whoever will be first, must be last, whoever is the leader of all, must be the servant of all. Linda gets that. You've put that into her. She walks in that beautifully, Lord. We affirm that. We affirm the gifts of servanthood, of mercy, of grace, and love, compassion, and focus on others and not on herself. We thank you God for all that, and at the same time, we recognize how the enemy has tried to use her gift against her, use that to try to crush that out of her at times, and tried to distort that and misuse that against her at times. We bring all that to You, to the foot of the cross and under the blood of Jesus.

We believe that You have said that along with that needs to be an outpouring of boldness! Holy boldness to go with Linda, that she is just as tenacious for herself, when you lead her to be, as she is for others, Lord. She is just as hungry for herself as she is for others to be hungry for You—in that godly and holy way.

So we pray that You would give her a holy boldness. Boldness to take a firm stand, not be pushed around, not give in, not compromise, not settle for less than the fullness of what You desire for her or for others Lord, in the name of Jesus.

Lord, just as Your first disciples prayed after the pouring out of Your Spirit, we just pray this prayer, we join in this prayer for ourselves, and for Linda and Your body of Christ in these days from Acts 4: 29–31: "And now Lord, look at their threats, and grant to Your servants to speak Your word with all boldness, while You stretch out Your hand to heal, and signs and wonders are performed through the name of Your holy servant Jesus. When they had prayed, the place in which they were gathered together was shaken; and they were all filled with the Holy Spirit and spoke the word of God with boldness!"

O yes, Lord! Release that anointing of boldness in the Name of Jesus! Boldness and all that speaks of—a holy boldness, a holy, courageousness, tenacity to not compromise, not settle for anything less! She needs it, Lord! She needs it to walk in this in order to release Your signs and wonders and healing and Your power and the Word of God to go forth with Boldness! We seal that to her, we impart that to her, release that though her and impart that to others, Lord, in the name of Jesus!"

Ave: Be strong and courageous, for the Lord your God is with you wherever you go! Jericho! Go with God without fear!

Tommy: Strength and courage. Boldness of the Lord!

Linda: Yes, God! I am your bold and courageous warrior, Lord! I am bold and courageous, Lord! I take up my scepter—Deborah!"

Tommy: Deborah, Arise! Arise, Lord God! Thank you, God!

366

<u>Linda:</u> *Oh wow! I feel different!*

Free to Be Like Jesus!

Our Father has sent His Holy Spirit to prepare a Bride for His Son, our coming King, Jesus Christ. By the power of the grace of God, He's setting us free from everything that would hold us back from all He created us to be—***Free to Be Like Jesus*** through the transforming power of healing and deliverance.

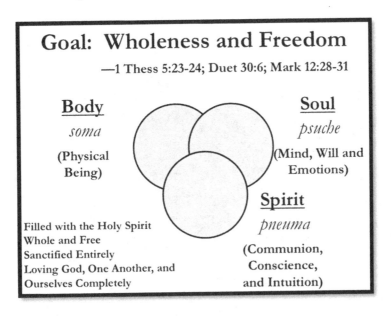

Goal: Wholeness and Freedom
—1 Thess 5:23-24; Duet 30:6; Mark 12:28-31

<u>Body</u>

soma

(Physical Being)

Filled with the Holy Spirit
Whole and Free
Sanctified Entirely
Loving God, One Another, and
Ourselves Completely

<u>Soul</u>

psuche

(Mind, Will and Emotions)

<u>Spirit</u>

pneuma

(Communion, Conscience, and Intuition)

Epilogue and Prayer of Impartation

We love to sing the beautiful song "Freely, Freely" by Carol Owen. We tend to sing that song at revivals and think that it's based upon the Scriptural call to evangelism. Really, evangelism is a part of this message, but the real context of this Scripture is the full ministry of the transforming power of healing and deliverance Jesus expects from His disciples:

> And as you go, preach, saying, "The kingdom of heaven is at hand." Heal the sick, cleanse the lepers, raise the dead, cast out demons. Freely you have received, freely give (Matthew 10:7–8 NKJV).

That's the Church of Jesus Christ, filled with the Spirit of Christ, continuing the ministry of Christ. That's the calling and destiny of the disciples of Jesus being His hands and His heart to the people of a broken, fallen world literally dying to see Jesus in the midst of their lives. So the Father heart of God longs to set us free to be like Jesus.

God clearly desires to release ever-increasing measures of His power upon the earth to display His glory through His people, as we enforce the victory of His cross. At the same time, though, God's desire to release miracles does not replace His desire to bring healing and wholeness through the sanctification of the hearts and lives of His children. He's preparing a Bride for the coming of Christ, and He's bringing many sons to glory. And in fact, the more sanctified the Lord's vessels become in the character and nature of Christ, the more He can entrust us with His power to do the "the greater works" He said we'd do, and bring about the restoration of all things. As Francis Frangipane, one of the great spiritual mentors of our day, loves to say, "Victory begins with the name of Jesus on our lips. It is consummated by the nature of Jesus in our hearts" (The Three Battlefields).

I'd like to close this book with a prayer the Holy Spirit led me to pray during my morning devotional time about going forth into our calling and destiny in Christ. From *Morning by Morning, A Prayer Journey with Tommy Hays,* this is my prayer named The God of All Comfort:

Good morning, Lord Jesus. Arise in newness of life in me today....

"Blessed by the God and Father of our Lord Jesus Christ, the Father of mercies and God of all comfort, who comforts us in all our tribulation, that we may be able to comfort those who are in any trouble, with the comfort with which we ourselves have been comforted by God" (2 Corinthians 1:3–4).

You care about us and comfort us and heal us and free us because You love us. You are a good Father, an "everlasting Father," the Father of mercies (Isaiah 9:6). And we are Your children. What parent can bear to see their children in pain, broken or bound, living life in anything less than their full potential. So You call us to Yourself, You hold us in Your arms, You heal our hurts and break our bonds, binding up the brokenhearted and setting the captives free (Isaiah 61:1; Luke 4:18). Because that's what a good and loving Father does.

But You also comfort us so that we can comfort others. You heal us and free us so we can go in the authority of Your name and in the power of Your Spirit to heal and free others. In the same way we have seen and known Your comfort, we have understanding, wisdom, empathy, and faith to see You bring that same comfort to others. You are "no respecter of persons" (Acts 10:34 KJV). You love each of us the same and You desire the same comfort and healing and freedom for each of us. So You empower us and send us to be Your "ambassadors," Your healing hands and heart in the lives of others who need Your comfort just like we did when You sent someone to us (2 Corinthians 5:20). "Freely (we) have received, freely (we are to) give" (Matthew 10:8 NKJV).

Thank You, Lord. I am Yours to be sent to freely give the comfort of Your love as You lead today and every day. In Jesus' name I pray, Amen. Be encouraged today! In the Love of Jesus, Tommy Hays

Prayer of Impartation and Anointing for Ministry

I invite you now to receive and embrace this Prayer of Impartation and Anointing for Ministry for you, with the cross and blood of Christ between us, so that you safely receive all that's of the Lord for you and nothing less (see 2 Kings 2:9; Romans 1:11; 1 Timothy 4:14; and 2 Timothy 1:6, among others):

370

Freely have I received, now freely I give. Such as I have, I give you. In the name of the Lord Jesus Christ, King of Kings and Lord of Lords, I pray an impartation and anointing of the Holy Spirit of the Living God to come upon you with power from on high. May you know how much God loves you. May you receive the fullness of His healing, freeing grace. And may you receive a double portion and more of every good and godly gift the Lord has poured into me. May you know the love of God, with His nature and power flowing through your life with ever-increasing measure, as you proclaim the coming of the kingdom of God, healing the brokenhearted and setting the captives free, to the glory of God our Father. God bless you! In Jesus' name I pray, Amen.

God bless you as He loves you and heals you and sends you to minister His healing love through you in the power of the name of Jesus! Through you and His glorious Bride, may the glory of the Lord cover the earth as the waters cover the sea!

—Tommy Hays

Principles and Model for Inner Healing Prayer Ministry
"Healing from the Inside Out"
Rev. Tommy Hays

Reveal, Remove, Replace

"Pray for one another, so that you may be healed" (James 5:16).

With the Love of the Father and in the power of the Holy Spirit, Jesus is still healing the brokenhearted and setting the captives free, through the Body of Christ in the authority of the name of Jesus (Isaiah 61:1-4; Luke 4:18-19; John 20:21).

1. Reveal: Ask the Holy Spirit to *Reveal* the root or source of the issue.

"Search me, O God, and know my heart; test me and know my thoughts. See if there is any wicked (or hurtful) way in me, and lead me in the way everlasting" (Psalm 139:23–24).

Bad roots produce bad fruit; "the tree is known by its fruit" (Matthew 12:33).

Often an earlier traumatic or emotionally painful experience or when some problem first began, in their life or in their past generations reinforced in their life.

Common roots issues: Pride, Rebellion, Control, Bitterness and Unforgiveness, Rejection, Shame, Fear, Infirmity, False Beliefs, Brokenness of Unhealed Trauma

2. Remove: Ask the Lord to *Remove* what the Holy Spirit has *Revealed*.

"Submit yourselves therefore to God. Resist the devil, and he will flee from you. Draw near to God, and He will draw near to you. Cleanse your hands, you sinners, and purify your hearts, you double-minded.... Humble yourselves before the Lord, and He will exalt you" (James 4:7–10).

373

Put the ax of the name of Jesus and power of the Holy Spirit to the root of the tree, cast it into the Fire of the Holy Spirit so it no longer bears bad fruit (Matthew 3:10).

Through prayer and taking authority in Christ, removing all that is not yet like Jesus, everything that would hold them back from being all God created them to be in their identity and destiny in Christ.

Often confession and repentance of sin, rejecting agreement with lies and evil spirits, renouncing words, curses and false beliefs, commanding the devil to flee.

3. Replace: Ask the Lord to fill their heart and life, *Replaced* with all God desires.

"He may grant that you be strengthened in your inner being with power through His Spirit, and that Christ may dwell in your hearts through faith, as you are being rooted and grounded in love.... to know the love of Christ that surpasses knowledge, so that you may be filled with the fullness of God" (Ephesians 3:16–19).

Ask the Lord to replace all that has been revealed and removed with His Holy Spirit, truth, light, love, blessings, gifting, anointing and the fullness of the Kingdom of God, which is *"righteousness and peace and joy in the Holy Spirit"* (Romans 14:17).

"Create in me a clean heart, O God, and renew a right spirit within me. Cast me now way from Your Presence, take not Your Holy Spirit from me. Restore unto me the joy of my salvation and renew a right spirit within me" (Psalm 51:10–12).

Speak a Father's Blessing and Mother's Nurture in prophetic words as the Holy Spirit leads to edify, exhort, and comfort.

"On the other hand, those who prophesy speak to other people for their upbuilding and encouragement and consolation" (1 Corinthians 14:3).

Principles and Model for Physical Healing Prayer Ministry

Rev. Tommy Hays

God's Will to Heal

Isaiah 53:4–5 fulfilled in Matthew 8:17; Isaiah 61

"Surely He has borne our infirmities and carried our diseases; yet we accounted Him stricken, struck down by God, and afflicted. But He was wounded for our transgressions, crushed for our iniquities; upon Him was the punishment that made us whole, and by His bruises we are healed" (Isaiah 53:4–5).

"That evening they brought to Him many who were possessed with demons; and he cast out the spirits with a word, and cured all who were sick. This was to fulfill what had been spoken through the prophet Isaiah, "He took our infirmities and bore our diseases" (Matthew 8:16–17).

Healing is at the Heart of the Ministry of Jesus

Isaiah 61, fulfilled in Luke 4:18–19

"The spirit of the Lord GOD is upon Me, because the LORD has anointed Me; He has sent Me to bring good news to the oppressed, to bind up the brokenhearted, to proclaim liberty to the captives, and release to the prisoners; to proclaim the year of the LORD's favor, and the day of vengeance of our God; to comfort all who mourn; to provide for those who mourn in Zion—to give them a garland instead of ashes, the oil of gladness instead of mourning, the mantle of praise instead of a faint spirit. They will be called oaks of righteousness, the planting of the LORD, to display his glory. They shall build up the ancient ruins, they shall raise up the former devastations; they shall repair the ruined cities, the devastations of many generations" (Isaiah 61:1–4).

God's Will to Heal Through His People

John 20:19–23; James 5:13-16; Mark 6:13; Luke 9:1–2; 10:17-19; 1 Cor. 12:28; 2 Cor. 1:4; Isaiah 61

Three Dimensions of Healing Prayer Ministry

1. Prayers of Faith

"Are any among you sick? They should call for the elders of the church and have them pray over them, anointing them with oil in the name of the Lord. The prayer of faith will save ["sozo"] the sick, and the Lord will raise them up; and anyone who has committed sins will be forgiven" (James 5:14–15).

2. Enforcing Our Authority in Christ

"Then Jesus called the twelve together and gave them power and authority over all demons and to cure diseases, and He sent them out to proclaim the kingdom of God and to heal" (Luke 9:1–2).

"I will give you the keys of the kingdom of heaven, and whatever you bind on earth will be bound in heaven, and whatever you loose on earth will be loosed in heaven" (Matthew 16:19).

3. Removing Barriers

"And by this we will know that we are from the truth and will reassure our hearts before Him whenever our hearts condemn us; for God is greater than our hearts, and He knows everything. Beloved, if our hearts do not condemn us, we have boldness before God; and we receive from Him whatever we ask, because we obey His commandments and do what pleases Him" (1 John 3:19–22).

A Basic Model for Physical Healing

1. Pray in humility with faith
2. Bind any afflicting spirit
3. Speak healing to the condition
4. Listen for any barriers
5. Pray blessings and affirmation

Contact

for Ministry Resources or Speaking Engagements

Tommy Hays
Founder, Messiah Ministries
Pastoral Director, Rapha God Ministries

4 Dominion Drive, Building 1
San Antonio, Texas 78257
www.messiah-ministries.org

CPSIA information can be obtained
at www.ICGtesting.com
Printed in the USA
FSOW03n0054030316
17383FS